ROUTLEDGE LIBRARY EDITIONS: WW2

Volume 19

MONTGOMERY THE FIELD MARSHAL

MONTGOMERY THE FIELD MARSHAL

A Critical Study of the Generalship of Field-Marshal, the Viscount Montgomery of Alamein, K.G. and of the Campaign in North-West Europe, 1944/45

R.W. THOMPSON

LONDON AND NEW YORK

First published in 1969 by George Allen & Unwin Ltd

This edition first published in 2022
by Routledge
2 Park Square, Milton Park, Abingdon, Oxon OX14 4RN

and by Routledge
605 Third Avenue, New York, NY 10158

Routledge is an imprint of the Taylor & Francis Group, an informa business

© 1969 R.W. Thompson

All rights reserved. No part of this book may be reprinted or reproduced or utilised in any form or by any electronic, mechanical, or other means, now known or hereafter invented, including photocopying and recording, or in any information storage or retrieval system, without permission in writing from the publishers.

Trademark notice: Product or corporate names may be trademarks or registered trademarks, and are used only for identification and explanation without intent to infringe.

British Library Cataloguing in Publication Data
A catalogue record for this book is available from the British Library

ISBN: 978-1-03-201217-9 (Set)
ISBN: 978-1-00-319367-8 (Set) (ebk)
ISBN: 978-1-03-204737-9 (Volume 19) (hbk)
ISBN: 978-1-03-204739-3 (Volume 19) (pbk)
ISBN: 978-1-00-319447-7 (Volume 19) (ebk)

DOI: 10.4324/9781003194477

Publisher's Note
The publisher has gone to great lengths to ensure the quality of this reprint but points out that some imperfections in the original copies may be apparent.

Disclaimer
The publisher has made every effort to trace copyright holders and would welcome correspondence from those they have been unable to trace.

Montgomery
The Field Marshal

A Critical study of the generalship of
Field-Marshal, The Viscount Montgomery of
Alamein, K.G. and of the campaign in
North-West Europe, 1944/45

BY
R. W. THOMPSON

London
GEORGE ALLEN & UNWIN LTD
RUSKIN HOUSE   MUSEUM STREET

FIRST PUBLISHED IN 1969

This book is copyright under the Berne Convention. All rights are reserved. Apart from any fair dealing for the purpose of private study, criticism or review, as permitted under the Copyright Act, 1956, no part of this publication may be reproduced, stored in a retrieval system, or transmitted, in any form or by any means, electronic, electrical, chemical, mechanical, optical, photocopying, recording or otherwise, without the prior permission of the copyright owner. Enquiries should be addressed to the Publishers

© R. W. Thompson 1969

SBN 04 355007 X

PRINTED IN GREAT BRITAIN
in *11 on 12pt Baskerville type*
BY C TINLING AND CO LTD
PRESCOT

ACKNOWLEDGEMENTS

The extracts from *The Supreme Command, Cross-Channel Attack, Breakout and Pursuit, The Lorraine Campaign, The Ardennes: Battle of the Bulge, Logistics*, vols I & II, *Command Decision*, are used by permission of the Chief of Military History, Dept. of the Army, Washington D.C.; from *Victory in the West, Grand Strategy*, vol. III, part II, *Grand Strategy*, vol. V, *Grand Strategy*, vol. VI, by permission of Her Majesty's Stationery Office; from *Closing the Ring*, vol. V, *Triumph and Tragedy*, vol. VI, by permission of *The Daily Telegraph* and Messrs. Cassell & Co. Ltd.

I acknowledge gratefully the value of the works listed in the bibliography in fortifying, and at times tempering my personal experience and knowledge of the Campaign in N.W. Europe, 1944/45.

R.W.T.

Frontispiece: Field-Marshal Sir Bernard Montgomery

CONTENTS

PART ONE THE GROUND FORCE COMMANDER

PROLOGUE	Cross-Channel Assault and the Supreme Command	*page* 15
ONE	Veni, vidi, vici ...	33
TWO	The Last Days ...	58
THREE	Montgomery's Ordeal	72
FOUR	The Tactics of Montgomery's Strategy	88
FIVE	The End of Strategy	102
SIX	The Parting of the Ways	110
SEVEN	The Nature and Anatomy of Victory	122

PART TWO THE FIELD-MARSHAL

EIGHT	The Art of the Possible	147
NINE	The Drive to the North	165
TEN	Arnhem	186
ELEVEN	The Price of Failure	203
TWELVE	Three Faces of the Field-Marshal	218
THIRTEEN	Counter-offensive: the Ardennes	233
FOURTEEN	Montgomery's Predicament	248
FIFTEEN	The Race for the Rhine	271
SIXTEEN	Plunder	288

EPILOGUE	313
BIBLIOGRAPHY	324
APPENDIX	327
INDEX	331

ILLUSTRATIONS

FRONTISPIECE
Field-Marshal Sir Bernard Montgomery

1. Eisenhower and Montgomery   *facing page* 96
2. General Eisenhower with General Montgomery at the latter's H.Q. in Normandy   97
3. General Montgomery touring units before D-Day   128
4. Army commanders confer in France: Generals Bradley, Montgomery, Dempsey and Hodges   129
5. Montgomery talks to men of the Black Watch before the Rhine assault   224
6. Montgomery directs the battle in northern Germany, April 1945   225
7. The C-inC, on tour of forward areas, interested in a fur jacket worn by a Canadian infantryman   256

PART ONE

The Ground Force Commander

PROLOGUE

Cross-Channel Assault
and the Supreme Command

I

On Christmas Eve, 1943, General Sir Bernard Montgomery, commanding the British Eighth Army in the field on the River Sangro, was appointed to the command of the 21st Army Group of Armies for 'Operation Overlord', the cross-channel assault on North-West Europe. He was under the Supreme Command of the American General Eisenhower. It had been agreed that Montgomery would command all the ground forces in the initial assault, and until such time as a U.S. Army Group was established on the continent. At that point the Supreme Commander would take over, and Montgomery would revert to the command of his Army Group. This arrangement was a minor triumph of some importance to the British, and a concession to their ideas of the functions of a commander. It might represent the thin end of a wedge, for Montgomery might succeed in maintaining his position and retaining control of the ground forces. Such a result must depend on success, and on the willingness not only of the Supreme Commander and his Army Group commanders to accept Montgomery's leadership, but on the agreement of the U.S. Joint Chiefs of Staff. Montgomery was not the man to relinquish any part of his power without a struggle.

The problems of Anglo-American command had not been easy to solve. They derived from different ideas of the functions of a commander. The Americans felt that the Supreme Commander 'should in some way control the assaulting army . . .'[1] but they had no clear conception of how this should be done. In British eyes the Supreme Commander would have his

---

[1] U.S. Army in W.W. 2, Pogue: *The Supreme Command*, p. 44. See also Morgan: *Overture to Overlord*, Hodder & Stoughton.

hands full with strategic and political problems of great complexity, combined with his function of co-ordinating the land, sea and air forces.

For Britain their choice of a commander for 'Overlord' was of great significance in the political, strategic and military context of the time. The realities of power had moved steadily out of British hands, to become little more than a shadow after the Quebec Conference in August, 1943. At Cairo and Teheran in the last days of November and the first week of December of that year even the shadow was gone, leaving no doubt that the United States and Russia would shape the future in war, and almost certainly in peace. It was an unpleasing prospect, boding ill for the future of Europe.

Thus, on the field of battle alone, might there be a chance for Britain to affect final decisions, and by military ardour and skill to influence the course of events. Prestige might be won, and even upon so fragile a foundation a reality of power in Europe might be built in the aftermath of war.

General Montgomery, therefore, would be Britain's champion.

Yet events had by that time developed a momentum of their own. It felt then, and it seems true now, that all that men could do would be to steer the ship of war as best they might. The engines were going, the gears engaged, the speed set. 'As a practical matter,' Richard Leighton observed, 'the war in Europe had progressed beyond the point of no return.' Even the date (for 'Overlord') was hardly any longer in the 'realm of strategic decision.'[1] In the end, as Churchill wrote, the date was fixed mainly by 'the moon and the weather.'

Immediately after reporting to his Supreme Commander, General Montgomery flew to Marrakesh in North Africa, where the Prime Minister was recuperating after a severe bout of fever. Churchill's condition had caused some alarm in his immediate entourage. Field-Marshal Smuts had wondered whether, for all his indomitable spirit, Churchill would stay the course. General Sir Alan Brooke, Chief of the Imperial General Staff, was gravely concerned.

Churchill had fought every inch of the way for his Mediter-

[1] Office of Chief of Military History, Washington, *Command Decisions*, p. 285.

ranean strategy at Cairo and Teheran, and the effort had cost him dear. He had thrived upon action and danger, and now, shorn of his power to shape the course of events, he suffered intolerable frustrations and anxieties. An *Aide-Mémoire* dated 11th November had expressed his views with force and clarity, while protesting his respect for the 'Sanctity of Overlord':

> With the Germans in their present plight the surest way to win the war in the shortest time is to attack them remorselessly and continuously in any and every area where we can do so with superiority.[1]

These views, totally opposed to U.S. strategic thinking, aroused their worst suspicions that the British were ready to 'ditch Overlord'. Only, some felt, the appointment of General Marshall, the U.S. Chief of Staff, to the Supreme Command would ensure the cross-channel assault.

Teheran marked the end of Churchill's Mediterranean strategy, but not of his dreams. *Anvil*, a new plan for an attack on the South of France as a subsidiary to 'Overlord', made the British Prime Minister wince. He would fight such nonsense to the bitter end with bitter words. But now, convalescing at Marrakesh, he sent for his new champion. Montgomery was good for him, for the general lived in a much smaller world in which he would never admit defeat. Moreover the general neither drank nor smoked, and he went to bed early. He had the knack of making up his mind swiftly and expressing himself with absolute conviction. It sustained and soothed the restless spirit of the Prime Minister.

'I had asked Montgomery to visit me on his way home from Italy to take up his new command in "Overlord",' Churchill wrote. '... I had offered him this task so full of hazard.... I was gratified and also relieved to find that Montgomery was delighted and eager for what I had always regarded as a majestic, inevitable, but terrible task.'[2]

It is a curious statement, reflecting Churchill's love of rhetoric rather than the substance of his thoughts, for no one knew better than the Prime Minister that Montgomery, supported by every agency of government, and the power of the Press, had

[1] Ehrman: *Grand Strategy*, H.M.S.O., vol. v, p. 109-110.
[2] Churchill: *Closing the Ring*, vol. v, R.U. Edn., p. 347.

been long resolved that this great military prize should be his.

'The immense labour expended by various authorities—not excluding Monty himself—had to be lived with to be believed,' wrote one of Churchill's principal aides.[1]

There were others with greater claims upon the succession than Montgomery, and there was also the man in possession. General Sir Bernard Paget, Commander-in-Chief Home Forces, and one of the Combined Commanders responsible for developing the basic information, material and plan for a cross-channel assault, had trained the 'Liberation' army for its task with unremitting zeal and foresight. He had produced the 'Skyscraper' plan upon which the Chief of Staff to the Supreme Allied Commander (Designate) had built 'Operation Overlord'.[2]

'It was with deep grief that I was replacing Paget with Montgomery,' wrote the Chief of the Imperial General Staff, General Sir Alan Brooke. '... Paget, of course, took it all in a wonderful way.'[3]

Nevertheless General Paget was 'upset and sad at being superseded'.

General Sir Harold Alexander, the obvious choice in American eyes for the command of 'Overlord' under Eisenhower, was quite unmoved by Montgomery's triumph. Alexander was the perfect 'amateur', concealing his considerable military gifts beneath a serene and imperturbable exterior, and an air of easy nonchalance. Yet, contemplating Alexander I find it difficult to be sure of his toughness of fibre. Perhaps he was too patently a 'gentleman' for his day and age. Perhaps he would have benefited from a more difficult passage to the top, and something harder than a 'golden spoon' to bite on. Alexander had a natural distaste for the limelight, and all that that must entail. Moreover it must be doubtful if he could have been adequately replaced as Commander of the 15th Army Group in Italy. General Mark Clark, commanding the U.S. Fifth Army, might well have found Montgomery intolerable.

[1] Personal correspondence to author.
[2] Lieut.-General Morgan, COSSAC, was appointed without a commander.
[3] Bryant: *Triumph in the West*, p. 130.

But to an enormous public, including the rank and file of the Army in Europe, the choice of Montgomery to command Britain's armies in the last great throw, seemed natural and obvious. His prestige was enormous, his image, his words and deeds, engraved upon the mind of a Nation.

Montgomery's performance in the Western Desert had won for him wide acclaim in the United States, but the American commanders and observers in the field had become progressively disenchanted. Montgomery's readiness to pontificate upon all military matters, his remarkable self-assurance coupled with his equally remarkable caution, caused many to question his 'genius' as a commander in the field, while few would question his genius in public relations. As a 'character', if not as a commander of an army, he was unique.

It was undeniable, as General Sir Alan Brooke observed, that Montgomery had never lost a battle. His record of victory was unblemished, and yet, when the record was examined it was difficult to discover a 'losable' battle. He had inherited not only a winning position against a beaten enemy, but also an overwhelming strength never before at the disposal of a British commander. To know Montgomery at his best some would look back upon his handling of his troops in the retreat to Dunkirk, and it is ironical that this man, so gifted and resolute in defence, should have been given the conqueror's attacking role.

In Sicily and in Italy Montgomery's use of his enormous fire power had been disquieting, not only to many observers in the field, but to those at home whose task it was to maintain production with a diminishing labour force, to provide shipping space, and generally to feed this voracious appetite. The Americans had observed with amazement that Montgomery would not move without such a superiority in every arm as to render defeat impossible.[1] Irrespective of the strength of the enemy confronting him, or the type of country, mountain, plain or desert, enormous supplies of ammunition were built up together with the transport to move them.[2] At the same time bombing had become a British obsession.[3]

[1] Butcher: *Three Years with Eisenhower*, p. 248.
[2] Fuller: *The Second World War*, p. 270.
[3] Buckley: *Road to Rome*, p. 107.

Nevertheless it was Montgomery's failure to work in close harmony with the Americans that had been the greatest source of worry, especially to General Brooke. General Eisenhower made no secret of the fact that he had expected to continue to work with Alexander, and the appointment of Montgomery came as a shock. Senior to Montgomery, Alexander had shepherded his difficult army commander from Alamein to the Sangro, smoothing out many difficulties on the way, while content to remain always in the background. He had commanded the 18th Army Group for the assault on Sicily and the 15th Army Group in Italy. From the first difficult days in Tunisia, when the Americans had been finding their feet and licking their wounds after their severe reverse in the Kasserine Pass, Alexander had been a tower of strength to the alliance.

It may be that in the back of Churchill's mind was the faint hope still that 'Overlord' would not take place, that a situation might develop which would render a cross-channel assault a virtual 'walk-in', planned for under the code name 'Rankin'. 'German strength in France next Spring may, at one end of the scale, be something which makes "Overlord" completely impossible and, at the other end, something which makes "Rankin" not only practicable, but essential.'[1]

In such a fortunate eventuality it might fall to Alexander to change the face of Europe and to forestall the Russian advance upon Vienna. British hopes for victory, and for peace, still lingered in the Mediterranean. The 'soft under-belly' had turned out to be more like the rugged back of a crocodile, but there, by way of the Ljubljana Gap lay a path to the heart of Europe which might still be opened to confound the dreams and ambitions of the Russian Dictator.

It is possible also that the choice of Montgomery was a symptom of British intransigence, for the cock-sure and plain-speaking general could be relied upon to argue every move with the Supreme Commander, and to maintain the course of the campaign for Europe on the lines most suitable for Britain. In a talk with Eisenhower at Carthage on 11th December, Brooke had noted the American general's preference for Alexander for 'Overlord'. 'He knew also that he could handle

[1] *Aide Mémoire*, 11 Nov., para. 3, G.S. vol. v.

Alex, but was not fond of Monty and certainly did not know how to handle him.'[1]

But perhaps there was no real choice. The bells pealing out to proclaim victory in the desert had pealed for Montgomery. He had become Britain's man of destiny, her soldier of good fortune, her 'lucky general'. Soon he would grasp the Field-Marshal's baton.

II

While it is not difficult to imagine others handling his armies with greater offensive skill, and many far more capable of oiling the wheels of Anglo-American understanding and co-operation, it is impossible to imagine anyone filling Montgomery's particular shoes. He was, in a peculiar way, an expression of his time, a triumph of the 'image' makers and projectors, and he answered a particular need in the British people. His eccentricities, real or imagined, however bizarre, inspired innumerable stories, all of them accompanied by chuckles of good humour, and usually of admiration. To a vast public he could do no wrong, or nothing to undermine their confidence in his ability. His immense sense of personal satisfaction and confidence, his remarkable flamboyance, suited the mood of a Nation, and boosted morale. Montgomery blew Britain's trumpet as well as his own.

All this was valuable, but the overwhelming need for Britain was for speed. Time was running out fast. Manpower and industrial production had reached, and were passing their peaks, and were becoming wasting assets. At the same time the enormous logistical demands of armies, growing alarmingly, mitigated against speed. The 'tails' of armies were becoming immense, and the wealth and variety of the materials of war threatened to become balls and chains dragging at the feet of generals and armies, and moulding strategy and tactics. Logistics had already set their seal upon war, restricting the 'art of the possible', and Montgomery was the willing slave of all this 'ironmongery'.

It was unavoidable that maintenance and supply, and all the

[1] Bryant: *Triumph in the West*, p. 115.

complex problems coming under the single heading of 'logistics', would determine the scale of assault in the evolution of 'Operation Overlord'. It had been observed in the comparatively unopposed landings of a British and an American army in Sicily, that '. . . the faster an army intended to advance, and the more violent the blows it desired to strike, the larger must be the administrative tail.'[1]

Every assault operation from the disastrous Dieppe Raid to the bitterly opposed American landings at Salerno, had added to the knowledge of the problems involved, and produced the means of countering or avoiding difficulties. No one had ever doubted that 'an army marches on its stomach', but the stomachs of armies were growing in complexity at an alarming rate, demanding great varieties of diet in huge quantities, and great skill in feeding. The finest minds available were heavily engaged, new departments were forming, each with its staff of experts and students, weapons were proliferating, many of them demanding specialists, or highly skilled craftsmen and technicians for their successful operation. By the time that the commanders for 'Overlord' were chosen it was apparent that war was entering, if it had not already entered, a new dimension. Logistics, rather than generalship, would govern the speed of advance and the nature of defeat or victory.

All this was complicating the deployment of manpower, and diminishing further the dwindling labour force engaged on the manufacture of weapons in their ever-growing patterns. Major-General Sir Percy Hobart,[2] recalled from his retirement and service as a corporal in the Home Guard, was training a new and complex armoured division in which almost every man must be a technician. Armoured fighting vehicles developed under Hobart included tanks capable of 'swimming' in to land under their own power, others with flails on revolving drums for beating minefields, with fascines for filling deep dykes, with bridges, with flame-throwers, in addition to bulldozers and an ever-increasing 'menagerie' of 'funnies', all capable of fighting in addition to their specialized functions.[3]

[1] U.S. Army in W.W. 2 Ruppenthal: *Logistical Support of the Armies*, vol. 1.
[2] Montgomery's brother-in-law.
[3] Many of these vehicles bore animal names. Troops usually referred to them as 'Funnies'. Hobart's command, 79th Armoured division, parcelled out its squadrons wherever needed.

On the water there were equivalent developments in assault landing-craft, many of them needing highly skilled personnel for their successful operation, and making demands upon naval manpower. The armed services, whether they liked it or not, were over-lapping on low levels as well as on high, and land, sea and air forces must fight under a single Supreme Command.

The reception and maintenance of a hundred new devices demanded highly skilled 'Beach Groups', engineers of many kinds, transport men, dockers, all trained to work under intense pressure, including enemy fire and bombardment from the air. Artificial harbours were under construction ready to be floated across the channel and 'planted' off the enemy shore, to provide dock facilities and anchorages, and all the needs of shipping in unique patterns and varieties.

Montgomery had become a general of an abundance inconceivable even in the days immediately prior to his first command of the Eighth Army. Perhaps he was the right man to deal with this mass of 'ironmongery', and all that served it; perhaps he would be less inhibited by it than many others who thrived on flexibility, speed and movement. It was unlikely that Montgomery would be frustrated by it as, for example, a Patton might be. He must comprehend clearly the nature of the weapon put into his hands, and use it to his advantage.

Montgomery had inherited an administrative organization of vast size and complexity, and it was unlikely that he would ever know many of the brigadiers and colonels under his command. Every week would add to the numbers of specialists and machines of war, and Britain would be restricted in a strait-jacket, not only of troops pouring into her coastal areas and inhabiting a high proportion of her countryside, but by materials of war beyond the scope of a small island to warehouse or to hide. From end to end Britain was becoming an arsenal of war, her woodlands stuffed with ammunition, her country lanes harbouring hosts of vehicles on their verges, her railway sidings massed with locomotives, her harbours crowded with types of shipping never before seen, while on the sea-approaches to the ports endless streams of shipping waited for harbour space.

Montgomery had the gift of seeing problems whole, and of

simplifying them down to their bare essentials. This trait might prove one of his greatest assets, but it could also be dangerous. Yet it was all a long way removed from what, so little time ago, and still in many theatres of war was the ancient art of generalship. Montgomery's position was akin to that of 'general manager' of an industrial complex embracing elements of an entire society, and subject to constant movement, and even to attrition. In the field it might be possible to break loose, for Montgomery to free himself and to free his army commanders, confident in the smooth working of the background organization in the hands of its innumerable heads of departments. Perhaps there had never been a greater challenge to generalship. The question was, would the tail wag the dog, or become such a weight upon it that the dog would be able to move only with great difficulty?

When Montgomery embarked upon his task it had been apparent for many months that Germany could not win the war, but there was no room for complacency in the Western camp. German industrial production continued to increase in spite of the Allied Strategic bombing programme, and it had been certain for many months that new 'secret' weapons were in production. 'Heavy water' had proved a disappointment and it was improbable that the enemy was engaged in any development comparable with 'The Manhattan Project', the atomic bomb.[1] Nevertheless the enemy was advanced in rocketry, and it was known that the launching of new weapons of this nature was imminent. Against this menace 'Operation Crossbow' was being mounted, and heavy bombers were diverted from their normal industrial targets to attack the suspected main production centre at Peenemünde. At the same time air photographs disclosed 'launching sites' over wide areas, and these too must be attacked. It was possible that 'Operation Overlord' might be wrecked before it could sail if the enemy launched a large scale rocket assault on south coast ports. The importance the enemy attached to his launching sites was evident from the powerful armament massed for their defence. At one site alone 50 Heavy and 76 Light anti-aircraft guns were observed.

Certainly Hitler's dreams of conquest and the establishment

[1] See: *The Virus House* by David Irving, Kimber 50s. Prof. Walter Bothe's remarkable miscalculation.

of a Third Reich would not be realized, but it would be doubly dangerous to under-estimate the strength and the will to fight of the German army and people in defence of their homeland. The rash and ill-considered announcement of 'Unconditional Surrender' had ensured a fight to a finish, welding the German nation, and cutting the ground from under those few who plotted the overthrow of the Führer.

Unconditional Surrender had bedevilled the 'Object' of the Second World War, and thereby blurred a clear vision of peace. This lack of an object frustrated the planners of the cross-channel assault throughout all 1943, and to the bitter end.

III

The nomination of General Eisenhower as Supreme Commander for the cross-channel assault quietened American fears that the British might still attempt 'to ditch' the operation. These fears were ill-founded. The appointment of General Montgomery to command the land forces still further allayed the powerful suspicions of those who had believed that only the appointment of General Marshall, the U.S. Chief of Staff, to the Supreme Command would keep the British to their word. Liked or disliked, Montgomery was Britain's hero, and would scarcely be chosen to command a non-starter.

The American resolution to mount a cross-channel assault upon the coast of France had been pursued with relentless determination, and very little appreciation of the immense difficulties involved. While the Americans had argued, and threatened to swing their main effort to the Pacific, the British had trained and planned, and harnessed a high proportion of their industrial capacity and technical ability to the project. While Allied shipping losses under German submarine attack had risen to the crippling total of 7,800,000 tons in 1942, the Americans had pressed angrily for the assault under the code name 'Sledgehammer'. While the losses worsened they insisted upon an assault code-named 'Round-Up' in 1943.

It must be true that if even one half of the build-up of men and matériel was essential to a realistic hope of success in 1944, an assault with any real chance could not have been mounted earlier than the late spring of that year. Above all, the shortage of landing-craft, persisting to the end, frustrated the planners, not only of 'Overlord', but of all operations from the North Sea to South East Asia. There was never enough to go round, and those available were shuttled from one theatre of war to another, even across half the world, and with dangerously narrow timings. Everywhere operations were prejudiced or abandoned. The campaign in Italy was always inhibited and finally bogged down. An operation against the Andaman Islands, promised to the Chiang Kai Sheks (M. and Madame operated as a 'team') was cancelled in order to free landing-craft for the Mediterranean, in their turn to be made available for 'Overlord'.

There was, therefore, a sense of unreality in the incessant American nagging of their British allies, and the constant mistrust. It revealed at the outset the gulf between British and American strategy. The Americans sought to come to grips with the enemy in the shortest possible time by the shortest route. The British, an island naval power, sought always the indirect approach. They sought to threaten the enemy wherever possible, striking at targets of opportunity with a combination of naval, military and air power. They sought to keep the enemy guessing, and by maintaining threats he dared not disregard from end to end of the enormous coastline he occupied, to contain more enemy divisions in defence than they might ever hope to meet or to defeat. The Americans persisted in regarding British menacing postures in the Mediterranean as intentions to mount operations to the detriment of the main chance.

The tragic casualties of the First World War, crippling Britain over the years between the wars, had underlined the only sane strategy open to them. The U.S. Secretary of State for War, Henry Stimson, was not very wrong when he said that the British were haunted by the shadow of Passchendaele and Dunkerque, and feared to come to grips with the German Army.[1] As a statement of sane fact it was worth understanding; as a gibe it was cheap and cowardly.

The British had used Indian troops in the defence of India, and in the Middle and near East, aided by Commonwealth

---

[1] Sherwood: *The White House Papers*, vol. ii.

divisions from Australia, New Zealand and South Africa. British divisions played their parts, but it was not for Britain to hurl her precious battalions against the great military power on the mainland of Europe. Russia and America were equipped for such a task, and the struggle for Russia had underlined German military power.

Thus the British saw the Mediterranean as her sea of hope and opportunity, while the Americans regarded it as a 'graveyard'. In January, 1943, General Marshall had insisted upon a British statement of intent to mount a cross-channel assault in 1943. At that time, as Marshall knew well, an import crisis of startling dimensions afflicted Britain, and was only relieved by President Roosevelt acting in opposition to his military advisers. 'By March, 1943, the danger to survival was as great as in April, 1917.'[1] Britain lived from hand to mouth.

At the same time the Western Allies were fully committed to the invasion of Sicily and Italy while the losses in the Atlantic mounted steadily to render a cross-channel assault impossible. Yet... 'In the light of developments in the Mediterranean, American military leaders discounted the repeated pledges of loyalty by the British to the cross-channel assault invasion strategy. They tended to gloss over or ignore the immense investment Britain had in the cross-channel operation, the heavy contributions of British shipping to the build-up of American invasion forces and material in the United Kingdom (almost half the entire tonnage used), and the persistent pleas of British leaders for a strengthening of the "Overlord" assault.'[2]

Ironically it was the Americans who were to insist upon a Mediterranean assault to compromise, rather than to aid, the mounting of 'Overlord'. The appointment of Lieut.-General Sir Frederick Morgan as Chief of Staff to the Supreme Allied Commander for 'Overlord', with the task of developing the organization and plans of General Paget and the Combined Commanders into a hard and fast plan for a cross-channel assault in the early summer of 1944, should have allayed American fears, but it did not. At Quebec in August, 1943, the Americans were in a dangerous mood, resolved on a 'show-down' with the British, and ready to switch their major effort to the

[1] *Grand Strategy*, vol. v.
[2] *Command Decisions*, p. 262. Leighton, Dept. of Army, Washington.

Pacific. Fortunately the British Chiefs of Staff were armed with Morgan's plan for 'Overlord', substantially the cross-channel assault to be mounted by Eisenhower and Montgomery in June, 1944. This was concrete evidence of intent, and there was much more. Morgan had constantly nagged at everyone from Roosevelt and Churchill downwards for the appointment of a Supreme Commander, for without a commander his demands lacked 'bite', and imposed severe limitations upon the scope of his planning and the strength of the assault. Only a Supreme Commander could provide the head to the body he had created, and take the whole enterprise off the 'drawing board', as it were, and make demands which would have to be answered emphatically.

It had been understood that General Marshall, the U.S. Chief of Staff, would be appointed, and Morgan had regarded Marshall as his 'Chief' to be, but the Americans were in no hurry to commit themselves. From first to last Morgan had also pressed for a firmly defined 'Object', for simply to assault across the channel is not in itself an 'Object'. That is a beginning without a clear-cut end, especially in the light of 'Unconditional Surrender'.

By the late Summer of 1943 it was clear that the Western Allies at last had the upper hand in the key Battle of the Atlantic, and the men and materials of war were pouring into Britain in ever-increasing quantities. Even so, and with a target date fixed for 1944, the Americans nursed their doubts and fears and failed to realize how deeply the British were committed. British hopes in the Mediterranean had not deterred them from 'turning their overcrowded island into a base for the greatest combined operation in the history of war'.[1] The production of the 'Artificial harbours' alone called for one million tons of materials and the development of special sites for their construction. All this was an almost intolerable burden upon industrial resources, factory space, shipyards, and the ordinary folk of Britain attempting to go about their business.

Nevertheless the Americans came to the Cairo–Teheran conferences of November–December, 1943, in an even more sour mood, and as full of suspicions as ever. 'The prospects of mounting "Overlord" as planned could not have seemed very

[1] The Price of Victory.

bright to the Joint Chiefs of Staff (U.S.) as they travelled to Cairo for the first conversations with the British...', wrote G. A. Harrison.[1] Yet an examination of all available material reveals the British as deeply committed and the Americans as vacillating between 'East and West'. At Cairo and Teheran they brought in the Chiang Kai Sheks, to the exasperation of General Alan Brooke and Churchill, and virtually ganged up with the Russians. Finally to the obvious delight of Stalin and his Marshals the Americans resolved on mounting an attack on the South of France (Operation Anvil) designed to assist 'Overlord'. This was, in Churchill's view, a major political and strategic blunder. It must hamper progress in Italy, remove the sting from British threats elsewhere in the Mediterranean, and would not, in Montgomery's view, bring aid to 'Overlord' for 90 days.[2]

At the same time the Americans had decided that a 'Supreme' Supreme Commander was urgently necessary to command the Allied Force Commanders in the Mediterranean, in North-West Europe, and the Strategic Air Forces. He should command all 'United Nations operations from the Mediterranean and the Atlantic...' The failure to set up such a command, they said, 'may lead to confusion and indecision at a critical time...'[3]

Where this 'master-mind' should form his headquarters, and how and from whence he would exercise his un-commandable command, they did not say.

Behind this very curious American suggestion there must have been President Roosevelt's earnest desire to secure a place in history for his Chief of Staff, General George Marshall. He had brooded to Eisenhower on the subject:

'Ike, you and I know who was the Chief of Staff during the last years of the Civil War, but practically no one else knows... I hate to think that fifty years from now practically nobody will know who George Marshall was. That is one of the reasons why I want George to have the big Command...'[4]

The Supreme Command in North-West Europe was not big enough for Marshall in the President's view, and in his desire

[1] U.S. Army in W.W. 2 Harrison: *Cross-Channel Attack*.
[2] Ehrman: *Grand Strategy*, vol. v, Appendix 10, p. 576. See also: *Command Decisions, The Anvil Decision, Matloff-Anvil Russian Inspired.*
[3] Ehrman: *Grand Strategy*, vol. v, H.M.S.O., pp. 169, 170.
[4] Sherwood: *The White House Papers*, vol. ii, p. 765, Eyre and Spotiswoode.

to create a niche for his Chief of Staff he would only have succeeded in 'kicking him upstairs'.

In rejecting this bizarre proposal the British Chiefs of Staff drew attention to its 'immense political implication', and pointed out quietly to their Allies that 'Total war is not an affair of military forces alone, using the word "military" in the widest sense of the term. There are political, economic, industrial and domestic implications in almost every big war problem...' It 'boils down', they stressed, to the virtual impotence of such a commander. Meanwhile the British patiently awaited the President's decision to appoint a Supreme Commander for 'Overlord'. The Russians waited less patiently. All expected General Marshall to have the job, but there were other candidates, and 'lobbying' was vigorous in the United States. Admirals Leahy and King, General Arnold and Secretary of War, Henry Stimson, were all anxiously inspired by suspicions of British intentions; yet, in a Memorandum to the President signed by Leahy, the name of the British Field-Marshal, Sir John Dill, was put forward, and known to have the support of General Marshall: 'He has worked on an intimate personal basis with the U.S. Chiefs of Staff since our entry into the war. We have the highest opinion of his integrity of character and singleness of purpose.'[1]

Stimson and his supporters would consider no other man than Marshall for the Supreme role: 'I believe that Marshall's command of "Overlord" is imperative for success,' Stimson wrote to Harry Hopkins, the President's personal confidante and friend. 'I anticipate that Marshall's presence in London will strongly tend to prevent any interferences with "Overlord" even if they were attempted...'[1]

The President held his peace until all the strategy for 1944, and the broad plans for the final destruction of Germany had been hammered out. On 6th December, 'just before they parted' Roosevelt told Churchill of his decision that Marshall should remain in Washington and that Eisenhower should command 'Overlord'. It was 'one of the most difficult and one of the loneliest decisions' the President had ever had to make.[2] With that the command structures for the Mediterranean and for

---

[1] Sherwood: *The White House Papers*, vol. ii, pp. 762-763.
[2] Sherwood: *The White House Papers*, vol. ii, p. 801.

North-West Europe fell easily into place. The plans and priorities for 1944 were fixed. 'Overlord' would be launched in May in conjunction with a supporting 'operation against the South of France on the largest scale that is permitted by the landing-craft available at that time.'[1]

Churchill had celebrated his 69th birthday in Cairo, and on the 9th December was clearly a very sick man, yet only to be deterred with difficulty from accompanying his Chief of Staff on a visit to his commanders in Italy. 'As I lay prostrate I felt we were at one of the great climaxes of the war,' Churchill wrote. 'The mounting of "Overlord" was the greatest event and duty in the world. But must we sabotage everything we could have in Italy . . .'[2]

On the 12th, Brooke left Carthage and the Prime Minister. He felt weary and in low spirits, and there was nothing in Italy to cheer him. 'The offensive is stagnating badly,' he wrote, 'and something must be done about it.'

Alexander was suffering the after-effects of jaundice, and Montgomery 'looked tired and in definite need of a rest.' In other ways Montgomery was his usual self, critical of Mark Clark, the U.S. General, and even of Alexander: 'I can see,' Brooke wrote, 'that he does not feel that Clark is running the Fifth Army right nor that Alex is gripping the show sufficiently.'[3]

When the British Chief of Staff finally made his way homeward, feeling that he had been away from England for months rather than weeks, the knowledge of the Prime Minister convalescing at Marrakesh was not the least of his anxieties. Churchill would not relinquish his Mediterranean dreams even at the point of death. He was fighting for a landing at Anzio in January to outflank the enemy in Italy and gain Rome, and on the 28th December he 'won' 56 Tank landing ships from Roosevelt for the purpose. They would be in England, he promised, in good time for 'Overlord'. Meanwhile he would contest the 'Anvil' assault on the South of France with all his might. Exhausted as he was '. . . events continued to offer irresistible distraction'.

[1] Ehrman: *Grand Strategy*, vol. v, p. 182.
[2] Churchill: *Closing the Ring*, vol. v, R.U., p. 334.
[3] Bryant: *Triumph in the West*, p. 120.

Early in the New Year, striving to launch 'Overlord' as a going concern, Brooke lamented, 'Most of the difficulties are caused by the P.M. at Marrakesh convalescing and trying to run the war from there... As a result a three-cornered flow of telegrams in all directions is gradually resulting in utter confusion. I wish to God that he would come home and get under control'.

But there was no confusion or frustration in the mind of Montgomery as he gathered the reins of his new command into his hands. General Brooke had had little difficulty in resolving the problems of the British Commander for 'Overlord'. I do not think there had been any doubt in his mind. Eisenhower was inexperienced militarily, and for the British a tough and uncompromising commander who knew his own mind was vital to take operational command of the ground forces. Before Christmas he had entrusted the task 'to his chosen lieutenant, Montgomery'.

No better tonic could have been devised for the little General. He had bobbed up like a cork, sparkling with enthusiasm on his visit to Churchill and Eisenhower at Marrakesh on the eve of the New Year. He had almost startled the Prime Minister with his 'leaping about the rocks like an antelope...' Churchill had warned his general that energy of mind does not depend on energy of body, but Montgomery had his own ideas, and stuck to them, while not denying that 'athletics are one thing and strategy another.' And he had won the Prime Minister's confidence.

'I must thank you for promoting me to command the armies in England,' he wrote to Brooke. 'It is a big job and I will do my best to prove worthy of your selection. There is a terrible lot to do and not much time to do it...'

CHAPTER ONE

Veni, vidi, vici . . .

I

THE appointment of General Eisenhower to the Supreme Command, and the naming of his principal subordinates, Lieut.-General Bedell Smith, his Chief of Staff, General Montgomery his commander of the 21st Army Group, and General Bradley to command the 1st U.S. Army and U.S. Army Group headquarters, at once brought Operation 'Overlord' to life. The frustrations of the planners, suffered with impatience and resolution over the years, were at an end. New targets, which even an hour earlier had been too far out of range to aim at seriously, became facts in Montgomery's sights. General Morgan with his COSSAC organization, and the Combined Commanders before him and with him, had built a sound edifice within the bounds of the possible, and these bounds they had questioned constantly. For months General Morgan and his dedicated Anglo-American staff had known that the assault upon the Normandy coast of France must be widened and strengthened, but the means did not exist. For this reason Morgan had never ceased to clamour for a commander to bring his work to life.

Montgomery, armed with powers to act on behalf of the Supreme Commander and to act as commander of the ground forces in the assault, was the immediate answer to Morgan's prayer. On the 2nd January the little general descended upon London, cherishing the piece of paper on which Eisenhower had written his authority, and all was changed. With a magnificent disregard for security Montgomery, hailed by a lively crowd, visited Norfolk House, COSSAC's headquarters. Up to that moment Morgan and all who worked with him had been at great pains to mask the importance of Norfolk House. The bounds of the possible were immediately extended, the framework of the assault swiftly expanded, and authoritative demands urgently made that this new framework should be filled. The Commanders-in-Chief of the Navy and the Air Force gave him blunt assessments of what his demands would mean in terms of ships and aircraft, and there were innumerable other factors. Montgomery was on safe ground. On his brief visit to Marrakesh the Prime Minister and the Supreme Commander had told him that the assault must be enlarged. The port of Cherbourg must be a vital objective. Montgomery had read a copy of the COSSAC outline plan and had readily agreed, although, as Montgomery saw it, the Prime Minister and the Supreme Commander had agreed with him and not he with them. Things invariably had to be that way round. The trait gave Montgomery his singleness of purpose, his immense drive, his uncompromising attitudes, his conviction of infallibility.

Within a month of Montgomery's arrival in Britain the planned assault had grown not only on paper but in fact. The little general, mountebank or Messiah, or a subtle combination of the two, had made his presence felt not only in every military establishment from Land's End to John o' Groats, and the outermost points east and west, but also in almost every household, factory, workshop, office, railway shed and dock. Very soon vast numbers of the populace, and of course the troops, would see him in the flesh and hear his voice. His presence in Britain in command was a remarkable and immediate stimulus. He had arrived, as Capt. Butcher (Eisenhower's indefatigable aide and diarist) put it, with a 'flare of trumpets', and there is a wealth of feeling behind the words, so that one seems to see the sardonic face of Bedell Smith, the faint grin of Bradley, over Montgomery's shoulder. All phrases seem inadequate to describe the arrival of Montgomery. There was no 'flare of trumpets', no whirlwind, no 'bombshell', but simply a little man in a black beret and battle-dress, at times seeming careless of his appearance and almost rudely unorthodox, at others as spick and span as a newly minted coin, breast resplendent with an 'herbaceous border' of medal ribbons which always seemed much larger than anybody else's. The contrast between Montgomery's flamboyant display and Eisenhower's engaging modesty and almost unadorned tunic became a source of amusement to British troops. They liked both men, seeing them in character. It did not escape them that the behaviour of these two generals in particular was a reverse of the popular 'National' images of the boastful 'Yankee' and the reserved Briton. The American seemed the perfect cosmopolitan, while Montgomery was a 'law unto himself', a remarkable mixture of puritan and panjandrum. Both men were ideally suited to their roles, if less suited to each other. Both inspired confidence.

Montgomery's Chief of Staff, Major-General de Guingand, had preceded his commander by 24 hours in London and had begun at once to set up shop. Twenty-first Army Group headquarters was established in St. Paul's School, and Montgomery's personal office in the Highmaster's study. It gave the general a curious little quirk of satisfaction to be sitting there, working there, as though in some way he had become 'one up' on the Highmaster who had never summoned his pupil to his presence in this room. It had been a crass omission. No feeling of nostalgia, no sentiment, no warmth is evident in Montgomery's account. In spite of his prowess in sport he had 'never entered that room before'.

On the 13th Montgomery called together all the general officers involved in operation 'Overlord' and told them the form in his inimitable manner. There would be, and there were, immediate changes in organization, even in the organization of a division. Montgomery didn't bother to consult with the War Office or with the Minister. After all, as he makes clear in his Memoirs, his battle experience and that of his own men was unique, and it would have been a waste of time to consult stay-at-homes about such matters. The General Headquarters Organization he had inherited suffered from the same malaise, and 'it was vital to inject new blood, and to bring in senior staff officers who knew my methods and would get on with the job without bellyaching'. Bellyaching was Montgomery's personal prerogative, and Eisenhower was destined to suffer a belly-full from his 'devoted subordinate'.

Heads of departments rolled in profusion, together with their assistants, with the implication that many of those who had dedicated themselves with devotion to the successful launching of 'Overlord', some since the days of Dunkirk, had failed. In fact, Montgomery had a passion for clean sweeps, for making his presence felt, for surrounding himself with his 'own chaps', and thereby to strengthen the illusion that it was all his. *Veni, vidi, vici* . . .

Similarly with the plans he inherited. 'The more I examined the proposed tactical plan of 21st Army Group, based on Morgan's outline plan, the more I disliked it,' he wrote.

He gives the impression that the COSSAC plan, and all the work of the Combined Commanders, was not much good. In fact Morgan's COSSAC plan, itself a development of Paget's 'Skyscraper' plan, was and remained the essential framework from which 'Overlord' was launched. To have given full credit to its value and to the work of his predecessors would have seemed to Montgomery to depreciate his own massive contribution. He could rarely bring himself to a gracious acknowledgement, and very swiftly he contrived to forget that there had been anything to acknowledge. His dislike of employing any senior officer who had not at some period in his career been one of his 'students' or 'disciples' was a sign of distrust of himself, rather than of the officer concerned. On 18th January, the C.I.G.S. recorded 'a sad interview with Kenneth Anderson to tell him he would not be commanding the Second Army in the forthcoming offensive, as Dempsey is to replace him. He took it very well.'

It is no reflection on the qualities of General Sir Kenneth Anderson that Montgomery should have appointed his own man to the most important command under him. The Commander of the British 2nd Army, officially 'The British Liberation Army', and the best equipped and trained military force ever to leave Britain's shores, was the one man above all others who must be able to work with the Army Group Commander. Dempsey was uniquely the right man. He was a fine soldier with a lucid and scholarly cast of mind and bearing, and a quiet and unassuming manner. His grasp of strategy was outstanding, and his plans the result of sound thinking. Among all those who knew him and served under him he inspired not only confidence, but a deep sense of loyalty based on genuine admiration for his character, and for his soldierly gifts.

Yet it was his rare qualities of character that made him the indispensable key figure in Montgomery's command structure.

In a sense he was a monastic figure, mentally and morally strong, quite fearless in his judgements, and equally fearless in expression. No man of Montgomery's calibre and difficult nature could hope to reach the top and stay there without help, and in this Montgomery was singularly fortunate, first in enjoying the support and guidance of General Brooke, the C.I.G.S., doubly fortunate in having General Alexander as his Commander-in-Chief in the Desert and his Army Group Commander in Sicily and Italy, and at last fortunate in his choice of Dempsey to command the 2nd Army. And this last choice reveals Montgomery's own percipience of his needs.

Temperamentally Dempsey was able to tolerate Montgomery's incessant interference—his 'usurpation of authority', Bradley called it—an interference Montgomery would not have tolerated for a moment in a like position. Alexander, if no one else, must have smiled. One may search British military 'memoirs' in vain, with the exception of Chester Wilmot's masterpiece,[1] for any light on General Sir Miles Dempsey, but the Americans appreciated both his character and his talents. Bradley observes that Dempsey, while absolutely competent to run his army did not object to Montgomery's habit of interference... 'this practice of Monty's had become a normal pattern of command. Dempsey knew how to tolerate it without jealousy or anger. Had Montgomery commanded his American subordinates in this rigid manner, we would have complained bitterly...' To imagine Montgomery commanding a George Patton is the ultimate phantasy.

I do not think it ever occurred to Dempsey that very few outside military circles knew of him. To the overwhelming majority of the public in Britain, and in the countries his army played a major role in liberating from the Germans, France, Belgium, and Holland, he was unknown. Montgomery was the liberator. He would have been the liberator had he commanded the 2nd Army, unless he had had the misfortune to have served under someone like himself, in which case, of course, he would not have served. Dempsey did not mind. He did his job quietly and efficiently. He provided Montgomery with an essential strength, with the benefit of lucid thinking, and with his loyalty.

Lieut.-General Horrocks, with his boyish enthusiasm and

[1] The Struggle for Europe.

unashamed adulation of the 'master', was Montgomery's favourite pupil; Major-General de Guingand, his lively and volatile Chief of Staff, standing in for his master at the many high level conferences Montgomery failed to attend, was his foil and 'maid of all work'; his young liaison officers, his 'cubs' round his camp-fire by night, replenished the master with their youth and deeds. But Dempsey was of very different calibre to all these, an adult, almost the solitary adult in what was essentially a 'schoolboy' world, the quiet man, unobtrusively putting his patience and wisdom at Montgomery's disposal, the tall slightly stooping figure, incongruously 'Bimbo' to his friends. The Asquiths in politics, the Wavells in the military field, do not need such figures in the wings, but to a man like Churchill in his much wider sphere, and to a man like Montgomery such men are vital. Like Churchill, Montgomery often deprived himself of the best men by his need to be served by his pupils and favourites. On one of his journeys in his special train, 'Rapier', visiting formations and units of the armies in Britain, Montgomery briefly interviewed Major-General Hakewill Smith, commanding and training the 52nd (Mountain) division in the Scottish highlands: 'You weren't one of my students, were you, Hakewill,' Montgomery said.

'No,' said Hakewill Smith.

Whereupon Montgomery at once lost interest. There was no more to be said. For months Hakewill Smith and his division despaired of being used in the war at all, and finally when they did come in, their role was in the below sea-level assault on Walcheren and the Bevelands.

Before January was out senior officers in the clubs were remarking that 'the Gentlemen are out and the Players are just going in to bat', and stories of this tremendous busybody of a General were rife, often told with resentment, even with angry contempt, but also, more often, with wry humour. Whatever one might think the man was certainly a 'card'. But never did a busybody appear less busy. At the heart of the activity Montgomery inspired and sustained, he remained relaxed, tranquil, serene. His life was austere, his personal habits unexceptionable, a 'Boy Scout' *par excellence* grown to man's estate, yet a Boy Scout with a blind spot about doing his good deed.

From his Memoirs covering this period one might gather that one of his major pre-occupations was the 'betting book' in which he recorded bets, mainly on the duration of the war, made by his brother officers. For his part he was sure that the war should be over in 1944, but since nobody would do the right thing, and would bungle, it would run on into 1945.

Montgomery's high-handed changes in military organization angered Sir James (P. J.) Grigg, the War Minister, his casual dress irritated the Sovereign, his speeches up and down the country irked Churchill. On 24th January, Brooke noted in his diary: '... I had to tell him off for falling foul of both the King and the Secretary of State in a very short time. He took it well as usual.'

A 'wigging from Brookie' had become a kind of routine.

The King was more amused than angry, and the War Minister responded to Montgomery's charm over a *tête-à-tête* luncheon. His exercise of charm was the more effective for its rarity; moreover it surprised those who imagined him incapable of charm. The bleak eyes warmed in nests of creases, the aspect of the sharp stern face softened, and there was suddenly the glimpse of a kind man, of boyish humour. It was a startling transformation. Perhaps it was a side of himself of which he was afraid, and which life, rightly or wrongly, had taught him to hide.

But it is Montgomery's exercise of power that demands thought. He was, without doubt, a tyrant, and one wonders how deeply he understood the intricacies of labour and effort his tyranny demanded. Perhaps ruthlessness was necessary. It was his duty to know everything, not in detail—which would have been impossible for any man—but in broad imaginative outline. His orders had their repercussions throughout the life of a nation, as well as of an army. His task was not to plan, not to do, but to think, to guide his planners, to assess constantly the desirable against the possible, and to extend with skill, care and humanity the bounds of the possible. In the thirteen days from 2nd to 15th January, supported by the authority of Lieut.-General Walter Bedell Smith, Montgomery was acting Supreme Commander. It was the nearest he would ever come to being Commander-in-Chief of the Ground Forces, and it irked him.

In his clashes with Monarch, Minister and Prime Minister and many others unable to hit back, he learned that in spite of, or because of, his great responsibilities he was no longer monarch of all he surveyed, as he had been as an Army Commander, thanks to Alexander's 'loose rein'. He was in a far wider world, in personal contact with politicians, with civilians, with industrial workers, as well as with troops. Few men understood more fully the elements of any army, but these are ponderable and amenable to discipline. There were three-quarters of a million U.S. troops in Britain in January, 1944, technically under his command, in addition to more than one million British troops. The numbers were increasing daily. They filled Southern England from the Wash to Milford Haven, occupying all the coastal areas with their camps, their hospitals, their aerodromes, their great vehicle parks and stores and workshops. Ramps and 'hards' augmented natural launching and landing-sites in many estuaries. The seaports bustled incessantly with the shipping to sustain the armies at a rate of 750,000 tons of supplies a month, supplies of great variety covering almost every need for war and peace from ammunition to bootlaces, from tanks, trucks and rifles to toilet rolls. All these supplies, long since bursting out of all available warehouse space, had to be organized in careful order of priorities and purposes. Each item had its particular place, and all this wealth of production had to be unloaded out of the holds of ships, moved from hundreds of production lines, and channelled away from docks, wharves and factories in an absolute precision, ready to be loaded back into ships and craft in precisely the correct order for use by tens of thousands of men in action fighting on alien beaches. Guns of many calibres must reach waiting hands with ammunition, trucks must reach those who needed them. Food and oil would be consumed in huge quantities. The smallest detail could not be overlooked.

Moreover the supplies for British troops must be kept quite separate from the supplies for U.S. troops. Lines of communication, lines of delivery, of storage, of re-delivery, must never cross. Chaos would ensue. Thus south-west England belonged to the United States armies and south-east England to British troops. Nor must it be forgotten that Britain served armies and garrisons in Italy, in the Middle and Near East, in Asia and over half the world, all of whom demanded constant sustenance.

Northward the ports belonged not only to war, but to a country striving to keep the channels of trade open, and to feed fifty million people, to clothe them, even to make life tolerable to them in small ways that might seem trivial to the thoughtless.

Montgomery saw the broad outline of it all on his indefatigable journeyings throughout the land. It was important to his handling of his armies, to the broad strategy and to the tactics of his troops, that he should understand it, that it should form a pattern in his mind; that he should know the kind of tasks facing the men working it all out, fulfilling it, dedicating themselves to it on all levels from Brigadiers to dock labourers, to the diggers of great pits to house the artificial harbours under construction on the banks of the Thames, to the railwaymen keeping locomotives on the move, to the makers and guards of camouflaged dumps extending over hundreds of square miles of forest and plain and country lane. And when all this is said no more than the fringes of this immense effort are touched, and the training activities of the troops on land and sea and in the air has not been touched at all.

The Commanders-in-Chief needed to combine ruthlessness and resolution with profound understanding. Whatever else may or may not be true I find it undeniable that in the five months from the 2nd January to the 6th June, 1944, when all this mighty force was launched upon the cross-channel assault, Montgomery's service to Britain was unique. Immune to the criticisms of politicians, generals, or indeed of anyone, he inspired not only the troops and the people, he inspired himself. He addressed scores of thousands of troops and workers in camps, workshops, railway stations and docks. Wherever he went men and women flocked to wave and cheer, to surround his jeep, his platform, wherever it was and filling all available space with seas of faces. His appearance amongst them meant that at last something was going to happen, that the last lap was at hand. Montgomery's words were always simple and perhaps he loved them at least as much as anyone. In effect he preached a simple gospel of Trust in Me; Trust in the Lord, and get your hair cut. He had something of the flare of a Baden Powell and a Billy Graham. He was a constant source of anxiety, an *enfant terrible*, but he bore a charmed life and knew it in his bones. He said things with a kind of innocence, yet it was a shrewd innocence.

The Americans in particular were remarkably patient, allowing him his head in areas where he exceeded his rights and privileges, and revealed his remarkable lack of tact. In mid-January, just after the Supreme Commander had reached England and assumed his command, Montgomery addressed the U.S. 29th Division:

> 'I came home the other day from Italy to take command of the British Army and the American Army of which General Eisenhower is the Supreme Commander, and he has put one army, the First American Army, under me for the battle.'

The newspapers were quick to question this statement, and to seek an explanation from Eisenhower. It was not the time for 'gamesmanship'. The Supreme Commander would not be drawn. He advised the newspapermen 'not to go off on the end of a limb'. Montgomery was undeniably the Ground Force Commander for the assault. After that, as soon as the Supreme Commander had established his headquarters in France, he would revert to the command of an Army Group opposite General Bradley. General Bradley, meanwhile, commanding the U.S. 1st Army from his headquarters in Bristol, and the U.S. 12th Army Group from its headquarters in London, watched sardonically from the sidelines, biding his time. 'Monty' was doing no harm, and his drive for the expansion of the assault, especially his emphasis on the rapid taking of the port of Cherbourg, earned Bradley's whole-hearted support.

Everyone, except Montgomery, was being very careful not to give offence, and the Americans often felt that they were walking on very thin and slippery ice. General Eisenhower commanded the entire resources of Britain on land, sea and in the air. It was as well not to rub it in. But the newspapers of Britain and the U.S.A. were quick to seize upon points of prestige, and to make 'news'. It was remarked, especially in America, that although Eisenhower was undeniably the Supreme Commander, the Commanders-in-Chief of the Naval and Air Forces, and the 'Ground Force' Commander were all British. Was it not clear that the British had yielded the 'figurehead' position while keeping the real power in their own hands?

It was not clear, and it was not true. Eisenhower, however modest he might be, was none the less the wielder of real power over Britain and all her war effort, even though it was difficult for him in the early days to realize the extent of his metamorphosis from a comparative nonentity to a world figure. For Eisenhower it was a situation of extreme delicacy, and if Montgomery was incapable of tact, others must exercise a greater tact to cover him. But there is no doubt that Eisenhower was irritated by Montgomery's constant travelling, and his absence from conferences.

The fact is that the command situation irked Montgomery. He alone of the three British commanders was not a Commander-in-Chief, and was never to be more than '*de facto* commander of the ground forces in the assault, but was never given the title of ground commander.'[1]

All this had been worked out carefully and agreed with the U.S. Joint Chiefs of Staff and by COSSAC, General Morgan, in November, 1943. But at that time an enlargement of the assault area and the forces involved had not been agreed. The enlargement would produce a U.S. Army Group on the Continent more swiftly than had been anticipated, and would set closer limits to Montgomery's ground force command. It never made sense to Montgomery.

II

Montgomery's immediate task upon arrival in Britain was to set his staff and the COSSAC staff to work on increasing the strength of the assault and enlarging the area of the *Overlord* plan. This brought him hard up against the basic facts of his command, and the immensity of the administrative, supply and maintenance problems involved. The repercussions were felt at once throughout the whole complex, and the strength of the structure and framework evolved over the years was subjected to severe stresses and strains, all of which it absorbed. In a very real sense the great operation was already under way, and would steadily gather momentum until the day when the Allied armies, with all the paraphernalia of war, would be

[1] Pogue: *The Supreme Command*, p. 45. Office of Chief of Mil. Hist. Washington.

launched against the enemy. Thereafter the momentum would have to be maintained until the end. Elaborate exercises involving assault troops, craft, vehicles and weapons were in constant rehearsal from the estuary of the Taw and Torridge to the East Anglian dunes. Tens of thousands of men assaulted the beaches in conditions carefully simulating the rigours and the din of battle. Convoys were incessantly on the move and the intricate machinery evolved for feeding troops, and all their gear, into and out of the 'pipe lines' of embarkation was tested, tinkered and improved. Organizations bearing curious code names—BUCO, TURCO, MOVCO, and even SPOBS, proliferated and strove by trial and error to perfect their vital functions for the day. Almost every kind of eventuality imaginable was imagined and the means of dealing with it considered and rehearsed.

Against such a background of constant growth and incessant activity the enlargement of the whole operation must be seen. It was like a vast subconscious whose intrusion upon the conscious mind of the commander might have proved daunting in the extreme.

In January, in agreement with the Supreme Commander's Chief of Staff, Walter Bedell Smith, Montgomery proposed to increase the weight of the assault from three divisions to five, and to drop three airborne divisions within twenty-four hours. The assault area would be increased from approximately twenty-five miles to fifty miles, from astride the River Orne in the East to astride the River Vire in the West, covering the Seine Bay between the Le Havre headland and the Cherbourg peninsula, from Caen to Carentan. Caen and Cherbourg would be the major objectives, the first as a road centre, the 'gateway to Paris', embracing many airfields, and offering minor port facilities by way of the Caen canal and the Orne; the second as a major port primarily for the direct supply of the U.S. Forces. Until these objectives were gained the supply of the invasion armies must take place over the Normandy beaches.

In discussions with the Naval and Air Force Commanders-in-Chief Montgomery learned from Air Chief Marshal Sir Trafford Leigh-Mallory that his enlarged plan would demand eight additional fighter squadrons to cover the new area and

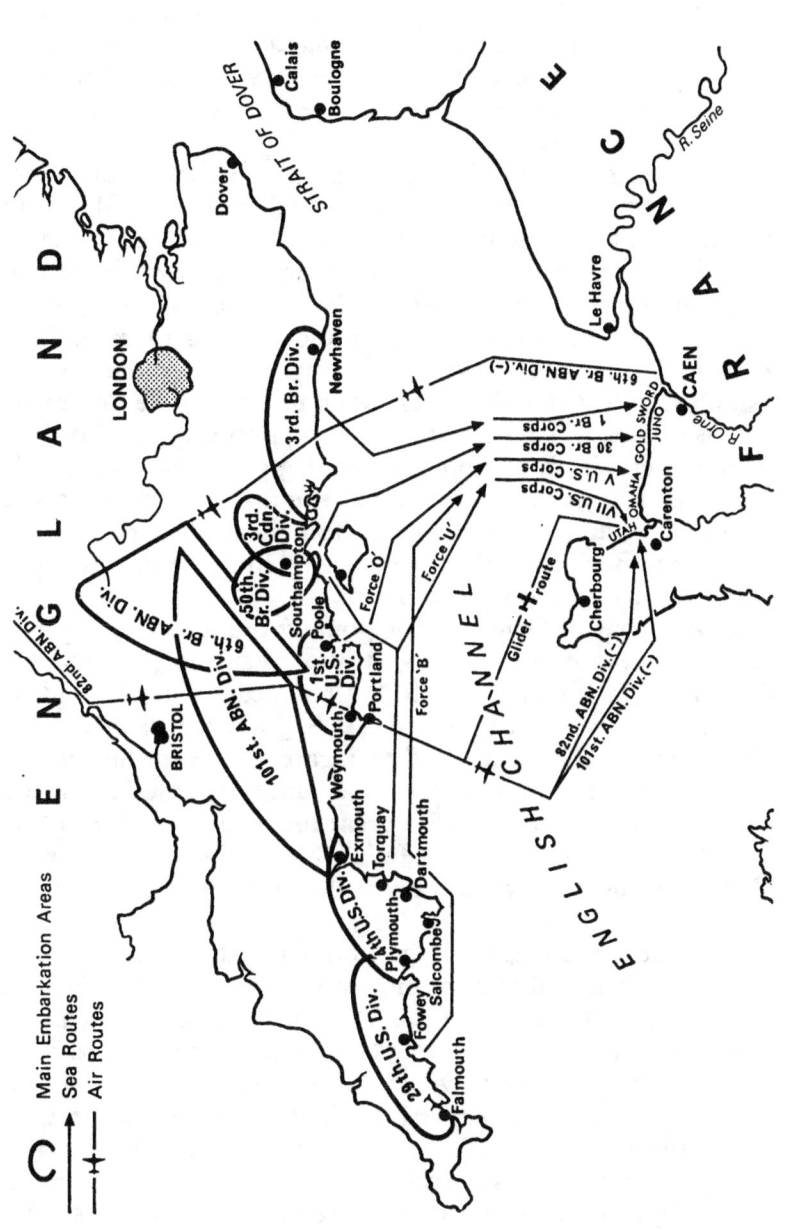

the shipping lanes, and at least two hundred more troop carrier aircraft must be ready in England two months before 'D day' to drop the three Airborne divisions in twenty-four hours. Crews would have to be selected and trained for gliders and troop carriers.

At the same time Admiral Ramsay, the Naval force commander, estimated the need for two additional naval assault forces to lift two divisions. The enlarged front would demand a considerable increase of naval bombardment. More Merchant shipping must be made available for the build-up, more mine-sweepers, more escort vessels, and above all more landing-craft—of which there were not enough even for the greatest assault COSSAC had been permitted to plan by the Combined Chiefs of Staff. The total naval and support shipping involved would increase from approximately 3,500 vessels to nearly 7,000, and 625,000 tons of coastal shipping would be pressed into service, and would directly affect the civilian population. The entire British people were involved in the war, and it had been so increasingly since Dunkirk.

It was clear to General Montgomery that operation 'Anvil' must go by the board. It was also clear independently to COSSAC, to Lieut.-General Walter Bedell Smith, and to almost all concerned except the U.S. Joint Chiefs of Staff in Washington. They continued to regard 'Anvil' as an integral part of 'Overlord', and not as a separate or subsidiary operation, yet they supported the great increase in the 'Overlord' assault. In a paper dated 6th January, COSSAC recommended that the whole strategical concept should be reconsidered:

(a) The assault against the South Coast of France should revert to a threat on the basis of one assault division as originally conceived . . . (At Quebec, August, 1943.)
(b) The additional requirements in landing-craft and other resources which would have been allotted to (the Supreme Commander, Mediterranean) to convert the threat into a two or three divisional assault should be re-allocated as early as practicable to strengthen Operation 'Overlord' and a reduction of air forces in the Mediterranean theatre in favour of the air forces in this country should be urgently considered.

Finally COSSAC requested 'the early concurrence of the Combined Chiefs of Staff to this proposal'.[1]

On the 10th January, Montgomery telegraphed to Eisenhower 'to hurl yourself into the contest and what we want, get for us'.

This was typical of Montgomery at his best, and thus far he was in agreement with the Americans in Britain. Thereafter their attitudes diverged. To Montgomery 'Overlord' was overwhelmingly all. On 5th January, Bedell Smith had telegraphed Eisenhower advising him that 'Additional lift can only be obtained at the expense of *Anvil*'. He was in agreement with COSSAC. In his view a one divisional threat would serve the Allied Purpose.[2] Eisenhower was no 'hurler'. He agreed that *Overlord* must be broadened and strengthened, but he clung to *Anvil* as a joint assault. It had been one of his last duties in December before leaving the Mediterranean to arrange the preliminary planning. It added to his difficulties in making an immediate decision; moreover the idea of a two-pronged attack, however far apart were the prongs, was in line with Eisenhower's strategic thinking, determining his belief in a 'Broad Front' approach to the defeat of Germany rather than the single powerful thrust favoured by Montgomery.

On the 15th January, Eisenhower arrived in England, and on the 21st he endorsed the enlargement of 'Overlord' in accordance with the demands of Montgomery supported by Bedell Smith. There is no doubt that Montgomery presented his views with the utmost force and conviction. Brigadier McLean, the chief Army planner in COSSAC, interpreted Montgomery's demands to mean 'Give me five divisions or get someone else to command.'[3] Broadly the COSSAC staff, including General Morgan, agreed with the British view on both *Overlord* and *Anvil*, and there were not seriously two views on the increased scale of the cross-channel attack. The Supreme Commander, as concerned for the success of *Overlord* as anyone could be, found himself in an increasingly difficult position. '... he was charged with the success of *Overlord* and from his

---

[1] *Grand Strategy*, vol. v, H.M.S.O., p. 234.
[2] Harrison: *Cross-Channel Attack*, Dept. of Army, Washington, D.C., p. 166-167.
[3] Harrison: *Cross-Channel Attack*, Dept. of Army, Washington, D.C., p. 166.

driver's seat the planning hazards began to make *Anvil* appear less feasible...'[1]

A long argument, basically at cross purposes and marked by extraordinary vehemence, was waged between Washington and London with the Supreme Commander trying to balance in the middle of the see-saw. The argument deeply concerned the campaign in Italy, which was meeting powerful enemy opposition. Against British insistence that the Italian campaign was the best and surest means of containing German forces, and thereby bringing aid to *Overlord* the Americans refused to abandon *Anvil*, until between a rapidly expanding *Overlord* and the minimum demands of Alexander in Italy, 'Anvil received the short end of the stick'. Nevertheless it was not abandoned. It was postponed until July, and finally took place in August under the code name *Dragoon*.

Montgomery's part in this long and complex affair was simple and definite. In his view an assault on the South of France would be about as much use in bringing aid to his forces in Normandy as an assault on the Marshall Islands. Moreover such an assault would not be possible as a joint operation. There were not enough landing-craft to go round, and there never would be. The U.S. Admiral King, the Naval member of the U.S. Joints Chiefs of Staff, held the key. He would either release landing-craft from the Pacific, or he would not. If he would not, then *Overlord* would be starved, and might only be sustained by releasing landing-craft from the Mediterranean.

Yet to see *Anvil* clearly it is necessary to consider many political and strategic issues. Had it been merely a proposed assault in conjunction with 'Overlord', and found to be impossible in the light of logistics, no one would have wasted much more breath upon it than did Montgomery. It marked, in fact, the end of British Grand Strategy and the dominance of the Americans and the Russians in deciding how the last phases of the war should be fought. For 'Stalin's stand (at Teheran) put the capstone on Anglo-American strategy. In a sense, therefore, he fixed Western strategy.' Moreover, as Maurice Matloff wrote, 'The Teheran decisions represented far more than the fashioning, at long last, of a grand design and a pattern

---

[1] *Command Decisions*, Dept. of Army, Washington, p. 390.

of victory. They marked a still subtle but significant change in the balance of military power within the coalition.'[1]

The Soviet Union was not only coming into its own, it had begun to call the tune. It was not a tune the British liked, and it generated fierce heat. In common with most rows, especially in the domestic sphere, the underlying cause of the trouble was never mentioned.

Meanwhile *Overlord* itself receded from its target date of 1st May to the end of the month, which would mean the first week in June. It was no more arguable than had been *Anvil*. Logistics determined not only the scale of the assault in *Overlord*, they determined its timing, and sign-posted the pace of its success.

Note: The Anvil arguments may be studied in the following books: *Command Decisions: The Anvil Decisions: Cross Roads of Strategy* Maurice, Matloff, Dept. of the Army, Washington, D.C.
Ehrman, *Grand Strategy*, vol. v H.M.S.O.
Pogue, *The Supreme Command*. Dept. of Army, Washington.
Ellis, *Victory in the West*, H.M.S.O.
Thompson, *The Price of Victory*, Chapter VII, *The Anvil Deadlock*, Constable, London.

III

All Britain was a miracle that year, or more truly the host of a miracle worked by the people. The full story has never been told, and probably it never will be. It involved the whole life of a nation, served by scores of anonymous and devoted men, many of drive and energy amounting to genius. It should not surprise, or provoke a grin of derision, when someone says, as someone sometimes does say, 'But for my father D-Day would not have been possible.' It may be true, inasmuch as the possible may be the work of a man.

The launching of the assault on Normandy, and all that

[1] Matloff: *The Anvil Decisions. Command Decisions*, Dept. of Army, Washington, p. 387-388.

preceded it, was known as 'Operation Neptune', and Britain had become Neptune Island.

By 1st February Montgomery and the Commanders-in-Chief of the naval and air forces had formulated the Initial Joint Plan, *Neptune*,[1] and the Initial Maintenance Plan. It was clear that the flexibility of armies, the objectives of armies, even the movements of armies, would be dictated by logistics, rather than by the enemy. An elaborate time-table of advance was growing. Tactically it would, and did, leave room for manoeuvre, but strategically it imposed severe limitations upon the Supreme Commander and his Army Group Commanders.

Suddenly time seemed very short. Scores of departments headed by practical men planned and laboured to achieve miracles, and confronted the statisticians on both sides of the Atlantic who were fighting with slide rules. The enormous quantities of shipping involved meant that loading capacities had to be examined down to the last detail. The Americans were inclined to cram in men or vehicles without considering the natural hazards of war and the sea, or the purely human problems. It was not simple arithmetic. Certainly it could be argued that so many men, or vehicles, could be fitted into so many cubic feet of space, but in practice it did not work out. The amphibious DUKW, for example, one of the finest general purpose 'work-horses' produced by the ingenuity of war, was grotesquely overloaded in trials, and with disastrous results. Men are not merely packages. Questions of weight were dependent upon how much equipment, rations, ammunition each man should carry. While some strove to strip men down to the bare necessities, others fought for latitude.

At times the enemy took a hand, reminding any who might tend to forget that the seas were dangerous. On the 28th April eight Tank Landing Ships were caught by enemy E boats in the channel. Two were sunk with tragic loss of life. 749 specialized highly trained men were killed and 300 wounded. Exercises and the 'real thing' were at times tragically mixed.

The vehicles essential to a division were cut from 3,000 to 2,500, and those immediately landed would be held down to carefully calculated minimum needs. Within the framework of

---

[1] Thompson: *The Price of Victory*, Chapter ix. *Neptune Island*. Ruppenthal: *Logistics*, vols. i & ii, Dept. of Army, Washington.

chance nothing must be left to chance. At one stage the specialized vehicles to be involved and in production seemed to demand so many for their service that Churchill exclaimed at the figures, and sent a memorandum to Montgomery on 27th January:

> 200,000 vehicles seem a vast outfit to attach to an army which, at thirty divisions of 20,000 men apiece would have only 600,000 men, of which less than three-quarters would actually fight. As each vehicle takes at least a man and a half to drive and look after it, here are 300,000 men already absorbed. One hopes there will be enough infantry with rifles and bayonets to protect this great mass of vehicles from falling into the hands of the enemy.[1]

The message reveals the ever-present dangers that the prodigious quantities of war material, and the increasing variety, could make planning go mad. Montgomery had sent a note of his priorities to the Ministry of Supply which included the waterproofing of all these vehicles. This entailed the training of 3,500 waterproofing instructors to supervise the laying on of a mixture of grease, lime and asbestos fibre.

These things are merely fragments in a jig-saw of vast complexity on which military, naval and air force staffs of two countries worked in with a host of civilian experts. By the end of January the whole process of detailed planning gathered momentum. It had been feared in the Autumn of 1943 that there would be a shortage of essential supplies in Britain. There had been a crisis due in the main to the inability of British ports to receive cargoes coming across the Atlantic in ever-growing fleets of ships. There had been a cut of half a million tons in 'peace imports' in a single month to make way for war imports. There was an even greater crisis of space. London itself had become a hive of war activity housing 30,000 United States troops. The three-quarters of a million men in Britain when Montgomery took over command rose swiftly to one and a half million before his eyes, and totalled three million at the end of May. Camps, spreading over thousands of acres, were growing with immense speed. Inland transport was strained beyond all previously imaginable limits, and so also were the

[1] Churchill: *Closing the Ring*, vol. v, Appendix C, p. 528 (R.U.).

creative and technical abilities of men. A single convoy coming in to one port in March, 1944, just before the very peak of import, consisted of 42 vessels with varied cargoes, comprising 1,500 vehicles, including tanks, 2,000 vehicles in cases, 200 aircraft and 50,000 tons of general supplies. All this, and the ships involved, had to be dealt with in eight days in a small port, and the berths cleared ready for more. This one batch of cargo demanded 75 special trains and 10,000 loaded cars, apart from movement by road. And it all had to be stored 'somewhere', camouflaged and in correct order, for soon it would be shipped again to France.

United States Army imports alone demanded 100 special freight trains with 18,000–20,000 loaded cars each week. Imported locomotives to bolster and sustain British rolling stock stood tender to tender in the sidings and yards.

The pattern was repeated in more than a score of ports handling 1,000,000 tons of war materials a month. Huge tracts of territory were requisitioned. Forests like Sherwood in Nottinghamshire became ammunition dumps. A tented camp for 1,000 men covered 34 acres. A hutted hospital, usually Nissen huts, for a similar number covered 50 acres. This must be multiplied in terms of 3,000,000 men and 300,000 hospital beds, and add the space for an additional 126 airfields provided for the U.S. Air Force. 56,000 civilians worked on these enterprises together with specialized military personnel.

> 'Even the smallest hamlets and rural lanes did not escape the feverish activity that characterized the operations of every depot and training area as well as of the various headquarters. A prodigious stocking of supplies and equipment took place in these months, evoking the comment that the British Isles were so weighted down with the munitions of war that they were kept from sinking only by the buoyant action of the barrage balloons which floated above the principal ports and military installations.'[1]

The ports were choked, the seas were choked, the country was choked, but it still breathed. The coastal belt was 'frozen' to a depth of ten miles from the Wash to Land's End, and from Dunbar to Arbroath in Scotland. On 10th March all

---
[1] Ruppenthal: *Logistics*, vol. i, Office of Co. Mil. Hist.

movement, communications and mail, became subject to strict control. On 6th April all military leave was stopped, and the censorship was drawn tight. Diplomatic privileges were severely restricted for all Embassies by the will of the Supreme Commander, and with the uneasy agreement of the War Cabinet.

On the East and South coasts elaborate deception plans were designed to mislead the enemy as to the direction and target of the coming assault, of which it was barely credible that he was unaware. The shortest distance between two points across the channel from Calais to the Somme bristled with men and armament on the enemy shores. The beaches of Normandy also sprouted a growing maze of lethal obstacles, observed and examined by men in midget submarines, and constantly reported upon.

All Britain seemed to hold its breath. Nobody knew anything, but everyone, in a sense, knew everything. Every man, woman and child lived with it. The troops lived in another world.

> 'Over the war years,' wrote COSSAC, 'indignity and inconvenience had been heaped upon the devoted backs of (the people) almost to breaking point.'[1]

Censors in their many hundreds, working on bare trestle tables in scores of dingy rooms, felt all this like the throb of engines in the tens of thousands of letters opened each day, and from which, more than anything else, they tried to gauge morale and the readiness of the leading troops for their ordeal. What mattered was 'the heart' of England, and it was sound despite war weariness after four years of struggle. The lot of the people, at its worst, was infinitely preferable to that of the citizens of Occupied Europe whose spirits were sustained by hopes that must too often have seemed fragile and unreal. For all Britain was an inspiration in its 'frenzied activities', and in the fertility of its brains. A dozen 'inventions' almost escaped notice. Among the most brilliant schemes was the project to construct ten three-inch submarine cables under the water from the Isle of Wight to Cherbourg, each pipeline capable of delivering 300 tons of fuel oil a day.[2] No one knew whether

[1] Morgan: *Overture to Overlord*.
[2] *Pluto*.

it would work, any more than they knew that the great harbours under construction to tow across the channel would work. If they didn't work, some sort of improvisation would be needed to fill the gaps. Few doubted that the gaps would be filled.

Winston Churchill, the Prime Minister and Minister of Defence, whose restless and questing spirit could not be subdued, seemed aware of 'everything'. He had even 'hatched' or assisted at the hatching of some of it. In the midst of considering and debating the strategies of a war embracing the world, the development of major plans, the movements of troops, he found time to send out a spate of memoranda reflecting his wide interests. The appendices of his war memoirs give constant startling glimpses of his immense versatility and fertility, even of his humanity. In his messages on 2nd April, 1944, for example, he is concerned with the niggling prosecution of a baker, the exhorbitant rents charged for letting houses to Americans, a trial under the Witchcraft Act, the use of D.D.T., prefabricated houses, and the organization of the Guards Armoured Brigades. Moreover he demanded answers to all his questions, great and small. You can practically feel Churchill's brains palpitating day after day.

Brilliant minds spawn ideas, often in droves, and many of them 'red herrings'. Churchill spawned his quota of 'red herrings', yet here and there were ideas of pure gold and of inestimable worth. High among these was his original idea to build harbours to tow across the seas into position tight up against enemy shores, to build a 'bridge', in effect, from England to Normandy. The idea had grown in his mind since Gallipoli.

In the Spring of 1944 the final activities to make the artificial harbours ready on the day were in full spate. They would ensure, given luck and reasonable weather, 12,500 tons of supplies to Montgomery's armies each day throughout the vital period of the 'build-up' and until major ports were won. If the harbours failed, whatever foothold might be gained must be sustained over open beaches. There were men who were not daunted by that prospect, and Montgomery was one of them. 20,000 men worked overtime day and night like beavers—literally like beavers—in twelve great holes excavated on Thames side below water-level, leaving a barrier of earth between them and the river. Pumps fought the encroaching water, and in these 'holes', as well as in eight dry docks and two wet docks, the harbours, in their various parts, took shape. Tens of thousands of tons of steel and concrete became known as Mulberries, Gooseberries and Phoenixes. There were also more than 3,000 craft, lighters and barges, manned by 15,000 men in this one 'artificial harbour' project. As for ships, they grew not only in the shipyards but in the streets, in alleyways, in workshops. The naked struts and skeletons were everywhere.

IV

From January to May, General Montgomery toured Britain in his special train, or out on the road, with all this panorama before his eyes. He spoke to groups of workers, great and small, at every opportunity, in factories, on the docks and railways. At London docks alone he addressed 16,000 men and thought that the people were showing signs of war weariness after four years of effort. The industrial side of his activities made him unpopular with politicians, but he did not care. His effect was electrical. He established an immediate audience-actor *rapport*. His self-confidence was infectious, and bred confidence. That he was clearly no respecter of persons was part of his appeal. He was the little man with teeth, and he could bite. He stood before his audiences of all types and conditions of men and women, supremely confident, an oracle, small in stature, distinctive of feature, crisp and positive in speech, a pocket-size fire eater. He gave the illusion of being 'matey'. He was a tremendous exhibitionist, a national hero, a phenomenon, His eccentricities had provided a fund of stories, mostly apocryphal, of his gall, his truculence, his ruthlessness, known in some measure to almost every man, woman and child in the island. Above all he was a winner, and his star was bright. He revelled in the warmth and confidence flowing out to him, and although he seems to have lacked a sense of humour, and it is impossible to imagine Montgomery seeing the funny side of himself, he gave laughter and chuckles to the multitude, and they loved him. He released the frustrations and buoyed the hopes of the ordinary man, and even now, a quarter of a century after, the chuckles linger on.

Montgomery's main concern was with the troops, and he has estimated that he saw and was seen by more than one million men. Wherever he halted troops formed great squares thousands deep, and he stood on the bonnet of his jeep, dapper, his breast swelling like a turkey cock's and as resplendent, his crisp military voice giving a new dimension to his *clichés*, absolutely in command of the situation. He made a point of walking slowly through the ranks of men, standing at ease, 'so that they could lean and twist, and look at me all the time if they wished to—and most did.' Indoors or out of doors no man coughed, for Montgomery did not permit coughing.

It is difficult from his writings to gain an idea of the impression made upon him by the unique performance of a nation in which he played a leading role. As an actor he was superb. At the Mansion House in March he paid a tribute to General Paget, his predecessor, 'who gave of his best in order that the army in England should stand ready at all times ... I find the army in England in very good trim. I believe that when it goes into battle it will prove to be the best army we have ever had.'

This tribute, unique, I believe, in Montgomery's record of high command, must be a measure of the deep impression the troops had made upon him. There were to be no excuses, no insurances against failure. There would not be failure. Whatever the forebodings in many minds, including Churchill's and General Brooke's, Montgomery did not share them.

General Eisenhower and his Army Commander, General Bradley, were also making the rounds, Eisenhower in his quiet and modest way gaining the confidence of British and American troops alike, while Bradley tramped the west country, where in the main his army lay, squatting on his haunches if he felt like it, to chew a blade of grass, watching, feeling in scores of units the essential fibre of his men, remarkably approachable, immune to flattery, difficult to fool, and not given to fooling himself. He forbade any kind of preparation for his coming, and observed his men as they were. The 'Enlisted Men' could and did speak to General Bradley without embarrassment. He had the mien of a soldier, a dour and natural simplicity recognized by the common man as a mark of the uncommon man. He might be a great general.

Bradley was profoundly aware that he had only one division under his command with battle experience, and that they were disgruntled men, wanting to 'go home'. This was not their Island, and not their war in the obvious sense that it was Britain's war. They could not share the British total awareness that they would be fighting for their country.

Bradley believed in men, more than in machines. He tended to dislike the new machines of war, and refused to use some of them, to his cost. But more often his judgement was true. He was very much aware of the initial difficulties that would face his troops, striving to cross the narrow causeways of the swamps behind the Western beaches code-named Utah and Omaha, and from which he must break out his army to take Cherbourg, to force his way through to the coast of Britanny and through the close country to the south and east, known as the *bocage*, at last to wheel on the British hinge and pivot on his left. Bradley knew that he needed, that he must have, an airborne division to drop close in, to help him to gain a foothold. Air Chief Marshal, Sir Trafford Leigh Mallory was all against it, convinced of disaster. He would prefer to use three airborne divisions on the left in the region of Caen, leaving Bradley's Army vulnerable in the extreme. The final decision rested with the Supreme Commander.

CHAPTER TWO

The Last Days . . .

I

ON the 7th and 8th April a scale model of the Normandy beaches was laid out on a floor as 'wide as a street' at St. Paul's School, Montgomery's 21st Army Group Headquarters. Montgomery dominated the model like a Gulliver triumphant in Lilliput, detailing his plan to his generals with the simple and precise virtuosity that had so impressed General Brooke and Churchill before Alamein. Once again it was not his own plan, but a marvellously sustained growth built upon the foundations laid by General Paget and the Naval staff, developed by General Morgan and his COSSAC staff, and brought to its final magnitude by the combined efforts of 21st Army Group staff, U.S. 1st Army staff, the Naval and Air staffs, and at last coordinated by SHAEF.[1] Nevertheless the mark of Montgomery was clear in its strategic pattern and in his tactical development of the 'lodgement area'. Three British divisions on the left and two U.S. divisions on the right would assault five beaches soon after dawn on the chosen day, and within one and one quarter hours of each other. Geography and the problems of supply had ordained the relative zones of the British and American forces first in Britain, and finally in the assault. Tidal variations on the Normandy coast between the rivers Orne and Vire further ordained that American troops should be the first to set foot on French soil. Thus, as it seems, by chance the Allied armies would be embarked upon roles admirably suited to the respective merits of their troops and their generals.

It was Montgomery's purpose to secure a foothold on D-Day embracing a strip of coast from Caen to Bayeux to Carentan. Thereafter by D 17 he hoped to have extended the lodgement in a loop from Cabourg at the mouth of the Seine to Granville.

[1] Shaef: G–4, *Logistics*, vol. i, p. 327.

A day or two later the Cherbourg (Cotentin) peninsula to Avranches would be in his hands. Thereafter movement would speed up, and by D 90 nearly all French territory between the rivers Seine and Loire would be his. That was the absolute limit of advance, according to 'Logistics', and there was no safety margin. By that time the Allied armies would be consuming 45,000 tons of supplies each day, and with a growing appetite, growing lines of communication, and almost certainly, growing congestion in the beach and base areas.

Very early in the logistical and in the military planning it had been realized that very shortly thereafter a second major port, the port of Antwerp, would become a necessity for 21st Army Group. Without such a port a drive eastward into Germany by the Northern armies, which the left wing of the Allied armies would have become, could not be seriously attempted. The Channel ports, whatever their condition, could not provide the base for such an enterprise. Thus Antwerp must be well in the sights of the Army Group Commander, and of course of the Supreme Commander, from the beginning. It must be an urgent priority of the 'second 90 days'.

Even so the time seemed very short if the war were to be won in 1944, and the urgency in General Montgomery's mind was very clear. Beyond 1944 the 'future' did not belong to Britain. Yet within this logistical and planning framework the entire upshot from D-Day to the end was unpredictable. The assault might fail, and despite all the overwhelming Allied air and sea power it might be contained in an area without room to move. The enemy might collapse, or partially collapse, and the whole road to the heart of Germany become 'wide open'. Or the enemy, faced with inevitable defeat, crushed between the armies of Soviet Russia in the East, and the Anglo-American armies in the West, might surrender. It was at this point of thinking that many minds, not previously troubled, began to regard 'Unconditional Surrender' with doubt, and even with dismay. This phrase might have condemned the enemy to suffer total defeat and destruction, and the Allies to inflict total defeat and destruction. Above all it might cost time that could not be spared.

At St. Paul's School in April no man could have misunderstood Montgomery's intention to draw the enemy armour and reserves to concentrate upon his armies on the left flank, while Bradley's armies, having secured Cherbourg, would cut Britanny in halves from Lannion to Vannes, investing Brest and Lorient, advance swiftly to the Loire, and pivot on the British hinge to the Seine. It was implicit that the role of rapid advance north-eastward was for the American armies, implicit also that if there should be an 'expanding torrent' they would provide its spearheads. No man was more suited to such a role than General Patton. It seemed possible that Montgomery–Dempsey with Bradley–Patton as a team in unison under one Supreme Command might prove to be a military team of all the talents. Rolled into one, if such an amalgam were possible, they would make a 'great general'. Everything might depend upon the quality of Supreme Command, and I believe Montgomery saw this from the beginning: a 'Ground Force' commander was needed, but where was such a man to be found? MacArthur was in the Pacific; Wavell was in India, too weary for such a command even if such a prospect had been considered. As for Auchinleck, he had the talents, but perhaps not the temperament, and he, too, was in India. There were no 'Napoleons', no 'Wellingtons', no 'Marlboroughs', and because of that there would be no 'Ground Force' commander, after Normandy.

Montgomery's strategy was unanswerable, and his plan made itself. Geographically and in the enemy distribution of forces the enemy strength could only be brought to bear upon the Allied left. A German army was in the Pas de Calais, awaiting the Allied assault north of the Seine. A German army was in Normandy. Enemy reserves must concentrate and converge upon the road centre of Caen. Montgomery must hold them and the hinge while the Americans wove their way through the *bocage* to emerge and strike. That was the way, and there was no other way.

Generals Bradley and Dempsey, in their turns, gave clear expositions of their more intimate tasks and intentions. Both men were very much aware of the difficulties their armies would encounter in the close *bocage* country, where, through centuries, the laden farm carts had carved deep channels between the small hedged fields. The branches of the hedgerows knit overhead, and in the summer the foliage made of the countryside a kind of maze. It was not the kind of country in which armour could hope to 'crack about'. It extended to a depth of 40 miles behind the beaches, and had an ominous and ancient reputation as 'Guerilla' country. Moreover the extensive swamps behind the beaches west of the Vire, and again embracing the river Aure from Isigny almost to Trévières, were a source of profound anxiety to General Bradley. Without powerful airborne support to secure the narrow exits over the causeways a landing on Utah beach might prove abortive.

General Montgomery supported General Bradley unequivocally. Yet this vital issue remained in doubt until the 30th May when Eisenhower, exercising the most difficult decision of his Supreme Command,[1] overrode the powerful and sustained objections of Air Chief Marshal Sir Trafford Leigh Mallory. Without success on Utah beach the capture of Cherbourg must be gravely delayed, and without Cherbourg the Allied armies, unable to grow and to be sustained, might be held in their 'lodgement' area indefinitely. It was a reminder that the artificial harbours had not been tried, and might even meet disaster in the long and difficult tow across the channel.

A tremendous assault from the air had been in progress for some months, working up to a crescendo as D-Day approached, designed to hammer the enemy into the ground and to deny him reserves. The German Air Force in the West was over extended and lacked the power seriously to hinder the Allied missions over France. Radar installations had been severely damaged or destroyed, communications disrupted, and even the enemy meteorological equipment was crippled. Railways, bridges, road junctions, and enemy movement in daylight suffered continuous bombardment from the air, and it seemed a miracle that enemy troops, armour and artillery could move at all. In their static defences troops were given little rest. 18,000 men of the Todt organization were moved away from work on strengthening the 'Atlantic Wall' to assist in the more urgent repair of railways. At the same time the French Resistance embarked upon plans of subversion and sabotage, known

---

[1] Harrison: *Cross-Channel Attack*, U.S. Army in W.W. 2, pp. 185-186. Pogue: *The Supreme Command*, U.S. Army in W.W. 2, p. 139.

as *Vert* and *Grenouille*, to aid the allied landings. 150 men and 1,500 tons of arms and supplies were dropped in France in the three months before D-Day to assist these activities.

Yet in spite of all these things Field-Marshal Rommel, commanding Army Group B from the Zuider Zee to Nantes on the Loire, had greatly strengthened the coastal defences. In particular the beach and under water obstacles had proliferated in number and complexity along the Normandy Coast. It was Rommel's belief that the Allied armies must be denied a foothold, and he wanted to mass all possible strength to this end. Neither von Runstedt, Commander-in-Chief West, nor Gehr von Schweppenburg, commanding Armoured Group West, agreed. All three men had access to the Fuehrer, whose decisions would be final. It was an unhappy situation, aggravated by the obvious need to expect the assault and to prepare to receive it anywhere between the Hague and Brest, particularly in the Pas de Calais, and secondly in Normandy. Those who believed that the Pas de Calais must be the Allied target continued to believe it long after the Normandy landings had been established, and Rommel's 15th Army was held partially immobilized for many days.[1]

Nevertheless Rommel was deeply concerned with the threat to Normandy, and demanded heavy reinforcements. 'If I am to wait until the enemy landing has actually taken place, before I can demand, through normal channels, the command and dispatch of the mobile forces, delays will be inevitable.'[2]

His demands were not answered. Similarly his demands for enormous quantities of mines to complete his beach defences were unfulfilled. His achievement in the face of obstruction was remarkable. He had planned for four main belts of obstacles from 'six feet of water at mean high tide' to 'twelve feet of water at low tide.' His first two belts were completed, and more than half a million obstacles, more than thirty thousand of them mined, successfully in place.

British naval reconnaissance units watched them grow and explored their nature, landing teams of specialists with astonishing daring on enemy beaches, and reporting on the vast jig-saw of lethal obstacles out beyond the low tide marks.

[1] Thompson: *The Price of Victory*, chapter viii. (*Air Power and Overlord*.)
[2] *The Rommel Papers*, Edn. L.H., p. 470.

General Sir Percy Hobart, commanding the 79th Armoured Division, and working closely with highly skilled engineer beach groups, devised the means to counter or to overcome each new threat. He was a man of great ingenuity, and immense drive. 'Some of the staff under me,' wrote de Guingand, Montgomery's Chief of Staff, 'would become terrified when they knew General Hobo was about.' General Hobart was not an easy man to deny. He was also Montgomery's brother-in-law, and there was a bond between the two men, almost certainly unique in Montgomery's personal relationships. For his part Montgomery pinned his faith on Hobart's great variety of armour. The swimming (D.D.) tanks would lead the assault of the infantry. Numerous armoured fighting vehicles of the 79th Armoured division would follow. All these would be Montgomery's 'tin-opener'. The first day would be, in its way, decisive.

No one under-estimated the enemy. He had 58 divisions in the West, and even half-blind and crippled as he was, almost helpless at sea and in the air, a great surge of armour might hurl the invaders back into the sea before a firm foothold could be established. In the final analysis the issue must depend upon men on their feet, and all the overwhelming fire power from the sea and sky, would not make it otherwise. Montgomery was well aware of his extreme vulnerability in the early stages. There was no way of knowing in advance that the enemy had been completely deceived by the deception plans and expected the assault in the Pas de Calais. There was no way of knowing the remarkable lack of co-ordination between the enemy land, sea and air forces, and not even the most sanguine observer would have gambled on the Allied achievement of surprise.

Moreover, all would depend upon the ability of the Naval forces to lift *Operation Neptune* out of Britain, across the channel, and onto the Normandy beaches, and keep the vast concourse of men and materials moving. Admiral Sir Bertram Ramsay left no one in any doubt of the immensity of the task.

On the 15th May the Supreme Commander conducted the final Presentation of Plans, again at St. Paul's School, in the presence of the King, the Prime Minister, General Smuts, the British Chiefs of Staff, and the Air Marshals, Admirals and Generals. General Eisenhower seemed to have a complete grasp of the situation. His task, in accordance with paragraph 2 of the Directive given to him, dated 12th February, 1944, was simply stated:

'You will enter the Continent of Europe and, in conjunction with the other United Nations, undertake operations aimed at the heart of Germany and the destruction of her armed forces.'

The rehearsals were over.

II

Early in May the Supreme Commander and his commanders-in-chief had established their headquarters in the vicinity of Portsmouth, and there they were not only able easily to keep in close personal touch with one another, but also to feel the final phases of the preparation as a vivid, living experience. At his Main headquarters in the area Montgomery had created the relaxed atmosphere in which he chose to live, and amidst all the 'frenzied activities', anxieties and tensions inseparable from the final days, the Ground Force Commander preserved his remarkable serenity, contriving an oasis of calm. There he entertained the King and the Prime Minister, and infected both men with his quiet confidence. Smuts also was a visitor, and the two of them had lamented that it was not possible to mount the assault in the fine and ideal May weather. In retrospect the failure to do so may have cost the winning of the war in the vital year for Britain, and whatever the shortages and 'last touches', it seems that the risk would have been worthwhile. The King, Churchill and Smuts had never fully reconciled themselves to a cross-channel assault, and to some extent the C.I.G.S., General Brooke, shared their unease.

For months Churchill had worried about the inordinate demands on manpower for the servicing of the hosts of armoured vehicles, and had expressed himself forcibly, it will be remembered, in a memorandum to Montgomery on 27th January. The Prime Minister had arrived at Montgomery's headquarters determined to pursue the matter further, but Montgomery had shown himself the absolute master in his own house. Quietly and firmly he told the Prime Minister to mind his own business, and leave him and his staff to mind theirs. It was evident that Montgomery had grown in stature during the final months. He had become accustomed to walk with Kings. The magnitude of the events in which he was playing a leading role had impressed themselves deeply upon him. His popularity had not waned, but it had changed key. He was no longer a 'mascot', no longer a 'Card', but Britain's chosen commander to lead the Allied ground forces in the greatest assault in the history of warfare. Soon after the final 'Presentation of Plans' on 15th May General Smuts had talked to Montgomery rather like a 'Dutch Uncle' over a tête-a-tête luncheon, and awakened him to a new view of his image. The wily old statesman had carefully planted the seeds of ideas in Montgomery's mind, and inspired him 'seriously to think.' Smuts had emphasized his immense prestige with the British people. It was unique, and it would grow. 'He was emphatic that when the war was over, I must speak out,' and say the things that statesmen could not say. Europe would need 'a framework on which to rebuild itself... Britain must stand forward as the corner stone of the new structure.'[1]

At the end of April the whole vast and complex machine of war had been set in motion towards its climax on the chosen day, the 5th June. The whole of Southern England seethed with men and machines in constant movement. It was like a gigantic human ant-heap, and as purposeful. The hideous thought occurred to some of how this mass of men and materials moving in innumerable channels, might be halted, and even put into reverse. It was a possibility almost too terrible to contemplate, involving not only prodigious problems of organization and improvisation, but the morale of tens of thousands of men brought carefully to a pitch of readiness. On the 4th, 5th and 6th June moon and tide would serve, and on the 7th the assault would still be possible. After that ideal conditions would not recur for two weeks, and more probably a month. The implications of such a postponement, including the loss of vital time, became a nightmare to the Naval Commander-in-Chief whose ships must begin to move, in some cases five or six days in advance. The Commanders of the Air Forces shared some of these anxieties, and their meteorological experts

[1] Montgomery: *Memoirs*, pp. 236-237.

watched their charts with the utmost care. Nearly 20,000 men were ready to be dropped in their target areas in advance of the assault from the sea. Elaborate close support bombing programmes would be jeopardised by cloud conditions that might not prevent an assault from the sea.

Only Montgomery seemed to preserve a genuine calm. The decision to delay or not to delay would not be his. If the Navy would support his troops and the great armada of ships would carry them, he was prepared to go. Meanwhile the final preparations gathered momentum. 150 'Hards' had been constructed of concrete and steel wire mesh to reinforce the southern ports from which nearly 200,000 men and all their armoury of war would sail in the first waves of the assault. While the minesweepers swept the channels to Normandy nearly 7,000 ships, from landing-craft to Capital ships, assembled at their anchorages, and it seemed inconceivable that such activity could escape the attention of the enemy. Yet in the last two weeks not a single enemy reconnaissance was flown over England.

On the 26th May the invading forces, moving as though on invisible conveyor belts, began to divide into embarkation groups to be sealed off in their last marshalling areas. No one in the ranks of men and junior commanders knew the day, but all could feel it. Weapons were checked. 170,000,000 maps were ready for distribution, and more were coming off the presses in infinite diversity. The waterproofing of tens of thousands of vehicles, together with artillery and even wireless sets, consumed an astronomical number of man-hours, and since this operation impaired the efficiency of machines it was left to the last moment, warning all involved that the last moment was at hand.[1] Moreover every item would have to be de-water-proofed as soon as possible after landing.

It was this kind of thing that caused the Prime Minister to blench, but as May gave way to June all men at the top watched the weather with an anxiety that transcended all else. It was astounding to realize that all this prodigious effort, this long and meticulous planning and organization over the years, coming at last to its fulfilment, could be denied by the weather. The weather could not only prevent the assault from sailing,

---

[1] The water-proofing of one tank took 286 man-hours.

it could overwhelm it on the way, it could maroon it on the beaches. In the mid-twentieth century not all the ingenuity and invention of men could overcome, or even predict with certainty, the weather.

III

The hours of the weather crisis have been explored in detail many times. On the 2nd June, the meteorological men observed the first signs that the fine weather was breaking up. A depression over Iceland was moving south. High winds and heavy cloud might form over the channel to threaten the airborne landings, and deprive the assault of air cover on the beaches. The sea-sickness certain to affect many throughout a rough passage would endanger efficiency and morale.

Nevertheless it was too early, and the evidence too inconclusive to slow the machine. On the 3rd June, 300,000 men were embarking or embarked on the great array of vessels which would carry them to their appointment with the enemy. The first convoys of the groups from south-west England sailed towards the sea assembly area off the Isle of Wight, known as 'Piccadilly Circus'. The mine-sweeping flotillas had cleared the channels of 'The Spout' to Normandy and placed 830 marker buoys in position.

There had been anxious conferences on the 3rd June presided over by the Supreme Commander at the Naval Headquarters of Admiral Ramsay, and in the early hours of 4th June the forecast for the next twenty-four hours was so bad that the Supreme Commander ordered a postponement. Montgomery's was the lone voice in favour of the assault going in. It was an attitude that amazed and shocked Air Chief Marshal Tedder,[1] the Deputy Supreme Commander, who at once cast his vote for postponement. I think he misunderstood Montgomery. The Ground Force Commander was not stating that the assault should sail, but simply that he was prepared to go. It was not intended as a reflection on the enormous importance of air support.

An agonising twenty-four hours followed, while destroyers

[1] Tedder: *With Prejudice*, Cassell, 1966, p. 545.

and a 'Walrus' aircraft raced to turn back two entire U.S. forces heading for France, and unaware of the postponement. 128 tank landing-craft were 25 miles south of St. Catherine's point, and likely to show up on the enemy radar screens. In the teeth of a Force 5 wind and heavy seas these ships turned about to seek the shelter of Weymouth Bay. Not all of them found even a brief shelter and respite.

For many of those upon whom the fortunes of Europe would depend the three days from the 3rd to the 6th June were the worst of their lives. 'Some of them had been shuttled, blind to sea and sky, daylight and darkness, sick, weary, wondering, aware that a moment would come when they would be spewed up like Jonahs upon an alien shore, bristling with devices of death and destruction and beaten with shot and shell. Yet it was a moment to be wished for; an end.'[1] On the morning of the 5th, while half a gale and high seas whipped the channel and low unbroken cloud lay grey over grey ships, the Supreme Commander made his brave decision that 'Overlord' would sail. It was none the less brave because the alternative was horrifying, and would almost surely prolong the conflict. Group Captain Stagg, the Chief meteorologist, forecast a break in the weather for the 6th June. He could not predict its duration, but it would be there. That night the airborne divisions took off for their dropping zones on the flank of the assault. The die was cast.

If General Montgomery suffered any grave anxieties in these last critical days he did not reveal them. On the morning of the 5th, soon after Eisenhower came to his decision, Montgomery went off to visit the guardians of his son in Hindhead. They were old friends with whom he had made his temporary home. He dressed in plain clothes. In a sense it was a gesture of calm and confidence on the eve of the most important adventure of his life. In the last meetings with the Supreme Commander he had been asked, not so much for his opinion, but whether he was prepared for his forces to assault in face of the weather. His answer was an unqualified 'Yes'. It did not imply that he was less than fully aware that the real burden of decision must rest with the Navy, the Air Force and the Supreme Commander, nor did he discount the great importance

[1] Thompson: *The Price of Victory*, Constable, 1960.

of air support. It seems fair to believe that Montgomery was simply taking the military weight off the Supreme Commander's shoulders, and saying, don't worry about us, we'll go if the Navy can take us.

It is clear now that Air Chief Marshal Tedder regarded Montgomery's attitude as a slight on the Air Force, and records his feelings with honest prejudice:

> 'Montgomery, knowing full well that weather conditions would prevent the air forces from giving any real support, amazingly asserted his willingness on the part of the Army to take the risk.'

Throughout the Battle for Normandy Air Chief Marshal Tedder was one of Montgomery's most severe and uncompromising critics. His views influenced and were partially shared by General Morgan, one of the principal architects of 'Overlord', and Deputy Chief of Staff to the Supreme Commander. They also influenced the Supreme Commander, and may have had a decisive effect on the pattern of the whole campaign.

But Tedder's attitude is important because it reveals the rivalries and fundamental problems in combined operations. Montgomery knew very well of the immense effort made by the air forces. In the last two months before D-Day, as Tedder recalls, 'nearly 2,000 aircraft and 12,000 air force lives had been lost in the tremendous efforts in support of the assault.' It was facts like these that gave Montgomery confidence to go in even if good air support might be lacking on the day. He would have the fire power of the naval forces at his back. Montgomery had the right, and even the duty, to believe that his troops could win a foothold. He was a military man, almost pure and simple. The army would do the fighting on the ground, and only the army could win the war. Its units, its multitudes of men, would live and fight in conditions, day after day, week after week and month after month, no airman or even naval rating would ever suffer or know. In combination the three services had an enormous potential, not simply adding to each other, but multiplying, and they had achieved a remarkable combination. That it was not perfect is not surprising. The air force, as Montgomery commented in

Normandy, 'wanted the airfields in order to defeat Rommel, whereas I wanted to defeat Rommel in order, only incidentally, to capture the airfields.'[1]

In Tunis, Kesselring had opposed Rommel's desire and urgent need to shorten his lines on the grounds that too many airfields would be lost. It was the position in reverse. The happy marriage of land and air forces would demand great wisdom and a commander-in-chief of genius. The Germans had failed to achieve any kind of marriage, and all partners, navy, army and air force lived apart, thought apart and fought apart. The British had achieved great things, and would achieve greater.

The Royal Navy, secure in its role for centuries, did not share the extreme sensitivity of the Royal Air Force, nor was it concerned to define its role. The Royal Air Force was unique, and it was young. Some of its commanders had suffered from the illusion, shared by Churchill, that it could win the war on its own, bombing the enemy into submission. It is a dangerous heresy, and it persists. The death of an enemy and of an enemy country is not a victory. Only men on their feet may win and consolidate victory, and there is no other way.

The inter-service difficulties both before and after D-Day were marvellously slight, and they derived from attitudes only time and experience might change. Montgomery was too casual in explaining his points of view, and a bad mixer with his equals. Tedder notes that at a special meeting on 29th May to discuss the use of the Airborne Divisions in support of Bradley's troops assaulting 'Utah' beach, Montgomery did not attend; de Guingand spoke for him. It may be that Tedder took Montgomery's absence as a slight, but it was a pattern continued by Montgomery. He disliked meetings, and discussion. He was the boss or he was the subordinate. He did not really know how to be an equal, and in command, it must be true, there cannot be equals. Wars and battles are not won by consortiums.

Montgomery, I believe, was also a very shy man. On the 6th June, while the spearheads of the first five divisions led the great assault on the beaches and battled for a foothold, he relaxed alone in the garden of 'Broomfield House', his head-

---

[1] Montgomery: *Memoirs*, p. 257.

quarters near Portsmouth. A destroyer was standing by to take him to Normandy, and at 9.30 that night he embarked to make contact with his Army Commanders. He had cut a record of his last message to the troops for the B.B.C. He felt cheered by the first news coming in. It was evident, he thought, that the landings were going well.

CHAPTER THREE

Montgomery's Ordeal

I

AT 9.30 on the night of the 6th June, Montgomery went aboard the destroyer, H.M.S. *Faulknor*, at Portsmouth and sailed across the channel to meet his army commanders. The long loneliness of his day of vigil was almost done. He had spent the day, for the most part alone, walking in the grounds of Broomfield House, pottering into his office now and then to see the latest reports, building up a pattern in his mind. He was at the 'eye' of the hurricane. The intense labours of months were over, and a new ordeal awaited him. He was on the eve of the greatest challenge of his life, but for the moment, the arrow had left the bow, and there was nothing more to be done. He had, as it were, put his affairs in order.

'... It has not been an easy time—for anyone,' he wrote to Brooke. 'My great desire throughout has been to justify your confidence in me and not to let you down and I hope I have been able to do this to your satisfaction.

'I cross over to France tomorrow night—if all goes well—and may not see you again.

'So good-bye and good luck.'[1]

In the event of disaster he would almost surely have been the scapegoat, for there were many in high places bearing him ill-will, and it was not one of his talents to make friends. Yet, unlike Brooke, he was quietly and genuinely confident of success. Brooke had confided his great anxieties to his diary:

'... I am very uneasy about the whole operation. At the best it will fall so very far short of the expectation of the bulk of the people, namely all those who know nothing about its difficulties. At the worst it may well be the most ghastly

---

[1] Bryant: *Triumph in the West*, pp. 205-206.

disaster of the whole war. I wish to God it were safely over.'[1]

There is a tendency, I think, to under-estimate the hazards of D-Day, and thereby, perhaps, to underestimate the great achievement of the landings. The overwhelming fire power at sea and in the air in support of the landings make it seem impossible that an enemy, however dedicated, however deeply entrenched, could have prevailed against the gigantic onslaught. Tens of thousands of tons of high explosive drenched the Normandy beaches, and moved steadily inland, a lethal carpet of destruction. A host of landing-craft with Hobart's armour, spear-heading the assaults, added the searching weight of smaller arms to the deluge. The remarkable resilience of men is one of the miracles we are slow to recognize and to understand, but I think Montgomery knew it, and recognized it in spite of his lavish use of artillery, and at times, of bombing. We have discovered how to desecrate the earth and all life, but men on the ground may only be defeated by men on the ground.

The phenomenon of D-Day was the failure of the German command. It was a failure of leadership on the highest level reflected downwards. It promised the disruption of the Nazi regime. The machine had begun to go to pieces, and the cancer had revealed itself. Field-Marshal Rommel had believed that the Allied assault might only be defeated on the beaches. Field-Marshal von Runstedt had thought otherwise. General Gehr von Schweppenburg, commanding Panzer Group West, held a third view. All had the ear of the Führer, and at the crucial moment the Führer slept.

'The main reason for the failure of the German defence was lack of a single, clear-cut plan, carried out under the responsibility of a single, experienced commander.'

Even so, as these German historians conclude, 'it is doubtful if they could have entirely beaten off the invasion of Normandy'.[2]

Nevertheless the presence of three Panzer Divisions forward, as Rommel wished, instead of one—the 21st—would have been a formidable challenge.

All luck was with the Allies on that day, and at the heart

[1] Bryant: *Triumph in the West*, pp. 205-206.
[2] *Decisive Battles of W.W. 11*. The German View. Jacobsen and Rohwer, p. 337.

of it was the unimaginable failure of enemy 'Intelligence' and Reconnaissance. This gave the Allies tactical surprise, and it also held the German 15th Army immobile in the Pas de Calais guarding against an assault which never happened, nor ever could have happened. It reveals, not simply the success of the Allied Deception plan, but an over-estimate of Allied strength bordering on dementia. On the first day—even in the first week—it is barely conceivable that the vast assault on the Normandy beaches could have been mistaken for a feint, or subsidiary attack.

Yet it was a hazardous day, an almost total commitment of great daring, whatever the odds, a gamble above all on the weather, perhaps the most fickle weather in the world. The weather could have disorganized much of the great fleet of little ships. It could have rendered assault landings almost impossible. It could have isolated the spearhead troops on the beaches to be captured or annihilated. It could have grounded Allied air power, and aroused the enemy to an urgency that would have overcome the dissensions in the command and unleashed a torrent of armour against a second attempt. In less than two weeks the worst weather in the Channel for forty years would do its worst, but by then it was too late to defeat the Allies or to afford more than a mild relief to the enemy.

The 6th June is one of the most momentous days in European history, and it would have been so whatever the outcome. The day was not in itself decisive in the sense that Waterloo, for example, was decisive. Nor was it '. . . a damned nice thing—the nearest run thing you ever saw in your life'.[1] It held the promise of victory rather than victory, and it was Montgomery's task to grasp that victory. All that he knew as he crossed the channel was that a foothold had been gained, and that nearly 200,000 men at sea were supporting and reinforcing those on shore. Casualties were far less than had been feared, and it seemed certain that 100,000 men, including the airborne troops, were engaging the enemy. That night it seemed a near miracle to many.

It was an exhilarating journey for Montgomery, giving him a sense of power. On these narrow seas the vast concourse of nearly 7,000 ships, 1,200 of them ships of war, sailed about their

[1] Wellington after Waterloo. *The Creevey Papers*, p. 236.

business almost immune from enemy interference. Four old enemy torpedo boats had sailed boldly out of Le Havre in an attempt to harass the weaker vessels. No enemy U boats reached the Channel, and enemy destroyers operating in the Bay of Biscay were easily intercepted. Overhead the sky was heavy with the sustained roar of Allied aircraft, as unmolested as the ships at sea. Only on land might the enemy hope to impose a serious check upon the overwhelming strength of the Allies, and on the night of D-Day it seemed clear to Montgomery that the enemy had failed. The enemy shore batteries had proved ineffective, and the immense thunder of gunfire was almost exclusively from the bombarding fleet, including the heavy armament of seven battleships.

The reports coming in, first of the airborne landings, and of the footholds being steadily established on four out of the five beaches, brought a sense of relief and sober optimism. Few had put words to hopes or fears. The target figures of men and materials landed had fallen short, but not dangerously short. The 'Objectives' of D-Day had not been gained, but these were not true guides to success or failure, nor on that day did anyone so regard them. They were not 'Objects', but thereafter they would be confused with objects by almost everyone except by Montgomery and his generals.

Montgomery had launched his armies into battle with his accustomed panache, and had not forgotten to evoke 'The Lord Mighty in Battle'. As his destroyer approached the Normandy coast in the unusually heavy seas still running, Montgomery did not under-estimate the ordeal he must face, not only for days and weeks, but probably for months.

'I had no qualms or doubts about the successful showing that this mighty force would make on the Normandy beaches,' he wrote.

But he was not without qualms. He was concerned that many of his senior staff officers were intensely weary after their sustained exertions to heave the invasion force into action. There was no time for rest. Moreover, Montgomery was acutely aware of time, of the lack of experience in battle of the bulk of his forces. He was aware, too, that his army, the British 2nd Army, was the last army Britain could put into the field. There were no more armies, and barely enough reinforcements available to keep his divisions up to strength. He knew that he must fight with this army, and win with it, while husbanding its strength. Above all he must preserve it. For the first month, perhaps for two months, its role would be paramount, and upon its success or failure victory must depend.

The British 2nd Army was a magnificently trained force, but it had not been tempered. Perhaps Montgomery set too high a value upon battle experience, and did not fully appreciate the virtues of men who had not yet drawn upon their resources of nervous energy and courage, nor learned the survival tricks of the veteran. The assault troops had needed all their resources on that day. Too much had been asked of them, even though it had not been expected. They had been cooped up for more than 24 hours in their landing-craft.[1] They had had a rough crossing, many knowing the miseries of sea-sickness in spite of the lavish issue of 'pills'. It had been a rough landing through a maze of obstacles in heavy surf on an alien shore bristling with devices of death and destruction, and beaten by fire. Engineer groups, D D (swimming) tanks, and Hobart's marvellous variety of armour, fighting, flailing, flame-throwing, bridging and laying tracks, blasted ways off the beaches, and burst through the enemy outer crust. The outer crust had been brittle in the extreme. Three enemy infantry divisions, the 709th, the 352nd and the 716th, took the weight of the Allied assault. A desperate shortage of cement and labour had left them excessively vulnerable to air attack and heavy bombardment. 'Of the installations in the sector of the 352nd division only 15 per cent were bombproof; the remainder were virtually unprotected from the air,' wrote Gordon Harrison. The 716th division was even worse off.[2]

By nightfall leading British troops had advanced up to six miles inland, and only the inspiration of victory within grasp, or of despair, might have maintained the momentum of weary men to fight another yard that night. Moreover, the congestion on the beaches was hampering and delaying the follow-up of infantry and armour in the second and third waves

[1] 287,000 men had been embarked, some of them since the first day of the month. Hundreds of thousands more, together with all their vehicles, armour, ammunition and supplies, were in the pipe line. The pressure was tremendous.
[2] Harrison: *Cross-Channel Attack*, U.S. Army in W.W. 2. Thompson: *The Price of Victory*.

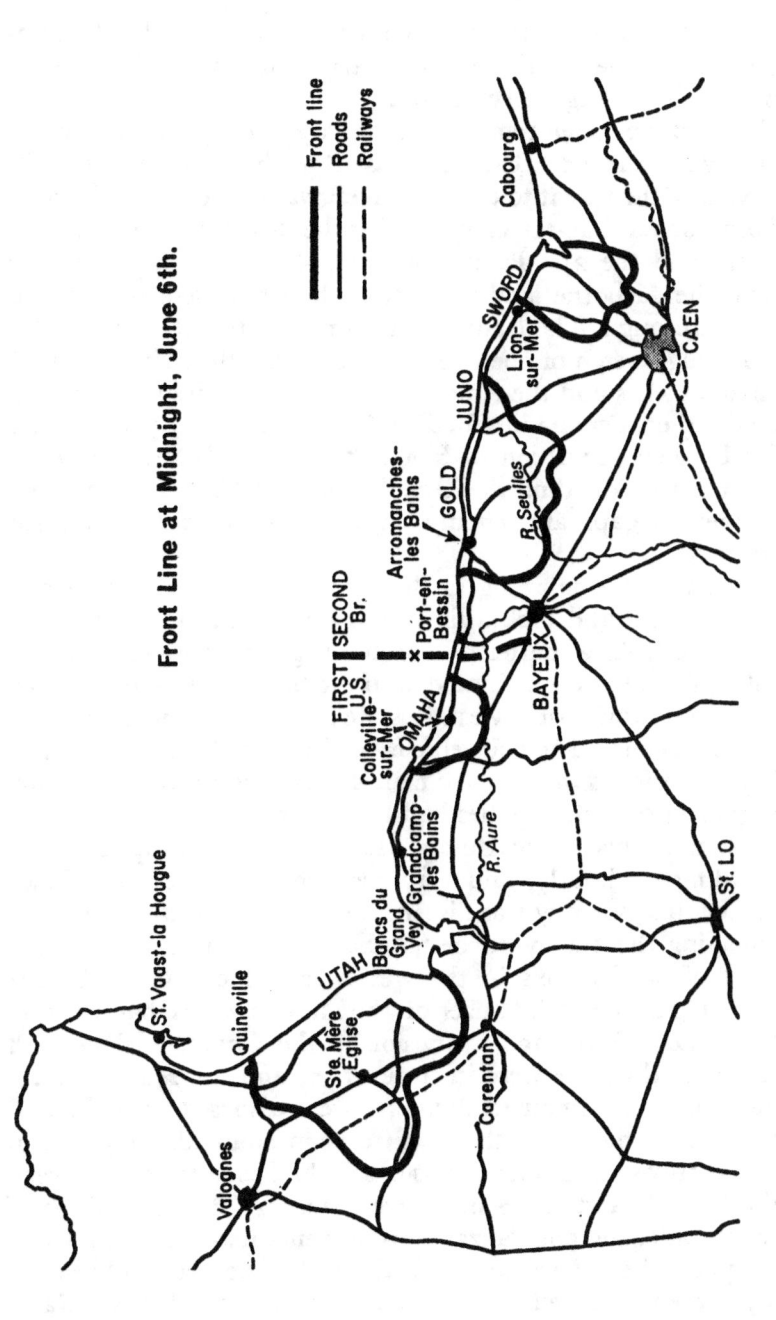

Front Line at Midnight, June 6th.

of assault. It was a factor of vital importance in the development of the battle, limiting the 'Art of the possible', and ever present in Montgomery's mind.

The city of Caen remained a long way off on that first night, and with the 21st Panzer division within the city and its environs, the threat to the British left was immediate. The road from Caen to Luc-sur-mer, splitting the British centre, remained open, and the 21st Panzer division, striving with its right to hold the Airborne landings east of the Orne, sent 90 tanks to break through. The leading detachment 'smelt' the sea.

A long stretch of open coast lay between the British right at Arromanches and the American left, fighting desperately for a toe-hold on Omaha beach. The Americans were paying dearly for Bradley's rejection of Hobart's armour. Isigny marked a danger area dividing the U.S. V and VII Corps. There were dangerous gaps and enemy pockets holding out with great courage.

Early in the morning of the second day Montgomery met his generals, and took a firm hold on the battle. He was not displeased. As a matter of extreme urgency the gaps must be filled, the pockets eliminated, and the bridgehead forged into a solid front from east to west. In spite of the heavy seas there were 187,000 men and 19,000 vehicles on shore by the end of the day. The Americans were 20,000 men short of their target, and only a quarter of their supplies had been landed.

None of this was alarming. Men, armour and supplies were building up hourly, and very soon the threat of abundance rather than scarcity was discernible. Five Allied divisions were engaging the enemy on better than equal terms. The enemy total of 60 divisions in the west was reduced to 58 by the re-fitting of the 19th Panzer division after a severe battering on the eastern front, and a division in the Channel Islands. Of these, 31 divisions were in static roles, and the remaining 27, including ten armoured divisions, were disposed from Holland to South of the Loire, the 88th Corps in Holland, the powerful 15th Army with nineteen divisions in the Pas de Calais, between the Scheldt and the Seine. Seven Infantry divisions, three of them static, and one Panzer division, remained in the 7th Army, to oppose the full weight of Allied attack. The reserve of armour lay in the rectangle Mantes-Gassicourt, Chartres, Bernay, Gacé, and subject to the vacillating will of the Führer. Moreover, the massive air attacks rendered movement by day almost impossible, and by night difficult, as Rommel had anticipated.

Within 48 hours Montgomery understood clearly the nature of the battle he was about to fight. The enemy armour must be contained on the left, and but for Rommel's insistence on holding the 21st Panzer division forward in Caen against von Runstedt's wishes, Caen might have fallen. It had become of secondary importance. The immediate need was for depth to the south to gain the high ground and the key points of Villers Bocage on the 2nd Army front and St. Lo on the American front. These were the vital objectives, and the winning of the first was essential to the winning of the second.

The presence of the 21st Panzer division in the immediate area of Caen had been a compromise, and a mistake. When Rommel's plan to defeat the Allies on the beaches had been rejected, the enemy would have been wise to accept von Runstedt's plan of holding back the armour for massive counter-attack, however crippling Allied air supremacy might prove. As it was the enemy was committed to defend Caen, and it was at once a magnet to draw the armoured reserves onto the British left. Montgomery must see to it that the way round to the south was swiftly blocked. The weight of enemy armour and reinforcements would then batter against the British shoulder, and crumble to pieces. The British shoulder must hold at all costs while the Americans confronted the enemy 91st division, with the 6th Parachute Regiment under command, covering the left flank of the 352nd division. The 709th division covered the eastern coastline of the Cherbourg Peninsula, and the 243rd division covered the western coast, facing west. One infantry division, one Panzer Grenadier division and one Parachute division would attempt to reinforce, but they were a long way off.

Montgomery had to maintain this position for the Americans, giving them time to gain space and strength. This was, in fact, the way Montgomery wanted it. The battle would be fought in his way. Above all he must keep control of the 'pattern', if need be at the cost of time and space.

In four days the Allied bridgehead was solid, and on 12th June, Montgomery welcomed the Prime Minister and the

C.I.G.S. to his headquarters. He had already established himself as he liked, and was on the best of terms with the chatelaine of Creuilly, in whose grounds he had come to rest. He had even borrowed a chamber pot from his hostess, having sent one of his aides in search of a *vase-de-nuit*, which was soon understood as a *pot-de-chambre*. There was, as nearly always, a remarkable tranquillity, like a cocoon surrounding Montgomery. He was brimful of confidence, as he had a right to be. His front was more than 50 miles long and from 8 to 12 miles deep. Already he knew that he would win, and von Runstedt and Rommel knew that they would lose. On the 7th June the 12th Panzer division, badly battered en route, had been committed on the left of the 21st. Two days later a Panzer Lehr division began to trickle into the battle on the left, already severely mauled on the way. The enemy was committing his armour piece-meal.

'... we were greatly assisted by the immense strategic importance of Caen,' Montgomery wrote. 'It was a vital road and rail centre through which passed the main routes leading to our lodgement area from the east and south-east. As the bulk of the German mobile reserves were located north of the Seine, they would have to approach our bridgehead from the east and would thus converge on Caen.'[1]

It was fortunate, I think, that Caen had not fallen, nor was its fall a matter of urgency, nor even desirable in the early stages of the battle. Montgomery's priorities were clear: first to defeat the enemy in battle; second to gain space to relieve the congestion in the Bridgehead, and speed up the deployment of reinforcements as well as the establishment of adequate base areas; and third, to gain airfields. But neither the pressing need for space, nor the desire of the Air Force Commanders for airfields must be allowed to divert the ground forces from their struggle to maintain the initiative and to attain Montgomery's strategic object. In my view more airfields would have been a hindrance, consuming labour, materials and transport. While their possession could not affect the progress of the battle, they would have added greatly to transport problems, and still further added to the congestion of the limited areas essential for the military build-up.

Perhaps Montgomery had not forgotten Foggia, when the

[1] Montgomery: *Memoirs*, p. 254.

Fifteenth Strategic Air Force had consumed 300,000 tons of shipping space in a very short time. Logistics were already multiplying at an alarming rate, impelled by some inherent momentum of their own rather than by the genuine needs of men.

The priorities provide an essential key to an appreciation and understanding of Montgomery's generalship. The Chiefs of Staff at Supreme Headquarters, unable to disentangle their minds from earlier plans, continued to attach a misguided importance to the conquest of Caen and a break-out to the east. The men struggling to clear the congestion on the beaches, to establish base areas and dumps, hospitals, posts, transit camps, training and reinforcement areas, and much of the paraphernalia of a modern society, grumbled incessantly. To keep supplies and reinforcements flowing to the battlefield on time was like forcing camels through the eyes of needles. But so long as reinforcements in men, armour, artillery, ammunition and fuel (POL), did reach the battlefield, so long as Dempsey, dourly husbanding his manpower, was able to find room to manoeuvre, to shift the weight and direction of his attacks, consistently to contain and 'write down' enemy strength, Montgomery was justified. Even Montgomery's caution in not pressing attacks on major objectives until his reserves were in the line and he was fully satisfied, ultimately resulted in a greater victory.

With all the delays, caused not only by the congestion in the bridgehead, but by slow turn-rounds of transport shipping, the inevitable hazards of the seas, harbour and transit problems, tight schedules, the Allied reinforcement and supply situation was much better than that of the enemy. The Channel was less hazardous than the roads and railways from the north-east on which the enemy must rely.

The War Diaries of the enemy commanders from von Runstedt, Rommel and Gehr von Schweppenberg, downwards, testify to the devastating effects of Allied air superiority. To this was added the great weight of Allied artillery and Naval fire power. Day after day enemy attacks were broken up in their assembly areas, so that enemy tactics became a matter of agonising improvisation. In the air, in spite of the lack of airfields in the bridgehead, the Allies outnumbered the enemy by 30 to 1. The 'Air Transportation Plan', which had wrought havoc with major roads, railways and bridges in the weeks before D-Day, continued so to harass the enemy that new divisions were fed into the line piece-meal, and often reduced to bicycles as their final means of transport. All this fully justified Rommel's appreciation of the situation, but with the Fuehrer refusing to consider any kind of withdrawal and re-grouping there was nothing the commanders on the spot could do about it. Fortunately their scale of equipment and supply was not more than one-third of the tonnage available to the Allies.[1]

By the end of the first week the Allies substantially, if not decisively, outnumbered the enemy in the field in every department of war. 60,000 tons of ammunition were safely put ashore in the first five days. In eleven days the Allies could deploy 650,000 men served by more than 90,000 trucks, and supported by more than 225,000 tons of supplies. These remarkable results had been achieved over the beaches while the artificial harbours were taking shape. Nevertheless the management of the vast flow of supplies was consuming manpower. Beach groups grew to 5,000 strong, to become sub-areas, to become base areas as the chain of supply grew.

II

Immediately after the visit of the Prime Minister and the C.I.G.S. on the 12th, the British suffered a minor set-back. It was the first of many set-backs, more apparent than real, and which Montgomery seldom if ever troubled to explain. He would always accept a tactical delay as a strategic gain, as Ehrman and others observed, and he could almost certainly have silenced much of the criticism directed against him from all sides had he bothered to do so. Instead he maintained a curious, and often dangerously ill-mannered isolation.

On the 13th June, advanced elements of the enemy 2nd Panzer division, having arrived mysteriously undetected from the Somme, imposed a check on offensive operations Dempsey

---

[1] A German division in battle consumed between 250-300 tons per day compared with 700 tons by an Allied division. A factor in this was the enemy lack of artillery.

was developing on the Caen Road. At the same time von Runstedt, with the Führer's belated consent, was moving all available armour to the Normandy battlefield. The 2nd Panzer division had been in Army Group B reserve, but the 1st SS division was in O.K.W. reserve, and thus under the direct control of Hitler, while the 2nd SS division, was in Army Group G reserve near Toulouse. By the 12th June, these divisions were struggling forward, and the 9th and 10th Panzer divisions were on their way from Poland, taking to the road on the French border on the 16th. Before the end of the month they were all building up against the British on the left.

While it was clear to Montgomery that a decisive battle on a very big scale was in the making, it was difficult to take it at its face value or to make an appreciation of enemy tactics and strategy. If he could grapple the enemy to him, and not let him go, he would fight a battle exactly suited to his talents. No one who had studied Montgomery's generalship, and had not been blinded by the blaze of propaganda that had obscured the nature of his victory and advance in the Desert, would have believed that it was Montgomery's intention to break out on the left.

Yet confronted with Rommel and von Runstedt it seemed to Montgomery that the enemy must shorten his line, attempt to disengage and re-group for counter-attack. Few doubted that a great battle would be fought on the line of the Seine, and thereafter would develop into a series of struggles on the water lines, back to the Rhine, the last great obstacle. Perhaps Montgomery, almost alone, might have predicted that the Battle for Normandy would be the decisive battle of the campaign. I believe that it was Montgomery's resolution that it should be so, and he could not know that the enemy would play into his hands.

As late as 6th August when Hitler issued his orders to press his abortive and hopeless attempt to break through to Avranches, Montgomery was quite rightly still thinking and acting on the premise that the enemy must withdraw and re-group. Any other course would mean the suicide of an army.

It may be that if, as some assert, it had been Montgomery's intention and hope to take Caen and have his spearheads well advanced on the Falaise road on the first day, the campaign would have developed more on the lines, and in accordance with the timings, of the 'Overlord' plan. The battle for Normandy would not have developed in the way that it did. In my view the failure to take Caen—and it was, I am convinced, never more than a hope, a possibility to be reckoned with—was fortunate. It did not trouble Montgomery. By the end of June the whole development and shape of the battle was pleasing to the Ground Force Commander. On the right the Americans had taken Cherbourg and were securing their supply lines. But progress through the *bocage* on the American left and centre was slow.

Throughout June the enemy generals, von Runstedt, Rommel and Gehr von Schweppenberg, united in adversity, urged the Führer to permit them to withdraw and re-group. It was the only sane course, but the Führer, beyond sanity and with the spectre of total defeat haunting him, demanded the impossible. The enemy must be hurled back into the sea. All else was defeatism. Early in July all three generals had disappeared from the scene, Rommel destined to be first wounded and then 'murdered' by suicide. Old von Runstedt, handing over to his successors and asked for his advice, replied dryly, 'Make peace, you fools!' But peace would have been even more impossible to make than war.

Thus Field-Marshal Gunther von Kluge replaced von Runstedt in a grim frame of mind. Heinrich Eberbach, replacing Gehr von Schweppenberg, was no happier. On the 17th August, von Kluge, believed to have been implicated in the July plot to kill Hitler, was replaced by Field-Marshal Model. Two days later von Kluge took cyanide. Long before then the German 'Commanders knew that their military decisions would be viewed in the light of a murderous and implacable political suspicion'.[1]

Yet in spite of this terrible command background and incessant bombardment from the air, land and sea, the German soldier continued to fight with great fortitude, inflicting heavy casualties, disquieting in the extreme to the British. To a great extent mortars had replaced conventional artillery in the establishment of German infantry divisions, corps and G.H.Q. troops. In close support these weapons were hard to detect and

---

[1] Ehrman: *Grand Strategy*, vol. v, H.M.S.O., p. 343.

devastating in their effect. Few British soldiers who fought in Normandy and through to the end at Luneberg are ever likely to forget these deadly and psychologically disturbing weapons.

In addition to establishing 60 81mm and 20 120mm mortars to an infantry division for close support, there were five *nebelwerfer* regiments confronting the British in Normandy. Each regiment had between 60 and 70 multi-barrelled quick-firing mortars from 150mm to 300mm calibre, capable of hurling 75lb, 248lb and 277lb bombs up to a maximum of 8,000 yards.[1] These weapons took a greater toll of the British than all other weapons added together, and before the end of July the losses were causing concern and adding to Montgomery's problems. His concern is evident in his messages to the C.I.G.S. before launching his heavy attacks in mid-July.

'... The Second Army is now very strong (he wrote); it has in fact reached its peak and can get no stronger. It will in fact get weaker as the manpower situation begins to hit us. Also, the casualties have affected the fighting efficiency of the divisions; the original men were very well trained; reinforcements are not so well trained, and this fact is beginning to become apparent and will have repercussions on what we can do. The country in which we are fighting is ideal defensive country; *we* do the attacking and the Boche is pretty thick on the ground. I would say we lose three men to his one in our infantry divisions...'[2]

At the same time Montgomery sent Colonel Dawnay to London to ensure that there could be no misunderstanding of his intentions in the mind of General Alan Brooke, for it was becoming clear that his intentions were increasingly misunderstood by almost everyone else, especially by the Supreme Commander, whose reply to a telegram 'seems to view Montgomery's plan upside down'. Dawnay was to explain to the C.I.G.S. that:

'The real object is to muck up and write off enemy troops. On the eastern flank he (Montgomery) is aiming at doing the

---

[1] This does not imply that the Germans were without conventional artillery. Their standard field gun was 105mm, the medium 150mm, and the heavy 170mm. In addition there were Light and Heavy A.A. guns.
[2] *Victory in the West*, vol. i, H.M.S.O., pp. 329-330.

greatest damage to enemy armour . . . General Montgomery has to be very careful of what he does on his eastern flank because on that flank is the only British army there is left in this part of the world. On the security and firmness of the eastern flank depends the security of the whole lodgement area.'[1]

The British anxiety to preserve their manpower was observable on the battlefield to an acute observer in early June. 'On the morning of June 10th,' wrote Gehr von Schweppenberg,[2] 'I visited a regimental headquarters near an Abbey on the top of the hill just north of Caen. There I saw a Panzer Regiment in action against the Canadians. It was hellish, but in this case the hell came from the sky. The British and Canadian troops were magnificent. This was not surprising when one knew the type of man, and when one knew that a large part of them had been trained by that outstanding soldier (and old friend of mine) General Sir Bernard Paget.

'However, after a while I began to think, rightly or wrongly, that the command of these superb troops was not making the best use of them. The command seemed slow and rather pedestrian. It seemed that the Allied intention was to wear down their enemy with their enormous material superiority. It will never be known whether Montgomery had received a private instruction from his Government to avoid for the British troops another bloodbath such as they had suffered in the First World War on the Somme and at Passchendaele. However, it seemed to me that the command of the British and Canadians failed to make the best use of these magnificent troops.'

Perhaps no one will ever know how best to avoid heavy casualties in war, whether caution is to be preferred to boldness. It may be a matter of temperament. Nevertheless I question Gehr von Schweppenberg's conclusions. It served Montgomery's strategy not to press too hard, but simply hard enough. Even so casualties were severe, and at the end of July 'A number of infantry battalion Medical Officers, from four different divisions, all agreed in placing the proportion of mortar casualties to total casualties among their own troops as above 70%. This

---

[1] *Victory in the West*, vol. i, H.M.S.O., pp. 329-330.
[2] General Leo Freiherr Gehr von Schweppenberg: *The Spectator*, 5 June, 1964.

figure is widely accepted among infantrymen, and it is thought if anything to be an underestimate.'[1]

By the end of the year the Americans would also suffer manpower problems, and in the New Year, Alexander would have to strip down his armies and his hopes in Italy in order to strengthen the Western front.

[1] *Victory in the West*, Appendix iv, Part vi, H.M.S.O., p. 550.

CHAPTER FOUR

The Tactics of Montgomery's Strategy

I

THE Battle of Normandy was fought in three main phases, falling naturally into the months of June, July and August. June was the month of solid establishment of the Allied armies in the bridgehead, and confronting the enemy with inevitable defeat; July was the month of bitter, close fighting in country riven with thickly wooded hills, valleys and streams, and confused with mazes of narrow lanes, deeply hedged fields, and with few good roads. It was the kind of country to favour the defenders, to add to the deadliness of their mortar fire, and to limit the role of armour. Moreover it was a battlefield whose intricacies were well known to the enemy, and in which he had established himself with great skill.

Twice the worst summer weather in living memory had a decisive effect upon the pace and timings of the tactics of Montgomery's strategy. On each occasion the weather favoured the enemy, allowing him some respite from the otherwise incessant Allied air attacks, and giving him time to strengthen his defences. But the weather did not effect the outcome of the battle, nor did it postpone the final victory. Early on the 19th June, a 30 knot gale began to rage in the channel, and persisted in growing intensity for three days. The American artificial harbours were hopelessly wrecked in course of construction, and the beaches became a shambles of shipping, small craft and supplies. The British harbour installations, somewhat more advanced and enjoying some shelter from the full force of the gale, suffered far less severely, nevertheless the first impressions were of a disaster on a massive scale. The supplies landed fell by 40,000 tons in the week of the gale, but were always adequate. Thereafter, until the Port of Cherbourg was finally opened, remarkably high tonnages—far beyond the most sanguine expectations—were landed over the beaches. The most serious effect of the storm was to delay the arrivals of reinforcements, already falling behind schedule owing to the normal hazards of a cross-channel shuttle service of such gigantic proportions. All this havoc coincided with the mounting of a major attack by Montgomery. His armies were three infantry brigades short immediately before the storm. Three days later they were three divisions short. The delay in the arrival of 43 (Wessex) division, coupled with a disaster to its reconnaissance Regiment on the beaches, set back Montgomery's intention to take the key village of Villers Bocage.

Again on the 20th July appalling weather conditions over the battlefield held up the third main phase of Montgomery's plans, and led to remarkable misunderstandings of his intentions and of his achievement.

Thus there were many factors beyond the control of the Allied commander. He could not know of the dire and destructive High Command situation afflicting the enemy commanders in the field, and greatly aggravated by the abortive attempt on the Führer's life on the 20th July. Montgomery had to dictate a battle based on a sober appreciation of the tactical and strategic skill of his enemy. Thus, while attempting to mask his strategic object from the enemy, he had to assume, not only at the end of June, but also at the end of July, that the enemy would attempt a planned withdrawal, and re-group his forces. Similarly towards the middle of August he could not take it for granted that the enemy, driven by a man in a state of hysteria, would delay withdrawal from a clearly disastrous position well beyond the eleventh hour. Nor could Montgomery budget for the wastage of enemy generals, not simply by the normal hazards of war, that would remove Rommel, von Runstedt and Gehr von Schweppenberg, and even remove their successors before they were able to make their marks upon the course of the battle.

Even had all these things been known it must be doubtful if the battle could have been better fought, or brought to a more successful conclusion. From the beginning Montgomery was under fire for his handling of the battle, but he was never misunderstood by his commanders in the field.

Many of the criticisms arose not only out of the contrast between his concise and lucidly expressed intentions and directives to his commanders, and his carelessly phrased communiques and public statements, but also, and basically, out of his eccentricities, his isolation and withdrawal into his private world, his peculiar arrogance, his inability to suffer 'military' fools gladly, and his failure to realize the importance of 'diplomacy' if he were to retain the 'Ground Force' command with all that that implied. In short he had risen to a position in which more than purely military talents were needed.

He found it difficult to discuss. He formed his judgements swiftly and stated them with a dogmatism that was often intolerable to his associates.

Thus, before D-Day Montgomery's role of Ground Force commander was accepted with reluctance by the Americans, and might have been terminated in July had Eisenhower felt completely competent to take command himself, or to find an alternative. In a sense he failed to realize, or to understand, his own possible importance.

It was greatly in his favour that he treated General Bradley with marked courtesy and unusual tolerance. Close associates observed that he seldom 'ordered' Bradley, but made suggestions with tact while keeping Bradley clearly informed of his intentions. Bradley, for his part, co-operated loyally and to the utmost of his ability, at least until the arrival of General Patton to command the U.S. 3rd Army and Bradley's assumption of Army Group command. On 10th July, for example, at a meeting with his field commanders in his caravan, Montgomery soothed Bradley's fears of failure. The American commander was depressed at his slow progress, and felt that he had failed in his attempt to break-out to the South. Montgomery urged him not to worry and to take 'all the time you need'.[1] He was on the eve of launching his own most misunderstood operation, designed to give Bradley time and space and freedom from enemy interference on a more powerful scale. This was the operation, known as GOODWOOD, which Eisenhower persisted in seeing 'upside down'.

But while Montgomery kept his relationships in the field on

---

[1] *The Tanks*, vol. ii, B.H. Liddell Hart, p. 359.

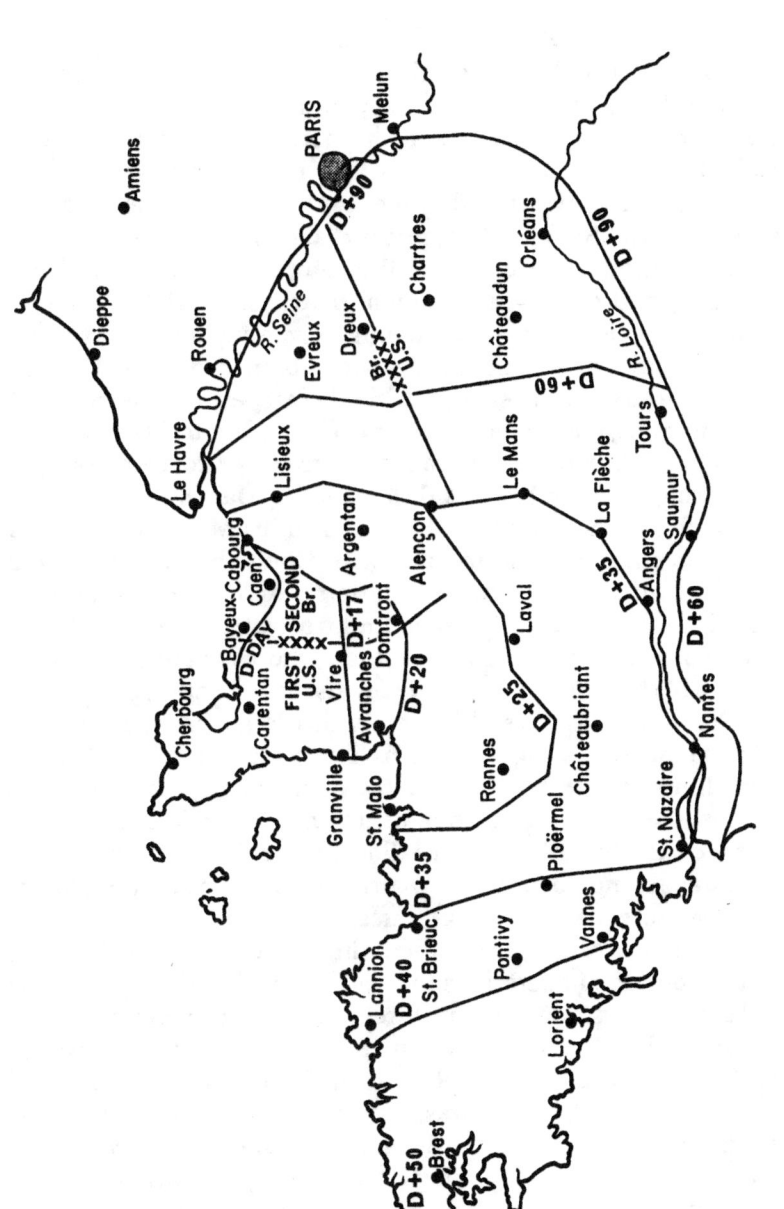

21 Army Group Forecast Phase Lines

an unexceptionable basis, his equally important 'liaison' personal relationships, essential to a military commander in his 'political', as well as military position, were deplorable. He seemed to save his charm, his vitality and his infectious self-confidence almost exclusively for the Monarch, who visited him in Normandy on 16th June, and for the Prime Minister and the C.I.G.S. Had Montgomery taken half as much trouble with Eisenhower the course of the campaign might have been changed, and the British position greatly strengthened. When Eisenhower visited Montgomery in Normandy for the first time his 'Ground Force' commander was absent from his Tactical Headquarters. The absence was deliberate, even if the personal slight was not, and Eisenhower was furious. Similarly when Lord Trenchard visited him he failed to greet, or to take leave of his distinguished guest. His dislike of Air Marshal Coningham was such that he would not have him in his Mess, even though it was at times essential to liaise with Coningham. In the same vein he disliked discussing air matters with Sir Arthur Tedder, perhaps the most distinguished and frustrated of the Air Force commanders, or with Leigh Mallory, whose contribution to the success of the Transportation Plan, and the constant dislocation of the enemy's lines of communication, was paramount. Montgomery, having formed a liking for Air Vice Marshal Broadhurst made him one of his own 'chaps', and offended against the Air Force chain of command. When he should have worked closely with Leigh Mallory, the only senior Air Force commander not bemused by airfields, and with Coningham, he chose to work with Broadhurst.

In this way Montgomery did a disservice to the development of the combined operations in which he believed. The genuine balanced integration of the three Services in combined command, while still far from fulfilment, was a long way in advance of the enemy's almost complete isolation of his Army, Navy and Air Force. Montgomery was a military man, and his counterparts could easily be found in the Navy and Air Force. Senior commanders, while all paying lip service to, and with a genuine belief in the development of combined operations, all had their own ideas of exactly what this should mean. Each tended to see his own Service as paramount.

II

It is difficult—perhaps impossible—to 'see' the shape of a battle of the dimensions of the Battle of Normandy from day to day. The shape is in the commander's mind, as a picture is in the mind of an artist, but it is true, as I have emphasized often, that a battle is an exercise in confusion. Lieut.-General Walter Bedell Smith, Chief of Staff to the Supreme Commander, and a man of an acute and perceptive intelligence, a dry humour, and chronic stomach ulcers, is said to have remarked of a campaign that it went according to plan 'from end to beginning'. There is always truth in that for the winning side. Nevertheless Montgomery never lost sight of the 'shape' of the battle he fought in Normandy, and he held it to the shape he wanted with rare fortitude. It was a close, clearly defined battlefield, and on that close battlefield the opposing armies were in constant collision, but the collisions were in a series of patterns initiated, if not devised, by Montgomery. From beginning to end he controlled the battle.

Thus, although named objectives were not often gained, and results seemed too often disappointing to observers, the enemy was steadily manoeuvred towards a disaster from which his High Command constantly refused to permit him to withdraw. It was a tight battle fought in a very tight way, the enemy constantly striving to stabilize his position, to 'rope off' the Allies, and failing. Moreover the enemy was misled in his appreciation of Montgomery's intentions, sharing with the Allied Supreme Commander, his Deputy, and most observers, the belief that Montgomery was resolved to break-out to the east while the British commander never wavered from his resolution to break out to the South on his western front.

No commander in the history of warfare had had to conduct a battle of comparable magnitude in such a glare of publicity, his day to day tactics observed, known to, examined and commented upon by scores of amateurs making balance sheets of battle as they went along. In all previous campaigns, save perhaps for Montgomery's own in North Africa and Italy, the checks and balances, the confusions, the triumphs and disasters, the currency of battle, had been the sole concern of the commanders in the field, and of no one else. All that would have been known, before the military historians came to dissect the development of the battle or campaign, would have been the outstanding fact of victory or defeat. In North Africa Montgomery's verbal excesses and tactical miscalculations could be easily forgotten, or become the subject of humorous comment, in the light of continuous success. But in Normandy continuous success was far from obvious even to some members of Montgomery's staff. Objectives were too often confused with Objects, and not as means whereby the Object might be achieved. Few close observers had the military experience to comprehend the relationship between tactics and strategy, and especially, as it often seemed, the contradictory tactics of Montgomery's strategy. The Supreme Commander, whose overwhelming longing was for a tactical opportunist, and not for a military Chess player who seemed glad when he appeared to fail to take an enemy 'piece' in his carefully planned advance to 'Check Mate', spent much of his time in a fever of frustration.

III

In the twelve days from the 6th to 18th June both sides had suffered frustrations, but those afflicting the enemy had been far more serious than the failure of the Allies to establish the strong positions they had hoped for. Montgomery had strengthened his bridgehead across the Orne at Ranville, but had failed to expand the bridgehead to the River Dives. Nevertheless Dempsey had built up a good attacking position south of Caen, and westward through Tilly-Sur-Seulles to Caumont. There he had a solid flank with Bradley's left wing. For their part the Americans, while making slow progress towards St. Lo, and taking heavy casualties in the *bocage*, had cut the Cotentin peninsula, and were ready to mount their attack on Cherbourg.

Thus, although Montgomery had made slow progress towards the Dives to the east, and towards the Odon to the south, he was meeting a stubborn enemy in the whole region of Villers Bocage, and compelling all enemy reinforcements to his front. These twelve days had been decisive. The Allied bridgehead in

THE TACTICS OF MONTGOMERY'S STRATEGY

Normandy was solid, although restricted, and with great skill Dempsey had manoeuvred his troops in position to mount the first major attacks since D-Day. The enemy were in a grave position, compelled to react to Montgomery's moves, and with time no longer on their side. The incessant assault from the air coupled with heavy and accurate naval gun fire, had made it almost impossible for von Runstedt and Rommel to move troops by day and difficult by night. Reinforcements on the way to the battlefield were forced to de-train often 100 miles short of their destinations, thereafter to face devastating assaults from the air. Counter-attacks were broken up in their assembly areas, and their timings and strength disrupted. The enemy had been forced to commit his armour and infantry piece-meal to contain Dempsey's continuous aggressive moves and threats. Messages from von Runstedt and Rommel individually, and by mutual agreement between the two commanders, had left the Fuehrer and the High Command in no doubt of the gravity of the situation. The American drive to cut off the Cotentin and to move upon Cherbourg could not be frustrated, and the British could be partially held only by concentrating all available armour against them. Infantry were scarce at this stage on both sides. Thus the Germans had been compelled to try to plug holes, instead of mounting moves of their own, and this, as Montgomery said, suited him very well.

Nevertheless to the millions of onlookers hungry for decisive news, the Allied progress seemed slow and disappointing. Perhaps the greatest omission of the observers was their failure to consider the enemy. They failed to note that the enemy had failed constantly in his intentions, and could not credit these failures to Montgomery. For Eisenhower and Tedder to begin to talk of crisis was absurd and dangerous. In these early days the seeds of frustration were sown, and swiftly nurtured by the Channel storm.

On 13th June, Montgomery had given tongue rather too soon in announcing his intention to establish his eastern flank from the Channel to Thury Harcourt, and to develop the American attack westward. The unexpected appearance of the 2nd Panzer Division frustrated Montgomery's plans, but, 'It (2nd Panzer Division) plugged the hole through which I had broken (in the Villers Bocage-Caumont area),' Montgomery wrote to Brooke, the C.I.G.S. 'I had to think again.' At the same time Montgomery was short of the necessary strength to attack simultaneously on both flanks of 2nd Army, and had decided to mount his greatest offensive effort on his right flank to strengthen his junction with Bradley's left, and block the movement of enemy reinforcements to the west.

On the 18th, Montgomery issued a directive announcing his intention to capture Caen in the east while the Americans would take Cherbourg in the west. Caen, he had written, 'is really the key to Cherbourg.' It was an unhappy and misleading statement, and the operation, known as EPSOM, had an unfortunate beginning, the channel storm compelling a delay of four days. This situation sparked off Eisenhower's 'vivid' fears of a stalement, and disturbed Churchill. At such times Montgomery's 'gratification' seemed somewhat out of place and ill-timed. Confidence was vital, but Montgomery's confidence seemed almost calculated to infuriate Eisenhower. A perverse element seems to have intruded into the relationship of these two very different types of men, and at times it seems that Montgomery was deliberately teasing the Supreme Commander.

Nevertheless Eisenhower should not have been misled by the tactical failure of operation EPSOM, for EPSOM was a strategic success beyond all doubt. It had frustrated the massive counter-attack with which the enemy had hoped to disrupt the Allied beachhead. When the battle was over Rommel and von Runstedt knew that their last hopes of holding Normandy and the territory west of the Seine had gone.

Montgomery's military language addressed to his commanders was impeccable, but his unmilitary language was too often open to wide misconstruction. His major operations of June and July, 1944, EPSOM and GOODWOOD, were both written small and spoken very large. His excuse might be—and it has been advanced by historians—that he wanted all the Air support he could get, and that he had to talk big to get it. It is a pity. He allowed his enthusiasm to run away with his tongue, or permitted the 'Romantic Cavalier' I have sometimes imagined to be lurking within the 'Puritan', to take temporary control. Or again, it could have been guile to deceive the enemy, and it may not have occurred to him that the Supreme Com-

1. Eisenhower and Montgomery

2. General Eisenhower with General Montgomery at the latter's H.Q. in Normandy

mander and his Deputy could be deceived. Certainly Montgomery deceived the enemy in regard to his intentions, but he would not, I think, have been capable of concealing his successful use of guile from a wider public. As it was, the use of colourful language, even when he had carefully and lucidly explained his intentions in messages to Eisenhower, was dangerous—

'My whole eastern flank will burst into flames on Saturday.'

The newspapers certainly began to burst into flames on Monday, even if the eastern flank did not.

The misunderstandings in regard to EPSOM were far less serious than the complete failure of the Supreme Commander, and the Press, to understand the object of GOODWOOD. GOODWOOD was never more than a sustained assault mounted against the most powerful concentration of the enemy forces, and designed to hold the ring while Bradley went into action to break out through St. Lo to the south. But Bradley's progress continued to be very slow in the face of a resolute enemy and appalling weather conditions. Meanwhile the British 2nd Army and the Canadians on their left held on against growing concentrations of enemy armour. Montgomery's first attack had coincided with Field-Marshal von Kluge's order to Army Group B on the same day:

> 'To deliver a concentric attack with all available forces against the enemy that has thrust down towards the south between the Dives and Caen and at all costs to push him back northwards to his starting position.'

It was a grim battle waged over many days, and at the end of it the British had gained Caen, and had improved their positions east and south of Caen from the Channel coast to Troarn on the west bank of the Dives, south to Bourgebus and west to Caumont. They now held a deep bridgehead south of the Odon, and were in position to mount an attack southward on Falaise. Moreover they had held enemy reinforcements in infantry and armour clear of the Americans in their bitter struggle for St. Lo.

On the 19th July, Bradley captured St. Lo and could only then begin to re-group his forces for operation COBRA—the break-out. That was the point and purpose of operation

GOODWOOD. Throughout the battle Montgomery showed no signs of impatience with Bradley's slow progress. He was prepared to go on 'writing down' enemy strength and holding it in the east, while improving, however slowly, his own position. On the 25th July, he ordered the Canadians to begin to move towards Falaise. The attack was to be 'limited', almost in the nature of a feint. It was the kind of attack which, perhaps, had slightly misled General Gehr von Schweppenberg more than a month before. The enemy reacted at once to this move of Montgomery's, swiftly re-grouping the 9th, 116th, and 10th Panzer Divisions to strike at 'the flank of a British southward thrust.'

The 25th July was the first decent day for a week, and 600 fighter-bombers of the U.S. 9th Air Force concentrated on a 300 yard strip of the enemy defences covering the St. Lo-Lessay road. 1,500 bombers of the 8th Air Force followed up with 3,400 tons of high explosive, and medium bombers of the 9th Air Force carpeted the whole area with fragmentation bombs. 3,000 aircraft had concentrated this holocaust into 90 minutes, and in its wake the U.S. VII Corps, its forward troops shaken and having suffered casualties from their own bombers, began to advance. There was nothing to stop them. An enemy Regimental headquarters had disappeared and the German General Bayerlein compared his front with 'a landscape on the moon—all craters and death'. At least 70% of his troops were dead, wounded, 'crazed or stupefied'. His entire tank force had been destroyed. It was the beginning of the end.

The American advance entered upon its decisive phase on the 27th July. On the 30th, the long awaited break-out to the south had been achieved. Montgomery's patient, thoughtful operation GOODWOOD, long sustained in fair weather and foul against all the strength the enemy could bring to bear, had reduced the enemy facing the Americans to a pitiful remnant, with no reserves worth speaking of and no plans for any possible withdrawal. Communications had broken down.

On the 27th July, seeing the whole battle developing in the way he had planned, Montgomery ordered Dempsey to re-group, to concentrate against Caumont, and to drive for Vire. This was to deny the enemy a rallying point in the Pincon hills, and the British were now fighting in the worst *bocage* country. It was an operation mounted with the least possible signalling to the enemy or to anyone else. It made steady progress, and a sense of excitement began to be felt throughout the Allied armies.

By the 31st July, the German High Command, with the exception of the Führer, was convinced that withdrawal was the only possible course to avert disaster. The Führer would not hear of it. Abnormal at the best of times, he was now almost certainly half out of his mind. General Warlimont was his emissary to convey his orders to the unfortunate von Kluge.

> 'Tell Field-Marshal von Kluge that he should keep his eyes riveted to the front and on the enemy without ever looking backward.'[1]

O.K.W., or Herr Hitler himself, would be the sole arbiters of what should happen next, but with every hour the options were fading.

On the 1st August, there were highly significant changes in the nature of the Allied command. General Bradley assumed command of the U.S. 12th Army Group, and General Patton took command of the U.S. 3rd Army. Montgomery remained 'Ground Force Commander', but his control over the Allied armies had begun to weaken. The tight battle was over, and the Americans were showing signs of reacting to freedom after long confinement. The final phase was about to begin. While the Americans finally cleared the Brittany peninsula Patton swung swiftly south and east. At the same time, while Montgomery watched intently for the first signs of the withdrawal of the enemy, Herr Hitler prepared his last attempt to drive the Allies back into the sea. With all available armour von Kluge must drive westward to Avranches. While von Kluge was striving to plan his impossible task in the light of reason, Montgomery ordered a rapid advance in the opposite direction. The American right would 'swing rapidly eastward towards Paris', the Canadians on the British left would press on astride the Caen-Falaise road, and the 2nd Army would heave steadily in a south-easterly direction against the still powerful enemy right flank. The enemy would then be hemmed in against the Seine without a single bridge to aid further withdrawal. The trap could not be escaped.

[1] Pogue: *The Supreme Command.*

At least until he assumed command of 12th Army Group and Patton's 3rd Army became fully operational, Bradley had never misunderstood Montgomery, or failed to give him credit for his handling of the battle.

> 'While Collins was hoisting his VII Corps flag over Cherbourg, Montgomery was spending his reputation in a bitter siege against the old university city of Caen. For three weeks he had rammed his troops against those Panzer divisions he had deliberately drawn toward the city as part of our Allied strategy of diversion in the Normandy campaign... For Monty's primary task was to attract German troops to the British front that we might more easily secure Cherbourg and get into position for the break-out.
> 'In this diversionary mission Monty was more than successful, for the harder he hammered towards Caen, the more German troops he drew into that sector. Too many correspondents, however, had over-rated the importance of Caen itself...'

Bradley's next passage gives some support for 'guile' theory.

> '... had we attempted to exonerate Montgomery by explaining how successfully he had hoodwinked the German ... we would have also given our strategy away. We desperately wanted the German to believe this attack on Caen was the main Allied effort.'[1]

But surely it was not necessary for Eisenhower, Tedder, and senior members of Supreme Headquarters to believe it also! Bradley goes on to explain that the more successful Montgomery was in his plan—that is, the more enemy strength he attracted to his front—the less 'likely he was to advance'.

Montgomery bore his long ordeal with equanimity, maintaining a stoic, and even a good humoured, calm. While it is difficult to fault his conduct in the field, his conduct off the field—or his lack of it—was a major blunder. It revealed his essential weakness and his limitations. He does not seem to have understood the importance of the Supreme Commander, and this was a failure as serious in its way as the Supreme Commander's failure to understand Montgomery's strategy. Apart from winning the battle for Normandy, Montgomery's

---

[1] General Omar N. Bradley: *A Soldier's Story*, Eyre and Spottiswoode, p. 325.

most important task was to gain Eisenhower's full confidence and respect. In this he failed. It was a grave and irreparable error of judgement, for by this means alone might Montgomery, and through him Britain, have done more to shape the course of victory.

So long as General Brooke, the C.I.G.S., General Kennedy, the DMO, the Prime Minister, and his army commanders in the field, knew exactly what he was doing, that was all that Montgomery seemed to care about. He did not even play to the gallery. From the 6th June to the end in Normandy Montgomery was a dedicated commander of the ground forces. He fought a hard battle, 'made for him', and a battle he made for himself.

CHAPTER FIVE

The End of Strategy

I

DAILY throughout the first week of August Montgomery watched the triumph of his strategy unfolding before his eyes. At last, as he said, the Allied armies had 'unloosed the shackles that were holding us down and have knocked away the key rivets'.[1] On the extreme western flank Patton's 3rd Army had moved swiftly out of its positions in the area of Coutances to drive through Avranches, crossing the See and Selune rivers. Even though Patton said it himself, it was a considerable feat. 'The passage of two Army Corps (VIII and XV) through Avranches is one of those things which cannot be done, but was,' he wrote.[2] The way was open. Faced by enemy groups lacking cohesion and overtaken by the sudden speed up of events, Patton detached his VIII Corps to clear the Brittany Peninsula while he swung his XV Corps south and east on Laval and Le Mans. At the end of the week the Seine was almost in his sights, and there was nothing to stop him as XX Corps and VII Corps joined his massive thrust. This was the 'expanding torrent' Montgomery had always feared, and which he had set in motion.

Meanwhile the 1st Canadian Army, the 2nd British Army and the First U.S. Army were locked in the last stages of the desperate struggle against the enemy in Normandy. The First U.S. Army under General Hodges strengthened the British western flank on Vire, and moved south through Mortain with its right to turn east through 90 degrees on a line Domfront-Alencon, parallel with the Allied front from south of Caen. The entire enemy forces south of the Seine were now in extreme danger, partially surrounded in a narrowing salient while

[1] Pogue: *The Supreme Command*, p. 206.
[2] Patton: *War as I knew it*, p. 98.

Patton, advancing at will on the southern outside track must inevitably anchor on the Seine. But there were no clear signs of enemy intentions, or of confusion. The Canadians mounting their attacks with great urgency astride the Caen-Falaise road encountered a powerful and growing opposition. General Dempsey, increasing the British 2nd Army pressure on Thury Harcourt with the object of advancing on Argentan, constantly identified new enemy units. At last von Kluge had persuaded the Führer to release units of the 15th Army to pour into the battle immediately south of the last real enemy hinge at Falaise.

On the 4th August, with good reason, Montgomery confessed himself 'mystified as to how he (the enemy) was endeavouring to conduct his withdrawal'. And 'There was no evidence to show on what line he was intending to reform his front.'[1] No other reasonable course but withdrawal had been open to the enemy since early in July, yet the signs—such as they were— were of an opposite intention. In fact, the desperate situation that had alarmed the German commanders in the field from the end of June, and which now harassed von Kluge, Hausser and Eberbach almost beyond endurance, seemed to the fevered and chronicly suspicious mind of the German Fuehrer to present, 'A unique, never recurring opportunity for a complete reversal of the situation.'[2] Rommel and von Runstedt in their day had tried to bring home to the Führer the decisive factor of Allied air power over the battlefield, and far beyond. And now von Kluge, emphasizing in an urgent message to O.K.W. the Allied 'absolute and unmistakable air supremacy, with our forces bombed to bits'[3] made his loyalty suspect. Ignoring the true position both in the air and on land, Hitler ordered von Kluge to mount an attack, massing all available armour. He was to break through at Mortain and thrust powerfully between the See and Selune rivers to Avranches, cutting the communications of the U.S. 3rd Army, and stabilizing a new front from the Cotentin to the Dives. At the same time he wanted to change his commanders in the field.

By this order Hitler condemned the German armies south of the Seine to almost certain annihilation, prejudicing irrevocably

---
[1] Montgomery: *Normandy to the Baltic*, p. 94.
[2] Pogue: *The Supreme Command*, p. 207.
[3] Ellis and others: *Victory in the West*, vol. i, H.M.S.O., p. 423.

their slender chances of orderly, or even organized, withdrawal. To add to the extent of the tragedy Hitler, overcoming his fears of Allied landings in the Pas de Calais, permitted the movement of troops not only from the 15th Army, but also from the Brittany peninsula, and from wherever they might move, even on bicycles. On the morning of the 6th August, the remains of six armoured divisions, pitifully under strength and all severely mauled, had been assembled facing west ready to strike at the 'hinge' of the U.S. 1st Army at Mortain. Finally not more than 80 tanks mustered for the 'last throw' under the command of General von Funck.

Yet all that was clear to Montgomery up to the night of the 7th August was that the enemy was pouring all available troops into the 'bag', or 'balloon', as Bradley called it, which was the final shape of the Battle for Normandy, which had become the Battle for France. It seemed as though the enemy marched open-eyed into an obvious trap, and as a result was reinforcing his shoulder south of Caen, resolved to hold Falaise at all costs, and to keep open his line of communications. This in itself could be the prelude to a last minute attempt at withdrawal.

But Montgomery could afford to disregard enemy intentions. The initiative was his, and he prepared to administer the *coup de grâce*. In successive Directives to his army commanders, and his 12th Army Group commander, Montgomery ordered his armies to begin the final encircling movement he had always envisaged and to force the enemy back to the Seine. The terrible trap forming as the enemy escape route narrowed between Falaise and Argentan under the weight of Allied pressure from the North and South was not yet clear. Thus at the precise moment that von Kluge ordered the attack to go in Westward on Avranches, Montgomery ordered his armies to advance with all possible speed 100 miles in the opposite direction. Watching developments with care he fixed new Army Group boundaries through Tinchebray, Argentan, Dreux, Mantes Gassicourt.

II

On the night of the 8th August, when it was already clear

that the enemy attack was held in the Mortain-Jubigny area by the U.S. 30th division, Montgomery signalled the C.I.G.S., 'If only the Germans will go on attacking for a few more days it seems that they might not (repeat not) be able to get away.'[1] His 'repeat not' emphasized his clear understanding of the developing situation.

Field-Marshal von Kluge agreed with Montgomery. On the night of the 8th, he informed O.K.W. that the thrust to Avranches was not only 'scarcely feasible', but would also 'be welcome to the English'. The 8th August was a fateful day. Montgomery, no longer treating Bradley as a subordinate, suggested that Patton should strike north from Le Mans upon Argentan with his left flanking corps. Excitement was rising, particularly with Bradley and Patton with their open view from the south, as the pattern of the enormous success took shape. The abortive attempt of the enemy to break through to the west had not caused the Americans to pause for a moment in their advance, but as the trap formed round the enemy, narrowing to the jaws of Falaise-Argentan, Bradley became anxious for the security of his long open flank. There, if anywhere, the enemy might burst out towards Alencon. At this stage Bradley began to blame the British in the North for squeezing the enemy out of the tube by their intense and growing pressure. The accusation was not true, and never justified.

From beginning to end Montgomery fought his battle with total dedication, too involved to permit himself the close and continuous contacts with Eisenhower and Bradley, the changing command situation demanded. He was in his element. His task above all was to finish the job. From the 8th to the 16th August the enemy continued to play into Montgomery's hands, but the awareness of the magnitude of the impending defeat his armies must suffer had begun to penetrate the mind of the Führer, like a canker. For eight days the remains of his spearhead troops in the attack on Mortain, despite their appalling experience on the opening day of their assault when British Typhoons had battered their armour into the ground, fought with magnificent courage and tenacity in the very bottom of the 'bag', and three-quarters surrounded. They had become the rearguard, and they knew it.

[1] Ellis and others: *Victory in the West*, vol. i, H.M.S.O., p. 416.

In spite of the tremendous pressure exerted by the British, and the rapid progress of the U.S. 1st Army, compressing the enemy ever more firmly in the west while advancing with its right flank upon Mayenne, and turning tightly upon Putanges, the enemy intention to withdraw was not yet evident. On the 9th, Hitler blamed von Kluge for bad timing in his attack, and on the 11th, he ordered von Kluge to mount an assault towards Alencon-Le Mans. It was already too late. Movement within the diminishing 'bag' was severely restricted. Von Kluge had done his best. He had kept O.K.W. fully informed, and thereby signed his death warrant. Like his predecessors he knew that the only sane course was surrender. Kesselring and Model were on their way to Hitler's headquarters, and one of them would be chosen for the impossible task of replacing the doomed Field-Marshal.

Meanwhile Patton had swung his left flank due north from Le Mans on Alencon and Argentan, while thrusting on unchecked in three prongs on Dreux, Chartres and Troyes. His right flank had easily closed the Loire.

Almost to the end the German order in the diminishing pocket remained remarkable, a triumph of discipline in face of hopeless odds and insuperable problems of supply. At last on the 16th, Hitler ordered the withdrawal, ordering his generals to attack with all their strength on the jaws of Falaise and Argentan. That night Field-Marshal Model replaced von Kluge, and on the 17th, von Kluge took cyanide. It was an impossible end-play for Model. At his headquarters at Lisieux he briefly contemplated a defence line on the Somme, or anywhere in France. His hopes were over-run before they could be committed to paper. But the last hours of the battle from the 16th to the 19th saw fighting as desperate as any since the first days. An infantry division from the 15th Army strengthened the dug-in and experienced defenders of Falaise, giving the Canadians a tremendous struggle. Montgomery, seeing clearly the situation, moved two armoured columns swiftly east and south on Trun and Chambois with Bradley conforming to the pattern. These two columns, one Polish and one Canadian, sustained one of the worst ordeals of baptism by fire experienced by any troops in the course of the campaign. As the enemy retreat gathered momentum, confined within the narrow corridor, bombed and battered by high explosive on all sides and devastatingly assaulted by limitless squadrons of Typhoons and Spitfires, retreat became rout, and rout near annihilation. In the midst of the enemy torrent the leading Canadian armour fought desperately for St. Lambert sur Dives. At last on the 19th, the gap was closed. Spitfires and Typhoons were attacking all the escape routes and the road to Lisieux. It was time for Field-Marshal Model to seek a new headquarters. There was no room in France.

III

Unhappily there were signs of disunity in the Allied camp. Bradley's sober judgement and impeccable loyalty to Montgomery, so clearly marked throughout the June and July battles, had suffered a change with his promotion to Army Group Command. General George Patton was going to the new Group Commander's head, and as the 3rd Army raced on spectacularly Bradley seemed like a man clinging to the mane of a half-wild stallion, dazzled and confused by the opportunities growing with every hour. Montgomery's control was clearly nearing its end. The set-piece battle so suited to his talents was over, and the area of war was rapidly expanding. Moreover the problems of commanding an Army Group commander whose forces already outnumbered his own, and whose praises were being sung in headlines inches deep, demanded tact of a high order.

From the 14th to the 19th August, Generals Bradley and Patton were highly critical of Montgomery and the British armies. On the 14th, Patton praised himself for his swift progress. 'As of August 14,' he wrote, 'the 3rd Army had advanced farther and faster than any army in history.' It is difficult, if not impossible, to discover an army in all military history with such a magnificent opportunity. 'We never had to regroup, which seemed to be the chief form of amusement in the British armies.'[1] Filled with contempt for his British Allies he urged Bradley to let him move his XV Corps out of Argentan upon Falaise to drive the laggard

[1] Patton: *War as I knew it*, p. 105.

British back into the sea. Two or three weeks later Patton was destined to sit down and cry like a child on the banks of the Moselle, having entangled his army in the maze of Metz in search of the headlines he could never resist. 'George was stimulated by headlines,' Bradley wrote. 'The blacker the headlines the more recklessly he fought.'[1]

At the crucial hour Bradley kept his head, halting Patton's XV corps at Argentan and pulling back its advance guards on the road to Falaise. For a long time, perhaps for the rest of his life, he wondered whether he did the right thing, and blamed Montgomery for his caution in shifting the weight of his attack on Trun and Chambois, but it was his own V corps which was slow to move. The closure of the Argentan-Falaise gap might have resulted in a greater slaughter, but it is by no means certain. It would almost certainly have delayed Montgomery's wide encirclement to the Seine, and the resulting disasters to the remnants of the enemy striving to cross the river. In fact Montgomery had swiftly understood the great triumph with which the Führer was presenting him by persisting in his abortive attempts to break through to Avranches. His slow but sure handling of the last phase, which so infuriated Patton and to a lesser degree aroused intense frustration in Eisenhower and Bradley, was wholly justified. In any case Eisenhower had the power to intervene, and would have done so had he thought it necessary.[2] Even had the retreating enemy reached the Seine through a wider corridor and in greater strength, he would inevitably have suffered a series of disasters in his endeavours to cross the river. As it was, the scene in the Elboeuf pocket as the enemy strove to escape by ferry was only less terrible in degree than the appalling 'shambles of Chambois'.

Meanwhile the separation and steady loosening of Montgomery's Ground Force Command, which had begun with Bradley's promotion and the advent of Patton, had deteriorated to the point where it had virtually ceased to exist. Immediately upon the end in Normandy, Bradley 'rolled EAGLE TAC 112 miles on up the road from Laval to the tree-shaded city of Chartres'. In so doing he was outstripping his signals

---

[1] Bradley: *A Soldier's Story*, p. 393.
[2] *Command Decisions*, p. 412. Office of Chief of Mil. Hist. Washington D.C.

communications, and keeping contact with Supreme Headquarters by radio telephone. 'With the break in telephone lines to the rear, 21st Army Group became even more inaccessible than SHAEF,' he wrote. 'This, however, we did not regret.'[1]

No one present at Chartres in those days harboured the illusion that Montgomery could, or even wished, to exert any influence in that quarter. Paris was entered on 25th August. It was a political-military decision which could only be made by the Supreme Commander. Militarily it involved daunting problems of supply to complicate a 'logistics' situation of ominous, and even decisive, proportions. It must have reminded the Americans, although they would never admit it, that military and political problems, the twin 'Arts of the Possible', are inextricably mixed.

Politically the decision to enter Paris was more complicated. General de Gaulle, after his triumphant reception in Bayeux, and his immediate appointments of Civil authorities, had already left the whole complex apparatus of U.S. civil planning for France in ruins. As for Paris, Paris belonged in the first instance to General Le Clerc's armoured division after its long haul from Lake Chad, and Eisenhower at once saw that this must be so. But above all Paris belonged to General de Gaulle. On 27th August, triumphant in the midst of the Republican Guards 'in their resplendent uniforms' General de Gaulle greeted Eisenhower and Bradley at the hub of his City. The Americans would long regret the constant snubbing they had given to this 'so-called' Free-French leader.

Montgomery had refused Eisenhower's invitation to join him on that Sunday, pleading somewhat pointedly that he was in the throes of directing his armies. He was the Ground Force Commander in name, if no longer in fact, and he was doing his job. The substance of command had given way to the shadow. His elevation to the rank of Field-Marshal was a poor compensation.

[1] Bradley: *A Soldier's Story*, p. 393.

CHAPTER SIX

The Parting of the Ways

I

It is often more difficult to pin-point the precise hour of a deterioration in affairs than it is to pin-point success. In this case the hour coincided. A rift had been growing between the Allies for a long time, and it was outwardly manifest in the disturbing pro and anti attitudes of War Correspondents in both camps. From the first day of August the correspondents sparked a crisis. The American newspapers greeted General Bradley's promotion to Army Group Commander with enthusiasm, and the event released all the pent-up discontents with British Command, not only on land, but on the seas and in the air. The appointment of General Eisenhower was seen more as a cunning British move to mask the fact that they had consolidated effective power of command in their own hands, rather than as a command reality. The British, it was said, had merely wished to set up a figurehead, destined to become little more than a spectator of operations beyond his control. This kind of criticism, threatening to reach Congressional level, alarmed the U.S. Secretary of State for War, and the U.S. Chief of Staff. At the same time the promotion of General Bradley, clearly agreed from the outset, and its timing ordained by events, was seen as a demotion for General Montgomery, arousing the keen resentment of British newspapers, and a corresponding pleasure in the United States. Not all the protestations of the Public Relations staff at Supreme Headquarters could convince public opinion otherwise on either side of the Atlantic.

In the course of the month of August, as the scope of victory became apparent, General George Marshall wrote to Eisenhower urging him to take over Supreme Command at the earliest possible moment. 'The astonishing success of the campaign up to the present moment,' Marshall wrote on 17th August, 'has evoked emphatic expression of confidence in you and Bradley.'[1]

Setting aside in this context the enormous contribution to the victory in Normandy of the Air and Naval forces involved, the military victory on the ground was never credited fully and firmly to General Montgomery. It is a strange quirk of fate and fortune. His cautious battle of attrition at 2nd Alamein in 1942, and his pedestrian progress thereafter to Tunis over the 'Tedder Carpet',[2] had earned him extravagant praise. Now his fine, if unglamorous, performance over three exhausting months in Normandy, again with an inestimable debt to the air force, brought him little more than a slow hand-clap. It was very rough justice.

In substance, if not in intention, Bradley's promotion was a demotion for Montgomery, the defining of the true command position and the necessary preliminary to the assumption of the Supreme Command in the field by Eisenhower. While the Eisenhower-Bradley relationship strengthened on a new note, the Eisenhower-Montgomery relationship, always uneasy, grew more and more tenuous. The war correspondents in full cry clinging to Patton's gun-belt, and extolling his deeds with understandable, if extravagant, pride, turned the closing phases of the battle into a competition, rather than the end-pattern of a co-operative effort so carefully worked for, and outwardly maintained. At the same time the balance of power in France moved in ever-increasing ratio in American favour. Bradley's twenty divisions in August gave him a decided advantage, destined to grow rapidly while the British were hard put to it to maintain their strength.

In early September the situation in the Far East and the minimum demands of General Auchinleck in India in order to fulfil his planned commitments in South-East Asia, would force Churchill and Brooke to consider how soon they might hope to withdraw three divisions and two brigades from N.W. Europe. At the same time three British-Indian divisions would

---

[1] Pogue: *The Supreme Command*, p. 264.
[2] The clearance of a pathway through the enemy defences by pattern bombing. 'To Tedder must be given the main credit for the consistency of the application of air power both for the campaign in the Mediterranean and for the re-entry into Europe.' *The Times*, 5th June, 1967.

be withdrawn from the Mediterranean theatre. There was no way out of these commitments, 'thus placing the whole burden of reinforcing Europe on the Americans alone'.[1]

Meanwhile, in August the long delayed and bitterly debated operation ANVIL, re-named DRAGOON, was about to be launched in the South of France in spite of Churchill's strenuous efforts up to the eleventh hour to induce the Americans to change their minds, to fortify Alexander's impoverished command in Italy, and to enable him to move, finally, through Jugo Slavia with Austria and Hungary, and above all Vienna, in his sights.

'I believe... that this may become a decisive front,' Alexander telegraphed to the C.I.G.S. 'I have only to get through the Ljubljana Gap and it will be.'[2] Such an intention if carried out successfully would have challenged Stalin's political-strategic aims in South-Eastern Europe, and have had a profound effect on the balance of power in the aftermath.

Thus in the last days of August and the first days of September, decisions were made irrevocably to fix the pattern of victory, and the pattern of power and command.

II

It is almost certain that nothing General Montgomery had done, or could do, would have changed the command situation more than marginally in the British favour. His Ground Force command was never more than a pipe dream in the manner he envisaged it, quite apart from whether such a command was practical in the circumstances prevailing in August-September, 1944. From early August onwards public opinion in the United States exerted a powerful—perhaps a dominant—influence on tactics and thereby on strategy. This power was greatly enhanced by the susceptibility of American commanders to public opinion and the plaudits of the multitude. From time to time a clamour was raised, or the threat of a clamour, which Eisenhower was not the man to resist.

Early in August, Montgomery had begun to develop his

[1] Ehrman: *Grand Strategy*, vol. v, p. 507.
[2] Bryant: *Triumph in the West*, 18 July, p. 255.

plan for the next move, the total defeat of Germany. That he should do this revealed his reluctance, or inability, to understand the true command situation. In the middle of August, General Eisenhower had stated in a message to General Marshall:

> 'No major effort takes place in this Theater by ground, sea or air except with my approval and no one in the Allied Command presumes to question my supreme authority and responsibility for the whole campaign.'[1]

Montgomery should have been planning in the closest possible co-operation with the Supreme Commander. His difficulty was that he planned as an Army Group commander while seeing himself in a much more important role. He did not seem to recognize that he was not commanding two Army Groups in the last phases of the Battle for Normandy. After 1st August, Montgomery tried to co-ordinate his Army Group's tactics and strategy with Bradley's Army Group. But this was not the way to command two army groups. To command two army groups, nearly 40 divisions strong, it would have been necessary to form a new headquarters, perhaps a 'Ground Force Command headquarters'. But it would have been too late to attempt to form such an H.Q. in mid-August, 1944, or even earlier, for as Ehrman points out:

> 'To perpetuate Montgomery's sole command of the land operations, for which the original plan had not allowed ... might be to sacrifice the amity of command—possibly of the Alliance—to a controversial venture which might well not succeed.'[2]

Thus there was a sense of unreality about Montgomery's ambitions, and a failure in himself to understand, to evaluate— and finally to accept—his position in the hierarchy of command. He went ahead, seemingly unaware of any fundamental objections to his plans and without considering the probability of genuine disagreement. On the 17th August, he visited General Bradley at 12th Army Group headquarters and put forward his proposition, of which the basic idea is clear in the first paragraph:

[1] Pogue: *The Supreme Command*, p. 264.
[2] Ehrman: *Grand Strategy*, vol. v, p. 380.

'i. After crossing the Seine, 12th and 21st Army Groups should keep together as a solid mass of some forty divisions which would be so strong that it need fear nothing. This force would move north-eastwards.'[1]

Montgomery returned to his 21st Army Group H.Q. under the impression that General Bradley was in agreement—'... on the 17th August, Bradley had expressed his complete agreement with my suggested plan.'[1] He was mistaken. Bradley had been doing his own thinking with Patton, and in close liaison with the Supreme Commander. The U.S. forces had already begun to part company with the British forces, and were oriented on a different line of thrust. Meanwhile General Eisenhower was shown Montgomery's notes:

'i. The quickest way to win this war is for the great mass of the Allied armies to advance northwards, clear the coast as far as Antwerp, establish a powerful air force in Belgium, and advance into the Ruhr.

'ii. The force must operate as one whole, with great cohesion, and be so strong that it can do the job quickly.'[1]

Montgomery then began to elaborate his plan.

'If we could maintain the strength and impetus of our operations beyond the Seine sufficiently to keep the enemy on the run straight through to the Rhine, and "bounce" our way across that river before the enemy succeeded in re-forming a front to oppose us, then we should achieve a prodigious advantage.'[2]

In attempting to evaluate Montgomery's generalship in the field the key words in this passage are 'impetus' and 'bounce'. Assuming that the plan was a good plan—and I think it was—was Montgomery the man to maintain the essential impetus, and to 'bounce' the river Rhine? In any case Montgomery's plan might have been a better plan than the Bradley-Patton idea to drive through in the centre on Frankfurt. It was certainly a better plan than the 'No-Plan' known as the Broad

---

[1] Montgomery: *Memoirs*, pp. 266-267.
[2] Montgomery: *Normandy to the Baltic*, p. 119.

Front strategy, which was very little more than a policy of letting things take their course, so that the campaign was destined to deteriorate into a piece of tactical improvisation from day to day with the Supreme Commander rationing out supplies as fairly as possible with the aim of keeping everyone as happy as possible. Of course it satisfied no one. Within a week or two Patton's officers referred to General Eisenhower as 'the best general the British ever had'.[1] The British, and Montgomery in particular, were even more certain that the dice were loaded against them.

Perhaps there was never a real chance that things would be different, and at this distance there is a sense of unreality about Montgomery's persistent nagging of Eisenhower. 'A bold strategy, as proposed by Montgomery, must carry the conviction, or at least the assent, of his fellow-commanders: unfortunately it was unlikely to do so. His relations with the Americans . . . were not particularly happy.'[2]

From the beginning Montgomery seems to have been unaware of the feelings he aroused in his American Allies, and in August, 1944, it was far too late to repair the damage.

On the 18th, Montgomery telegraphed his views to General Brooke, the C.I.G.S.:

'Have been thinking ahead about future plans but have not (repeat not) discussed subject with Ike . . . When I have got your reply will discuss matter with Ike.'

But the C.I.G.S. had left for Alexander's headquarters in Italy on the night of the 18th, and was unable to reply. On the 22nd, Lieut.-General Nye, V.C.I.G.S., visited Montgomery in Normandy to discuss the plan and the ideas of command. These are briefly stated in paragraphs 3, 4, 5 of Montgomery's note to Nye:[3]

3. Single control and direction of the land operations is vital for success. This is a *whole time* job for one man.
4. The great victory in N.W. France has been won by personal command. Only in this way will future victories

---

[1] Butcher: *Three Years with Eisenhower*, p. 568.
[2] Ehrman: *Grand Strategy*, vol. v, p. 380.
[3] Ellis and others: *Victory in the West*, vol. i, H.M.S.O., p. 460.

be won. If staff control of operations is allowed to creep in, then quick success becomes endangered.
5. To change the system of command now, after having won a great victory, would be to prolong the war.

The last paragraph fails to recognize that the system of command had not changed; nor did Montgomery recognize that his personal command position had changed upon Bradley's assumption of the command of 12th Army Group. Moreover it was not envisaged at any time that Montgomery should have the command of the two army groups. In a message to the Combined Chiefs of Staff, Eisenhower stated his intention to take over Supreme Command in the field on 1st September. There was no secret about it: It was 'as foreseen from the beginning of the campaign...' and General Montgomery's responsibility 'for co-ordinating actions between 21st and 12th Army Groups' would cease.[1]

Montgomery, in the light of his thoughts and actions, could not have accepted this translation of his position, or he had chosen to consider it overtaken by events, notably his success in Normandy. In fact events had underlined the original intention of the OVERLORD command, and had justified them without further directive or emphasis.

Meanwhile on the 19th August, Montgomery again visited General Bradley and learned that 'Ike wants to split the force and send half of it eastwards towards Nancy.' In fact Bradley and Patton had worked out their own plan for a thrust to the Reich, through the Saar, to the Rhine and Frankfurt. Bradley was no more enamoured of 'The Broad Front' than was Montgomery. In these circumstances a rivalry between Bradley-Patton and Montgomery was inevitable.

On 20th August, Montgomery sent his Chief of Staff, de Guingand, to represent him at a conference at Eisenhower's headquarters. At the same time he issued a Directive stating his intention: 'To complete the destruction of the enemy forces in north-west France. Then to advance northwards, with a view to the eventual destruction of all enemy forces in north-east France.'[2]

[1] *Victory in the West*, vol. i, p. 460.
[2] *Victory in the West*, vol. i, p. 450.

THE PARTING OF THE WAYS

Montgomery's failure to attend the meeting with the Supreme Commander on the 20th, coupled with his failure to understand his position, is inexcusable. The meeting, he must have known, was the vital meeting to reach some preliminary decisions on operations in the immediate future. Nothing could be of more urgent and vital interest to Montgomery, yet he was not there. There is no word in his writings to explain why. Perhaps he awaited some word from the C.I.G.S.?

Meanwhile, before the arrival of the V.C.I.G.S. on the 22nd, Montgomery knew that Eisenhower had stated his intention that the 12th Army Group would be 'directed towards Metz and the Saar'.[1] Montgomery also knew that Eisenhower was sticking to the intention clearly stated on 27th May, before D-Day, for an advance into Germany on two axes. This had been approved. Of course this is a poor reason, for on the 27th May, the nature of the victory in Normandy was not foreseen, and intentions had to be based on assumptions. Nevertheless it is a pointer to the inflexibility of the logistical pattern, and therefore to the tactical and strategic patterns. This would put the Supreme Command in a strait jacket.

On the 22nd, Montgomery sent de Guingand back to Eisenhower to discuss the plans and ideas already well known to the Supreme Commander. On the 23rd, Eisenhower, accompanied by his Chief of Staff, Lieut.-General Bedell Smith, visited Montgomery. It was a case of the mountain coming to Mahomet, or half of Mahomet, for Bradley was the other half. Montgomery asked Eisenhower to see him alone. He had flown that morning to Bradley's headquarters to find 'to my amazement that Bradley had changed his mind'.[2]

The meeting with Eisenhower on the 23rd was nevertheless far from barren, or it would have been far from barren if Montgomery had been able to understand clearly his own position. In a message to the C.I.G.S., reporting the meeting, he stated:[3]

'Ike came to see me today. After a long and weary discussion he agreed on our left flank we must clear the channel coast

---
[1] Montgomery: *Memoirs*, p. 267, p. 269.
[2] Montgomery: *Memoirs*, p. 269.
[3] Ellis and others: *Victory in the West*, vol. i, p. 461.

and establish a powerful air force in Belgium and invade Ruhr ... he agreed that left flank movement must be strong enough to achieve quick success ... It seems public opinion in America demands Bradley shall hold his command directly under Ike and shall not be (repeat not be) subordinated to me ...'

In addition the Supreme Commander promised priority and all possible logistical aid to Montgomery's drive to the north with the U.S. 1st Army on his right flank. In fact Eisenhower had given way a great deal, and modified his own plans accordingly. Montgomery's comment in his Memoirs[1] is most strange: 'But my arguments were of no avail ... And so we all got ready to cross the Seine and go our different ways ... Everyone was to be fighting all the time.'

This does not accord with his message to the C.I.G.S. that, 'I think discussion was valuable and cleared the air and there is a good hope that directive will be what is wanted.'[2]

In fact, it is possible that Eisenhower had given Montgomery the chance—if he would take it—to prove his point and gain the victory. Many years later Montgomery ruminated on his behaviour to Eisenhower, wondering whether he had gone 'a bit far in urging on him my own plan, and did not give sufficient weight to the heavy political burden he bore ... Looking back on it all I often wonder if I paid sufficient heed to Eisenhower's notions before refuting them ...'[3]

But there is no hint that Montgomery seriously questioned his behaviour, or his handling of his armies, and was able to conceive that he might be wrong.

III

In spite of protesting that 'I do not (repeat not) propose to continue argument with Ike,'[4] Montgomery continued to badger the Supreme Commander on the whole subject until

---

[1] Montgomery: *Memoirs*, p. 269.
[2] Ellis and others: *Victory in the West*, vol. i, p. 461.
[3] Montgomery: *Memoirs*, p. 269.
[4] Ellis and others: *Victory in the West*, vol. i, p. 463.

the end, returning to the argument with unabated vigour on 4th September and again on 18th September.

Eisenhower continued to act with great restraint and patience. He had reason to do so, but I feel that in doing so he sacrificed a great opportunity to take powerful and decisive command of his armies, and thus denied himself the prospect of military immortality. He could only be himself, and he was a conciliatory man, a man of compromise.

'... While Field-Marshal Montgomery was the leader of a British Army Group, and as such occupied the same level of authority as Generals Bradley and Devers,' wrote Forrest Pogue, 'he was also the Chief British commander in the field, in close contact with the British Chief of the Imperial General Staff and in a position to know and defend the British strategic point of view.' In the upshot Eisenhower did not feel able to say to Montgomery, 'Here is an order: execute it.'[1]

It is startling to see this statement put down in black and white by one of the most trustworthy of military historians. Such considerations should not—must not—apply on the field of battle in any circumstances whatsoever. The Supreme Commander had been given the command and the power to command. It was for him to grasp it, and to wield it ruthlessly without fear or favour. Demonstrably he failed to do so, and the campaign inevitably deteriorated into a 'free-for-all' race to the Rhine, ironically destined to be won by the dark horse outsider Hodges, in command of the U.S. 1st Army.

In Montgomery, Eisenhower had the most insubordinate of his subordinates, while General Bradley appears to have been almost mesmerized at times by his 3rd Army commander, General Patton. The perpetual tug-of-war rivalry between Montgomery and Patton dominated, and to a great extent dictated the pattern.

In private both Eisenhower and Bradley perceived the British Army Group commander's fundamental weakness, even if completely unaware of their own failings. 'Monty did not wish to surrender his Army Group command to become Eisenhower's deputy for the ground at SHAEF. He would retain 21st Army Group, and take on the dual role of Super Ground Force

[1] Pogue: *The Supreme Command*, p. 289. (General Devers commanded 6th Army Group, coming up from the South.)

commander as an added function,' wrote Bradley. He goes on to quote Eisenhower, 'Monty,' Ike said in exasperation, 'wants to have his cake and eat it too.'[1]

Montgomery's view of the campaign was undoubtedly narrow, and Eisenhower was perfectly justified in saying, 'General Montgomery was acquainted only with the situation in his own sector.'[2] In fact, Montgomery's view was even narrower, for his constant tight control of the 2nd Army made of General Dempsey the 'unknown' soldier. Montgomery's conception of Ground Force command was: (a) To command 21st Army Group, concentrating on the 2nd Army. (b) To co-ordinate the movements of the 'alien' (U.S.) flanking army. (c) To 'ground' the rest.

The Supreme Commander's Directive following his talk with Montgomery on the 23rd August, conceded a great deal. It gave 21st Army Group undoubted priority, and all the flank protection he could possibly need. 'He has given me power to co-ordinate action of forces being used for northward drive to the Pas de Calais and Belgium including those divisions 12th Army Group which (word omitted) taking part in this movement.'

It was not the forty divisions of which Montgomery had dreamed, but it was the maximum strength that could be adequately supported and deployed, and surely it was strong enough 'to fear nothing'. Indeed it is difficult to see how Montgomery could have used another man to advantage.

On the 26th, Montgomery issued a Directive in his role of co-ordinator of the left flank. The U.S. 1st Army would 'operate' on his right flank 'with the object of getting established in the general area Brussels-Maastricht-Liege-Namur-Charleroi.' He quickly modified the army boundary to give Brussels to the British 2nd Army. The 2nd Army would cross the Seine 'with all possible speed, and forge ahead whatever happened on its flanks'. The Canadian 1st Army would clear the left flank, opening up le Havre, Dieppe and north, clearing the Pas de Calais of 'V' bomb sites, a matter of great urgency to the people of Britain. The race was on. Antwerp and Brussels were in Dempsey's sights, and of these Antwerp was of

---

[1] Bradley: *A Soldier's Story*, p. 355.
[2] Eisenhower: *Crusade in Europe*, p. 336.

vital importance, the great port by which and through which the war could be won, if the immediate prospect of quick victory should fade.

It was clear then, and it is clearer now, that Montgomery had been given a great opportunity. When he saw clearly that he could not get the command he wanted, and believed desirable, he should have stopped 'belly-aching', and made the best of what he had, concentrating his whole mind on the job. If there was a true quick winning position to win the war in 1944, Montgomery should have won it. In his shoes I think Patton might have done so. Even had Montgomery found his own shoes he might also have found the faith and drive for the job. Of one thing I feel sure: in Patton and Montgomery the Allies possessed the combined talent capable of winning the war in 1944; but to have achieved this meant the existence of a commander powerful enough in personality, in strategic vision and tactical opportunism, to have welded these two—or driven these two—ill-matched and difficult characters as a team. Montgomery was clear-headed in aggressive defence; Patton was fearless and acute in rapid advance, often to the point of extreme rashness, but Patton alone of those available could have freed himself from the worst chains of 'logistics', and driven his army beyond the point where all men want to stop.

The skills of these two generals were complementary, as had been embryonically revealed in Sicily. Unhappily there was no one of the stature to command such men, and there were other probably insuperable difficulties. Patton, in effect, would have had to have been switched to the command of the U.S. 1st Army. The speculation serves no purpose now other than the assessment of generalship.

CHAPTER SEVEN

The Nature and Anatomy of Victory

I

IN the 79 days from the 6th June to the 24th August, the British and U.S. armies commanded by General Montgomery inflicted an overwhelming defeat upon the German armies in Normandy, and won the battle for France almost at a stroke. Rejecting the advice of his generals in the field and ignoring their warnings and appeals, Herr Hitler committed his forces piece-meal west of the Seine. Montgomery held them there, fought them there, beat them there, and virtually destroyed them there.

On the 24th August, the Allied armies closed the Seine, seized bridgeheads at Troyes and Mantes Gassicourt and prepared crossings at Vernon and Elbeuf. Before them the remnants of the German 7th Army and 5th Panzer Army fled in a confusion that caught up others in its torrent and cleared most of France and Belgium of the Nazi incubus. It was a victory on a scale none had predicted or foreseen. It belonged to Montgomery.

This astonishing victory confounded the planners of *Overlord* and confronted the army commanders with dazzling opportunities they could not take and were reluctant to yield. The successive struggles on the water-lines back to the last great barrier of the Rhine would not take place. Instead the Allies faced a vacuum they could not fill, and could not ignore. Henceforth logistics dictated tactics as well as strategy. The Brittany ports through which it had been planned to supply the U.S. armies beyond the Seine were still held by enemy garrisons. Cherbourg and the beaches were not enough. The Allied Deception Plan which had held the German 15th Army anchored in the Pas de Calais throughout most of the battle of Normandy predicted a struggle for the Channel ports. From the outset of his 'Ground Force' command Montgomery had won the confidence of his army commanders, Dempsey, the Englishman, Crerar, the Canadian, and Bradley, the American. He had retained that confidence throughout the battle, exercising his command with authority, tact and skill. The enemy had sustained more than 400,000 casualties[1] and lost an enormous quantity of *matériel*, including armour and artillery. The survivors of two armies had escaped almost empty-handed from the battlefield. The price had been high, but 'appreciably lower' than had been expected. At times it had been necessary to trade two men for one in constant attack against a resourceful enemy handling heavy mortars with great skill and often devastating effect in a countryside like a maze, criss-crossed with deeply wooded valleys, sunken lanes, tiny fields and tall hedgerows. The battle had cost the Americans nearly 126,000 men, including 21,000 killed, and the British 84,000 men, including 16,000 killed.

The Allied dead had lain on many battlefields and beaches, but in the narrow funnel between Trun and Chambois the enemy dead lay in a ghastly chaos of torn flesh, tangled steel and shattered equipment. Horses still harnessed in teams to ammunition and supply wagons festooned the trees in grotesque and hideous confusion, like frescoes woven into the foliage of high summer. The Typhoons, swooping low over the massed enemy in the narrow lanes, had inscribed their fearful trademark to become indelible on the mind. The dead lay in their hundreds on the green verges, in the ditches and over the fields, sharing the pastures with the swollen corpses of the cattle. Seldom before or since has it been possible to see so grimly the ultimate story of a battle engraved so starkly upon a countryside in full bloom. In Winter the rotting dead too often seem to match the rutted mud and the stark, naked trees.

There is a curious anonymity in the slaughtered on a battlefield. It is as though these corpses have no more relevance to life than the shed skins of snakes; and life itself seems as ephemeral and vulnerable as a candle flame. At a puff it is gone, and there is nothing. Even a photograph in a pocket seems meaningless.

The Ency. Brit. puts the figure at 500,000.

II

By the end of August, supply problems had become 'frantic'. There were more than two million troops in the 'lodgement area' between the Seine and Loire, served by half a million vehicles of all kinds. More than three million tons of supplies had been landed and fed to the armies by prodigious efforts. Meanwhile the immense appetites of the armies were growing rapidly as the supply lines lengthened from the Normandy beaches. The U.S. 3rd Army commanded by General Patton consumed more than 200,000 gallons of petrol a day when relatively quiet. On the move these demands were often more than doubled. In addition tens of thousands of tons of food, ammunition and general supplies had to be moved hundreds of miles by trucks over rough roads growing rougher.[1]

At the same time the nature of the battle of Normandy had restricted the development of Base depots, railheads and forward supply points and dumps. By D plus 50 the whole bridgehead had become like a boil at bursting point with the front line roughly at the 'Phase line' estimate of D plus 20. None could know that this deficit of 30 days would become a gain of 11 days in one great bound forward. When the boil burst it left a 'scar' that was not healed before the new year. The hour demanded a genius, and perhaps even genius would not have been enough.

At this crucial moment, on the 1st September, 1944, General Eisenhower took over the Supreme Command of the Allied armies in the field, relieving General Montgomery of the command of the 'Ground Forces'. General Montgomery, promoted Field-Marshal, became the Supreme Commander's left hand, commanding the 21st Army Group. General Bradley became the Supreme Commander's right hand, commanding the 12th Army Group. From the South of France General Devers, commanding the 6th Army Group, made rapid progress to take his place on Bradley's right. Thereafter, inevitably

---

[1] Cherbourg and other U.S. supply points were discharging 35,000 tons a day—well below requirements at the beginning of September. At 650 tons per day per division 12th Army Group consumed between 20-25,000 tons per day (October figure) and demanded a 100,000 ton 'cushion' of supplies forward. It was impossible. There was a 60-day time lag.

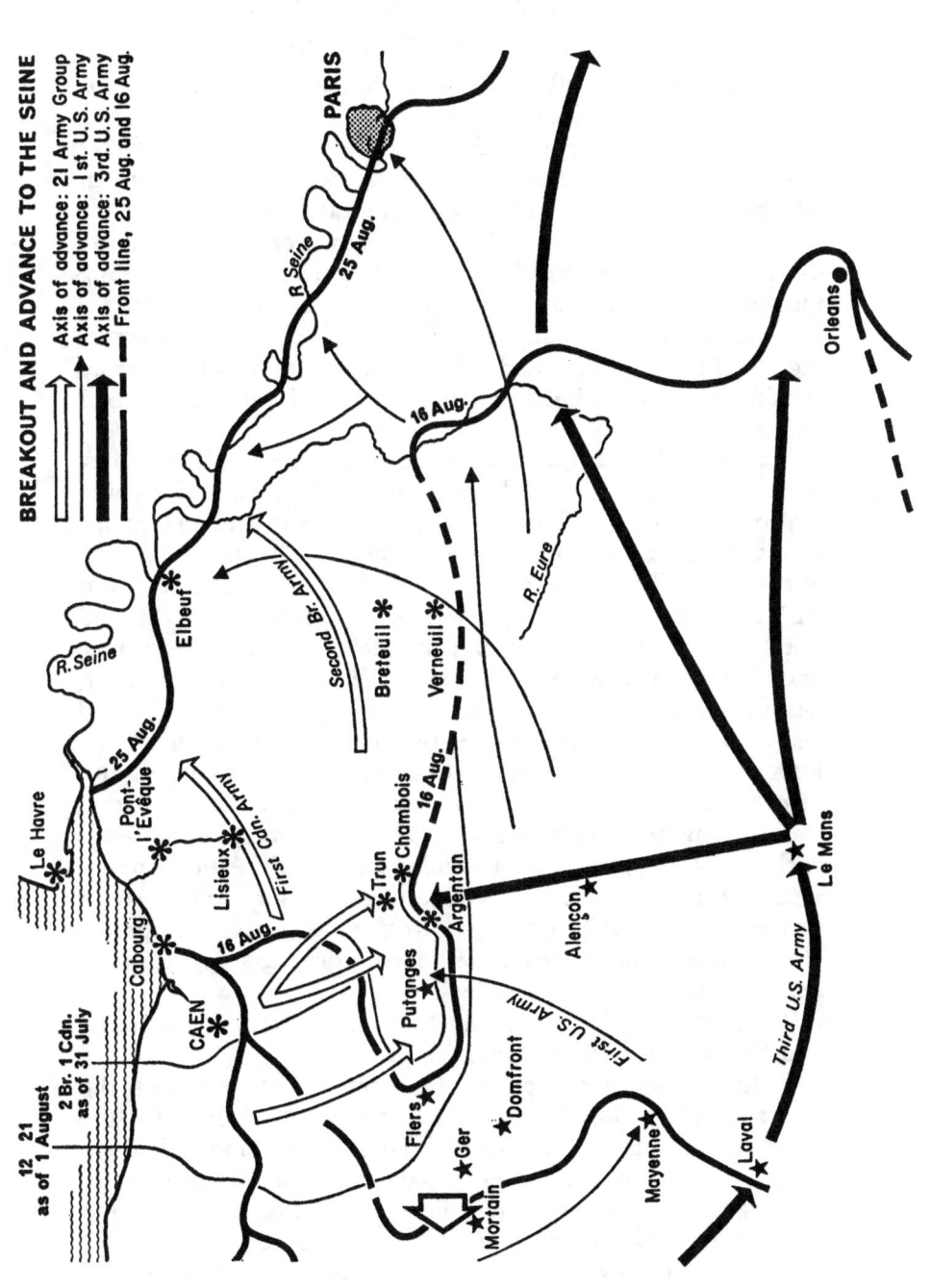

it seems, seven armies began to line up to close the Rhine from Emmerich in the north to Basle in the south. General Montgomery had known his finest hour.

In two weeks the new Supreme Command, with forces already outnumbering the enemy in the west by two to one in effective strength, and with an almost total authority in the air, saw the prospect of swift and devastating victory over Germany disappear. For the British, acutely aware of their dwindling manpower and hard put to it to maintain an effective strength of 20 divisions, the disappearance of swift victory was agonizing. All that they did, and all that they tried to do, must be considered in that light. Their writ would not run beyond 1944.

For the Americans almost the reverse was true. Time, they felt, was on their side. Their immense strength was coming swiftly to fruition. Their 20 divisions at the end of August would become 60 divisions, and more, by Christmas, or soon afterwards. Their generals began to feel their strength, and with their growing experience were not prepared to play second fiddle to any man. They were, they felt, no longer beginners, and more than capable of standing on their own feet. Moreover, despite the harmony of command in Normandy, rivalries had begun to grow, and were fanned by a vast public, fragmentarily informed and unashamedly partisan. War was played out before a huge audience on both sides of the Atlantic, and it was not simply 'a game' fought against an enemy, but a 'game' with rival armies and nations racing for the kill. A new dimension (at the least!) had been added to generalship, and it would demand remarkable qualities from an American Supreme Commander who might have to consider stopping General Patton 'with the ball at his feet'.

Thus, profoundly, the nature of the command, of the battle and the battles, had changed.

Field-Marshal Montgomery, from his vantage point on the left, supremely confident, as he had a right to be, with the powerful flavour of the 'Ground Force' command still upon him, and imbued with urgency, saw clearly a way through to the heart. There must be no splitting of armies, or of 'Ground Force' command at this vital and crucial stage.

General Bradley, from his vantage point on the right, and

in effective command of two armies (one of which was a flyer), saw equally clearly another way.

The Supreme Commander, unlike Solomon, cut the baby in halves. Or perhaps the baby was twins, each twin naturally short of weight. Even so, it may be argued, they should have been allotted to one parent.

III

From the first unfolding of his strategic plan and his method at St. Paul's School on 7th April, Montgomery had stuck to his purpose with a fortitude and perseverance that had been wholly justified. He had stated clearly exactly what he would set out to do, and he had done it. In the final upshot he had done a great deal more. Yet for nearly fifty of the seventy-nine days of the battle, even on the very eve of his success, he had been subjected to harsh criticisms, ill-judged promptings, and some genuine misgivings. These criticisms were on several levels, and could have been dangerously disturbing to a commander in the midst of the most important battle he would ever fight. He was misunderstood, above all, by Eisenhower, the Supreme Commander. 'That he (Eisenhower) *did* misunderstand it (Montgomery's conduct of the battle) is revealed in his report to the Combined Chiefs of Staff after the war was ended.'[1]

Yet 'misunderstand' seems a strange word to use, for it is clear that Eisenhower had not understood Montgomery's strategy from the beginning. 'His military thinking,' wrote Chester Wilmot, 'like that of most American commanders, was essentially straightforward and aggressive, so much so that it might have been expressed in the simple formula, "Everybody attacks all the time".'[2]

Bedell Smith, Eisenhower's Chief of Staff, said of his commander that 'he was up and down the line like a football coach, exhorting everyone to aggressive action'. This was the Supreme Commander's invariable attitude.

To General Brooke, the C.I.G.S., it was clear that Eisenhower

---

[1] *Victory in the West*, H.M.S.O., p. 494.
[2] Wilmot: *The Struggle for Europe*. (Reprint Soc.), p. 371.

knew nothing about strategy. 'Bedell Smith, on the other hand, has brains, but not military education in its true sense.'[1]

No one seemed alarmed that Eisenhower was the man chosen and destined to command seven armies in the field, but the Supreme Commander's attitude was often disturbing in his personal relationships with the British. He was shy of approaching Montgomery directly and expressing his anxieties forthrightly. Instead he grumbled to General Brooke and to Churchill, showing his extreme frustration, using such phrases as that Montgomery should 'get on his bicycle'. As early as 16th June, he had begun to show his distrust in Montgomery's conduct of the battle on the left. By the middle of July, according to his indefatigable amanuensis, Captain Butcher, he was 'blue as indigo' over Monty's slowness, and on the 20th of the month Butcher describes the Supreme Commander as 'like a blind dog in a meat house—he can smell it, but he can't find it'.[2]

Unfortunately Eisenhower was fortified in his attitude by the Deputy Supreme Commander, Air Chief Marshal Tedder, by Air Chief Marshal Sir Trafford Leigh Mallory, and on a slightly lower level by Air Marshal Coningham. Most serious of all he was supported by General Morgan, the Deputy Chief of Staff, Supreme headquarters, who, as COSSAC, was one of the principal architects of the original *Overlord* plan. The substance of Morgan's implacable antagonism to Montgomery and his extended plan was in his belief that Caen must be taken and that the British must break-out to the east. He regarded the *bocage* country as virtually impassable, and appeared to be blind to Montgomery's clear intention to take Cherbourg, to clear the Cotentin peninsular while the U.S. Centre fought through the *bocage* to pivot on the powerful British left as soon as they were clear. Meanwhile the British task was to hold the enemy armour, and keep enemy reserves from reinforcing his front against the U.S. forces.

But Morgan's attitude was complicated by his dislike of Montgomery coupled with an attitude to the Americans little short of idolatry. His attitude to General George Marshall is comparable with that of a very junior schoolboy to the Captain of School. In the U.S.A. visiting General Marshall on 8th

[1] Bryant: *Triumph in the West*, p. 243.
[2] Butcher: *Three Years with Eisenhower*.

3. General Montgomery touring Army units before D Day

4. Army Commanders confer in France. (Left to right) General Bradley, General Montgomery, General Dempsey and General Hodges

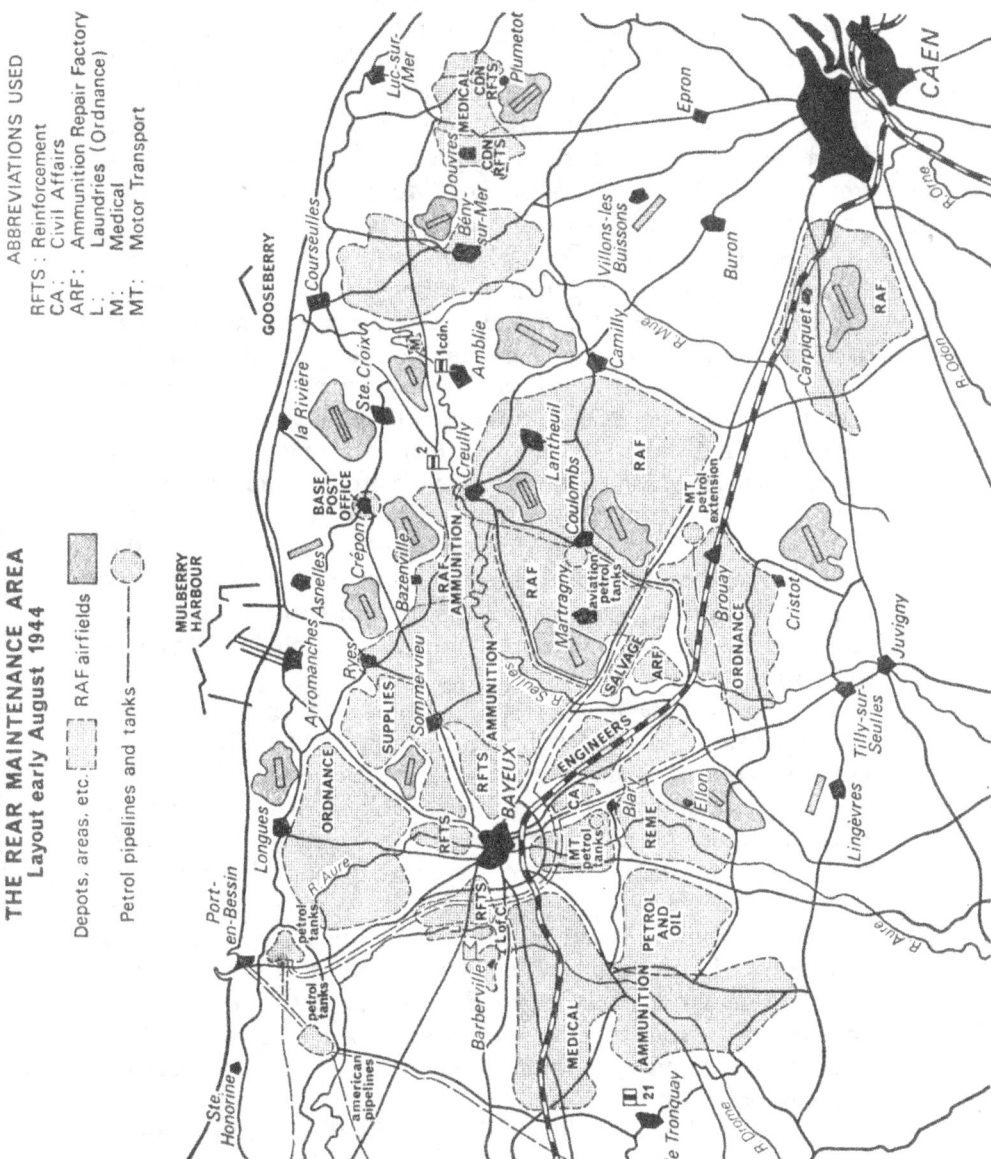

October, 1943, Morgan wrote, 'I found myself in the presence of greatness'. Summing up his attitude, Morgan concluded, 'our main body lay here in America in the full sense of that term, our main reservoir of men, material, energy, spirit and everything else'.[1] When Eisenhower was appointed to the Supreme Command Morgan rejoiced, 'There was a man sent from God and his name was Ike.' Morgan saw no reason to revise this opinion, and was fond of repeating it.

Air Chief Marshal Tedder, however, was an even more dangerous critic and opponent of Montgomery. As early as the 14th June, Tedder had said that the situation 'had the makings of a dangerous crisis'. Air Marshal Coningham, commanding the Second Tactical Air Force, was even more definite. At the end of the first week he announced categorically that 'the army plan had failed'.[2] He continued to propagate this view *ad nauseam*. Air Chief Marshal Sir Trafford Leigh Mallory's opposition to Montgomery and his conduct of the battle began farther back. With Morgan he had disagreed with the decision to expand the bridgehead, and the consequent shifting of the emphasis away from a break-out to the east to a break-out to the south on the right flank, and the subsequent envelopment of the enemy.

It is not surprising that all these powerful critics infected the Supreme Commander, but it is surprising that Eisenhower remained blind to the true state of the battle up to the very eve of Montgomery's triumph. The lack of space for airfield building blinded Tedder and the air force critics to a balanced view of the battle. Moreover they were remarkably ignorant of land warfare. On the 23rd July, Tedder wrote to the Supreme Commander virtually suggesting Montgomery's dismissal, and promising his support 'in any action you may consider the situation demands'.[2] He urged Eisenhower to take over direct control, and wrote that he saw no signs of the 'bold offensive action' demanded by circumstances. The airfield programme was still only half-complete.

Possibly Tedder may be partially excused for his ignorance, if not for his action. Eisenhower, however, is an enigma. In spite of close contact with Bradley and a visit to Montgomery

[1] Morgan: *Overture to Overlord*, pp. 199-200.
[2] *Victory in the West*, H.M.S.O., pp.265-355.

on the 20th July, he was as much in the dark as his Deputy. On the 21st, Eisenhower wrote to Montgomery to 'insist that Dempsey keep up the strength of his attack ... In 1st Army the whole front comes quickly into action to pin down local reserves and to support the main attack. Dempsey should do the same.'

The Official History comments:

'A somewhat curious remark since Dempsey's sustained pressure was successfully pinning down almost all the German armour and most of the infantry reinforcements.'[1]

It is, in fact, astounding that Eisenhower could not observe the major offensive action going on, if not before his eyes, at least clearly marked on 2nd Army battle maps. There was the story for him to read. He did not read it. Perhaps the sense of orderliness and peace pervading 2nd Army headquarters and Montgomery's Tactical headquarters deceived him. He was used to bustle and a sense of drama. U.S. 1st Army was certainly constantly active all along the line, and these tactics had resulted in heavy casualties. Moreover on the day Eisenhower wrote his letter of complaint, U.S. 1st Army was roughly at the point it had hoped to reach on D plus 5. The sense one has from Eisenhower of swift movement and great gains on the right is wholly false. The *bocage* was very hard going indeed, and the Americans were steadily fighting their way through it. It was slow. It meant that the British were forced to hold an ever-increasing weight of enemy armour and infantry away from the western flank for seven weeks, and this they did with remarkable success.

General Bradley, at any rate, had no doubt about the situation. 'For another four weeks (from end of June) it fell to the British to pin down superior enemy forces in that sector (Caen) while we manoeuvred into position for the U.S. break-out. With the Allied world crying for blitzkrieg the first week after we landed, the British endured their passive role with patience and forbearing ... In setting the stage for our break-out the British were forced to endure the barbs of critics who shamed them for failing to push out vigorously as the Americans did. The intense rivalry that afterwards strained relations between the British and American commands might

[1] *Victory in the West*, H.M.S.O., p. 354.

be said to have sunk its psychological roots in that passive mission of the British on the beachhead.'[1]

'Passive' is perhaps a curious choice of a word to describe the hard (and vigorous!) British struggle, and General Dempsey's brilliant shifting of the weight of the 2nd Army attack in a very confined space constantly to frustrate all the endeavours of the enemy armour, and a high proportion of enemy infantry, to seize the initiative. Nevertheless Bradley's heart seems to have been in the right place, and his good intention is clear. His final personal tribute to Montgomery is no less clear, for Bradley was no back-scratcher:

'During these operations in the lodgement where Montgomery bossed the U.S. 1st Army as part of his 21st Army Group, he exercised his Allied authority with wisdom, forbearance and restraint... I could not have wanted a more tolerant or judicious commander.'[1]

Perhaps Bradley's attitude helped Montgomery to maintain an admirable sangfroid under constant Service criticisms and Eisenhower's incessant fussing both on and off the battlefield. His final comment on General Morgan's curious aberration has a dry humour, and is without malice: 'He considered Eisenhower was a god; since I had discarded many of his plans, he placed me at the other end of the celestial ladder.'[2] Montgomery had grown in stature from the days of his first army command in the desert. In Normandy he showed none of the anxieties and nervous 'cracking of the whip' that had driven his armoured commanders to anger and frustration. If, as the Americans thought, he interfered unduly with Dempsey, Dempsey did not seem to mind, and the performance of the 2nd Army was not disturbed.

Yet a man of lesser calibre and confidence must have been deeply disturbed by the weight of opposition constantly aligned against him in the Supreme Command. The power 'dice' were in any case heavily loaded against the British as American strength grew swiftly on the battlefield, and it seems unfortunate that the Deputy Chief of Staff, and many of his British staff, should have been so blatantly Americanophile. With the Deputy Supreme Commander also opposed to

---

[1] Bradley: *A Soldier's Story*.
[2] Montgomery: *Memoirs*, p. 256.

Montgomery personally, the British Commander's isolation would have been serious but for the constant and loyal support of the C.I.G.S., General Brooke. Even Churchill, with his American blood and liking for the signs, if not the substance, of aggression, was inclined to waver in support of his general. But Brooke was a rock, and Montgomery had no difficulty in restoring Churchill's confidence in the wake of Eisenhower's anxious sorties.

Perhaps one result of all this criticism and lack of confidence in his strategic plan, and conduct of the battle, was to confirm Montgomery in his liking for privacy in his Tactical headquarters, and to strengthen his belief in his group of young liaison officers. He was very much a professional soldier, content with his 'eyes and ears' and with his close contact with his field commanders. Let others look upwards or sideways, he would look to his front. Perhaps also these experiences throughout the Battle for France confirmed him in his dislike of high level conferences in which he would be always in a minority. If he had anything to say he would say it, in or out of season, press it to the limits, and abandon his idea, when he had to, with an outward show of grace.

Montgomery understood very well the need for space in the bridgehead, not only for airfields, but for the full development of the communications zone, the establishment of the base and service depots, for R.E.M.E. workshops, for ordnance, ammunition, for petrol and oil dumps, for transport and reinforcement areas, for hospitals and medical services, and for all the needs of a million men rapidly becoming two million men on the move. As an item little short of the miraculous most of them were able to send and receive letters with regularity. This was not a luxury, but a vital ingredient in morale.

Space was important, but the overwhelming priority was to engage and defeat the enemy. It was Montgomery's unfaltering aim to draw the enemy on to the British shoulder in the east, and to gain time for the Americans to win through the coastal swamps and the *bocage* to open country. Territorial gains were slight, but were not a measurement of Montgomery's success. Those who had the misfortune to see phase line maps, and those—and they were legion—who misunderstood the importance of the city of Caen, wondered very seriously and honestly what had gone wrong. They did not appreciate that Montgomery was drawing the enemy strength on to him, was holding the enemy, was winning, and it was up to the supply and maintenance men to make the best possible use of the space available. There was barely room to swing the proverbial cat by the end of June and anyone having the misfortune to catch a senior 'logistics officer' off guard might have felt that the situation could scarcely be worse. The bridgehead grew by inches. It did not grow as fast as the troops within it.

Ruppenthal quotes a frustrated staff officer who wrote:

'The general principle is that the number of divisions required to capture the number of ports required to maintain those divisions is always greater than the number of divisions those ports can maintain.'[1]

There was very little flexibility in the 'Overlord' logistics plan, and perhaps that was inevitable, but there was little comfort in it for the British, or for Montgomery. Under the 'Overlord' plan it would not have been possible to defeat Germany in 1944, short of a total enemy collapse and the overthrow of Hitler and his regime. The Allies had not given serious thought to such a possibility (save in their planning of *Rankin*), nor had they given any support or comfort to those who planned the overthrow of Hitler in order to save their country.

By the end of May, 1945, the *Overlord* logistics planners had budgeted for the support of armies 200 miles beyond Paris and equivalent distances. That would have been on D plus 350. The armies had reached that point on D plus 98, more than 250 days ahead of schedule. For the British the war had to be won by Christmas, and no one was more aware of it than Montgomery, whose strength had reached its peak in July, 1944. It was a bleak prospect, but Montgomery was optimistic. Before the end in Normandy he had already planned the only possible way—if there were a possible way. Antwerp and Rotterdam had been in the sights of the planners long before D-Day. Without one or other of those great ports, or both, the final military defeat of Germany seemed impossible.

---

[1] Ruppenthal: *Logistics*, vol. i, U.S. Army, Washington, Chapter iii.

IV

In all these factors and facts there was clearly room for genuine misunderstanding, and only a highly trained military mind with access to plans, to commanders, to battlefields, might have reached a sober judgement of the march of events. War Correspondents, however brilliant, however accustomed to warfare they had become, could not, even in the rarest of cases, genuinely understand and report day by day, or week by week, the progress of the Battle for Normandy, for the Lodgement area, for France. Through the War Correspondents in Normandy, and throughout the campaign in North-West Europe, the general public on both sides of the Atlantic received and absorbed their views of varied battlefields, of the performances of the generals, and the progress of the Allied armies. On D-Day there were 530 War Correspondents accredited to Supreme headquarters, and the British, Canadian and U.S. armies, and on that day the censors on the beaches, on the assault craft, and in the Ministry of Information, cleared 700,000 words of messages to newspapers. In May, 1945, nearly 1,000 War Correspondents representing newspapers and magazines in Britain, the United States, France and Canada, were sending millions of words each day of very uneven quality and uneven censorship. In the nature of things it was difficult, if not impossible, for any man on the spot to write a balanced account of events as they were taking place. Some saw, others listened, and often the events men saw did not match the things to which men listened. Inevitably prejudices were fed, and I believe that it was impossible for a general reader of a newspaper to form a balanced view of the progress of war. Nevertheless, for the first time public opinion, especially public opinion in the United States, rapidly made itself felt on the battlefield, and became a powerful factor in strategy. At times it constrained, at others it instigated the very tactics of warfare, and the campaign was destined to become a vast tactical improvisation played out before a 'world' audience cheering on its favourites. It was one of the assets or liabilities of what is loosely called 'democracy'. It split the Alliance before the Allied armies reached the Seine, and made a united effort impossible.

Few men were more publicity conscious than General Montgomery, yet it is unthinkable that he would have permitted public opinion to have any kind of impact upon his tactics or strategy. General Eisenhower, a modest man, normally content to remain on the fringe of the limelight, feared and was powerfully influenced by public opinion. Generals Bradley and Patton played unashamedly to their huge galleries of supporters, while General Dempsey was almost as unaware of the public as the public was of him.

From the first it had been the determination of Supreme headquarters 'to keep the public informed of operational developments without compromising the security of operations'.

Thereafter it strove 'to reconcile these opposing interests'. The most trivial errors of censorship, or of taste, or judgement, could and did arouse angry outbursts from the public, as well as misunderstanding. The general rule that the description 'Allied troops', or 'Allied Aircraft', should be used was often broken and American or British troops were named with sad results. A reference to American troops liberating Carentan created anxiety very early on, and in August, Colonel Dupuy, acting Chief of Public Relations, Supreme headquarters, warned General Smith that unless the approaching American break-out was summarized and depicted as part of an integrated assault, 'the importance of the British-Canadian offensive in its zone may be minimized, with resultant embarrassment to Anglo-American relations, as well as distortion of the over-all picture'.[1]

The warning was only partially effective, as it was bound to be with so many involved, and with censorship failing to maintain a consistent pattern. Before the end of June the seeds of bitter rivalries had been sown in millions of minds, and were soon to become manifest on the battlefield.

War Correspondents, greedy for news and answering the incessant demands of editors, and the insatiable public, for dramatic stories, wrote (in the main) honestly of the struggle as they saw it. The best of them, not content with official handouts and briefings, strove to see, to discuss, to discover for themselves. Some few had achieved fame, not only as first-class

[1] Pogue: *The Supreme Command*, Dept. of Army, Washington, Appendix A, p. 520.

reporters, but as military analysts. Such mantles were cast upon them, rather than sought. Others, accredited to Supreme headquarters, or to Army Groups, perforce attempted to interpret official briefings, and to stamp their work with their personalities. Censorship seemed a challenge to ingenuity.

It seemed to many that after the first relief of the landings and the establishment of a firm foothold that progress was slow, and falling far behind schedule and expectations. They saw the growing congestion in the beach-heads, and lived with the packed transport on the battered roads and by-ways. It was more than possible to waste a whole day in covering half a mile, and to return to camp empty-handed only to find that one had missed an important official progress report. Indefatigable pursuers of action managed to talk with brigade and battalion commanders, but these gave very narrow views of limited sections of a confused and tenuous front covering more than 100 miles from the Orne to the West Coast of the Carentan peninsula. To become involved in action would mean failure to reach camp and communications in time to tell a story. Frustrations were the common lot. Moreover, there were two distinct 'fronts', one British and one American, each with its dedicated and increasingly partisan correspondents. In an International undertaking of such colossal dimensions, involving tens of thousands of men and tens of thousands of tons of supplies it was painfully simple to discover 'scandals'. For example 15 million out of $17\frac{1}{2}$ million 'jerrycans' shipped to Normandy disappeared by Autumn. Armies were maintained on a lavish scale that would have astonished Russians, Italians and the German enemy. Waste seemed almost the natural order.

In the very early days Supreme headquarters was the principal source of official progress reports, especially until the public relations departments, the hordes of censors, and the communication channels were fully organized and operational. And Supreme headquarters, while tending to bend over backwards in its efforts to be fair, was none the less biased and highly critical of General Montgomery in its higher stratas.

In the first weeks, 21st Army Group headquarters, and 1st Army headquarters were main sources of official 'news'. Inevitably only very small groups of favoured correspondents enjoyed access to commanding generals and their Chiefs of Staff. Long before the end of June, it was apparent that the War Correspondents were creating a rivalry that would soon alarm General Eisenhower. It was, I think, the optimism emanating at all times from 21st Army Group that laid the foundations for the widespread newspaper criticism which infected the public on both sides of the Atlantic. Unfortunate comparisons were made, especially at the end of July and in early August, with the speed of advance of the British and American armies. It was forgotten that the American left wing had slogged slowly through the *bocage* while the British held off the great weight of enemy armour and reinforcements. It was forgotten also that the American break-out was Montgomery's plan. The higher American casualty figures were also stressed and translated as a measure of greater effort, rather than as a reflection of the difference between British and American methods. The American 'cowboy' approach to war was exciting and dangerous, but costly. Often units plunged into combat without much thought as to where they were going and why. With luck the pieces came together in the end. The performances of units varied widely. Platoons, companies, battalions were often magnificent, while others were willing, but bewildered. Many seemed to confuse common-sense with cowardice.

On the 10th July, with misunderstanding of the true situation and Montgomery's intentions growing to dangerous proportions, Montgomery stressed to his generals that his broad strategy remained unchanged, and again underlined his unfaltering intention:

> 'It is to draw the main enemy forces in to the battle on our eastern flank, and to fight them there, so that our affairs on the western flank may proceed the easier.'

Fighting had been particularly heavy on the eastern flank since the 1st of the month, and on the 7th July, an attack by 460 bombers upon Caen had led to great expectations amongst the onlookers. On the 10th, the city of Caen was still incompletely in British hands, and it seemed that hopes were not realized. War Correspondents did not know of Montgomery's orders at this important time, nor were they clear about his intentions.

Most of them shared the view of Eisenhower, and many others that Montgomery had intended to break-out to the east. The heavy bombing attack had confirmed them in this view.

It was in Montgomery's words, or in his lack of words, not in his deeds, that the long-range audiences, the great galleries of the public in Britain and the United States found the ammunition for their 'barracking'. Moreover, it may be too easily forgotten that these were days of great anxieties, and the initial success coupled with the near American disaster on Omaha beach had released powerful emotional tensions of relief, followed by a rush of over-optimism which it was difficult to adjust to the harsh realities of the struggle.

In his statements for publication Montgomery tended to use expressions like 'crack about' and 'burst out', giving false impressions of intended break-throughs and territorial gains which did not occur, nor were they expected to occur. He announced his satisfaction with operations which appeared to have failed, or had patently failed to gain the tactical objectives he had named. His satisfaction, which was genuine, could have been simply explained. It meant that the operation had broken up enemy counter-attacks, had lured the enemy, or induced the enemy to commit reserves, or had foiled enemy attempts to move strength westward. Steadily and surely the enemy strength piled up against the powerful shoulder he had established.

A good deal of Montgomery's reticence was natural. The fact is that he was deceiving the enemy, and it would have been madness to undeceive him. Thus Montgomery, Dempsey, and their troops bore the growing criticisms, and were not greatly moved. In my personal view at least five War Correspondents knew almost exactly what was going on, and probably wished that they did not. These were Moorehead, Clifford, Buckley, Woodward and Wilmot. They enjoyed Montgomery's confidence, and had established close friendships with de Guingand, Montgomery's Chief of Staff.

Whatever the true background to the widespread criticisms, they posed new problems for generals compelled to plan and deploy their armies in the full glare of publicity, while subjected to day-by-day comment.

On the 19th July, *The Times* headlines read: *Second Army*

breaks through—Armoured forces reach open country—General Montgomery well satisfied.

Three days later it headlined:
Lost momentum of Break-In.

Three days later *The Times* lamented the use of the expression 'break-through' to describe a limited operation.

No one seems to have reminded, or informed, the public that the good weather had broken, and that violent storms dominated the battlefields and blotted out the sky and air support. Ironically, on the 25th July, the skies having cleared, *The New York Herald Tribune* announced:
Allies in France bogged down on entire front.

Montgomery and the British were accused of over-caution. It was, in fact, the very eve of Montgomery's triumph. Even Supreme headquarters did not seem to realize the impending fulfilment. On the 27th July, Churchill wrote to Montgomery: 'It was announced from S.H.A.E.F. last night that the British had sustained "quite a serious setback". I am not aware of any facts that justify such a statement.'

Montgomery replied at once under the same date: 'I know of no "serious setback".'

On the 3rd August, Churchill wrote again: 'I am delighted that the unfolding of your plan, which you explained to me, has proceeded so well.'[1]

On the 7th, the Prime Minister joined his General in the field. Montgomery had wisely taken great care not only to keep Churchill fully informed of his intentions and of real progress, but to ensure that General Brooke, the C.I.G.S., was never in doubt. The Prime Minister was capricious and fickle, and was susceptible to Eisenhower's complaints. In mid-July, he was moody in his attitude to Montgomery, for as the C.I.G.S. pointed out, 'Winston had never been very fond of Monty; when things went well he put up with him, when they did not he at once became "Your Monty".'

In addition Eisenhower had given Churchill the impression that Montgomery would not welcome a visit from him, whereas Eisenhower himself had advised Montgomery not to have visitors for a week or two. Henry L. Stimson, U.S. Secretary of War, had just visited Bradley's headquarters,

---
[1] Churchill: *Memoirs*, vol. vi, p. 26.

and had wasted so much time (according to Montgomery) that orders were held up and an attack had to be postponed.

'Just at this time,' wrote Brooke in his diary,[1] 'Eisenhower had been expressing displeasure and accusing Monty of being sticky, of not pushing sufficiently on the Caen front with the British whilst he made the Americans do the attacking on the right.'

General Brooke at once visited Montgomery to warn him, and found his general in 'grand form', and ready to write an immediate letter to invite the Prime Minister to visit him. Churchill was at once delighted. The feeling of active physical participation and involvement on the battlefield, for in Normandy the battlefield was never far away, always roused Churchill's spirits. Moreover he understood very well what Montgomery was doing.

The truth is that while the Supreme Commander was denigrating Montgomery, and the newspaper headlines and comments lamented his lack of success and extreme caution, seven Panzer divisions, two-thirds of the entire enemy armour in France, were massed against the British 2nd Army almost entirely on a twenty-mile front from Caumont to Caen. Only elements of one weak Panzer division were able to confront the U.S. Forces, and even in Hitler's desperate attempt to break through to Avranches in early August only 70–80 tanks could be mustered for the task, and these were hammered mercilessly from the air. The attacks of the fighter-bombers were reported by the enemy to be 'unendurable'.[2]

Not once in the course of the long battle did Montgomery lose the tactical initiative. He made mistakes, in his original over-optimism in regard to Caen and Villers Bocage, and later in the massive close support bombing, of Caen, sadly reminiscent of Sicily and Italy. But Montgomery's strategy had proved sound and flexible, and it had brought devastating victory.

In late August, Montgomery believed that he had won and retained the confidence of Bradley. He was sadly mistaken. On 13th August, near Argentan, Bradley and Patton were near to revolt.

[1] Bryant: *Triumph in the West*, pp. 234-235.
[2] Army Group B War Diary.

'If Monty's tactics mystified me,' Bradley wrote,[1] 'they dismayed Eisenhower even more. And (at LUCKY FORWARD)[2] where a shocked 3rd Army looked on helplessly as its quarry fled, Patton raged at Montgomery's blunder.'

But Montgomery had not blundered, nor were Bradley and Patton watching as the 'quarry fled'. The quarry had not fled. To Montgomery's satisfaction and astonishment Hitler refused to abandon his thrust on Avranches until 16th August, and not until late on that day did the enemy begin to organize withdrawal. 'That Bradley claimed to have seen this as early as 13th August is due either to bad memory or to over-anxious expectation of what, in his opinion, the Germans would have to do.'[3]

Nor were Bradley and Eisenhower 'mystified', for the same U.S. Official analysis comments: 'If Patton in a subordinate role, could only rage at Montgomery's tactics, and if Bradley thought he might offend a sensitive Montgomery by requesting permission to cross the Army Group boundary (to close the gap between Argentan and Falaise), Eisenhower, who was in France and following the combat developments, might have resolved the situation had he thought it necessary. Yet General Eisenhower did not intervene.'[3]

Patton's tanks of the XV Corps under Haislip were already moving out of Argentan on the 12th on a collision course with the British, who were involved in hard fighting against very strong enemy positions on the Falaise road. Bradley had to act very fast to halt Haislip's armour. 'Let me go on to Falaise and we'll drive the British back into the sea for another Dunkirk,' Patton urged.

In spite of Patton's raging and his expressed contempt for the British, Bradley did not really believe that it would have been wise for him to attempt to close the gap. His long flank was extremely vulnerable should the enemy attempt to break-out to the south, nor did he believe that Patton could have held the neck of the 'bag'. 'Although Patton might have spun a line across that narrow neck, I doubted his ability to hold it,' he

---

[1] Bradley: *A Soldier's Story*, p. 377.
[2] Near Laval.
[3] *Command Decisions*, U.S. Army in W.W. 2, Washington, p. 413.

wrote. Moreover he preferred, he said, 'A solid shoulder at Argentan to a broken neck at Falaise.'[1]

Before August was out the rivalries between the Allies had been fanned by Press and public, and enhanced by the personalities involved. It would have been virtually impossible to have maintained Montgomery as 'Ground Force Commander' over Bradley or Patton, and almost as difficult for the British armies to have served under Bradley, had either course seemed desirable. I think that it is true that even before the destruction of the German armies west of the Seine, not only 'logistics' and Eisenhower's incurable tendency to compromise, but public opinion, particularly in the United States, dictated strategy, and saved Germany from the complete disaster that seemed about to overwhelm her at the end of August, 1944.

I doubt whether ever before the Press and public of a nation have had so profound an impact upon the conduct of war.

[1] Bradley: *A Soldier's Story*, pp. 376-377.

PART TWO
The Field Marshal

CHAPTER EIGHT

*The Art of the Possible—
The Situation*

I

WHILE Montgomery and the Western Allies had been winning their victory in Normandy, inflicting more than 300,000 casualties on the enemy, the Russians, in Churchill's colourful phrase to the House of Commons, had been 'tearing the guts out of the German army'. The final aggregate of German losses on both fronts in the months of June, July and August totalled approximately 1,500,000 men. Nor was this all. A quarter of a million more officers and men of quality had gone into the fortresses, the besieged ports of Brittany and the Channel coast, many of them to be bottled up to the war's end. The 'casualties' in senior commanders had been tragic, Rommel, Dollmann, Hausser, Eberbach,[1] Chevallerie, von Kluge, Blaskowitz were all dead, wounded, captured or relieved. Old von Runstedt was under a cloud. Warlimont at O.K.W. was suspect. Few of the survivors could feel secure, and on the Eastern front casualties in senior commanders had been severe. The German losses in munitions of war had been enormous, while throughout almost every day and night the homeland was under incessant bombing from the air. By all the normal criteria of warfare Germany had suffered defeat on a scale to render recovery impossible, and to demand surrender as the only sane, or civilized course. Yet because of the total commitment of the Nazi Führer, the fanaticism of the German people, and the Allied demand for Unconditional Surrender, both sides were condemned to fight to the bitter end. The only hope of alleviating the scope of the tragedy lay in quick victory. Such a victory was not only a matter of extreme urgency for Great Britain in the early Autumn of 1944, it was also a matter of urgency for humanity.

[1] Captured 31st August when his Tac H.Q. was overrun outside Amiens.

The great question was, and remains, could the Second World War have been won in 1944? And if it could have been won, why was it not won?[1]

By the 31st August, the spearheads of General Patton's U.S. 3rd Army had crossed the Meuse, and a day later reached the Moselle. It was 'pursuit warfare at its best, a headlong pell-mell rush that swept Allied troops irresistibly toward the German border'.[2] Patton and his commanders were resolved, in General Haislip's words, 'to push all personnel to the limit of human endurance'. This is a phrase to remember.

On the left flank of the Allied advance the pursuit was no less spectacular. On 3rd September, Brussels was liberated by the right wing of General Dempsey's 2nd Army, while the U.S. 1st Army, covering his right, collected an enormous bag of enemy troops, occupied Liege and Namur, and drove for Aachen. On 4th September, the great port of Antwerp was captured with its vast docks virtually intact by the left wing of the British 2nd Army drive to the north, and on the 5th September, the Canadian 1st Army entered Ghent.

The Germans were horrified, for with the fall of Antwerp 'the door to north-western Germany stood open', and there was a gap 100 miles wide facing the British, and with barely an enemy to offer so much as a token defence. The German hopes of organizing defences of the river lines north of the Seine to check the speed of the Allied advance had evaporated before defences could be formed. Now, desperately, they attempted to improvise a defence of the Scheldt estuary, the Meuse-Escaut and the Albert Canals. Leaving the Scheldt estuary to the still formidable remnants of the 15th Army under von Zangen, Hitler ordered General Student to form a scratch army using a motley collection of garrison troops in the Netherlands, 'stomach battalions' of the middle-aged and semi-sick, newly recruited youths of 16 and 17 years, and every man, able-bodied or not, he could lay his hands on. While General Student organized and inspired his bravely named 1st Parachute Army, Field-Marshal Model strove to create a last ditch defensive screen to block the road to the Ruhr and Allied victory.

---

[1] These questions are unanswerable. They are in the realm of 'if' history. Yet the questions will be asked as long as military history is a study.
[2] Blumenson: *Break-Out and Pursuit*, U.S. Army in W.W. 2, p. 668.

Meanwhile the enemy pursued by Patton to the Moselle, trading ground for time, had almost miraculously organized five poorly armed skeleton divisions to oppose Patton's six divisions at full strength.

All along the line the tasks confronting the enemy seemed hopeless. All that remained of his armies in the west were the remnants of eleven armoured divisions mustering barely 100 tanks between them, and disorganized bodies of men ('a disorganized corporal's guard,' in Bradley's phrase) from which a possible twenty divisions might be formed. There were no enemy reserves. Weapons and ammunition were in desperately short supply, and communications were under heavy attack from the air. It would take months rather than weeks to rebuild the armoured divisions.

'The rapid loss of the Western fortifications (Atlantic Wall),' Guderian wrote, 'compelled us to fight a mobile war with almost immobile units, a bombed communications network in our rear, and the enemy in command of the air above us. While our Panzer units still existed, our leaders had chosen to fight a static battle in Normandy. Now that our motorized forces had been squandered and destroyed, they were forced to fight the mobile battle that they had hitherto refused to face. The favourable chances which the boldness of the American command occasionally offered us we were no longer in a position to exploit.'[1]

Against this enemy condition the Allies mustered 38 divisions at full strength, with new divisions arriving almost daily. In the air, in artillery and armour Allied power was overwhelming, giving an effective superiority of 20 to 1 in tanks and 25 to 1 in aircraft. In addition, the 1st Allied Airborne Army, commanded by Lieut.-General Lewis Brereton, was ready and anxious to fly an airborne corps of three airborne divisions commanded by General Browning at short notice.

If this were all, the Allied failure to seize and consolidate victory would be both incomprehensible and unforgivable, convicting the Supreme Command of gross incompetence. But it is not all. Maintenance and supply problems had become 'War's Mistress', as Ruppenthal wrote, and summed up: 'The Allied forces had become the victims of their own success;

---

[1] Guderian: *Panzer Leader*, p. 373 (and quoted by Jacobsen and Rohwer).

logistic limitations had clearly come to dominate operational plans.'[1] Moreover, the allies had used up their operational reserve on reaching the Seine. And again, in the opinions of the U.S. Official historians commenting upon the drive of the U.S. Third Army to the Moselle, 'Adequate gasoline at the end of the month (August) would probably not have sustained the dream of unlimited pursuit terminating in quick victory.'[2]

Nevertheless the last week of August and the first week of September was a time of 'glittering opportunities', and the frustrations, hopes and dreams of these two weeks are reflected in every military history.

How real were these opportunities? Could any of them have been taken? Did the Allies realize the extent of the disaster that had befallen the German armies in the West? Did the Allies appreciate the resilience, the recuperative powers and the fanatical resolution of the enemy? Above all, perhaps, did the Allied Supreme Command respond to the great challenge? Or, could it have responded?

Or, did the German collapse confront the Allied Supreme Command with an insoluble problem in terms of logistics, national vanities, rivalries, jealousies, available strength, and war and peace aims?

'On the field of battle,' Clausewitz said, 'everything depends on a decision made in a few minutes.' Napoleon agreed with him.

II

The collapse of the enemy in the West did not take the Allies by surprise. As early as the middle of July the Joint Intelligence committee concluded that 'all the elements for a collapse of Germany already exist', and it was 'difficult to see' how Germany could hope to continue the war into 1945.[3] Mid-July, therefore, must be seen as the time of challenge to the Supreme Command. From that time a Supreme authority in close contact with the rapidly developing situation should have taken control of the battle, or, if this were impossible, supreme

---

[1] Ruppenthal: *Logistics*, vol. ii, U.S. Army in W.W. 2, p. 12.
[2] Blumenson: *Break-Out and Pursuit*, U.S. Army in W.W. 2, p. 670.
[3] Ehrman: *Grand Strategy*, vol. v, H.M.S.O., p. 398.

authority and the responsibility for the vital decisions should have been delegated.

The optimism of the committee continued to grow as the extent of the defeat suffered by the enemy in Normandy took shape. This optimism was stimulated by reports from SHAEF. The SHAEF G–2 intelligence summaries were jubilant before the end of August: 'The August battles have done it and the enemy in the West has had it.'[1] The end was not only in sight, but 'almost within reach'. The German army was 'no longer a cohesive force'. The conclusion was that 'no recovery is now possible', and that organized resistance could not continue beyond 1st December, 1944.

These exuberant intelligence reports failed to stress the need for speed, but almost alone Colonel Koch, G–2 U.S. 3rd Army Intelligence, sounded a warning note. Despite his enormous losses and the disruption of his communications the enemy, he pointed out, was managing to 'exercise an overall control of his tactical situation'. It was not a rout, or a mass collapse, the Colonel argued, and summed up: 'It is clear from all indications that the fixed determination of the Nazis is to wage a last-ditch struggle in the field at all costs. It must be constantly kept in mind that fundamentally the enemy is playing for time.' Finally, Colonel Koch believed that the German armies would continue to fight until destroyed or captured. The weather would soon be on their side.[2]

The conclusions of Colonel Koch did little to temper the optimism of Montgomery, Bradley and Patton, but they did underline the need for speed, and revealed a clear understanding of the nature of the struggle ordained by 'Unconditional Surrender'. The SHAEF conclusion that 'organized resistance under the control of the German High Command is unlikely to continue beyond 1st December, 1944 ... It may even be sooner', is unrealistic and very near to irresponsibility. Victory could only be won by bringing about the total collapse of the enemy, and the Supreme Commander, focusing upon his brief, '... to undertake operations aimed at the heart of Germany and the destruction of her armed forces' warned newspaper reporters against over-optimism.

[1] Pogue: *The Supreme Command*, U.S. Army in W.W. 2, pp. 244-245.
[2] Pogue: *The Supreme Command*, p. 245.

Since the failure of the July plot to assassinate Hitler, and the attrition of the German generals, the order could be seen in all its stark, unequivocal reality. Nevertheless, as late as 5th September, the Joint Intelligence Committee had not modified its conclusions, but its report was being rapidly overtaken by events. On 8th September, Churchill stressed that the Intelligence summary 'erred on the side of optimism' and pointed out that some of its paragraphs already needed rewriting. He concluded with the statement that 'it is at least as likely that Hitler will be fighting on the 1st January as that he will collapse before then. If he does collapse before then the reasons will be political rather than military.'[1]

It is significant that Churchill and Eisenhower were among the very few to question the appreciations of the enemy situation. President Roosevelt agreed with them. The Combined Chiefs of Staff were optimistic but guarded. As late as 7th September, Field-Marshal Brooke, the CIGS, informed Churchill that 'although he considered the Joint Intelligence Committee's report to be slightly optimistic, he saw no reason to disagree with it'. Nevertheless the Chiefs of Staff 'had not ignored the possibility that German resistance would be prolonged into the winter'. The U.S. Chiefs of Staff held similar views.[2]

In fact, by 7th September the chances of quick victory had already cooled. The intelligence reports had not been far wrong, but no one seems to have realized the astonishing ability of the enemy to improvise a defence, and the speed and determination of his reactions. Before mid-September, 200,000 labourers were strengthening the defences of the West Wall (Siegfried Line) while Student's 1st Parachute Army fought desperately for every yard of ground. Too much time had been lost.

III

On 15th August, almost everyone in the Western world believed that victory would be won, not only in 1944, but within a few weeks. One month later the Allies were locked in a

---
[1] Ehrman: *Grand Strategy*, vol. v, p. 401.
[2] Ehrman: *Grand Strategy*, H.M.S.O., vol. v, p. 401.

battle of attrition that would endure for many months, culminating in the German counter-attack through the Ardennes. Thereafter, slowly, painfully, the Allies slogged forward to the Rhine, their eighty-five divisions straining their manpower to the limits. At last the end was near. Seven months of bitter fighting replaced the dreams and hopes of August, and in those months the Allies suffered 500,000 casualties to add to their 250,000 losses in Normandy.

The primary problem is to consider the decisions of the Supreme Commander, and to examine what he did; what he might have done; what was possible for him to have done. But it is important in the nature of this account to consider the responsibility of Field-Marshal Montgomery, and to examine what he made of his opportunities.

It becomes an assessment of the possible, and of what one means by the possible. I shall take the possible to mean the attainment of victory with the means available in the last ten or eleven days of August, which means the commanders and men, the transport and communications, the munitions of war. It is not, therefore, within the possible to imagine what might have been possible, given say a Napoleon leading the Allied armies, and served by Marshals of the calibres of Ney and Soult. The question is would it have been possible for General Eisenhower, served by his 'Marshals', Bradley and Montgomery, and his army commanders, Dempsey, Hodges and Patton? These are the commanders concerned with victory in those vital days.

But since it is impossible to know exactly what could have brought victory, short of the total collapse of the enemy forces and the collapse of Hitler, the problem is to discover what would have, and should have, been possible to achieve in the month between the 15th August and 15th September. And would such an achievement have brought victory nearer.

There are many relevant factors, and one of them is the landing in the South of France, under its code name DRAGOON, which took place successfully on 15th August. Very soon, as General Devers and his generals, pursued the enemy up the Rhone valley, the U.S. 6th Army Group would form the southern flank of the great line-up in the West, from Nijmegen on the Neder Rhine or Waal, to Basle. In the first three days of September, Hitler was furiously urging his generals to re-organize Army Group G to meet this threat to his left flank. The event may have influenced the thinking of the Supreme Commander, tending, by distracting his gaze southward, to lessen his concentration upon the scene of enemy disaster and Allied opportunity in the north. It may have broadened Eisenhower's concept of the campaign at a time when the 'glittering opportunities' were essentially narrow, demanding swift, devastating action—if such action must be decisive. The mauling and bludgeoning of the enemy had been achieved, and the time had come for the death thrust.

It seemed to some, the writer among them, that the advance of the 6th Army Group, even the mounting of DRAGOON at all, dictated the 'Broad front' strategy, and emphasized the inflexibility of the logistical plan. Was it possible for the Supreme Commander to break out of the strategic strait-jacket designed for him? Or were there alternatives?

Before considering the principal factors governing Allied possibilities, and the thinking of the Supreme Commander and his generals, it is worth taking a look at the 'other side of the hill' to discover the enemy appreciation of the situation on various levels, and what the enemy was doing about it. In discussions with Sir Basil Liddell Hart,[1] Generals Blumentritt and Westphal gave their carefully considered opinions. General Blumentritt was Chief of Staff on the Western front up to 5th September, when he was replaced by General Westphal. Both generals believed that the way was open almost anywhere over the whole front and that the region between Metz and Aachen—the Ardennes—was extremely vulnerable. The way was open to the Rhine at Coblenz. Both generals believe that Patton blundered in attacking Metz instead of by-passing this collection of fortresses, and that Hodges blundered in getting himself bogged down in the Aachen complex. Above all, perhaps, both generals saw the powerful argument for a powerful thrust to the north.

'He who holds northern Germany,' Blumentritt said, 'holds Germany. Such a break-through, coupled with air domination would have torn in pieces the weak German front and ended the war. Berlin and Prague would have been occupied ahead of the Russians.'

[1] Private Papers, B.H.L.H. 14.8.54.

In regard to Patton's involvement at Metz, Blumentritt said that an advance further to the north through Luxembourg 'would have caused the collapse of the right flank of our 1st Army followed by the collapse of the 7th Army, which would have been cut off entirely before it could retreat to the Rhine.'

When General Westphal took over from Blumentritt the Allies had already carried out the northern thrust as their main effort, and crucial days—perhaps even a crucial day—had been lost by Montgomery's failure to seize the locks of Antwerp, to cross the Albert Canal, and to seal off the narrow neck of the Bevelands. The pause of 21st Army Group from 4th to 7th September, took the bite out of the northern thrust. A pause even of hours on the left flank was, in fact, indefensible. Nevertheless victory would still have been possible in General Westphal's view, given flexibility in the Allied strategy, and the governing factor of logistics.

'A heavy defeat anywhere along the front, which was so full of gaps that it did not deserve this name, might lead to catastrophe if the enemy were to exploit his opportunity skilfully,' said Westphal. 'A particular source of danger was that not a single bridge over the Rhine had been prepared for demolition, an omission which took weeks to repair. Until the middle of October, the enemy could have broken through at any point he liked with ease, and would then have been able to cross the Rhine and thrust deep into Germany almost unhindered.'

This is a serious indictment, for the chance of quick victory appeared to fade long before the middle of October.

4th September is not only a crucial date in the Allied calendar but also in that of the enemy. It is improbable that Hitler and the High Command were aware of the gravity of the situation at Antwerp. On that day Hitler was giving his personal orders to General Student in Berlin, and the enemy had a wide open flank from Antwerp to Maastricht until Student's hastily assembled force began to reach the zone, detraining and rushing straight into action. His 'Army' mustered 18,000 men, lightly armed and almost without armour. Hitler was very far from giving up, and a statement from his Ministry of Propaganda dated 4th September reflected his resolution. He believed that the difficulties of transport, maintenance and supply, would hold up the Allied advance and give him time. He at once recalled von Runstedt as Commander-in-Chief West, while Model retained command of Army Group B in the north. Neither von Runstedt nor Model minced words in their urgent reports to Hitler and the High Command. They both emphasized that it would take at least six weeks to put the West Wall in minimum readiness to withstand the Allied armies, and that reinforcements were needed with extreme urgency to slow down Montgomery's 21st Army Group, including the U.S. 1st Army driving on Aachen. In fact the German generals knew that they were faced with imminent disaster.

The German High Command promised four infantry divisions ready for action between 13th and 25th September, and two Panzer Brigades, and various odds and ends, between the 15th and 30th.

The situation in the East was even more serious. With the Russians pressing hard in the first days of September, Finland sued for peace. The Baltic States were almost cut off, and Russian troops had reached Warsaw. At the moment of maximum Allied pursuit in the north on the western front, the Russians in the south had seized the Ploesti oil-fields, forced the collapse of Rumania, and added Bulgaria to their side. Two million Germans confronted the victorious Russians in growing desperation, and not one could be spared. Every man and boy deemed capable of bearing arms was rounded up for the defence of the Reich.

At the same time the Germans over-estimated the strength of the Western Allies, crediting the Supreme Command with 54 divisions available. It was unimportant, for very soon it would be true, and what mattered was not how many divisions were immediately available, but how many the Allies might sustain in a pursuit of the enemy which should carry them to the Rhine.

A maximum of twenty divisions, including a minimum of five armoured, at full strength would have been more than enough hopelessly to outnumber the troops the enemy could hope to throw in their path. In fire power, armour and in the air, as I have emphasized, Allied strength was overwhelming.

It seems, therefore, that it would have been impossible for the enemy to prevent a deep penetration by 21st Army Group in the ten days from 4th to 14th September, and very difficult for some weeks thereafter. Whether a rapid penetration to the Rhine would have brought victory, it is impossible to say, but it is certain that the Ruhr would have been gravely threatened in October, 1944, rather than in March, 1945.

IV

General Eisenhower officially took over as Supreme Commander in the field on 1st September, 1944, and on that day his advanced headquarters, recently established at the small township of Joullouville, near Granville in the Cotentin peninsula, became operational. On the same day Montgomery, with the rank of Field-Marshal, relinquished all that remained of his 'Ground Force Command', and became Bradley's 'opposite number' as the commander of an Army Group.

It must be borne in mind that these bare factual statements do not imply that there was any fundamental or recognizable change in the command on the battlefield. The grip—or the various grips—on the reins of command remained very much the same as they had been since 1st August, except that they had steadily become more tenuous. On that date, 1st August, the U.S. 3rd Army had become operational under General George S. Patton, and General Bradley had assumed command of U.S. 12th Army Group. While Montgomery remained in nominal command of the ground forces throughout August he had, in fact, ceased to command Bradley and U.S. 12th Army Group. In Forrest Pogue's words, 'he (Montgomery) consulted General Bradley increasingly as a partner instead of a subordinate'.[1]

Thereafter the courses of the two Army Groups diverged at ever-increasing speed, and before Eisenhower took over nominal command in the field both army group commanders, again to quote Pogue, 'conscious of the opportunities on his own front and desirous of seizing them quickly, favoured single thrusts into enemy territory'.[2] It must be clear that such attitudes were natural and inevitable, reflecting the true command positions of the Army Group commanders.

[1] Pogue: *The Supreme Command*, p. 263.
[2] Pogue: *The Supreme Command*, p. 250.

General Eisenhower, while asserting that nothing went on without his direct authority, was either unable, or had very little real power, to reverse these trends. Nor had he on 1st September.

Meanwhile the collapse of the enemy and the pursuits to the east and to the north by 12th and 21st Army Groups had shifted the area of battle up to 200 miles from the Seine in two weeks, and put an increasing distance between the two Army Groups, partly bridged by the U.S. 1st Army on Montgomery's right flank. This opening pattern left the Ardennes almost bare, a region defended at the time by six weak enemy battalions, and destined to become the chosen point of enemy counter-attack. At the same time nearly 400 miles separated both Army Groups from their base areas, and from the beaches over which they still received the bulk of their supplies and reinforcements.

Eisenhower's headquarters at Joullouville was impossibly placed for command, and the Supreme Commander was 'attempting to keep in touch with his commanders by jeep and plane'.[1]

Montgomery, who expressed his frustration uncompromisingly and almost incessantly, remarked of the headquarters near Granville, that it was possibly a suitable place for a Supreme Commander; but it was useless for a land force commander who had to keep his finger on the pulse of his armies and give quick decisions in rapidly changing situations. He was over four hundred miles behind the battle-front.'[2]

Moreover at this crucial time Eisenhower was half laid up with a bad knee, and there were very sketchy and slow communications between Supreme headquarters and the Army Group commanders. The Supreme Command and the Supreme headquarters situation had been inherently bad, and ill-conceived. On 7th August, General Eisenhower had a small advance headquarters in a camp near Tournières in Normandy. This had enabled him to keep in touch with his commanders in the field, and to watch the development of the battle. Finally on 15th September, Supreme headquarters began to move to Versailles. It was an enormous task, involving many thousands of officers and men, and with its signals units multiplying

[1] Pogue: *The Supreme Command*.
[2] Montgomery: *Memoirs*, p. 271.

rapidly. Forward headquarters had numbered 750 officers and 2,500 men by the end of August, and on 1st October, it was finally and firmly established.

The Supreme Commander's authority is not in question, but his power to command the immense proliferation of armies, air forces, and ancillary troops and services, must be questioned. One fact is clear: there was no 'Ground Force commander' in N.W. Europe from 1st August to 1st October, 1944, nor, at any time thereafter, was there anyone capable of exercising full direction, command and control of the armies. This is not to question General Eisenhower's ability. He was the victim of a system of command doomed to compromise and consultation from the beginning. Nevertheless the failure of the command was the major factor in denying victory to the Allies in 1944.

V

It emerges in the development of this story that the middle of July was the last possible moment for recognition of the pressing need for a 'Ground Force commander', but even then it would have been very late to attempt to establish the necessary headquarters for such a command. Neither Bradley nor Montgomery was equipped for a task of such magnitude. Such a commander would have needed to be a strategist of exceptional ability, and with a character of rare quality. Perhaps only a MacArthur or an Auchinleck among living men at the time, might have filled such a role, and there were no men of that calibre available or discernible.

Nevertheless the recognition of the need for such a man on the part of the Combined Chiefs of Staff might have given cohesion and drive to the armies involved, and silenced the grumblings and rumblings emanating constantly from the rival camps of Montgomery on the left, and the Bradley-Patton partnership on the right. Moreover the creation and employment of the 1st Allied Airborne Army in the summer of 1944 was a factor second only in importance to the problems of command in the achievement of quick victory. It was also closely linked with the command factor.

The creation of the 1st Allied Airborne Army arose in part

from American suspicions of the British command position. With Admiral Ramsay, Commander-in-Chief at sea, Air-Marshal Leigh Mallory, Commander-in-Chief in the air, and General Montgomery, Commander-in-Chief on land, it seemed to the Americans that the British had made a clean sweep of effective command. If the Americans were not ever watchful they feared that Eisenhower would become a mere spectator. It was this near-obsession, accentuated by the American dislike and distrust of Montgomery that provoked the rather hasty formation of an Airborne Army under the command of the American General Lewis Brereton. Brereton's appointment at once strengthened the U.S. command position. He was a man of great experience, and with his British second in command, General Browning, it seemed that the use of the powerful airborne forces could be one of the vital factors in victory. From the end of July, the Airborne Army was striving to get into the battle, and the commanders in the field were anxious to use its resources. So also was the Supreme Commander. A number of plans were made throughout August, but all of them were discarded or overtaken by the speed of events on the ground. A plan to seize Boulogne was abandoned, and the decision to drop on Tournai was cancelled at the last moment on 2nd September, only to be replaced immediately by a plan to seize powerful advanced positions in the Aachen-Maastricht Gap.

The responsibility for these decisions rested in the main with Montgomery and Bradley, and of the two generals, Bradley was the most realistic. 'This Allied Airborne Army,' he wrote, 'showed an astonishing faculty for devising missions that were never needed.'[1] Moreover, Bradley was deeply concerned with the supply problems of his ground troops, and air transport was the key to a partial solution. The question in his mind was, could the use of the Airborne Army as a fighting force at this stage be as valuable as the use of its transport aircraft for the supply of the advancing armies? Bradley's comments on the proposed Airborne drop on Tournai are illuminating. The withdrawal of transport aircraft cost him an estimated 823 tons of supplies a day for the 3rd Army, and 'demolished our last faint hope for the support of Patton's offensive'.[1]

[1] Bradley: *A Soldier's Story*, p. 402.

THE ART OF THE POSSIBLE—THE SITUATION

Bradley expressed the view that Tournai, in any case, would be, or could be, overrun on the ground before the airborne attack could go in. He went out of his way, at the risk of infuriating Montgomery, to prove it, and ordered Hodges to take Tournai even though it was in 21st Army Group territory. Montgomery was quick to react, and Hodges withdrew at once. Bradley had proved his point, but had not gained his transport aircraft.

The decisions to use the 1st Allied Airborne Army in various operations, all but one of them abortive, and that one too late and disastrous for a British Airborne Division, helped to rob the ground troops of the maintenance which might have heaved them through to victory. Moreover, the existence of the Airborne Army disturbed the concentration of the commanders on the ground forces, and on what might have been achieved by these troops alone.

The possibilities of the Airborne Army do not seem to have been fully considered. The alternatives were not simply to use this powerful force in its full fighting role, or to use its air transport for the supply of the ground forces. Three of its airborne brigades, for example, could have been held in readiness under Army Command for immediate use in the tactical opportunities which seemed certain to present themselves, and which in fact, did present themselves. An airborne brigade could serve as a key to the other side of a difficult door, and open it. If such a scheme had been adopted, two-thirds or more of the Airborne Army's air transport could have been pressed into maintenance of the ground troops, while three brigades remained in instant readiness for action.

This, in my view, would not have been a compromise, but the most natural way of using airborne power in that particular crisis.

Nevertheless, none of the factors, however important, may be considered in isolation, for all are part of a whole of which the basic, and probably decisive, factor is 'logistics'. The logistical problems coupled with the corollary of transport, were monumental, intensified and complicated by the rivalries of Bradley and Montgomery, but they were not insuperable. While Montgomery fought for maximum support for his northern thrust, Bradley moved five divisions forward from

F

Normandy unnecessarily, and added 12,000 tons of supplies a day to his demands.[1] It is not in dispute that the Allies had outstripped their logistical plans, that ports notably in Brittany had not been opened as hoped for, and that a tremendous congestion had built up in the base areas. This problem underlined the urgent need for the Allies to gain and to open the port of Antwerp, without which it would be impossible to mount a massive drive eastward into Germany.

The fall of Paris and the need to feed the population complicated the supply problem. Yet it was not so much that supplies were not available, but that the difficulties of transport made it almost impossible to move them far enough and fast enough. The startling discovery that 1,400 British 3-ton trucks were defective cost the 2nd Army 800 tons a day. A loss of 15,000,000 'jerrycans' added greatly to the problems of moving fuel by road. French railways were in ruins, and would take time to bring into helpful service, and until this was done the Channel ports, even when opened, would not be fully effective. Nevertheless, by 'grounding' certain formations and using their transport, the difficulties could have been overcome, and to a great extent were overcome.

But the question that should have been asked, and faced with the utmost ruthlessness, was: Was the lavish supply scale of Allied divisions really necessary? If the enemy, under constant attack from the air, harassed incessantly by guerillas and saboteurs, could put up a magnificent resistance in Normandy on 200 to 250 tons per division per day, why could not the British and Americans manage on much less than 700 tons per division per day?

Moreover at this critical point in time at the end of August the enemy was in defeat, in flight, disorganized and very poorly armed. Surely in these circumstances ammunition could have been scaled down drastically? There was no question of fighting 'pitched' (or 'set-piece') battles, of employing medium or heavy artillery. The ammunition for the main armament of the armoured spearheads should have been reduced to a bare minimum, and all troops limited to 'iron rations'. Every single vehicle employed in the actual advance, including all fighting vehicles, could have been loaded to the limits. Fuel was the vital

[1] Ruppenthal: *Logistics*, vol. ii, U.S. Army in W.W. 2, p. 15.

necessity, and all else should have given way to it. The thing to do was to keep going far and fast, disrupting the disrupted enemy still further, denying his opportunities to rally.

If ever there was a time for boldness that time was the end of August, 1944. Thus, in the final analysis, the decisive factor must be the Supreme Command, and secondly the Army Group Commanders, notably Field-Marshal Montgomery. But even on 1st September, General Eisenhower was not in a position to exercise effective control and effective command. 'It would seem,' wrote Pogue[1] of this period, 'that immediate and firm control were sometimes lacking.' Bradley and Montgomery, agreeing on very little else, agreed on that point. Indeed Eisenhower did not have the command situation in hand—inasmuch as that was possible—for a further month. 'By 1st October, the Supreme Commander had gathered firmly into his hands the control of Allied forces from Holland to the Mediterranean and from the German frontier westward to the Atlantic. He commanded as well U.S. air and ground forces in the United Kingdom. Under his direct control he had one British, one Canadian, one French, one Allied airborne, and four U.S. armies as well as the British and U.S. tactical air forces. While he no longer controlled any part of the strategic air forces, he still had first call on them for necessary support of his ground operations. With his headquarters set up on the Continent and with an adequate radio and telegraphic link to his chief subordinates, he could now personally direct operations against the Third Reich.'[1]

It was more than a month too late, and it was far too much. No wonder Montgomery cried out for a Ground Force commander, for never was a commander more necessary on the ground.

In these circumstances General Eisenhower did support Montgomery to the limits of the possible, and in spite of the demands of Bradley and Patton. Chester Wilmot, a close observer of these events, thought that the Americans did not support Montgomery whole-heartedly because they thought him too timid for the role he had conceived for himself. There is no doubt that this is true, but the question is not whether the Americans were 'whole-hearted', but whether in fact Mont-

[1] Pogue: *The Supreme Command*, pp. 275-276, p. 278.

gomery was given enough, and enough for what? Sir Basil Liddell Hart's summing up of the Allied failure to gain victory in 1944 is also both lucid and true:

'The root of all the Allied troubles at this time of supreme opportunity,' he wrote, 'was that none of the top planners had foreseen such a complete collapse of the enemy as occurred in August. They were not prepared, mentally or materially, to exploit it by a rapid long-range thrust.'[1]

Patton's comment is perhaps the most important of all in this context: 'One does not plan and then try to make circumstances fit those plans. One tries to make plans fit the circumstances. I think the difference between success and failure in high command depends upon its ability, or lack of it, to do just that.'[2]

It is time to leave the Supreme Command, and to concentrate upon Field-Marshal Montgomery.

---

[1] Analysis: B. H. Liddell Hart, 14.8.54. Privately circulated.
[2] Patton: *War As I Knew It*, p. 116.

CHAPTER NINE

The Drive to the North

I

From Port-en-Bessin in an arc southward to Vire, eastward through Argentan, and curving again to the sea, embracing the tragic rubble of the city of Caen, the close Normandy countryside of hill and valley seethed with men and armour, guns and vehicles, choked beneath the vast impedimenta of an army in victory, and the refuse of an army in defeat. Great dumps sprawled over the countryside, piled high with ammunition, petrol, and all the needs of men, the wealth of a nation. Within the great beachhead, now swollen and swelling to bursting point there was a feeling of suffocation, the sense of a great boil, oozing slowly through the narrow waist of the Falaise gap, forcing its way behind bull-dozers through the dust and rubble of Caen, probing for outlets in a slow but sure crescendo through to the Seine from Mantes Gassicourt to the sea.

The advance demanded prodigious feats of skill, speed and endurance, especially from the engineers in the manifold tasks of bridging. In Normandy 3,000 yards of bridging had sufficed, mainly in the spanning of the river Orne. The Seine was a major challenge. An infantry division could cross initially using folding boat equipment to carry loads up to 9 tons, but armour demanded Bailey bridges capable of bearing 40 tons, while armour on transporters needed a bearing capability of 70 tons. Eight Bailey pontoon bridges between 450 and 750 feet long, using 7,500 tons of bridging material, were thrown across the Seine by Field Companies and bridging platoons in a time span of 14 to 34 hours, four of them in tidal water.[1]

---

[1] The Establishment of a division included in its divisional engineers, three Field Companies and a Bridging platoon. Corps and G.H.Q. engineer establishments greatly increased these resources.

There was a kind of frenzy, an unbroken and incessant turbulence through every hour of the days and nights, as the great mass of men, armour, artillery, trucks, fed constantly with more men and machines from the heartland of England, strove to break loose.

It was a bitter harvest in Normandy that year, but here and there a field of ripe corn shone in golden relief against the grey face of death and destruction. People lived here, life had burgeoned here. It was their native land, not simply a battle-field. It was difficult to remember.

In the middle of August a new vista of war and peace marvellous and irresistible had begun to move into the view of the soldier in the line. Troops hemmed in to narrow and dangerous salients, harassed by incessant bursts of mortar fire, began to move, to find elbow room, and the way ahead clearing, the dangers subtly lessening as the enemy, at last overwhelmed, barely paused to fire over his shoulder in headlong retreat. It was clear to every man advancing to the Seine that the enemy had suffered an appalling disaster. They saw, day after day, the human and material wreckage of an army with a sense of awe, which would turn into elation, a knowledge of victory. But the going was slow for the British all along the line. The intense congestion in the British and Canadian bridgehead had been imposed by the shape and strategy of the Battle for Normandy, compelling them to hold the shoulder against the enemy on the left, long after the way had opened on the right. The British and American ordeals had been different in kind. From the beginning of August, following Patton's break-through at Avranches, the right wing of the American armies had steadily gained momentum, and was speeding for the Moselle while the British were still struggling through the debris to the Seine. The right had cracked wide open; the centre was about to burst; but on the left the Canadian 1st Army with the British 1st Corps under command confronted the German 15th Army, 150,000 strong, and resolved to defend the Channel ports from Le Havre to the Scheldt estuary.

In his orders of 26th August, Montgomery had made it clear that the immediate tasks confronting 21st Army Group, 'were the destruction of the enemy in north-east France, the clearance of the Pas de Calais with its 'V' bomb sites, the capture of airfields in Belgium, and the opening of the port of Antwerp.'[1] The Field-Marshal could not tell how long these moves would take, but it is clear that he expected a pause in Belgium for a build-up of supplies. Meanwhile on 25th August, General Bradley, enjoying some freedom of movement with his left flanking troops, and chafing for action, sought and gained General Dempsey's permission to pass four U.S. divisions across the line of march of the British 2nd Army, and to operate in the area of Elboeuf. If this was intended as an example of Anglo-American co-operation it was singularly ill-conceived, ill-timed and wasteful, and it is astounding that Dempsey agreed. The idea is best expressed in General Bradley's own words:

'Thinking to trap those units that had escaped through Falaise,' he wrote, 'and at the same time break ground for the British advance . . . and rather than miss this opportunity for a second encirclement of the enemy west of the Seine, I proposed that we turn our U.S. forces north into the British sector and cut the enemy off on the left bank.

'We anticipated beforehand that any such maneuver of U.S. troops across the British line of advance would entail an administrative headache. For the 80,000 troops that eventually marched up north would have to march back down again, this time across the British columns that in the meantime were closing the Seine . . . By 25th August they had driven 35 miles across the British front to the vicinity of the Gothic city of Rouen.'

Anything more hare-brained it is difficult to imagine. Thus on the day before Montgomery ordered the 2nd Army advance 80,000 friendly troops were blocking the way. The unscrambling of the U.S. divisions imposed rigid and complex road controls, and there was a stop-go progress for some days, so many hours for the lateral movement of the U.S. divisions back to their own areas, and so many hours for the British moving forward to the Seine over broken roads hideous with traffic. The result, it seemed to Bradley, was an undoubted bonus for Dempsey, but it imposed a serious delay on the 2nd Army advance, and brought Dempsey under criticism.

'Several days later,' Bradley wrote, 'when Dempsey was questioned by the British press on his advance to the Seine, he

[1] Montgomery: *Normandy to the Baltic*, p. 123.

complained that the movement could have gone faster but for the U.S. traffic that snarled his front.'[1]

Dempsey's 'complaint' which was no more than a straightforward explanation, 'piqued' Bradley. It is an example, relatively unimportant in itself, of the difficulties in the different approaches to command and tactics of different races and armies. Moreover it was a time of a growing awkwardness between the Allies, and Bradley might have been even more 'piqued' to have had a refusal to his generous gesture of 'aid'. It may seem curious also that Montgomery did not erupt at the very thought of a manoeuvre, offensive in every way to his sense of order. It is almost certain that the Army Group commander's gaze was already firmly fixed a long way ahead, and that nothing would move him from his vision of victory.

By the time the British 2nd Army crossed the Seine in strength to debouch almost unopposed through north-western France a subtle change was becoming evident in the mien and temper of the troops. It was manifest in a relaxation of tension, and the feeling that it was nearly over. In fact there was no room for complacency, no room for the slightest diminution of effort. Indeed, the demand was for all troops to face a new ordeal, no less exacting, but different in character and kind, and in some ways more subtly dangerous, especially to morale, than the ordeal they had sustained in Normandy. A battle had been won, but the war remained.

II

In the last hours of August the Canadian 1st Army with the British 1st Corps under command set about its difficult task in the Pas de Calais. While the 51st Highland division took St. Valery in its stride to avenge its tragic losses of 1940, the Canadian 2nd division over-ran the first of the 'V' bomb sites in a swift and triumphant progress to Dieppe. Nevertheless from the outset it was clear that there would not be an easy struggle on the left from the Seine to the Scheldt. The British 1st Corps encountered a resolute enemy on the difficult landward approaches to the fortress port of Le Havre, and it might prove

[1] Bradley: *A Soldier's Story*, pp. 380-383.

as hard a nut to crack as the worst of the Brittany ports still defying the Americans. The progress of the Polish and Canadian armour, thrusting deep into Flanders on the road to Ghent, was satisfactory rather than spectacular, while the infantry of the Canadian 2nd Corps was discovering the tedious, deadly and damp nature of the struggle ahead to free the Channel ports and to close the approaches to the Scheldt. Even though it soon became apparent that von Zangen, commanding the German 15th Army, was resolved to concentrate his main strength on the defence of the water-lines barring the way to the Scheldt estuary from Ghent to the sea, leaving the garrisons of Boulogne, Calais, Dunkirk and Ostend to fend for themselves, only Ostend was to be an easy prize.

There was no thunder on the left, and soon it seemed that the Canadian Army was forgotten, together with the British 1st Corps investing Le Havre. Events on the right completely overshadowed all that was happening, and all that might happen on the left, and even on the left prong of the 2nd Army advance. The hopes of Britain for quick victory, and of Field-Marshal Montgomery, were upon the British 2nd Army, and with the great drive of armour rapidly developing out of the Seine bridgeheads.

On the 29th August, the 11th Armoured division with 8th Armoured brigade led the advance out of the 30th Corps bridgehead at Vernon, and was followed by the Guards Armoured division brought up to the river on transporters. It seemed an indication that the Guards hoped to go farther and faster, and that the emphasis, and the vision of the command, was upon them. The 11th Armoured, having cleared the way, was on the left, the Guards Armoured on the right. Their orders were simply to drive on with all possible speed. Horrocks, commanding 30th Corps, had spurred the 11th Armoured to seize a bridgehead across the Somme at Amiens, and on the night of the 30th, responding magnificently, the division drove 55 miles through torrential rain in almost pitch darkness to 'bounce' the second of the great water barriers on the road to the north. All hope of the enemy organizing even a token resistance on the Somme had vanished, and on the morning of the 31st, a spirit of exultation began to light British troops. All France and Belgium felt wide open.

F*

For six days and nights five armoured divisions and five armoured brigades tore in a furious crescendo through towns and villages that had known only the Nazi invader for four years. It was not a pursuit of the enemy, not a battle. The British armour had broken loose after ninety days of battle within a tight perimeter, and on the 3rd September, while the 11th Armoured halted, dog-weary to laager at Alost a few miles outside the great city and port of Antwerp, the Guards roared into Brussels on the crest of a wave of triumph. The welcome all along the roads had been almost overwhelming. Flowers, fruit, wine and kisses became the new enemies, threatening at times to halt the columns. The young men, riding the open turrets of their tanks, their faces bronzed under their berets, looked like the chivalry of a nation, undefeatable and irresistible. The infantry mopping up in their tracks were more vulnerable, welcomed by a people delirious with joy. The Cameronians of 15th Scottish division, one example among many, ran into 'a mass of frenzied humanity' on their way through Lille, and were held up for nearly twelve hours, unable to move forward until two o'clock in the morning. Enemy horse drawn columns bewildered and losing all sense of direction were blasted to death and debris before they could find their bearings and civilians on short rations for years carved steaks from the dead horses for the feasting.

But on the seventh day the great drive halted, having travelled 250 miles from the Seine, and with the beginnings of its long 'tail' nearly 400 miles in the rear. The experiences of the 11th and the Guards Armoured divisions had been very different. The 11th had had by far the greatest ordeal, and on the night of the 3rd, they felt that they must have reached journey's end, sleeping where they lay or sat or sprawled by their vehicles. While the Guards advanced to Louvain on the morning of the 4th and began probing for crossings of the Meuse-Escaut and Albert canals, the 3rd Royal Tank Regiment seized the main bridge into Antwerp without difficulty, and by early afternoon the city was occupied and the great dock areas captured intact. It was the moment of truth, the moment when commanders needed to 'push all personnel to the limit of human endurance', in Haislip's words.

There was very little to stop the 11th Armoured division from seizing the bridges across the Albert Canal, and advancing to close the narrow neck of the Bevelands, and thus isolating the 15th Army.

'Had any indication been given that a further advance north was envisaged, these might have been seized within a few hours of our entry into the city,' wrote the historian of the 11th Armoured division. In fact, the divisional commander, and his corps commander, were dazzled by the astonishing fortune of seizing the great dock areas intact, and did not look beyond their orders. Liddell Hart commented: 'The omission to seize the Albert Canal bridges would seem to have been primarily due to concentration on the immediate objective and the dazzling effect of the triumphant race to gain it.'[1]

Major-General Roberts, commanding the division, might well have urged the situation strongly upon his Corps commander, and General Horrocks, despite his orders to 'refit, refuel and rest' ('the sound course if there had been any serious opposition ahead, but such did not exist at the moment—as was, in fact, correctly gauged by 30th Corps and the higher commands')[1] should have ordered the seizure of the canal bridges.

Nothing was done, and the blame cannot be attributed to the corps and the divisional commanders. They had been fully involved in the great drive, sharing to some extent the weariness and exultation of their troops. It was not for the twin spearheads to choose their courses, but for the army commander, and the army group commander. At the crucial hour leadership was lacking, the kind of leadership and decision only Montgomery could have exercised, and which the hour demanded. It was not a time for planning operations into a future that was unknown, but for seizing options and opportunities. If there could be a chance for quick victory, it was clear that these great armoured spearheads probing far and fast, overrunning enemy headquarters, and turning disruption into chaos, must discover it. And they did discover it. But the two prongs of the armoured advance were not probes, seeking the weakest points, ready to deliver a 'knock-out'. Montgomery was not probing. He was not even considering the possibilities which might present themselves on his left flank. His plans were already in the making, his direction virtually decided. On 3rd September, he

---

[1] Liddell Hart: *History of the Royal Tank Regiment*, vol. ii, p. 414.

issued new orders to 21st Army Group. '... the main object constantly before me was to "bounce" a crossing over the Rhine with the utmost speed before the enemy could reorganize sufficiently to stop us,' he wrote. 'Speed, and still greater speed, was the essential factor, and I now ordered 2nd Army to drive forward to the Rhine as quickly as possible.'[1] This order could have been taken as *carte blanche* for Roberts to press ahead with the 11th Armoured division, but this was not Montgomery's intention as his long message to the Supreme Commander on the very day of the entry into Antwerp underlines. His mind was on the Ruhr and Berlin, and upon 'the single full-blooded thrust' above all else. He did not consider the immense possibilities of quick victory in those few hours when the enemy was floundering, 'so unnerved by the tales of what had happened in France that they disappeared without bothering to blow up this most valuable prize of the campaign—Antwerp, third largest port in the world, and with its twenty-six miles of dock frontage, one of the main gateways leading into the heart of Europe'.[2] Without it no 'full-blooded thrust' was possible to mount or to sustain.

The failure to exploit the confusion of the enemy by pressing on through Antwerp to Woensdracht and Hoogesheide and cutting off the narrow neck of the Bevelands can only be explained in terms of Montgomery's pre-occupation with a thrust to the north on his right flanking axis, and his nagging involvement with the Supreme Commander for support. Had there been a commander following the battle 'hour by hour and day by day', as Montgomery was never tired of emphasizing to Eisenhower, and with the flexibility of mind to see the prospects, then the 'might-have-beens', justly lamented by General Bradley in his comment on Montgomery's failure to open Antwerp, are truly agonizing. Given the attention of the Army Group Commander, committed to the battle in progress and moving with great speed, and not to a problematical and highly speculative future, the quick victory Britain needed and Montgomery dreamed about, might have been achieved. There would be no second chance. The 1st Allied Airborne Corps was ready for action, its commander, Lieut.-General Browning

[1] Montgomery: *Normandy to the Baltic*, p. 128.
[2] John North: *N.W. Europe*, 1944-45, H.M.S.O., p. 128.

actually summoned to confer with Field-Marshal Montgomery on 3rd September. The 52nd (Mountain) division, after years of training for a role it would never fulfil, was alerted to be flown in to anywhere. Not only was the road to Bergen-op-Zoom open, but through to the whole north of Holland. Utrecht, Amsterdam and Rotterdam could have been freed, and the Maas and Rhine crossed before September was out. The German 15th Army would have been lost, and the positions of all the garrisons from Le Havre to Walcheren would have been hopeless. Not only the port of Antwerp would have been ours, but all north Holland, for Field-Marshal Model, denied the breathing space to work his miracle, and unready to meet an enemy in full cry, would have had no option but to retreat to the Siegfried Line, a line still far from secure.

The tragic failure of the Northern group of armies to seize all or any of these opportunities reveals Montgomery's severe limitations. He was a man incapable of self-criticism, and with an essentially tidy mind. He liked to plan well in advance from a known or fixed startline, his resources methodically gathered and overwhelmingly powerful. He strove to turn an exercise in confusion into a mathematical process. At 2nd Alamein, his first great traumatic military experience as an army commander, he was, as Horrocks noted, always planning the next battle. It tended naturally to take his mind away from the development of the battle in progress, and the variety of end patterns which might result. By deciding upon the end pattern in advance he denied himself the manifold opportunities and options of the hour of victory. Moreover, as I have underlined many times,[1] he had had always a fear of the 'expanding torrent', of troops and especially armour breaking loose, driving far and fast and beyond his immediate control. He would never give 'the horse its head'. This fear of loosing his armour, and turning deaf ears to the urgent pleas of his armour commanders, cost him the complete victory at 2nd Alamein that the heavy odds in his favour should have ensured. It also preserved Rommel and the nucleus of his army all the way to join with von Arnim in Tunisia.

Psychologically the great armoured break-out from the Seine would have filled Montgomery with misgivings. He wanted

[1] *The Montgomery Legend.*

them to stop, so that he could get things in hand again, regroup, and go ahead with his pre-arranged plan. He was incapable of handling swiftly moving armour tactically, or strategically, incapable of commanding the kind of break-out his armies had embarked upon by virtue of his great victory in Normandy, and which would have been meat and drink to a Patton.

Following his orders of 3rd September, Montgomery wrote that '2nd Army continued its advance from the Brussels-Antwerp area with minimum delay'. It did not. There was almost at once a sense of anti-climax, and the ordeal of liberation had begun to sap the morale of the troops. It was a strange and subtle feeling, growing upon men who had thought that the worst was over, and had begun to realize that a long winter of war lay ahead. No one wanted to be killed, and of course no one ever did, but in the midst of battle men do not think about it. Now they had time to think, hoping that it would all prove easy. It was manifest in a lack of drive, difficult to define or to pin-point, as infantry and armour probed for crossings of the Albert and Meuse-Escaut canals. Even as early as the 7th and 8th September the enemy had begun to stiffen up, to turn and fight with a new ferocity, not for the defence of the great gains in France, Belgium, Holland, but for the defence of the Fatherland. All the bridges were blown. Field-Marshal Model and General Student had wrought a miracle.

The iron should not have been permitted to cool, even for a day, and forceful leadership could have prevented it. No men in this world, except those dedicated to some individual task, will fail to rest when they have a chance, and weariness takes hold. They are not 'running the show'. They go when they are told, and they stop when a halt is called, but these troops of the Northern Group of armies had shown that they were good soldiers, capable of going on far beyond the point when men want to stop.

The fall of Antwerp was a wonderful opportunity to use an airborne brigade, but even without one the Bevelands could have been sealed off. As it was, there were nearly ninety days of gruelling struggle ahead for the Canadians, ninety days as bad or worse, in the mud and flood and bitter cold, as their days tight in the shoulder in Normandy.

While time was running out fast Field-Marshal Montgomery embarked upon a new phase of his long nagging exchanges with the Supreme Commander, which were to continue with various changes of emphasis until finally scotched in the New Year. Twice Montgomery provoked a command crisis, and finally exhausted the patience of the patient Eisenhower. These exchanges, usually at long range, were unsatisfactory in the extreme and often at cross purposes.

On 4th September, Montgomery telegraphed:
'... we have now reached the stage where one really powerful and full-blooded thrust towards Berlin is likely to get there and thus end the German war.'

This was the burthen of the exchanges throughout September. The 21st Army Group Commander wanted the full backing of the Supreme Commander, and all available resources allocated to his armies—specifically the 2nd Army. The rest would make do with whatever might be left over. Five corps would have to be grounded in Normandy, while Bradley, the 12th Army Group Commander, and his fiery 3rd Army Commander, Patton, would abide in patience. Apart from the physical possibilities of such a thrust, and its chances, the proposition sounded unreal and impossible to Eisenhower.

It is perhaps a pity that Montgomery did not attend the meeting at Chartres on 2nd September when Eisenhower had discussed his plans with Bradley, Patton and Hodges, and had given a qualified approval to Bradley for a drive to the east on the 3rd Army front. It would have been clear beyond all argument that the Supreme Commander was resolved to keep the 'enemy stretched everywhere', and his armies on the move all along the line. General Patton, aided by Bradley's 'blind eye', and with his notorious 'Rock Soup' methods, could be relied upon to 'make the greatest use of any loopholes in the Supreme Commander's orders'.[1]

But it is misleading to describe Eisenhower's mild directives,

---

[1] Pogue: *The Supreme Command*, p. 293 and footnote. Patton: *War As I Knew It*, pp. 125, 133 and 365.
'Rock Soup': 'In other words, in order to attack, we had first to reconnoiter, then reinforce the reconnaisance, and finally put on an attack.' Moreover, in order to frustrate Montgomery's intentions, Patton wrote: 'It was evident that the 3rd Army should get deeply involved at once, so I asked Bradley not to call me until after dark on the nineteenth.'

especially at this stage, as 'orders'. They lacked emphasis, and they lacked the bite, the clear thinking and the decision of command, but they did reveal very clearly the Supreme Commander's intentions and desires. The rivalry of his two Army Group Commanders (for Devers was still too remote to enter the competition), jockeying for position regardless, it seems, of enemy dispositions or intentions, produced a natural 'strategy' of compromise and convenience.

Attendance at the Chartres meeting might have convinced Montgomery of the realities of the situation, and the extent of the backing he might expect, or force out of the Supreme Command by his own brand of 'Rock Soup'. Nothing would have made Montgomery change his mind about what he regarded as the correct strategy, but direct confrontation might have persuaded him to concentrate upon the possible. His emphasis on Berlin was unreal, and so was his desire to halt the U.S. armies.

As it was, poor communications delayed the Supreme Commander's negative reply and his insistence upon the importance of Antwerp, but on the 7th September, Montgomery learned from his Chief of Staff that 80% of his demands for locomotives and rolling stock would be met, and there was no doubt that the Northern thrust would have top priority, including the 'Airborne Army as a means of capturing Walcheren Island and clearing the Schelde estuary in the hope of opening the approaches to Antwerp'.

But the Field-Marshal's thoughts and intentions were far from Antwerp, and he was already resolved to use airborne troops to bounce a bridge over the Rhine at Arnhem. With Brereton, commanding the Airborne Army, and Browning, his deputy, Montgomery had already devised one plan—COMET—using one and a half divisions. His whole mind was oriented upon his centre line and right, and nothing would induce him to look to his left flank. Unhappily his head was also in the clouds, for his vision was focused too much on the air and too little on the ground. General Dempsey, it was believed, favoured an airborne drop to seize Wesel. This eastern line of attack would have tended to consolidate the ground power and with the U.S. 1st Army would have given a more solid look to the possibilities.

On the 9th, news of the V bomb attacks upon England determined Montgomery upon his chosen course, and convinced him that Arnhem was the only possible target. The points of departure of the V weapons were believed to be in the Rotterdam and Amsterdam areas, and Montgomery's reasoning is not clear. His intention was to 'lay a carpet' of airborne troops from the Dutch town of Eindhoven to Arnhem, seizing the bridges over the Wilhelmina canal, and the rivers Maas and Waal at Grave and Nijmegen, while an airborne division landing on the right bank of the Rhine would secure the bridge at Arnhem and open the way to the Zuider Zee. It was a grandiose plan, virtually ignoring enemy strength. On the ground the start line across the Albert canal was not yet strongly secured.

On the 9th, 10th and 11th, the Supreme Commander conferred with his Naval, Air and Ground Force Commanders, and on the 10th at Brussels he endorsed Montgomery's plan while at the same time emphasizing the importance of Antwerp.[1] It should have been clear that Arnhem and Antwerp were mutually exclusive, and that the one must wait upon the other. Eisenhower only gave one small sign of his irritation by referring to Montgomery's 'full-blooded' thrust as a 'pencil-like' thrust. The description was justified, for whatever Montgomery might choose to call it, it was clear that his thrust to the north over 60 difficult miles of enemy occupied territory, and with enemy resistance stiffening almost hourly, would be very thin on the ground. To think beyond that to Berlin reduced the idea almost to absurdity.

A target date was fixed for the 17th of the month, but on the 11th, Montgomery telegraphed Eisenhower that he would be forced to delay the attack to the 26th unless further support were forthcoming, and absolute priority given to the northern army. This seems curious in the light of the personal meeting on the 10th, for surely the whole project should have been discussed fully. Nevertheless, the Supreme Commander immediately sent his Chief of Staff, Bedell Smith, to confer with Montgomery. An additional 1,000 tons per day of supplies were promised, to be delivered by air and U.S. truck companies. In addition three U.S. infantry divisions would be stripped of their

[1] The C.C.S. also emphasized the need for Antwerp and Rotterdam.

transport and 'grounded' in Normandy. At last Montgomery seemed to be 'mollified', and telegraphed his thanks to the Supreme Commander in the warmest terms: 'Most grateful to you personally and to Beetle for all you are doing for us.'[1]

Nevertheless, on the 18th, with the Arnhem operation already giving cause for anxiety, Montgomery returned to his attack on the strategy of the Supreme Command. Again he urged Eisenhower to strip all troops, except for those in 21st Army Group and the U.S. 1st Army, of all transport and 'everything else' to support one single 'knife-like' drive towards Berlin.

To Eisenhower this seemed like a return to the demands of the 4th September, which he had rejected, and he reacted with the first signs of mild asperity. He had agreed to the Arnhem operation because 'The attractive possibility of quickly turning the German north flank led me to approve the temporary delay in freeing the vital port of Antwerp.' The Combined Chiefs of Staff had also underlined the pressing need not only for Antwerp, but for Rotterdam.

'As I have told you,' the Supreme Commander emphasized, 'I am prepared to give you everything for the capture of the approaches to Antwerp, including all the air forces and anything else you can support.' At the same time he told Montgomery that Patton had not only repelled heavy enemy counter-attacks in his sector, but had taken 9,000 prisoners and knocked out 720 tanks.[2] This confirmed the Field-Marshal in the rightness of his arguments, and in his suspicions of Bradley and Patton. He replied at once, 'I have always said stop the right and go on with the left but the right has been allowed to go on so far that it has outstripped its maintenance and we have lost flexibility.'

On the 22nd, the Supreme Commander held a conference with his principal commanders at Versailles, and again Montgomery failed to attend. It is improbable that Montgomery intended a slight, but in his message to the Field-Marshal the Supreme Commander, while expressing himself in warm and friendly terms, reveals a personal hurt: 'Good luck to you. I

---

[1] See Pogue: *The Supreme Command*, pp. 283-284. Thompson: *The Eighty-five Days*, pp. 31-33.
[2] This *must* be pure hyperbole—a completely mythical figure.

regard it as a great pity that all of us cannot keep in closer touch with each other because I find, without exception, when all of us can get together and look the various features of our problems squarely in the face, the answers usually become obvious.'[1]

But Montgomery was not interested in such discussions, and was concerned simply to establish the rightness of his views.

The argument continued well into October, long after Montgomery had failed to 'bounce' a bridgehead across the Rhine at Arnhem. On 10th October, Eisenhower telegraphed:

'Let me assure you that nothing I may ever say or write with regard to future plans in our advances eastward is meant to indicate any lessening of the need for Antwerp, which I have always held as vital, and which has grown more pressing as we enter the bad weather period.'

Indeed the need for Antwerp was becoming so pressing that without it the Allied armies might be forced to grind to a halt. In further messages Eisenhower 'spelled out' the urgency, and on the 16th, the Field-Marshal at last 'gave orders—with, it may be presumed, an infinite reluctance—that his armies should turn their gaze west'.[2]

On the 18th, Eisenhower and Bradley conferred with Montgomery in Brussels, and on the 20th, the Combined Chiefs of Staff in Washington came to the conclusion that the chances of winning the war in 1944 had disappeared. Only the early capture of Antwerp might have made such a result possible.

IV

Two points demand attention. The first is why the Supreme Commander failed to *order* the opening of Antwerp on 4th September, or as soon as he became fully aware of the position. The second is why did Montgomery ignore Antwerp and insist upon his drive by air and land to Arnhem.

I have already referred to the reasons why Eisenhower failed to act forcefully. As Pogue pointed out, the reins of

[1] *The Eighty-five Days.*
[2] *North, North-West Europe,* 1944-45, H.M.S.O.

command were not properly in his hands until 1st October. He was not in close touch with the rapidly developing situation on the left flank, and communications were bad between Supreme Headquarters and both Army Groups, particularly 21st Army Group. Moreover there was the over-riding problem of 'logistics', the 'pattern' almost fore-ordained, and difficult to modify drastically to take advantage of the immense chance of victory which became apparent in mid-August. There was the need, or desire, of the Supreme Command to deploy the full power at his command and not to put more than half of his command, however temporarily, out of 'business'. And there was the enormous psychological problem of halting the U.S. 3rd Army 'with the ball at its feet'. The ball, in fact, was not at its feet, but it seemed that it was, or might be, in late August and early September, 1944.

By the time Eisenhower began to get the feel of his command, his armies and his subordinates, it was already too late. The iron was cold. But the Supreme Commander's greatest weakness at this crucial time was his sense of justice, of being 'fair' to his rapidly weakening ally.

Montgomery, for his part, was entirely without such inhibitions. It has been stated the he never disobeyed an *order*, and while the anti-Montgomery faction at Supreme Headquarters argued that he did, and that his attitudes and persistent arguments were the equivalent of insubordination, it must be clear that Montgomery did not disobey an *order*. An order had to be given simply and unequivocally. He argued, as he said, as long as he was permitted to argue. Perhaps his arguments went beyond the limits of reasonable intercourse between a subordinate and a Supreme Commander, and certainly beyond the limits of propriety, but Montgomery's position was in many ways unique in the hierarchy of command, and he was well aware of it. He was, as Eisenhower observed, in direct contact with the Prime Minister and the British Chiefs of Staff, and the figurehead on the battlefield of the host nation of the invasion, the nation, moreover, that had fought long and arduously against the enemy from the beginning, and whose powers were waning fast. These considerations while genuine and true were none the less emotional, and Eisenhower treated Montgomery with too much delicacy and circumspection. It was the Supreme Commander's task to command his armies irrespective of nationality, and without fear or favour, and it must be added that Montgomery was not the type of man to treat with 'kid gloves'. He needed command, and had suffered from a lack of it throughout his career as an Army Commander. Alexander had been too soft and easy-going with him. Powerful command might well have brought out the best in him, forcing him to see himself more clearly. It would almost certainly have been a 'kill or cure' treatment, but nothing less could have saved Montgomery from himself, and helped him to grow to full stature as a soldier. A leader—and Montgomery regarded himself as a superlative leader—must learn to accept leadership. This is one of the major flaws in Montgomery's professionalism.

The fact is that Eisenhower did not command Montgomery at any time in this crucial period from 4th September to the end of the month when powerful and courageous command were an absolute necessity, if there was to be a chance of winning the war in 1944. It must be remembered that the need for quick victory was not a matter of grave necessity to the Americans: they could afford to wait. Nevertheless the task of Supreme Command called for a man of iron, a Wellington or a Napoleon with the unique gifts of a Marlborough added; moreover, a man supremely competent and confident militarily. It would be ridiculous to blame Eisenhower for not possessing these qualities, and lacking them he did possess great qualities for his most difficult task. But in the crucial days, caught between the demands and urgings of Bradley-Patton on his right, and the nagging insistence of Montgomery on his left, Eisenhower vacillated. Logistics called the tune. Promising all possible aid to Montgomery, and giving more than a fair measure, he also turned a blind eye to the Bradley-Patton 'rock soup' performance.

Montgomery's obsession to strike due north on his right flank and to ignore the immense, and obvious, opportunities on his left, is less easily explained and must be largely a matter of conjecture. Montgomery himself, incapable, as it seemed and still seems, of self-criticism or of conceiving 'in the bowels of Christ' that he might ever have been wrong, is of little or no help in the matter. His voluminous writings merely underline his colossal egotism and egocentricity, his belief in the sublime genius of his generalship, and in the outstanding qualities of his leadership. I think Montgomery's eyes were fixed on the north and east because he more than any other man was acutely aware of the time factor, and the need for Britain somehow to gain victory in 1944. Rightly or wrongly he must have come to the conclusion that quick victory could not be gained on the western flank, and that it must be at least one month, say, before the Schelde estuary and the port of Antwerp could be opened to shipping. And even if bridgeheads could be seized over the Maas and Rhine and Rotterdam won, the line would lie too far to the west to threaten the enemy homeland. He may have foreseen that the enemy might be compelled to 'roll back' eastward behind the Siegfried Line, but this—if he did give it any thought at all—may have seemed to mark the preliminaries to an extended struggle, and perhaps he felt too weak to strike a powerful right-handed blow, say, on Wesel, to follow up his terrific left hook.

On the other hand the evidence is that he had come to his decision to strike due north with his right flank before the possibilities of Antwerp were apparent. He appeared to count too much on the possibilities of the Channel ports.

If all this is wide of the mark, I feel bound to speculate, fully aware that strategists and tacticians far more competent than I may disagree, and advance more cogent arguments for Montgomery's choice. Moreover I was there, and while in many ways this may be an advantage it may also endanger the objectivity, attainable by the uninvolved observer and student of a later generation. My hope is that my reporting of this campaign may be helpful. I was in very close touch with developments on the ground in the crucial days, in the dock areas and canal crossing points in Antwerp on the 4th September; in Brussels with the spearheads of the armour on the 3rd, at Louvain on the morning of the 5th, and closely observing the struggle for the bridgeheads at Gheel and Beeringen on succeeding days. For what it may be worth I knew the 'feel' of the situation as well as any man, and my opportunities from beginning to end of the campaign were unique. I was a trained soldier, a Captain in the 'Intelligence Corps' with a forced and tough training in the ranks, and as an infantry officer. I had done well on junior staff courses, not much less severe. In 1944, I was appointed a War Correspondent with a unique commitment to newspapers of the highest standing, whose Editor-in-Chief gave me *carte blanche*. Almost alone among my new colleagues I was able to 'get lost', and commit myself with forward troops without worrying unduly about 'dead-lines'. I was accepted as a soldier rather than as a War Correspondent by all those who knew me well, and had been my brother officers since 1940. At divisional, brigade and battalion levels I had many friends. Moreover, I had many opportunities to observe Montgomery at close quarters, while always remaining completely anonymous. My conclusion at the time, and my conclusion now, is that Montgomery saw a bold blow as his only chance of quick victory, and his decision to strike north ignored tactical opportunities. At the same time he was acutely conscious of his administrative difficulties and his lack of basic strength; his blow had to succeed, it had to take advantage of the almost total disruption of the enemy, and every hour was of vital importance. At any time up to, say, 8th September the drive to the north on Arnhem and the Zuider Zee might have succeeded, but to succeed the ground and airborne forces would have had to be closely co-ordinated, with the airborne forces used to support the ground forces, and not the other way round. General Brereton, commanding the 1st Allied Airborne Army, and frustrated by the many abortive plans, wanted to strike on the 4th, but Browning, his deputy, disagreed and threatened to resign. By the time it became possible to mount the drive it was already too late, and it felt too late. The impetus that had sent the armour surging north from the Seine, and the *élan*, had evaporated and could not be regained.

Finally the Supreme Commander had made it clear that his consent to the operation was based upon securing his line, and not as the first phase of a blow eastward by 21st Army Group 'on the general axis Rheine-Osnabruck-Munster-Hamm, with the main weight on the right flank directed to Hamm: whence a thrust would be made along the eastern face of the Ruhr'.[1] In short, Eisenhower was not prepared to change his 'Broad Front' strategy, and Montgomery's drive 'was thus a tactical

---

[1] Montgomery: *Normandy to the Baltic*, p. 136.

change of plan, designed to meet a favourable local situation within the main plan of campaign.'[1]

Thus, in a sense, Montgomery's 'strategic plan' was a 'tactical plan' to the Supreme Commander. Yet Montgomery's main fault lay, not so much in his conception of a drive to the north to 'bounce' the Rhine as his great opportunity, nor in his disregard of Eisenhower's clear intentions and strategic aims, his 'Broad Front' policy, but in his failure to recognize the vital importance of the time factor, and his unwillingness to abandon, or modify, any plan once he had committed himself to it. Tactical opportunities seldom prevail for fourteen days, especially in the fluid circumstances created by major armoured breaks-through against a defeated enemy in a temporary state of confusion. Furthermore, quite apart from the Supreme Commander's strategic plans, Montgomery's thrust, even if successful could not have been developed 'along the eastern face of the Ruhr' without the backing of the resources of the Port of Antwerp. That fundamental task might be postponed, but it could not be avoided.

Above all, Montgomery ignored the military principle expressed clearly by Patton, and to which I drew attention at the end of the last chapter: 'One does not plan and then try to make circumstances fit these plans. One tries to make plans fit the circumstances.'

One thing seems beyond argument: there was an almost complete failure of Supreme Command, progressively more serious from 1st August onwards. Perhaps it was unavoidable in the peculiar growth of the whole 'Overlord' plan and its massive logistical timings. However that may be, there was also a breakdown in command by the two principal army group commanders. Both Bradley and Montgomery were so concerned with their own opportunities, so jealous of the priorities of supplies, so suspicious, that they jeopardized the authority of the Supreme Command. And both men failed to command their army groups as groups. Bradley was virtually backing Patton and the 3rd Army, while Montgomery was more like a Commander-in-Chief of the 2nd Army, than the commander of an army group. Thus both the U.S. 1st Army and the Canadian 1st Army, pursued their courses on their

---

[1] Ehrman: *Grand Strategy*, vol. v, pp. 526-528.

own, the one doggedly involved in the complex of Aachen, the other even more doggedly involved in the muddy, dreary and bloody struggle on the southern approaches of the Schelde estuary.

In that light, whatever the merits of the Field-Marshal's arguments for a 'Ground Force Commander', neither Montgomery nor Bradley were fitted for such a role.

CHAPTER TEN

Arnhem

I

IT is, I believe, impossible for anyone to be completely objective about history, and especially about war. To regard events with a clear impartiality seems to demand a negation of self, the elimination of a personal point of view or attitude of mind. Moreover, war is a deliberate exercise in violence, involving death and obscenity, on a scale to numb the sensibilities of most men. While in the heat of battle these things may be 'forgotten', they surge into the mind in retrospect. The armies consist of people. Everytime they move against the enemy some of these people are blown to bits, mutilated, cleanly killed, while others take refuge in hysteria and various forms of shock. It is remarkable that the majority of men caught up in this monumental violence retain their balance, their *sang froid*, their humour, their will to advance day after day into death, and to kill without much thought, while living in conditions of discomfort, danger and squalor.

Within my limitations I attempt to recall the events and the 'feel' of the situation in the days between 3rd September and 17th September. In these fourteen days, even in the first seven of them, but in my strong feeling in the first three of them, the hopes of quick victory expired and the chances were lost. It is certain that the exultation infecting the armoured divisions gave way to more normal feelings, to a reaction, at first a kind of vacuum of relief, hard to define. The defences essential to a soldier in battle were down. In some way almost everyone had expected the war to be over, and it wasn't. There was a period immediately in the wake of triumph when troops adjusted to the likelihood, and finally to the certainty, of a long struggle ahead, and began to prepare themselves for further ordeals.

The infantry had not shared the exultation of the armour.

Their progress, inevitably, had been less spectacular, far more uncomfortable and seldom 'safe' in the sense that the armour had felt safe. As the armoured columns roared through the villages of France and Belgium the troops had tasted absolute victory. Here and there lorried infantry moved off the roads to round up a demoralized enemy. Enemy transport, mainly horse drawn, was blown to bits; individuals dashing out of side turnings like bewildered animals caught by the hunt were either crumpled to ugly heaps of old clothes, or simply ignored.

The progress of the infantry, 'mopping up', being shot at, however desultorily, was very different. In some ways it is very disconcerting to be under sporadic fire, fire without pattern, and coming from anywhere at anytime. A battle is a battle. But for many miles the infantry advanced through still dangerous country. Houses, barns, trees, gave cover to occasional fanatics or dedicated soldiers determined to 'take someone with them'. The will to die seems at times even more powerful than the will to live. Bridgeheads, though seldom if ever strongly held, at times offered brief and fierce resistance. In such conditions a man begins to think too much of danger, and acquires a conscious distaste for being killed, as it were by pure chance. And someone must be killed.

In short, it was a dangerous time for morale, and it is at such times that the rigours of training and discipline that most of us feel are ridiculous in peace time, may pay high dividends. I mean the training that calls men sharply to march at attention after a long and gruelling route march, combined with TEWTS,[1] and a period of marching at ease. This happens about one mile short of 'home'. That last mile must be covered as briskly and smartly as the first mile out of camp. Men intensely weary, sore, often with bleeding feet, must stride out, limps must disappear, shoulders must be braced, heavy rifles must appear to be weightless. And then, the slow and perfect dismissal. It seems like pure cruelty, but it is often the basis of winning a battle, particularly the next battle. The longing to rest must be brutally smashed, thoughts must be driven out, men must be driven, and in the end by themselves. War is a brutal and terrible business. It is about killing, and it has to be

[1] Tactical exercise with or without troops.

also about 'duty' unquestioned. In a very real sense the minds of all concerned, including the minds of leaders, must be converted to a new currency. Men must believe absolutely in the rightness of their cause. They must be ready to give their lives, and the moment they ask 'what for', all is lost.

Several factors became evident and obvious in the first few days of fighting on the Belgian-Dutch border country. It is flat open country, laced with waterways, and the maps are networks of blue lines. No man, one feels, could possibly talk about 'cracking about' in such country, and yet Field-Marshal Montgomery did talk about it in these terms, and especially in regard to the North German plain, his target. When his armies finally reached the North German plain they built five hundred bridges between the Rhine and the Elbe. Holland is worse. At Gheel, where the 15th Scottish division relieved 50th division in the bridgehead, there was stiff fighting. I do not know how stiff it was on the 5th and 6th September because I was not there, but on the 7th, the enemy was very definitely resisting strongly. We did not know then that the enemy was near his last gasp, almost without guns, ammunition, and totally without reserves, and that if the brittle crust of this renewed resistance on the canal lines was broken, there would be no enemy for miles. Indeed it is very difficult to believe the assessments of their condition made by the enemy commanders. The hopeless situation of the enemy was not apparent to the leading platoons and companies seeking to establish solid bridgeheads in the region of Gheel. It was a key point midway between the Albert canal and the Junction canal, and two roads out of Gheel to the north led to crossings of the Junction canal at places named Aart and Rethy, distances of $2\frac{1}{2}$ to 3 miles. At these points the infantry met mortar, machine gun and rifle fire, supported by self-propelled guns. By the 14th and 15th of the month the enemy was still resisting the establishment of a solid bridgehead across the Junction canal with intense ferocity. Counter-attacks came in against the British flanks. Looking back it seems that the enemy had discovered a higher morale than ever before at the moment when British morale was in decline, manifest in an instinct to move with caution. Perhaps, if it had been known that there was nothing more than a crust of enemy to break through the infantry would have found inspiration. Almost certainly lives would have been saved, for boldness usually pays. Yet some would have been killed.

It is not for me, or for any man, to criticize men for wishing to stay alive, but it is almost certainly true that what might have been achieved at a cost of ten men on 4th-5th September demanded the price of one hundred men by the 14th-15th—all along the line. Severe casualties were sustained by the lead battalions of the 15th Scottish at Aart and Rethy on the 15th.

There was a remarkable under-estimation of the difficulties of the water obstacles. The country on a 1 in 250,000 map looks vastly different from the same country on a 1 in 25,000. It is the difference between looking at an object with the naked eye and through powerful binoculars. On an 'enlargement' by a battalion I.O. the country is under a microscope, and this land of waterways, seemingly endless dykes, canal joins and junctions, saturated lands, swamps and exposed roads, was very depressing. Moreover it is flat. It was easily predictable that infantry would be faced with an arduous and deadly task as soon as the enemy found his bearings. By the 8th September, the enemy had begun to find new strength, and by the 17th, he had not only found his bearings, but had organized a defensive system, reinforced by elements of the German 15th Army escaping across the Scheldt estuary and through the narrow, but still open neck of the Bevelands. Whatever anyone may believe about the priority of Antwerp, or the choice between Antwerp and Arnhem, it surely must be clear that the German 15th Army should have been roped off. It was not.

By the 7th September Montgomery had begun to re-group, the 11th Armoured division moving east out of Antwerp to take up a position on the right, or eastern flank of 30th Corps on the centre line facing due north from Beeringen towards Eindhoven, and on. The 50th division, having been relieved by the 15th Scottish in the Gheel bridgehead, also moved east to the right flank. Thus in the minds of the beholders, anxious to know 'what next', it became clear that the form up was 30th Corps in the centre with 8th Corps on the right and 12th Corps on the left. The Guards Armoured division, gaining a bridgehead at de Groote completed the picture. The enemy could see it also. The strike would be due north out of de Groote. On the 17th September, with the British 1st Airborne division landing north of Arnhem, and the U.S. 82nd and 101st Airborne divisions landing astride the main road from Eindhoven to Nijmegen, the enemy knew beyond a doubt exactly the line and exactly what he had to fear.

On the 16th September, Lieut.-General Horrocks, commanding 30th Corps, held his 'O' (Order) Group at Bourg Leopold. The Corps Commander was in an exuberant mood:

'This is a tale you will tell your grandchildren,' he began, and grinned: 'And mighty bored they'll be!'

The broad outline of the plan seems to have been swiftly forgotten. A carpet of airborne troops would be layed astride the road from Eindhoven to Arnhem to seize crossings of five major water-ways, the Wilhelmina canal, the Zuidwillemsvaart canal, the rivers Maas, the Waal and Neder Rijn—the Rhine. 30th Corps, following an armoured dash through a corridor little more than the width of the road, and horribly vulnerable to counter-attacks on both flanks, would join up with the 1st Airborne division and advance out of the Arnhem bridgehead, establish a northern flank on the Zuider Zee, and on the Ijssel. Meanwhile the 52nd 'Mountain' division, having trained for an 'Air Portable' rôle, after years of training for mountain warfare, would be flown in north of Arnhem. At the same time 8th Corps on the right and 12th Corps on the left would fill the flanks of 30th Corps.

The daring and dangers of this plan were very clear, and even startling, quite out of character with Montgomery's extreme caution. While 30th Corps would advance with great speed (for if it failed to do so the whole plan must fail) up a single road, Eindhoven, Son, Veghel, Grave, Nijmegen, Arnhem, the flanking corps would be struggling up over the most difficult country, without benefit of airborne troops to pave the way. It was certain that the flanks would be open for a period of days, and that 30th Corps would be extremely vulnerable. In fact 8th Corps on the right was only level with Eindhoven when 30th Corps was at Nijmegen. 12th Corps on the left was even slower. Thus the escaped divisions of the German 15th Army were able to harass the 30th Corps line of march to some purpose while hastily formed 'battle groups' of enemy harassed very effectively from the east. These battle groups consisted of up to ten panther tanks with infantry in company strength, or

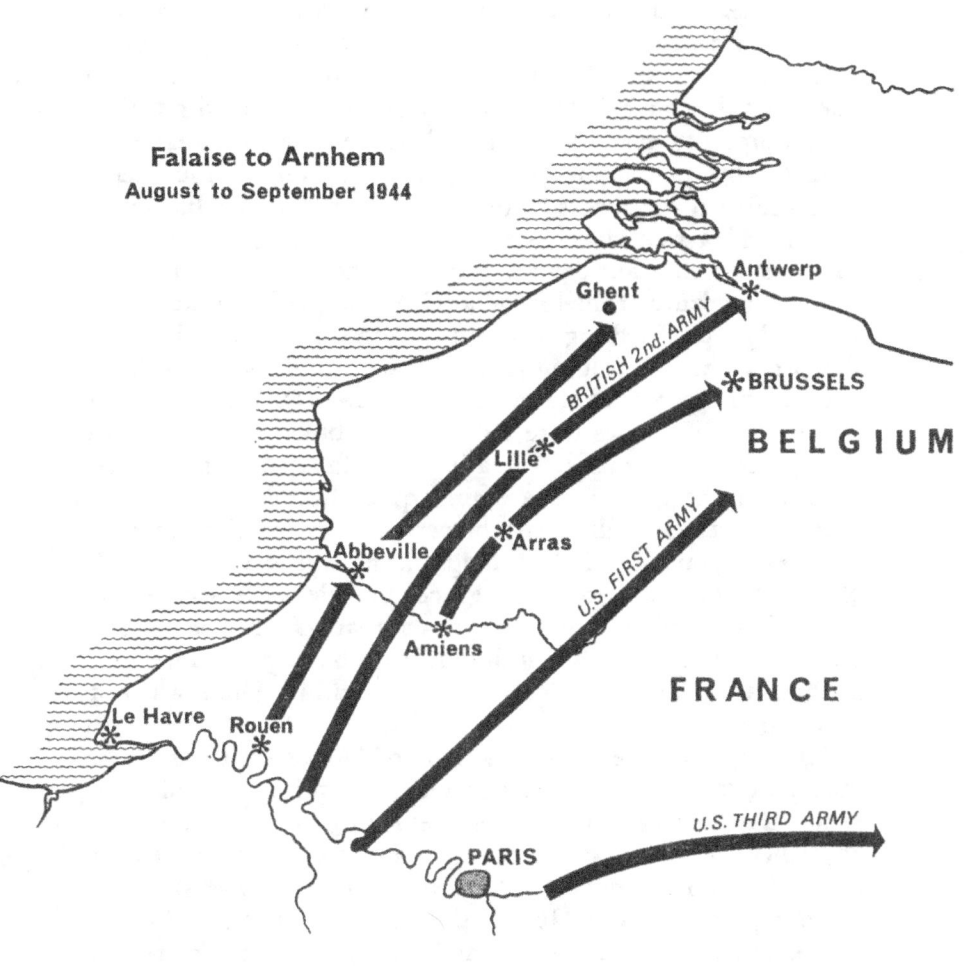

slightly more. One of these groups virtually held up an army between Son and Veghel on and off for two days.[1] At the same time the bridgehead at Grave remained vulnerable, and the pile up of vehicles on the road from Son to Hechtel, and indeed right back to the beaches, was unbelievable. One wonders what would have happened if it had been necessary to bring forward the transport with the bridging equipment, and how it could possibly have forced its way over a road solid with traffic. The immunity from air attack had been swiftly taken for granted, but one suddenly thought of the miracle the enemy had achieved for weeks, moving reserves into the Battle for Normandy across rivers without a single bridge, over roads subjected to constant devastation from the air.

Yet the seizure of the bridge at Grave seemed a miracle, and the bridge itself a thing of beauty. War is such an ugly thing that we have to deck it out in bright colours whenever possible, and it was easily possible on the three days from 18th to 21st September. The skies were still a gentle blue, and filled with many coloured parachutes floating gracefully to earth, spaced by little puffs of smoke, seeming quite harmless. It was as though the sky was filled with flowers. Nijmegen bridge seemed the greatest miracle of all, a magnificent object, its great arch of latticed steel soaring with grace and elegance astride the Waal. The gaping hole torn in its roadway by an enemy bomb seemed a minor blemish, adding a flavour of excitement as the leading armour edged bravely round it. There was not much to spare.

There was no feeling or thought of failure on those days. Surely these things were miracle enough, and how should one expect a further and greater miracle. And I think that on these days there was in all the leading troops a sense of relief that they had won so much. But in fact Nijmegen was the real beginning, not the end. It was the start line of the real plan, and understandably there was no 'start', and even this bridgehead was not secured without a long and bitter struggle.

---

[1] The author, driving a soft skin vehicle, ran the gauntlet of this battle group on the road from Veghel to Son. Burning vehicles along the way provided some sort of smoke-screen. Enemy armour was clearly visible and streams of tracer made a lazy arch over the open road.

II

This bold operation, bearing its rural code name, 'Market Garden', began on 17th September with the Guards armour breaking out of the de Groote bridgehead and speeding north, after an initial set-back, to relieve the airborne troops dropping from the skies from Eindhoven to Arnhem. There was very little time, say a maximum of three days from start to finish and with three major rivers, two canals and a score of lesser waterways to cross. Success must depend upon the ability of the airborne troops to seize all the major bridges intact. Bridging the three major rivers for the passage of armour would be an immense task, and it had to be faced, even expected. Three Army Groups Royal Engineers were held in readiness with 2,277 trucks loaded with equipment.

I think that it was predictable that if these resources had to be used the operation must fail.

Rocket firing Typhoons blasted the Guards out of the bridgehead, while an artillery barrage rolled ahead. It did not prevent well-concealed enemy self-propelled guns from knocking out eight tanks on the road. It was 'a glorious lazy Sunday morning' wrote the Commander of the 1st British Airborne division, preparing to embark upon his brave enterprise. 'Two days,' Montgomery had told him. 'They'll be up with you by then.'

'We can hold it for four,' General Browning, the Corps commander, had said. 'But I think we might be going a bridge too far.'

Too far or not it was the core and purpose of Montgomery's plan to go much farther.

It had become a matter of great importance to get the 1st Airborne division into action. It had suffered too many false starts and alarms. 'By September, 1944,' General Urquhart wrote,[1] 'My division was battle-hungry to a degree which only those who have commanded large forces of trained soldiers can fully comprehend. In fact, there were already signs of that dangerous mixture of boredom and cynicism creeping into our daily lives ... Certainly, it is impossible to over-emphasize

---
[1] Major-General R. E. Urquhart: *Arnhem*.

G

the ultimate significance of this procession of operations that never were. In the cold afterlight the historian and military critic has his licence to juggle the arithmetical equations of battle. Only the participant can adequately apportion the invisible factors, such as the effects of sixteen cancelled operations in a row.'

I doubt whether anyone, participant or not, may judge these invisible factors. They were there, and they always are. The most serious factor was the lack of sufficient air transport to drop the 1st Airborne division as a division. It would, perforce, land piece-meal. In the event some of it would not land at all, and its reinforcements, the 52nd Mountain division, would not progress beyond another cancelled alert. The responsibility for the decision to rob the 1st Airborne division of air transport, rather than either one or other or both of the 82nd and 101st Airborne divisions, must rest with the Corps commander. Possibly it was based on National prides and prejudices rather than a cool assessment of priorities.

Yet on that 'glorious Sunday morning' no one could have said that the omens were bad, and no one, I think, can ever honestly say that there was any bad luck attendant upon the whole operation. Its failures were inherent.

The plan was to use the 43rd division in the forward role as soon as the armour had opened the way, and it is worth examining the strength of the division and its orders. In addition to its normal Establishment of three infantry brigades plus divisional troops, the 8th Armoured Brigade,[1] the Royal Netherlands Brigade Group, plus 147th Field Regiment, R.A., 64th Medium Regiment, R.A. and one heavy battery, were under command for the operation. The mind of the division was focused *north* of Arnhem as its arena of battle. Its role was to seize crossings over the Ijssel, while an infantry brigade would take up a position south of Apeldoorn. The division would then face both east and west.

In fact the division was never within sight of its target, even though it found itself excused from major bridging roles by the success of the Airborne divisions in seizing the principal bridges. On the 19th, the division, still stuck in its forward assembly area, was warned that it must be ready to aid the hard pressed

[1] Less the Sherwood Rangers.

Guards armour and U.S. paratroops in the Nijmegen bridgehead. Thus by the time the division began to move on the 20th the operation was already on the brink of failure. Progress was slow, not only due to the monumental congestion on the single road north, and enemy action beyond Eindhoven, but also to the greetings of the wildly excited 'liberated' Dutch. In the streets of Nijmegen, when the leading troops of 43 division finally reached the town on the 21st, the exuberant inhabitants were a greater obstacle to speed than the enemy. On the afternoon of that day a troop of Irish Guards had crossed the great bridge over the Waal while paratroopers gained the railway bridge to the west. These were deeds of great daring in the face of a resolute enemy on the north bank.

Thus the way across the Waal and on to the 'Island' was open for the leading brigade of 43rd division. Less than ten miles remained over the 'causeway' road from Nijmegen through Elst to Arnhem, but the armour could not move on it. On the 22nd, the leading battalions of infantry, amply supported by artillery and with as much armour as they could use, were struggling to reach the Neder Rijn by way of Valborg and the network of difficult roads through the orchard and dyke complex of the 'Island' to Driel, Hetern and Randwijk. On the morning of the 22nd, two troops of Household Cavalry reached the banks of the Neder Rijn under cover of the morning mist. It seemed to indicate that where they might venture others might win through also. Tanks were too often 'sitting ducks' on the embanked roads. It was a task for infantry, infiltrating the enemy, overwhelming him 'at all costs'. It seemed very slow, and it was much too slow. Even on the 22nd the situation of the 1st Airborne striving to hold a diminishing perimeter on the north bank was desperate in the extreme.

But the slowness in essence was imposed from the outset. 43rd division lay massed with its 5,000 vehicles in the region of Hechtel. An enormous array of troops was assembling ready for the word 'go' from about 10th September. That was the time when everyone, in the know or not, had the feeling that something very big was about to happen. Every day the sense of tension, expectation and frustration grew. At the same time troops of 8th and 12th Corps were moving on to their start lines east and west of Hechtel, ready for action.

On the 19th, just before 43rd division began to try to move, an officer of *Phantom*[1] estimated that there were 18,000 vehicles nose to tail between Eindhoven and the de Groote bridgehead. Eindhoven itself was pack-jammed with vehicles from armour to jeeps. No division, not even a battalion, could have passed through this mass, and on the 20th, the road was cut between Son and Eindhoven. On that day the leading troops of 8th Corps had reached a point near Helmond, eight miles E.N.E. of Eindhoven, while 12th Corps was heaving itself slowly and doggedly over equally difficult country. Thus the flanks were wide open and unguarded over the vital road from Eindhoven to Nijmegen, and sections of the road were under fire from both flanks. As late as the 25th, a powerful group of enemy cut the road near St. Oedenrode, forcing the Guards to send back armour from Nijmegen. It was a dangerously uncomfortable situation, yet it is probable that the enemy groups south of Nijmegen had no clear direction and purpose, and were mainly concerned to link up with whatever forces remained to the north and east.

Thus the operation had seemed doomed to failure after the second day, yet it seemed then, and it seems now, that the Guards armour went farther and faster than anyone could have planned or reasonably expected. Up to and including Nijmegen the advance of the ground troops, and the seizure of the great bridge over the Maas at Grave, even though a detour was necessary to bridge the link canal at Neerbosch, three miles south of Nijmegen, was better than good. Yet it was not nearly enough. To have bridged the Maas and Waal would have imposed a further delay of at least 24 hours, and must have been expected. It never seemed likely that the 1st Airborne division could have been reached in less than four days, and that only by miraculous fortune.

Moreover it is difficult to argue that the Guards armour and the infantry of 43rd division failed to press on with sufficient resolution. They were not short of inspiration, but progress was agonizingly slow. Everyone knew that it was too late, and that the plan had failed. It was no longer a 'dash' to gain the vital bridgehead over the Rhine, but a desperate struggle to save the remnants of the only British Airborne division. Signals

[1] G.H.Q. Liaison. See R. J. T. Hills: *Phantom was There*, Arnold, 1951.

were appalling, and there was almost no news at all. The fact is that 'the island' between Nijmegen and Arnhem is a dirty piece of country, a tight patchwork of mud and water, with orchards making a maze of little islands giving fine cover to the enemy in possession. It was difficult, if not impossible, to deploy armour, and for the first time close air support was lacking. In short it was a hard slog for infantry in grim and depressing conditions, with the enemy having the advantage of terrain. And there was no time for a hard slog. If the 1st Airborne was to be relieved the armour would have had to burst through like a bomb, and the enemy 'exploded' out of their tight positions. It was not possible. It is doubtful if the Arnhem bridge could have been taken even as late as the 20th.

No doubt it seemed intolerably slow to the hard pressed paratroopers holding out in a steadily diminishing perimeter on the north bank of the Neder Rijn, without sleep, without news, and under incessant mortar fire. A desperate band of men had held on to the north end of the bridge, and finally survived in buildings in the vicinity. In all the circumstances Major-General Urquhart, commanding the airborne division, is fully entitled to his view:

'Even when one has taken into account every possible setback,' he wrote, 'the fact remains that we were alone for much longer than any airborne division is designed to stay. I think it is possible that for once Horrocks's enthusiasm was not transmitted adequately to those who served under him, and it may be that some of his more junior officers and N.C.O.s did not fully comprehend the problem and the importance of great speed. By and large, the impression is that they were "victory happy". They had advanced northwards very fast and had been well received by the liberated peoples, and they were now out of touch with the atmosphere of bullets and battles . . . At first, the opposition seems to have caused them a certain amount of shock and surprise.'[1]

There may be truth in this, but it is assumption, and not based on observation. The plain fact is that the 1st airborne division had been parachuted out upon a hopeless and impossible limb in accordance with a vain and irresponsibly optimistic plan, inadequately thought out. The 1st Airborne division

[1] Urquhart: *Arnhem*, p. 203.

held out for nearly nine days, and the 4th Dorsets, crossing the Neder Rijn under heavy fire on the 25th September, helped many of the survivors back across the river to safety. The greater task, the true role and object of 43rd division north of Arnhem had never been more than a mirage.

In summing up the roots of failure, Major-General Essame, the historian of 43rd Wessex division, and the commander of one of the brigades on the 'Island' north of Nijmegen, concluded:[1] 'That at the decisive moment the Corps commander lacked adequate forces was no fault of his, the Army commander's or the Field-Marshal's. It will be recollected that after crossing the Seine, the Supreme Command had compromised and given part of the Allied resources to General Patton's thrust and part to Field-Marshal Montgomery's. Had the entire effort been placed in the hands of the Field-Marshal he might have ended the campaign in the autumn of 1944. He himself thought so and he is not given to rash statements.'

As an assessment of military failure this is pure military claptrap of a kind to which the British people are addicted. There were far more troops available than could be brought to bear. The difficulty in an assessment now lies partly in the recognition of hindsight, and an attempt to think back to the situation as it seemed at the time, and the knowledge then available. The fault lay with the 'Plan'. First, an appreciation of enemy strength was bound to conclude that the enemy would muster his most powerful resources in defence of the great river lines of the Maas, Waal and Neder Rijn, while being unable to muster, or to organize, sufficient resources to form more than shallow delaying crusts on the canals and minor streams to the south. Thus it was clear at the time that the greatest available Allied strength would be demanded in the north, and that the strength available to, and deployable by, the commanders was concentrated at the wrong end of the operation, at the start and not at the finish. Those, therefore, who must hold out the longest at the focal points of enemy strength, and in the most exposed position, were the least equipped to do so.

If one is willing to concede that a bridgehead might have been seized at Arnhem as late as 17th-18th September, and that

[1] Essame: *The 43rd Wessex division at War, 1944-45*, p. 132.

a further advance to the Zuider Zee in accordance with the 'Object' of the operation, was a reasonable gamble, then it must be clear that the vital bridges are those at Nijmegen and Arnhem, and of these I would suggest that Nijmegen was of the greatest initial importance, for without seizing the Nijmegen bridge swiftly and eliminating the enemy between Nijmegen and Arnhem, all else must fail. Even had the 1st Airborne division been able to deploy its full strength as a division, seize and hold the bridge at Arnhem, and the airfield at Deelen for the landing of the 52nd Mountain division in support, failure at Nijmegen and on the 'Island' would surely enable the enemy to eliminate the isolated British troops. The sustained and substantial supply of such a body of troops from the air would have been supremely difficult, if not impossible. The presence of the enemy armoured divisions refitting in the vicinity of Arnhem was well known, and the fact that this would be in effect 'the last battle' (if lost), the virtual end of Nazi Germany in the west, would have forced Field-Marshal Model and the High Command to concentrate all possible force against this threat. Two divisions, isolated, lacking in air support and starved of supplies, would not have had a reasonable chance.

Thus I would conclude that the failure was not at Arnhem but at Nijmegen and on the 'Island'. First, the significance of the Reichswald forest immediately to the east of Nijmegen was fully appreciated. Powerful enemy counter-attacks were expected from that quarter, and it was this threat that forced General Gavin, commanding the U.S. 82nd Airborne division, to concentrate two of his brigades on that flank. This left him too weak to carry Nijmegen and the southern defences of the bridge by a *coup de main*. Even so, with the arrival of the Guards six battalions were immediately available for an assault on the road and railway bridges. At that time there was not more than a company of enemy, well dug in, and well supported by carefully sited flak and S.P. guns defending the northern exits of the road and railway bridges. They could not prevent U.S. paratroops forcing a crossing over the railway bridge and planting their flag at the northern end of the road bridge.

I do not believe that anyone may seriously question the achievement of the U.S. 82nd Airborne division, or the decisions of its commander. The division did all that could be expected of it. It secured and held the dangerous eastern flank. It kept the defenders of Nijmegen and the bridge very busy until the arrival of the Guards armour enabled heavy, and finally successful, attacks to be mounted. In short, it was not reasonable to expect the Nijmegen bridge to be taken, or a river crossing of the Waal to be established before the arrival of the ground troops, and yet the success of the Arnhem operation depended upon it.

For the operation to succeed the Nijmegen and Arnhem bridges had to be seized and the way opened. To succeed in this substantial forces would have had to be landed astride the bridges, that is, on the 'Island' as well as north and south of the rivers. The terrain of the 'Island' was well known. It was rejected as unsuitable for landing gliderborne or paratroops, 'a mistaken assessment' in the opinion of Major-General Urquhart. 'In fact it would have been perfectly feasible for a limited number of gliders to have landed in the vicinity of the bridge. Despite the flak, it might have paid us to have accepted even quite heavy casualties in order to get men south of the bridge. It would have been cheaper in the long run.'[1]

In the event the Polish airborne brigade did land south of the Neder Rijn near Elst. It was much too late, for the 1st Airborne had already lost control of the ferry point by which they could have crossed to reinforce. The landing near Elst was also unfortunate, for the Poles were immediately engaged not only by the enemy, but with some of our own troops of 43rd division whom they mistook for enemy.

Nevertheless a powerful force landing on the 'Island' on the first day, and not later than the second day, coupled with a powerful force on Arnhem itself, would have sufficed to seize the bridge. 'I doubt, however,' wrote Urquhart, 'in view of the strong opposition and the time taken by corps, whether anything less than a whole division, plus the Polish Brigade, would have been able to hold the bridge area until the arrival of the 2nd Army. We still would not have been able to prevent a certain amount of German movement towards Nijmegen from the Reichswald Forest.'[2]

In the event the 1st Airborne division never had more than

[1] Urquhart: *Arnhem*, p. 199.
[2] Urquhart: *Arnhem*, p. 201.

one brigade effectively available for the main task. The division was forced on to the defensive. The landing and dropping zones were too far away from the main target area, and the Reconnaissance Force, especially briefed for the task of seizing the bridge, landed without its transport, and its role was taken over by a battalion. The brigades coming in to land on the second and third lifts were immediately involved in the defence of the landing zones. The airfield at Deelen could not be captured. With or without supplies the venture was doomed.

Finally, could the Guards armour spearheading the advance of 30th Corps have made greater speed? I don't think so. The delays from Eindhoven had been no greater than must have been expected, and much less than many expected. How then would it have been possible to produce the Guards armour at Arnhem in time to support the 1st Airborne division on 19th September, as Montgomery had assured the divisional commander? Or on the 20th or 21st? On what possible appreciation of the enemy situation, and of the canal and river crossings, could such a result have been planned? It would have been a miracle, a fast run for armour unimpeded by an enemy, as it had been on much of the dash to Brussels. But in mid-September the enemy was no longer in confusion. There had been time to reorganize. Even so the enemy strength between Eindhoven and Nijmegen was very modest, and mainly of nuisance value.

To have turned the enemy flank in the north, seizing the bridgeheads on the way, would have demanded daring of a high order in conception, in leadership in the field, and in execution. The conception of such a plan was impossible for a man of Montgomery's innate caution. The painful truth is that the British 1st Airborne division was stupidly squandered, dropped into the enemy's lap beyond the limits of the ground troops in a doomed effort to make up for lost time. There had been a first chance, and it had been lost when the armour failed to drive on to seize the canal crossings while the enemy was on the run. It would have demanded an immense effort and outstanding leadership, and it is by such efforts and leadership at the critical hour that great victories are won.

In fact, Montgomery's decision to mount the operation aimed at the Zuider Zee was as startling as it would have been for an elderly and saintly Bishop suddenly to decide to take up safe-breaking, and begin on the Bank of England. He did not lapse again, but acted always with extreme caution, culminating in his massive build-up and preparation for his crossing of the Rhine.

Montgomery's misfortune was in the ease with which he was able to rationalize failure, and never to learn from it. Thus his failure to destroy the remnants of the Afrika Corps after 2nd Alamein was due, not to his extreme caution, but to the weather. His failure to turn the enemy flank in the Arnhem adventure, or even to rescue the Airborne division, became a 90% success. It was not difficult to sustain this view 'in the field' because very few of those involved had a sense of failure, which was not compatible with 21st Army group's official praise describing the operation as 'a magnificent achievement brought about by the actions, so brilliantly co-ordinated and executed, of the Guards armoured and the 82nd U.S. Airborne divisions.'

And finally, there was the 'Dunkirk' rescue of 2,000 men of the 1st Airborne division on the orders of General Dempsey. For more than a week survivors, weary, hungry, ragged and often soaked to their skins, straggled into the British lines, having swum two rivers and negotiated the difficult and dangerous country in between. Day after day the enemy mounted desperate efforts to destroy the Nijmegen bridge by air attack, and by the daring of 'frogmen' swimming to place explosive charges. Unflagging vigilance was demanded and given, and the slow work of consolidation began.

CHAPTER ELEVEN

The Price of Failure

I

By the end of September, Field-Marshal Montgomery had run out of options, and had lost the strategic and tactical initiative. Characteristically he failed, or refused, to recognize his condition, and while the urgent need to open the great port of Antwerp was grimly evident to everyone but himself, it was clear that he would abandon his vision of a major assault north of the Ruhr with great reluctance. This obsessive singleness of mind and purpose would prove a strength as well as a weakness, enabling him to maintain his objective through all the crippling vicissitudes of winter.

Meanwhile, ironically, he had established the 'Broad Front' strategy he abhorred, and the Supreme Commander, while expressing and experiencing growing concern about the long delayed opening of Antwerp, could accept Montgomery's jaunty estimate of his Arnhem failure as a 90% success.

This, of course, was to look at the whole operation not only out of its context, but with extreme myopia. It was also, I believe, an indication of a sense of relief. Things might have been a great deal worse, for the price of victory might have been far more grave than the price of failure. Without Antwerp no improvement in the supply situation all along the line could be hoped for, and it was a nightmarish thought that the British 2nd Army might have been stretched out over a narrow corridor 100 miles long from the Belgian-Dutch frontier to the Zuider Zee, short of supplies and reinforcements and horribly vulnerable. The plight of the four divisions north of Arnhem would certainly have been perilous, and possibly disastrous.[1] The enemy had revealed remarkable powers of recovery in the north and east, and was fighting with a new resolution and

[1] The Guards Armoured: the 43rd, the 52nd, the 1st Airborne.

ferocity, while in the west the German 15th Army, under the new leadership of General von Zangen, was not only virtually intact, but had successfully extricated 80,000 men and 600 guns across the Scheldt under constant air attack. At the same time powerful elements were still holding resolutely to a pocket south of the Scheldt from Breskens to the coast, and compelling the Canadians to a grim struggle for every yard of water-logged earth. To the north of Antwerp von Zangen had sealed off the narrow neck of the Beveland Isthmus and established powerful defensive positions based upon Woensdrecht. It was agonizing to remember that all this had been wide open a month earlier. A bitter struggle lay ahead, costly in time and lives.

The unescapable truth is that Antwerp and Arnhem had been a double failure, compromising the strategic and tactical possibilities of the 21st and 12th Army Groups, and dispelling the last hopes of early victory. The realities of Antwerp in early September had been sacrificed in exchange for Montgomery's unreal vision of Arnhem and the Zuider Zee.

For the enemy the overwhelming confrontation with total disaster had been dispelled, and the situation was one of immense relief. They had withstood the whirlwind and had won vital time. With the Russian armies pressing inexorably from the east and the Allied armies in the west certain to regain their balance, they could not hope for more. Field-Marshal Model, and old von Runstedt recalled to service on the western front, had every cause for grim satisfaction. They could look forward with some confidence to an autumn and winter of consolidation of the Siegfried defences, while the genius of von Speer provided replacements of arms, armour and ammunition. Manpower would be an increasingly pressing problem, but it would be a problem also for the Allies.

Thus the Allied position in early October was far from enviable. A bitter winter of attrition lay ahead, reluctantly and slowly understood, the Allies estimating hopefully the extent of the unbearable casualties they could inflict upon the weakening enemy, failed at first to pay sufficient regard to their own condition. Attrition was a double-headed coin. From October to the middle of December the Allied armies all along the line were locked in head on collision with an enemy defending a maze of concrete emplacements threaded through networks of villages and townships, the industrial complexes of the Roer and Saar valleys, and water-lines veining the entire battlefield from north to south and from east to west. It was hideous territory, made worse by appalling weather conditions, drenching icy rain, bitter cold, sleet and seas of mud, swollen rivers and the constant threat of disastrous floods. While the enemy controlled the Roer dams in the region of the Hurtgen forest on the U.S. 1st Army front, one hundred and sixty million cubic metres of water could be released to rage down the ravine of the Roer and create an impassable flood barrier to seal off the Cologne plain. Further north the water prospects were equally unpromising, and would enable the enemy to cordon off vast areas. Trench foot added significantly to American casualty figures, and all gains were measured in yards and lives. Steadily throughout November the weather worsened.

Meanwhile Montgomery's concentration on the east, and his evident reluctance to face the challenge of Antwerp, inhibited October planning and held the armies virtually to day-to-day tactical moves as supplies or opportunities offered. The Reichswald forest, confronting the British 2nd Army across the Maas, was almost the only dry land in the north, and the Field-Marshal's chosen battlefield. The flanks of the Allies were now clearly defined from Nijmegen to Basle, but it was necessary for the 2nd Army to anchor their northern flank securely. This called for a minimum of two divisions on the 'Island' between Nijmegen and Arnhem, and the elimination of the enemy threat from the Reichswald forest. It would take the 2nd Army at least six to eight weeks to 'tidy up' on the line of the Maas, and perhaps even longer to defeat the enemy stubbornly defending west of the Maas at Venlo and Roermond. Thus the immediate tasks of the 2nd Army and the U.S. 9th Army on its right flank were evident without definition. Both armies must close the Maas, and remember that beyond that great river lay the Ems and the Erft and a host of lesser waterways. Water everywhere was the enemy's most potent weapon. South of the Ardennes, Patton had enmeshed his army in the fortifications of Metz, while struggling to master the flood waters of the Moselle and move against the Saar. In the centre the 1st Army was becoming entangled in the defences of Aachen. The Ardennes was bare, inducing the Supreme Commander to remark a month later that there might be a danger of a 'nastly little Kasserine'.[1]

October threatened to be, and became, a frustrating month of re-appraisal, command arguments, and a loss of initiative all along the line. The promise of early victory had gone and a new strategy had to be established. On the 20th October, the Combined Chiefs of Staff meeting in Washington had finally abandoned all hopes of winning the war in 1944. Briefly they had considered the possible effects of the introduction of 'new weapons', and 'the elimination of those strategic air force operations which did not effect an immediate reduction in German capabilities.'[2] Yet the Combined Chiefs of Staff, while abandoning hope with evident reluctance, still clung to hope. In a personal message to Eisenhower, General Marshall urged the Supreme Commander to 'be frank with me', handing the final decision to him. The Supreme Commander, acutely aware of the serious logistical situation, had no hesitation in emphasizing the unlikelihood of early victory. Antwerp was the *sine qua non*.

At the same time the British Joint Planning Staff was reaching the conclusion that the earliest possible date for ending the war was the 31st January, 1945, or May, 1945. No all out effort would be possible without Antwerp.

On 28th October, the Supreme Commander, having reviewed the position, and basing his hopes on the early opening of Antwerp, to which at long last Montgomery was giving his attention, issued a Directive which was a clear expression of the Broad Front Strategy. He had discussed the possibilities with Bradley ten days earlier, and for the first time the main role was given to the U.S. armies. The U.S. 1st Army would attempt to establish a bridgehead south of Cologne, while the U.S. 9th Army under Simpson and now in the line would protect the left flank of the U.S. 1st Army and the right flank of the British 2nd Army from Sittard to Aachen. Operations throughout November would be directed south of the Ruhr

---

[1] A reference to the defeat of a U.S. Armoured division in the Kasserine Pass in Tunisia.

[2] Pogue: *The Supreme Command*, p. 307 '... release of weapons whose use had hitherto been restricted for security reasons ...'

with the object of closing the Rhine. This meant the final abandonment of the strategy to attack north of the Ruhr that Montgomery had urged upon the Supreme Command from the beginning. For the time being the British 2nd Army was too weak to play a major role. Montgomery had dug his own grave.

In the context of these deliberations Montgomery's behaviour seems unreal. He appeared to live in a world of his own, clinging to his dream of attacking north of the Ruhr long after the dream had lost all substance, but on the 10th October, he had at last begun to emerge and to look somewhat casually westward. In his own account he had 'underestimated' the task of opening Antwerp, and seems vaguely to have imagined that the Canadian 1st Army would do the job, when all the evidence proclaimed that a major effort would be demanded by land, sea and air. The Supreme Commander observed the Field-Marshal with growing misgivings and rising exasperation implicit in his urgent messages of 10th and 13th October in which he 'spelled out' the urgent priority of Antwerp over all other operations.

With an infelicity of timing that was becoming characteristic Montgomery launched into a massive criticism of the Command structure, insisting that operations north of the Ardennes should be under one commander, and suggesting that 12th Army Group's main role should be in the northern theatre. Moreover he continued to maintain that the correct line of assault was north of the Ruhr.

In 'one of his most explicit letters of the war' the Supreme Commander dealt politely but firmly with Montgomery's arguments. He pointed out that the commitments of 21st Army Group left it in no condition to carry out major operations to the east. The task of capturing the Ruhr should be given to 12th Army Group with 21st Army Group in support. These were bitter truths. The Field-Marshal's task was to open Antwerp, and quickly. The whole campaign depended upon it. That was the overwhelming priority upon which there could not be two opinions. Montgomery would not be able to regroup his armies until the task was done.

Finally, the Supreme Commander attempted to put an end, once and for all, to Montgomery's command criticisms. 'I am quite well aware,' he wrote,[1] 'of the powers and limitations of an Allied Command, and if you, as the senior commander in this Theatre of one of the great Allies, feel that my conception and directives are such as to endanger the success of operations, it is our duty to refer the matter to higher authority for any action they may choose to take, however drastic.' In conclusion, Eisenhower wrote: 'It is the job of soldiers, as I see it, to meet their military problems sanely, sensibly, and logically, and while not shutting our eyes to the fact that we are two different nations, produce solutions that permit effective cooperation, mutual support and effective results. Goodwill and mutual confidence are, of course, mandatory.'

Montgomery was not in the least put out. 'You will hear no more on the subject of command from me,' he wrote. 'I have given you my views and you have given your answer. I and all of us will weigh in one hundred per cent to do what you want and we will pull through without a doubt. I have given Antwerp top priority in all operations in 21st Army Group and all energies and efforts will now be devoted towards opening up the place. Your very devoted and loyal subordinate.'

Eisenhower, beginning to know his man, received this message with a sigh of hope, feeling assured of a temporary respite from Montgomery's nagging command arguments. No doubt Montgomery was sincere, but it was not in his nature to keep silent.

Meanwhile on the 18th October, Montgomery met the Supreme Commander in Brussels to discuss the 'modest' objectives to be pursued, and to become the substance of the Supreme Command directive of the 28th October. On the 16th, Montgomery had at last issued his own directive to his troops to open Antwerp and to clear the Scheldt estuary, and by the 23rd, the ugly battle was in full swing. The Canadian 1st Army, reinforced on the left by the 52nd Mountain division, finally going into action in a watery role below sea-level, cleared the Breskens pocket south of the estuary to mount the difficult assault across the Scheldt estuary on the Bevelands and Flushing, while the Canadian right, with the British 1st Corps screening its open flank and closing the Maas, broke the enemy defences barring the Beveland Isthmus at Woensdrecht

[1] Pogue: p. 297.

in one of the bravest and bloodiest battles on the Western front. In terrible conditions and opposed by a resolute enemy in a position of great natural strength, the Canadians together with the British units immediately involved suffered 13,000 casualties in a long and arduous struggle which might have been avoided by bold action two months earlier. The battles of attrition had been costly all along the line, and it was an ugly balance sheet even if it showed a credit in the Allied favour. The U.S. 1st Army had lost 21,000 men mainly in its involvement in the Hürtgen forest, while the U.S. 9th Army had paid with 10,000 men for its limited gains on the right flank of the British 2nd Army. Even in the extreme south de Lattre de Tassigny estimated French losses at 10,000 men.

Meanwhile, since the fall of the city of Antwerp on 4th September, naval diving teams, working in the mud and slime and bitter cold of the docks cleared mines of great variety and ingenuity, and on the 28th November, 85 days after the city and docks had fallen, the first ship sailed into Antwerp. The great build-up of supplies had begun and the stranglehold of logistics was at last about to be broken. This was the essential prelude to a successful assault eastward.[1]

II

At the end of November, and in the first two weeks of December, there was little cause for satisfaction and none for jubilation. The objectives defined on 28th October had not been gained and the enemy could claim the Scheldt, Arnhem, Aachen and Metz as defensive victories. In an abortive and tragically inept battle at Schmidt the U.S. 28th division of the 1st Army had failed to avert the threat to the whole Roer valley posed by enemy control of the Schwammanuel dams near Düren. Indeed the division seemed to have been unaware of the 'object' of its costly and demoralizing battle. This battle, bravely analysed by the Americans, was clear proof, if proof were needed, that the U.S. 1st Army was directly involved in the northern battle. Its failure to seize the Schwammanuel dams would inhibit and threaten the role of

[1] Thompson: *The Eighty-Five Days*, the Battle for the Scheldt.

the U.S. 9th Army on its left in direct support of Montgomery's planned battle for the Reichswald forest and the Rhineland.[1]

Slowly, tediously, in the appalling weather conditions, unprecedented in local memory, the British and Canadians in the north slowly closed the Maas and were still short of the enemy West Wall in the region of Venlo, Roermond and Maesyck. Only at Aachen was there a break-through, but this was of little or no advantage in the complex industrial areas of Düren and Jülich which had suffered some of the worst bombing and artillery bombardments of the war. It could be argued that the U.S. 1st Army involvement was a strategic error, even though it had provided the first landmark of some news value for many weeks. There had been an absence of landmarks throughout the miserable months of October and November when places with drab names no one had heard of became imprinted upon the memories of forward troops, and it was difficult to tell that there had been any gains at all.

As soon as they had been able to disengage from the battle for the Scheldt the Canadians had moved to take over the northern flank of Montgomery's armies, already confined by the release of the Rhine flood-waters. The immediate task of the Canadians was to consolidate and to plan the assault across the Maas from Nijmegen to Gennep, through the Reichswald forest, and to produce the British armies on the west bank of the Rhine from Emmerich to Wesel. The British 30th Corps under Horrocks with the bulk of British 2nd Army under command would provide the massive central push, while the U.S. 9th Army on the right would close the Rhine from Wesel to Dusseldorf and join with the U.S. 1st Army just north of Cologne. This would be the penultimate operation paving the way for the Rhine crossing in the north, the assault upon the Ruhr and the drive into the heart of Germany, the drive to the Elbe. It would demand logistical support on an awe-inspiring and extremely complex scale. The Battle for the Rhineland, code-named 'Operation *Veritable*', would be mounted, Montgomery hoped, in 1944, whatever the weather, and whatever the flood situation of the Rhine and Maas. Yet the speed and success

---

[1] U.S. Army in W.W. 2, 'Special Studies': *Three Battles*. R. W. Thompson: *The Battle for the Rhineland*.

of the whole operation was threatened by enemy control of the Schwammanuel dam complex which must inhibit, and might seriously delay the U.S. 9th Army in its supporting role. This meant that the enemy could wash out the battlefield and maroon the U.S. 9th Army at the crucial moment. It seemed, therefore, that 'Operation *Veritable*' should be planned to go forward without U.S. support if need be.

Throughout November there was a sense of great activity in the headquarters of 21st Army Group, 2nd Army, 30th Corps and Canadian 1st Army, and this sense of activity in the headquarters was in marked contrast to the inactivity and frustrations on the battlefield. It was a winter reminiscent to older soldiers of the 1st World War. Watery, ill-defined landscapes of miserable similarity, seared by biting winds, sleet and torrential rain; networks of dykes, canals, locks, windmills and exposed villages with names like Weert, formed the physical environment of troops for weeks on end. But it seemed to me that the frustrations in the north were less than those in the centre and south. This must be to the credit of Field-Marshal Montgomery. In spite of appearances the British soldier believed in a 'pattern' and in the generalship of the Army Group commander. In the American armies this kind of confidence in leadership was rare, and many men were neither disciplined enough, nor psychologically or physically conditioned to accept the miseries of a dull, and often deadly, routine.

In the south the U.S. 7th Army with the French 1st Army on the right had closed the Rhine from the junction point of the enemy 'West Wall' near Karlsruhe to the Swiss border. But here again was a resolute pocket of enemy holding on grimly west of the Rhine to a difficult area embracing Colmar and Mulhouse. At Strasbourg there was the satisfaction of looking out over the Black Forest, to observe with feelings of strange surprise the movements of ordinary people going about their business in the Nazi Reich. The last battle could not be far away. The 'winning post' was in sight.

To the north of the U.S. 7th Army, Patton's 3rd Army, having at last disentangled from the complex of the Metz fortresses and made good its crossings of the Moselle from Thionville to Nancy, was slogging in a north-easterly direction to come up against the last ditch enemy defences covering the

Saar. Mainz and the road to Frankfurt, always in the minds of Bradley and Patton as the most favourable route into the heart of Germany, remained a very long way off. Certainly they were not better placed than Montgomery in the north, even if it is conceded that there was nothing to choose between Frankfurt and north of the Ruhr. It seemed to be a case of whoever was first on the final start-line, and it was not difficult to see the lining up of the rival Allied armies for the last 'run in'. It was, indeed, manifest at the time especially in 12th Army Group and 3rd Army headquarters. It was the sense of this, rather than the knowledge of it, that so irked Montgomery.

Travelling north to the U.S. 1st Army there was a very real feel of partial isolation, a gap, a sense of detachment from north and south, so that 1st Army seemed to be fighting a battle on its own while the Army Group commander concentrated upon his right wing. Yet the 1st Army's struggle was of paramount importance, and the territory over which it had to fight was perhaps the worst of all, especially in the Hürtgen forest. Here, made clear by the painstaking analysis of the battle for Schmidt, the lack of clear planning and execution from 12th Army Group headquarters downwards reveals an absence of clear objectives and tight command which seriously hampered U.S. units. Whatever the frustrations of British troops there was always a faith in the existence of a clear plan; that if they didn't know what they were meant to be achieving, or where they were going, somebody did.

This great battlefield in its entirety was in the vision of the Supreme Command. This was broadly the shape of the command, compelling Eisenhower to the concept that he must be ready to lead with his right or left, to strike the final blow with either flank, and always poised to counter. This was why the Supreme Command could not, and would not, commit itself to overwhelming support of the northern thrust or the south-centre thrust on Frankfurt. It seems to me that the Supreme Command attitude must evoke understanding and respect. Moreover the Supreme Command must continuously weigh the demands of Bradley and Montgomery as carefully as possible, keenly aware that the two protagonists were of different nationalities with different aims and pressures. It was not an easy balance to maintain.

By the end of November it was clear that the autumn and winter battles had been very disappointing, falling a long way short of the targets outlined in the Supreme Command Directive of 28th October. Montgomery's failure to open Antwerp had been a contributory factor in these disappointments, but by no stretch of the imagination would the opening of Antwerp affect the November battles. The position had been perfectly clear to the Supreme Command at the end of October, and the appreciation on which the Directive was based had been unreal. The recovery of the enemy had been grossly underestimated, and insufficient regard paid to the effect on his supply problems of short lines of communication. The enemy was now operating on short internal lines, and was far less vulnerable to air attack than he had been throughout the campaign in Normandy. This, of course, was partly due to the weather. On top of that the genius of von Speer in keeping the factories going provided arms, ammunition and armour on a scale unrealized by the Allies. The powerful tendency of the Allies to exaggerate the effects of heavy bombing, which seems to have rested on hopes rather than facts, was to be a source of weakness for many years. Finally the enemy had at last gained some freedom of movement and was able to concentrate strength wherever it might be needed to block the holes and dents made by Eisenhower's strategy. Thus two Panzer armies were able to baffle Allied Intelligence and were able to 'hide', masking their final attack until the last moment.

On 28th November, Field-Marshal Montgomery re-opened his criticism of the Supreme Command in a blunt message spelling out the 'strategic reverse' suffered by the Allies, and calling for a new plan.[1] He insisted on a concentration of strength 'on the main selected thrust', appeared to be unaware that however valid were his criticisms, his failure to defeat the enemy west of the Rhine could not be attributed to lack of support from the Supreme Command. The Canadian 1st Army had moved to its new positions on the northern flank from 8th November onwards. There had been no room for more movement on the lines of communication of 21st Army Group. In fact the Supreme Command Directive at the end of October had been ridiculously optimistic, and it seemed evident that the

[1] Pogue: *The Supreme Command*, pp. 312-315.

enemy had been virtually 'written off'. Plans were made as though all initiative lay with our own troops. The reorientation of the Supreme Command to the changed situation after Normandy and the rapid advances in the north and centre, had been painfully slow, and there was no immediate prospect of improvement in the situation. The obvious physical factors of the battlefield, the direct threat of floods under enemy control, the deterioration in the weather, and the natural difficulties of the terrain seem to have been overlooked, or ignored. These things, and not a lack of troops or of logistical support, together with the failure to open Antwerp were the causes of the painfully slow progress all along the line. Montgomery's hope to mount 'Operation *Veritable*' in late November or early December had not been justified.

The Field-Marshal's vice was that he seemed to adopt the position almost of an 'armchair critic', as though he criticized a situation with which he had had little to do. He did not seem to speak as one of a team. His virtue was in his resolute determination to mount his battle, a resolution that would enable him to maintain his purpose throughout the battle of the Ardennes, and on into February. Once his eyes were fixed on a target it was almost impossible to deny him. The weakness of this strength was that it could leave him dedicated to a battle which might no longer be necessary.

Meanwhile the swollen river Maas confronted Montgomery's engineers with formidable bridging problems which they would be unable to meet until a massive build-up of bridging equipment became available. And beyond the Maas lay the river Niers, itself a considerable obstacle, and beyond that the flooded and unpredictable Rhine, and the hazards of its many 'meanders' in the north. In retrospect it is difficult to believe that operations could have gone forward more swiftly. The lull of the Autumn was inevitable, which is not to say that more could not have been done. That more was not done was due in the main to faulty appreciations rather than to faulty strategy, and a command failure to integrate the actions, large and small, all along the line. The Allied failure at Schmidt within easy reach of the Roer dams underlines this contention.[1]

On 30th November, Montgomery demanded a new plan.

[1] Thompson: *The Battle for the Rhineland*, 'Schmidt'.

He blamed the Autumn failures on the concentration of insufficient strength in the north, but the real burthen of his message was his strong belief that the Command structure was faulty.

'The theatre divides itself naturally into two fronts,' he wrote, 'one north of the Ardennes and one south of the Ardennes. We want one commander in full operational control north of the Ardennes, and one south.'

The Supreme Commander did not agree that there had been a strategic reverse, nor that the command was wrongly divided. 'Certainly,' he conceded, 'we have failed to achieve all that we had hoped by this time, which hopes and plans were based upon conditions as we knew them or estimated them when the plans were made.' In regard to the division of the command he wrote: 'We must choose the best line of attack to assure success ... from my personal viewpoint it would be simpler for me to have the battle zone divided into two general sectors in each of which one individual could achieve close battle co-ordination. I expressed some doubt whether this zone should be divided on the basis of our rear areas or on the basis of natural lines of advance into Germany. There was some question in my mind whether the Ardennes or the Ruhr should mark the dividing line, if such a plan should be adopted.'[1]

On the question of more strength in the north Eisenhower was, I believe, on safe ground. 'I do not agree,' he wrote to Montgomery, 'that more strength could have been thrown to the north than was actually maintained there during early September. Lines of communication in the north were so stretched that even delivery of five hundred tons to you at Brussels cost Bradley three divisions, the possession of which might have easily placed him on the Rhine in the Worms area.'

In fact Bradley's lines of communication would have had as much difficulty as Montgomery's to sustain three more divisions. But disagreements on strategy, and on command, were perhaps inevitable between two men, and two nations, looking at the battlefield and the 'shape' of the war from different angles. What might be right for Eisenhower and the Americans might well be wrong for Montgomery and the British. The British needed to win the war quickly. The Americans could afford—

[1] Pogue: *The Supreme Command*, pp. 312-313.

or thought they could afford—time. More important, the American picture of the defeat of the Nazi Reich did not accord with British ideas of victory.

Churchill, the British Prime Minister, worried about the progress of the war and suffering frustration in regard to the Italian campaign, quickly supported Montgomery, and expressed his disappointments to President Roosevelt. Tactfully noting the successes at Metz and Strasbourg, Churchill emphasized that the Allies 'had definitely failed to achieve the strategic object we gave our armies five weeks ago.' The Rhine was still a long way off, and would remain so for many weeks.[1]

The Supreme Commander and the President both minimized or brushed aside the British complaints. The truth is that the British wanted to achieve the impossible, and were fundamentally frustrated when the Allies failed to reap the harvest of the great victory in Normandy. Having failed they were loth to accept the delays and timings imposed by that failure. But they had to. For the moment the argument petered out with the usual protestations of misunderstanding and goodwill. All that he had pointed out, Montgomery explained, was that they had failed to carry out the Directive of 28th October. No one would deny it, and Eisenhower promptly apologized for giving Montgomery's message 'an interpretation' the Field-Marshal had not intended.

Nevertheless the shape of the battlefield lent real substance to Montgomery's desires and criticisms. Throughout November the campaign on the western front was in two distinct halves, north and south of the Ardennes, and Bradley's command position astride this difficult region was becoming increasingly uncomfortable. The U.S. 9th Army coming into the line on the right flank of 21st Army Group was clearly Montgomery's concern, and would inevitably come under his command. At the same time the U.S. 1st Army's operations on the right of the 9th had a direct bearing upon the northern battlefield, and were far removed from Patton's drive south of the Ardennes. Patton's drive had not only proved disappointing, it had pulled the campaign out of shape. Bradley's Army Group was not a cohesive force, and was nearly, if not actually, a geographical absurdity. Yet if Mont-

---
[1] Pogue: *The Supreme Command*, pp. 314-315.

gomery were to command north of the Ardennes, Bradley would be squeezed out, or Devers on Bradley's right would be squeezed out. Or if a new Army Group command had been created to embrace the U.S. 9th and 1st Armies Bradley or a new man would have had to give the U.S. 3rd Army to Devers.[1] This was unthinkable.

Perhaps, had Montgomery been an American, or even a much less cantankerous and difficult Northern Irishman—an Alexander, for example—he might have won and retained command of the entire northern front. The argument was by no means at an end.

[1] The U.S. 3rd and 7th Armies were at this time closely co-ordinated—Bradley had sent 6 divisions to the 7th. December attacks planned jointly—See Montgomery: *Memoirs*, Bradley's letter 3rd Dec., p. 301. Pogue: *The Supreme Command*, p. 317.

CHAPTER TWELVE

Three Faces of the Field-Marshal

I

IN endeavouring to understand the words and deeds of Field-Marshal Montgomery at the time, and in the succeeding years, I reached the conclusion that his behaviour must be explained by his absolute resolution to maintain the maximum British position at all costs. Thus he could not and would not accept a secondary role after Arnhem, which the distortion of his Army Group position and his relative weakness in the period to the end of November might have brought about. To give way—to acknowledge the immediate logic of the battlefield—and to accept an equality of strategic thrust with Bradley might have made it impossible for him, and for his armies, ever to regain priority for his northern thrust. Thus his attitudes must be understood in the context of Allied relations, and of the struggle for the end pattern. Right or wrong the hope for Britain lay in the maintenance of the main effort north of the Ruhr. Similarly the Supreme Command, with an immense panorama of battlefields in its vision, and with a massive complexity of para military and civil problems demanding immediate judgement and urgent attention, had to keep open various, options south of the Ruhr, and notably on Frankfurt. It would be a race, and in the late autumn and winter of 1944 the protagonists were jockeying for position. General Eisenhower was in the position of 'starter', striving to treat his generals without fear or favour.

No observer of the Field-Marshal's public behaviour in these difficult months when the campaign was in the doldrums, could have deduced from his bearing, often jaunty, always buoyant, and his general air of relaxed confidence, that he bore any anxieties at all, or was less than well pleased with the progress of his armies and of the campaign. Yet his anxieties were grave and real, and shared by Field-Marshal Alan Brooke, the C.I.G.S., to whom Montgomery frequently opened his mind. Neither man had confidence in Eisenhower as a commander of the land forces, and both were convinced that a land force commander, able to concentrate exclusively upon the battlefield, and in close touch with his commanders throughout every day and night, was vitally and urgently necessary. In their view the Supreme Commander, with his vast commitments and with his headquarters at Rheims and Versailles, was unable to exercise tight and effective command. Moreover Montgomery considered Eisenhower incompetent to do so, wherever he might be placed. These arguments reached their climax in the nine days from 28th November to 7th December.

But there are other aspects of Field-Marshal Montgomery worthy of some attention. There were, I think, three main 'faces' of Montgomery: the Montgomery as seen by the general, and a particular, public in his country, and the civilian public of the liberated countries. The Montgomery seen by his own troops, and the Montgomery in his association with the Supreme Command, his fellow generals, and the General Staff of Supreme headquarters. With the great body of the people at home his image was untarnished, if not enhanced. Certainly the war was dragging on, and war weariness was evident, but Montgomery was not the scapegoat of the British people. In more sophisticated, privileged, sections of Britain his stock and popularity had never been high. His fellow generals did not like him, and gossip in the clubs, especially the 'Senior', was often amusing, but with an edge to it when it concerned Montgomery. The mention of his name in the House of Commons, it was noted, was usually received in silence, or with an isolated and muted 'hear, hear'. P. J. Grigg, the Minister of War, a fervent admirer of the Field-Marshal, asked Harold Nicolson, 'Why is it that whenever I mention the name of Montgomery there is always a cold hush?'[1]

Harold Nicolson, who does not disguise, or excuse, his personal antipathy to Montgomery based upon a dislike of his general mien, manner of speech and behaviour, offered the

[1] *Nicolson Diaries*, vol. ii, p. 441.

opinion that there was a fear on the Left that Montgomery 'is a political general'. At the same time there was a dislike of his immodesty, and his blatant self-advertisement, on the Right and Centre. It was feared that Montgomery would seek a political role for himself after the war, and might enjoy massive popular support if things were going wrong, or too slowly for an impatient public.

On the Continent, in Belgium and Holland in particular, admiration for 'Monty' was simple and lasting. He was the symbol of liberation, the 'Liberator'. Moreover his presence was a promise of victory, dispelling all doubts. The attitude of tens of thousands was almost lyrical not only towards the Field-Marshal, but also embracing the spearheads of the troops who had surged in their triumphant advance through scores of towns and villages. They had looked like conquerors, and the image stuck. Even now, twenty-five years after, the picture, though faded by time, remains in the hearts and minds of the old and the middle aged.

In the aftermath of Arnhem, a failure already regarded as an heroic triumph, more impressive in a curious way than victory, and more memorable, the arrival of the Monarch upon the scene added to the Field-Marshal's aura. The presence of King George VI seemed a double guarantee of security. In a field just outside Eindhoven an investiture was held in the presence of a fortunate few, and the Field-Marshal's faithful Chief of Staff, Major-General de Guingand, was among those to receive the accolade of knighthood. It seemed like a piece of 'history' marking the liberation of southern Holland. Montgomery was master of ceremonies, the host of his monarch, and delighting in his role. The King bestowed the accolades, but it was Montgomery, no one doubted, who named the knights.

On the Sunday following this event King George VI and his Field-Marshal attended Morning Service in a small Anglican church tucked away in a residential corner of the predominantly Roman Catholic Eindhoven. Montgomery took his place a few feet back from the chancel steps kneeling 'to attention at the King's side, the two men 'dressing' carefully as they nibbled forward on their knees, resolved possibly to be absolutely level, or to stress their equality 'in the sight of God'.

It was very clear that the King's visit was a happy occasion, and a gesture of confidence in Montgomery at a critical time in the British military situation. It seemed to confirm to anyone who might doubt it that Montgomery was not only the commander of victorious armies, but the chosen champion and favoured 'ambassador' of his Sovereign.

Throughout the Autumn and Winter months the Field-Marshal was often to be observed visiting his brother-in-law, Major-General Hobart, at his headquarters in Eindhoven. Hobart, whose great and growing armoured division, with its unique and versatile 'engines of war', had opened the way into North-Western Europe, commanded a force of the utmost importance, capable of overcoming many of the hazards and obstacles the enemy, the terrain and the abominable weather, were producing. The success of the 79th Armoured division and the wealth of uses to which its herd of armoured fighting vehicles could be put, many of them amphibians, fully justified frequent visits by the Army Group commander. But it may be also true that Hobart was Montgomery's nearest and most important friend, a living link with the brief but tragic idyll at the core of Montgomery's adult life. One had the impression, induced by Montgomery's relaxed off duty mien on these occasions, his readiness to sign autographs for small boys and girls, and his obvious pleasure in the young, that Hobart was a firm and intimate friend as well as a military adviser of great experience, and the commander of a unique force ever more prominent in British success.

Montgomery would squat on his heels to bring himself down to eye level with the children who often surrounded him on the pavements. He was not playing to a gallery, but was completely at ease and 'alone', so that looking through the curtained windows one felt an eavesdropper on some personal private matter.

To the men in the field, and especially to the vast army of line of communications and support troops, the Field-Marshal was popular in an unusual way. He dispensed cigarettes freely, but his popularity was not dependent upon 'bribery'. He was a potent tonic, a unique personality, unmistakable, a talisman. His visits to troops, occasionally to give lectures to all ranks, were welcomed and a source of interest. Most men did feel that

Montgomery was not only lucky, but honest, and that his presence promised success, however badly things might seem to be going. His apparent tight grasp of the situation and his lucid expositions gave confidence, and few were in a position to question his assumptions, his reasoning, or his conclusions. Nor did anyone wish to. The Field-Marshal's crisp diction and confident bearing left no room for doubt. I felt that he was regarded with an amused affection, his tremendous showmanship fooling nobody while in fact fooling almost everybody. But none doubted his expertize, his tight grasp of command, his promise of victory.

Yet in one respect his words were unpopular, especially with front line troops. His references to 'killing matches', a phrase he seemed to use with relish, revealed a curious lack of understanding of the psychology of men whose work was to kill or be killed. A remark attributed to a G.I., an American 'Enlisted Man' or Private soldier, referring to General Patton may properly be transposed to apply to a Private Soldier's reaction to the Field-Marshal.

'Yeh! Your guts, our blood!' The G.I. growled behind old 'blood and guts' Patton's back. Similarly a British soldier might have remarked of old 'killing match' Montgomery, 'Your match, our killing!'

I believe that the notion that generals of the type of Patton and Montgomery are liked by their troops is a myth. They may gain the admiration and respect of those who fought under them, but it is not liking. They are too exalted to enter the consciousness of soldiers as 'fellow soldiers'. Their popularity, or the reverse, is akin to that of the politician. In war society becomes regimented into battalion families based upon the platoon and the company, and in this society the Lieut.-Colonel is supreme, the absolute head of his battalion family, the 'Seigneur' to the fighting troops. Army commanders, corps and divisional commanders, and all but exceptional and daring brigadiers, exist on the outer periphery of the soldier's world, only tenuously associated with tribulations in the field. Captains and subalterns often earn great loyalty from their men, but even these have their distinctive separateness. The below stairs hierarchy of Warrant officers, and non-commissioned officers in general, are the foremen on the factory floor of war, the field of battle. They reflect the absolute power emanating from the top. None of this is questioned.

II

Montgomery's life in the field in his own command was assuredly a happy one. He liked the quiet austerity of his Tactical headquarters, his caravan, his memories, his faithful personal servant, his busy and gregarious Chief of Staff, de Guingand, and his youthful personal entourage of picked junior officers, his élite. Relaxed round his own 'camp fire', as it were, a circle very rarely penetrated by outsiders, apart perhaps from his favourite and loyal War Correspondent, Alan Moorehead, his behaviour was in tune with the gravity of war. His young men lived dangerously in his service. They kept him in the closest possible touch with the progress of fighting troops, and enabled him to feel that he had his fingers on the pulse of battle. Yet this was in some measure an illusion. In this setting he enjoyed unqualified admiration and loyalty, and not one of his personal staff would criticize the Field-Marshal in an ungenerous way. It is not surprising that he preferred all this to the company of senior Allied generals and their staffs, whose attitudes to war and whose manners, customs and conversation, were often uncongenial.

In this way Montgomery felt that he kept himself in the closest possible touch with his battlefield. It is no part of a commander-in-chief's duty to put himself within range of enemy fire in forward areas, or worse still in danger of capture. Yet there is no way of knowing about a battle without being physically involved in it, and even Montgomery's young men, his eyes and ears, for all their undoubted courage, were involved as observers and not as fighters. Things are rarely what they seem in war, and it is very easy to gain wrong impressions. With the great commanders and the great leaders of men there is a kind of instinct, a real total involvement of the whole man, transcending logic and even common-sense, which enables them to know exactly what men can do, what they are doing, what they will do. Montgomery did the best he could. I think he erred in his belief that veteran seasoned troops were the best in almost all circumstances. He omitted to consider the belief that men have a stock of courage, of nervous energy, and that it may run out. Moreover seasoned veterans are often very resolute in their determination to stay alive, and very skilful in doing a minimum duty, especially as a war draws to an end. Well-trained troops, inexperienced in battle, are often magnificent in attack.

On the 14th November, two weeks before he opened his barrage of criticism of the Supreme Command, and when he was disenchanted with the progress of the campaign, Montgomery visited his old division, the 3rd British Infantry division, held an investiture in the field, and addressed the officers and men. There was little doubt that he was in his element. He spoke with absolute confidence, his clipped dry phrases carrying absolute conviction. He stood in his characteristic pose, feet slightly apart, hands behind his back in an 'at ease' position, body balanced on his heels, tending to curve backwards, and his piercing blue eyes searching his audience. The 21st Army Group front was almost tidy, and the great battle for the Rhineland—the penultimate battle—would soon be launched, according to plan. No detail would be overlooked, and the masses of ammunition and munitions of war would soon be moving out of the port of Antwerp to the stock piles. The 3rd division had played its part in the hard preliminaries to the coming battle for the Rhineland at Overloon, Venraij and Deurne. It had held fierce enemy counter-attacks. It was happy with itself.

'You want to know,' Montgomery said, 'how long the war is going to last. I have some money on it myself. The Germans fought the battle for France on our side of the Seine. Will the battle for Germany be fought on our side of the Rhine? If the answer to that question is "Yes", then I say "That's easy".'

But it wasn't easy, even though the enemy had shot his bolt when at long last the Allies closed the Rhine. U.S. and British intelligence officers were attempting to follow the movements of two enemy Panzer armies seeming to threaten a powerful counter-attack in the Roer valley. Yet this might be a deception plan. It was impossible to detect unease in the Army Group command or the Supreme Command. Bradley recognized that he was particularly weak in the Ardennes, but believed that it

5. Montgomery talks to men of the Black Watch shortly before the assault over the Rhine

6. Montgomery directs the battle in Northern Germany, April 1945

was safe enough, a 'calculated risk'. Meanwhile the Allied armies were re-grouping for the heave to the Rhine, singularly ignoring the possible 'courses open to the enemy' and the tentative warnings of intelligence officers that something big was brewing, even though they could not say exactly what and where and when.

III

The third face of Field-Marshal Montgomery was the one to cause the gravest concern. This was the face he showed to the Supreme Command, to his rival Army Group commander General Bradley, and to Supreme Headquarters. At Supreme Headquarters his adherents in the higher echelons were greatly outnumbered by his opponents. General Walter Bedell Smith, while striving to be absolutely fair, found it difficult to conceal his disenchantment and dislike of Montgomery. General Morgan, his British deputy, made no secret of his personal antipathy, and his critical attitude. Fortunately Montgomery enjoyed the confidence of General Whiteley and the impartial and considered support of General Strong, the chief of Intelligence. Within a month these two men were destined to play a vital part in the developing fortunes of the Commander of 21st Army Group.

But in general, Montgomery's churlish attitude to General Eisenhower, his bluntly phrased criticisms of strategy, his failure, more often than not, to attend conferences in person, his ill-timed (as it seemed) criticisms of the command structure and the strategy of the Supreme Command, coupled with the aloof austerity of his military life, earned him dislike and ill-will. From the middle of November onwards the Field-Marshal was full of complaints, frustrated by his assurance to Eisenhower at the beginning of the month that the argument was closed, and 'You will hear no more from me . . .!' A decent period had to elapse before he could begin nagging again, and Brooke, the C.I.G.S., restrained him while recording his own grave misgivings in his diary. On 17th November, Montgomery complained to the C.I.G.S. 'that he had neither seen nor spoken to his chief on the telephone since October 18th, and had only met him four times since the end of the Normandy campaign.'

Despite the difficulties and distances involved the blame could not be laid upon Eisenhower. In the nature of his immense command it would have been impossible for him to have been in close personal contact with his senior commanders much more frequently.

'He (Eisenhower) is at a Forward headquarters at Rheims,' Montgomery wrote. 'The Directives he issues from there have no relation to the practical necessities of the battle. It is quite impossible for me to carry out my present orders . . . Eisenhower should himself take a proper control of operations or he should appoint someone else to do this. If we go drifting along as at present we are merely playing into the enemy's hands, and the war will go on indefinitely . . . He has never commanded anything before in his whole career; now, for the first time, he has elected to take direct command of very large scale operations and he does not know how to do it . . .'[1]

This is unjust and should be read as a measure of Montgomery's frustration and not of his judgement. The Field-Marshal was, I believe, having a good grumble, doubtless hoping for a disposition of troops more in his favour. Field-Marshal Brooke, on the other hand, lacked all confidence in General Eisenhower, and voiced his anxieties not only to his diary, but to the Prime Minister. The C.I.G.S. was even contemplating his resignation.

'Eisenhower completely fails as commander,' he wrote. 'Bedell Smith lives back in Paris quite out of touch; as a result the war is drifting in a rudderless condition. Had a long and despondent letter about it from Montgomery over the weekend. Am preparing a case, as we shall have to take it up with the Americans before long.'[2]

But Churchill was not prepared to 'gang up' against Eisenhower, especially since Eisenhower had the support of his Staff and of the Deputy Supreme Commander, Air Marshal Tedder. Moreover Churchill did not share Brooke's anxieties. He rather liked Eisenhower and had mixed feelings about Montgomery. As for Montgomery's idea of dividing the battlefield into two parts, one north of the Ardennes and one south, this did not seem a solution of the problems to the C.I.G.S.

---

[1] Bryant: *Triumph in the West*, pp. 333-334.
[2] Bryant: *Triumph in the West*, p. 334. Tedder: *With Prejudice*, p. 616.

'I don't think much of your plan,' he wrote to Montgomery. 'You have always told me, and I have agreed with you, that Ike was no commander, that he had no strategic vision, was incapable of making a plan or running operations when started.

'Now you state that, "this solution is so very simple and would solve all problems. Ike would allot forces to each front as demanded by his plan." Further, "He must decide on his strategic plan *now*, lay down objectives, allot resources, and so on." Is that not exactly what he has proved himself incapable of doing?

'And again: "Bradley and myself then carry on, and Ike co-ordinates as necessary." Can you see Ike judging between the requirements of the two fronts, overriding American clamour for their Commander being in charge of the main thrusts, etc. etc.? I can't!'[1]

The letter is a long one, and should be read in full, for it reveals that Montgomery was doing all in his power, consistent with his beliefs, to achieve some sort of compromise, and to make the best of it.

On 28th November, Montgomery had a personal meeting with Eisenhower, and was able to put forward his views in the most forthright manner. It was a key day in Allied fortunes. The first cargo ship had sailed up the long Scheldt estuary in the wake of two coastal vessels, and docked at Antwerp to unload the first 9,000 tons of cargo. It spelled the beginning of the end of shortages all along the line. Two weeks later the daily flood of supplies through Antwerp reached 20,000 tons. Only the growing shortage of manpower, Americans as well as British, and the scarcity of reserves, marred the prospects. Montgomery was in excellent form, lucid and convincing. Eisenhower was patient, a good listener. When the two men parted Montgomery believed that his troubles were over and wrote at once to the C.I.G.S.:

'We talked for three hours in a most friendly way and I proved to him that we had definitely failed and must make a new plan ... He admitted a grave mistake has been made and in my opinion is prepared to go almost any length to succeed next time. *Hence his own suggestion I should be in full operational*

[1] Bryant: *Triumph in the West*, pp. 335-336.

command north of the Ardennes with Bradley under me and 6th Army Group in a holding role in South.'[1]

This was a complete misunderstanding. Montgomery had mistaken his own convictions and Eisenhower's polite listening for agreement. At best the Supreme Commander must have been non-commital. Yet forceful arguers with strong opinions will have suffered similar misunderstandings.

Field-Marshal Brooke was at once doubtful, and wrote in his diary, 'If only all Monty thinks he has settled materializes we shall be all right, but I have fears of Ike going back when he has discussed with Bedell Smith, Tedder, etc.' A day earlier he had noted, 'Ike is incapable of running a land battle and it is all dependent on how well Monty can handle him . . .'[2]

But it should have been clear that no amount of handling would change the situation. On 3rd December, Bradley had written frankly to Montgomery of his dispositions in the South. The U.S. 3rd Army could not spare a single division for transfer to the North. 'Because of our inability to receive, equip, and supply troops through our Channel ports,' Bradley wrote,[3] 'it has been necessary to divert seven divisions to Devers' Army Group. Naturally we wanted to get as much out of these divisions as possible, and the attack of the 6th Army Group, in conjunction with Patton's attack, has so far achieved satisfactory results. I believe that between the 7th Army and the 3rd Army this very important attack can be kept up.'

Thus Montgomery could have been in no doubt of the situation when he went to Maastricht on 7th December to confer with the Supreme Commander, his Deputy, Air Marshal Tedder, and with Bradley. The meeting was abortive, as it was bound to be, but it was surprisingly cheerful. 'I may say that we all had a very cheery lunch, and parted with much laughter,' Montgomery wrote. He had stated his convictions, but in attempting to persuade the Supreme Commander to concentrate his force on the northern attack he knew that he was crying for the moon. Bradley was committed, and there was no doubt that he would be supported to the hilt if his efforts

---

[1] Bryant: *Triumph in the West*, p. 342.
[2] Bryant: *Triumph in the West*, pp. 343, 345.
[3] Montgomery: *Memoirs*, p. 300.

justified it. The Frankfurt line was at least as important in Eisenhower's mind as was the major assault north of the Ruhr. He would be free to strike with his right or his left, or with both. He saw no reason why both attacks should not take place. In any case the proposition that his armies south of the Ardennes should adopt static roles was unthinkable; nor was this a solution to a problem that had its roots in a logistical pattern planned long in advance. Montgomery, of course, believed that only one main line of attack could be adequately supported. That was the 'fundamental' difference between Montgomery and the Supreme Command.

'In terms of complete understanding and agreement, these view-points were never really reconciled,' wrote Forrest Pogue, pointing out that Eisenhower was 'in a position to make his view prevail. For this reason, if for no other, there was never a deadlock between the Commanders-in-Chief.'[1]

Immediately after the Maastricht meeting Montgomery and Bradley went their different ways, Bradley to conduct his southern battle from his headquarters in Luxembourg, Montgomery to concentrate upon his northern attack from his headquarters north of Eindhoven.

'I played a lone hand against the three of them,' Montgomery wrote to Brooke. 'They all arrived today and went away together.' He felt sure that any points he might have made with Eisenhower, 'would be put right by Bradley and Tedder on the three hour drive back to Luxembourg ... if you want the war to end within a reasonable period you will have to get Ike's hand taken off the land battle.'

These are very strong words, and they increased the anxieties of the C.I.G.S. to the point where he would do all in his power to 'take Eisenhower's hand off the land battle'. I do not feel that Montgomery shared the urgent anxieties of his Chief although he had stimulated them. He had said his piece once more, and his own position in the north was very sound with vast supplies pouring in from Antwerp. He was maintaining his strength and nothing would prejudice his battle for the Rhineland. It is doubtful whether he wanted a change in the Supreme Command. He would have been content to command the forces north of the Ardennes, and in effect that was his position.

[1] Pogue: *The Supreme Command*, pp. 316-317.

The U.S. 1st and 9th armies were tied in to his battle rather than to Bradley's.

The C.I.G.S. meanwhile had put Montgomery's letter before the Prime Minister, and arranged for the Supreme Commander and his Deputy to visit London for talks with the Chiefs of Staff and the Prime Minister. But Churchill's attitude was unusually detached, almost euphoric, brooding on Greece and forgetting to read Montgomery's letter. 'Found him (Churchill) in bed eating his breakfast. He was quite incapable of concentrating on anything but the Greek situation... I tried to explain, but he kept returning to Greece,' Brooke confided to his diary.[1]

Dinner with the Chiefs of Staff, the Prime Minister, the Supreme Commander and his Deputy, was a happy occasion for all but Brooke, who discovered, among other things... 'that Ike does not hope to cross the Rhine before May!' All Brooke's attempts to open critical discussion were blocked by Churchill in one of his benign 'cherubic' moods, and enjoying his company. The next day he told Brooke calmly that he hadn't wanted to 'gang up' against Ike: 'He was one American against five of us with only Tedder to support him.'

Nevertheless, Alexander was soon to be alerted to leave his Italian command to 'come to the aid of the party'. Perhaps, fortunately for Alexander, it didn't happen, and he was able to bring his Italian campaign to a successful[2] but disappointing end. Neither President Roosevelt nor General Marshall would have tolerated a change in command, although they might have been induced to agree some modification of the command structure. It was, in any case, too late.

IV

Montgomery's relationship with the Supreme Command, and his attitudes to Allied generals and their staff officers, was the subject of wide comment at the time, often humorous, but invariably highly critical. It is a subject on which there has

---

[1] Bryant: *Triumph in the West*, p. 532.
[2] See Decision Malta Conference, 2nd Feb., 1945—transfer of troops and aircraft to Western front—Chapter 15.

been considerable comment in the succeeding years. The general verdict at the time was that Montgomery was boorish, and unnecessarily inaccessible, and that this was to his disadvantage. The wisest and most perceptive observations about his personal characteristics and behaviour were made, I think, by Chester Wilmot of the British Broadcasting Corporation. From the outset of his army command in the desert Montgomery had been keenly alive to the immense value of the B.B.C. in the building and maintenance of his 'image'. Moreover his taste for 'cutting discs' of some of his special pronouncements and speeches tended to endow B.B.C. war correspondents with some special privileges in the way of access to the Field-Marshal and his entourage. Montgomery's manners and methods, Wilmot observed, 'would have been equally distasteful (to the Americans) in an American. General Douglas MacArthur, who also exercised his authority with an autocratic hand, as though it were his by more than mortal dispensation, was heartily detested by many Americans.'

Of course, in common with Montgomery, MacArthur was also hero-worshipped by many more. The fact is that Montgomery, Wilmot observed, 'was not as other men. He revealed no trace of ordinary human frailties and foibles. He shunned the company of women; he did not smoke or drink or play poker with 'the boys'. He could never be slapped on the back. Because he lived in a small Tactical H.Q. with a few aides and liaison officers, he was looked upon as setting himself apart from (and therefore above) his fellows. The impression seemed to be confirmed by his practice, resented as much by other British services as it was by the Americans, of sending his Chief of Staff, de Guingand, to represent him at conferences.'

Many would regard some of these traits as to be desired in a man carrying great responsibilities. It does not follow that he was a 'kill-joy', simply because he did not like being slapped on the back, smoking and drinking, and playing poker with the boys. He was, or had become, something of a recluse, relaxing in his own fashion at his own fireside, often at the expense of his military social duties. But he could be, and sometimes was, a first-class host, entertaining and amusing, providing wine and cigars, and giving brief glimpses of his rare charm. As for shunning the company of women, most soldiers must do so in the field unless they keep 'mistresses' somewhere on the side, and it might be a dangerous and distracting practice. Montgomery had been a one woman man, and there is ample evidence that he responded warmly to women, but not as intimate companions. That lay in his memory, never to be forgotten.

It was his 'what a good boy am I' attitude, in de Guingand's phrase, that most stuck in the gullets of his American colleagues. The worst was yet to come. The enemy was about to take a hand.

CHAPTER THIRTEEN

Counter-offensive; the Ardennes

I

THE background to the Battle of the Ardennes underlines one of the important factors in the failure of the Allies to defeat the enemy in 1944. From the break-out across the Seine at the end of August there had been a consistent failure to assess or to appreciate enemy intentions, or capabilities, to consider the 'courses' open to the enemy, his ability to re-group and re-arm and to reinforce his shattered infantry and armour, while sustaining an incessant bombing bombardment of his home front. The Supreme Command, the Army Group and Army commanders pursued their plans almost as though the enemy had ceased to exist as an organized force, and even when confronted with organized resistance they failed to change, or even to modify, their conclusions. Apart from their overwhelming power on the ground and in the air, their awareness of the bombing offensive, and the tide threatening to engulf the German armies on the eastern front, made them complacent.

While it is improbable in the extreme that the enemy counter-offensive could have succeeded in its grandiose plan to drive through to Antwerp, or that the enemy could have done more than delay disaster in that event, it is certain that the offensive exposed Allied troops to avoidable dangers and minor disasters. It disrupted the 3rd Army offensive, and opened a dangerous gap into Alsace. It relieved the threat to the Roer dams and postponed Montgomery's planned offensive in the Rhineland. At the same time the enemy, despite his enormous commitment in the Ardennes, contrived to exert dangerous pressures from Nijmegen to Strasbourg. A serious delay in the fulfilment of Allied plans might have been imposed.

Field-Marshal Montgomery estimated at the end of the affair that the Allied plans had been set back by six weeks, and while that is true of the planned offensive either under way or in active preparation, it may not be true in the final analysis. The enemy had cast away his entire strategic reserve on that one hopeless throw, and the heavy losses sustained in the Ardennes gravely prejudiced his ability to defend the approaches to the Rhine, and sustain the final battle for Germany. The delays suffered by the Allies at the outset may easily have been made up at the end.

It was the belief that an enemy offensive on the scale of that launched on the Eifel-Ardennes front in December was militarily beyond enemy resources that resulted in the Supreme Command and the 12th Army Group command being taken unawares. However reasonable this may have been it was not reasonable to discount the probability of a counter-attack. As a counter-attack the enemy assault would have been a great success if a withdrawal had been set in motion as soon as 1st and 3rd Army troops had become committed, and Montgomery had begun to deploy the British 30th Corps and detach the U.S. VII Corps from the 9th Army. After a week all that could be won had been won. It had been snowing in the north for more than a week and it would snow in the Ardennes at any moment. The heavy overcast sky, which had kept Allied aircraft on the ground, must one day clear. At that moment it was certain that the deeper the enemy penetrated into the Ardennes, the worse would be the disaster that must inevitably overtake them. This was very clear to Field-Marshal von Runstedt. He had few illusions before the attack; he had none after the first forty-eight hours.

Thus the failure of the Supreme Command to appreciate the counter-offensive is understandable, but the failure to appreciate the very real threat of a counter-attack is not. It was a failure comparable with the failure to anticipate the enemy armoured attempt to break through to Avranches in the final phase of the Battle for Normandy. But perhaps it is unreasonable to expect the Allied military commanders to appreciate the probable courses open to the mind of a madman in a state of despair, and in Supreme Command. Montgomery thought in terms of military sanity. His opponents were von Runstedt, Model, and highly experienced soldiers of that calibre. Certainly it would have been inconceivable that such men would have launched the counter-offensive in the Ardennes. But Hitler would and Hitler did, and nothing that von Runstedt, or Model, or Manteuffel, another of his privileged commanders directly concerned, could say could shake his resolution. Nor could they persuade him to withdraw when the offensive was clearly hopeless.

The handicaps under which the Germans operated were grave. In spite of their almost superhuman efforts petrol was dangerously short, and American supplies and dumps would have to be overrun if the armour was to keep going for more than a few days. Transport was almost comically inadequate, of great variety, and short of spares. There were more horses in some of the German divisions than there had been in 1918. 'Not only were there too few trucks but many divisions were equipped with poor worn-out booty vehicles that simply fell by the wayside along the bad roads of the Ardennes and had to be abandoned because there were no repair parts.'[1] Ammunition was in short supply, and the shortage of transport made the situation desperate for many units in the first week.

It was, as von Runstedt said, 'all or nothing.'[2] Indeed it was much worse, for it could not be all, and it could not be nothing. 'We should go down on our knees and thank God if we reach the Meuse,' old von Runstedt added. It was worse than a desperate throw.

In a sense the Allied commanders could not believe the indications, however strong, even when fully aware of the existence of, and the approximate locations of the 5th and 6th Panzer armies, and of the threat their existence must pose.

The threat was well appreciated by Intelligence staffs, notably of U.S. 1st Army, and by Supreme Headquarters Chief of Intelligence. U.S. 3rd Army refused to take these views seriously, and it was evident that in the days before the German attack there were constant irritations on a personal level between 1st and 3rd Army staffs. Forrest Pogue, who questioned the officers concerned after the war, remarked cautiously:

'There seems little doubt that some personality conflicts, and

---

[1] Cole: *The Ardennes*, pp. 664-665.
[2] 'Es geht ums ganze.'

sometimes a tendency to question the validity of predictions existed between 12th Army Group and 1st Army G–2's.'[1]

Colonel Dickson, Chief of Intelligence, U.S. 1st Army, reported enemy troop movements of an ominous nature, particularly in the Bitburg-Wittlich area, right up to the eve of the attack. He also reported the presence of engineers with bridging equipment. His file on the subject had been growing since October when a captured German order calling for speakers of the 'American dialect' to report to Waffen SS Colonel Otto Skorzeny's headquarters for special training by 1st November indicated to Colonel Dickson the development of enemy plans for sabotage behind the American lines.

Small pieces of the puzzle painstakingly put together increased the uneasiness of 1st Army Intelligence, and two days before the enemy offensive Colonel Dickson's warnings grew more urgent. On 15th December, the 1st Army Intelligence estimate read (in part): 'Reinforcements for the West Wall between Düren and Trier continue to arrive. The identification of at least three or four newly-formed divisions along the army front must be reckoned with during the next few days... It is possible that a limited scale offensive will be launched for the purpose of achieving a Christmas morale victory for civilian consumption. Many PW's now speak of the coming attack between 17th and 25th December.'

General Hodges, commanding the 1st Army, reacted to the reports of his Intelligence chief by asking General Bradley for two extra divisions. He was refused. Nevertheless Hodges did not expect an enemy offensive or counter-attack through the Ardennes. 'All of us,' he said, 'thought they were getting ready to hit us when we crossed the Roer.'

Supreme Headquarters Intelligence had been increasingly concerned by the reports coming in, and had noted the movement of enemy armour towards Bitburg in the Eifel. For at least two weeks before the enemy counter-offensive Major General Strong, Supreme Headquarters Chief of Intelligence had drawn attention to the situation. At the Chief of Staffs' morning conference 'daily for a period of at least a fortnight before the attack, I called attention to the possible three uses of the reforming Panzer Army. (a) to go to Russia; (b) to

[1] Pogue: *The Supreme Command.*

counter-attack an Allied penetration; (c) to stage a relieving attack through the Ardennes... Course (c) so impressed General (Bedell) Smith, (Chief of Staff to the Supreme Commander) that he asked if General Bradley was aware of this possibility. I replied in the affirmative but nevertheless General Smith instructed me to go to 12 AG and see General Bradley personally and warn him. This would be about the first week in December. I saw General Bradley for about ¾ hour and he told me he was aware of the danger but that he had earmarked certain divisions to move into the Ardennes area should the enemy attack there...'[1]

General Bedell Smith confirmed the statement: 'General Strong... said the attack might come in the Ardennes or east of the Vosges whenever the Germans had a prediction of six days of bad weather... As a consequence of this I sent him to see Bradley and Bradley said, let them come...'

General Eisenhower also agreed that 'the possibility of a break-through was certainly made known to him by General Strong.'

Yet these warnings were not strong enough to impress General Bradley to the extent of persuading him to modify his plans or to take precautions. 'At that moment nothing less than an unequivocal indication of impending attack in the Ardennes could have induced me to quit the winter offensive,' he wrote; but his attitude appears to be equivocal and uncertain, the attitude of a man who feels that he should have done something, but was damned if he was going to. His attitude to Intelligence was not uncommon among Commanders, and Bradley commented: 'Had I gone on guard every time Dickson, or any other G2 called Wolf, we would never have taken many of the riskier moves that hastened the end of the war.' Bradley would not permit himself to be influenced by detail, and he leaves the powerful impression that he had very little time for intelligence reports. 'I commanded almost three quarters of a million men on a 230 mile front,' he wrote. 'It was impossible for me even to scan the intelligence estimates of subordinate units.'[2] The views of the commander impregnated the attitudes of his staff, and his chief of intelligence was the last man to 'cry wolf'.

[1] Pogue: *The Supreme Command*, pp. 365-366.
[2] Bradley: *A Soldier's Story*, p. 464.

Yet whatever justification Bradley had for ignoring not only the many intelligence summaries adding up over the months, surely the very definite personal warnings delivered by General Strong at the request of the Chief of Staff to the Supreme Command should have persuaded Bradley to take some precautionary measures against the strong possibility of enemy attack. No commander on Bradley's level should permit himself to become immersed in detail; that is the business of his staff.

'In analyzing the intelligence situation before the Ardennes offensive,' Forrest Pogue wrote, 'one may well ask what additional information the Allies would have needed to predict the 16 December attack.'[1]

In fact Bradley did believe that there might be an enemy attack, but simply would not believe in the enemy capability of mounting an attack on a massive or embarrassing scale. His remark to General Strong, 'Let them come', and his reaction to General Bedell Smith's remark to him at Supreme Headquarters when the counter offensive had begun, bear this out. 'You've been wishing for a counter-attack. Now it looks as though you've got it,' Bedell Smith said.

'A counter-attack, yes, but I'll be damned if I wanted one this big,' Bradley replied.[2]

At first Bradley and Patton believed that the German offensive was no more than 'a spoiling attack to force a halt on Patton's advances into the Saar', and it was almost a week before they realized that 'Hitler, in fact, was out to split the Allied armies apart.'

Bradley has been frank about his reactions, and his attitude is important. His statements are inconsistent and difficult to reconcile. 'Indeed no one came to me with a warning on the danger of a counter-attack (the Ardennes),' ignores the testimony of Generals Walter Bedell Smith and Strong, and even of the Supreme Commander.

It is clear that Patton's offensive in the South predominated in Bradley's mind to the extent that he refused to consider any possible situation which might force him to modify his plans. Fearful that his attack, which held priority, might be halted in

---

[1] Pogue: *The Supreme Command*, p. 365, p. 376.
[2] Pogue: *The Supreme Command*, p. 455.

favour of Montgomery in the North if he failed to make swift progress, he turned a blind eye to other important sectors of his front. It is understandable. The Maastricht conference represented a triumph for Bradley, at least in his own mind. For the first time the priority had been moved away from the north, and the chance to lead the way to final victory was his— and Patton's. Yet he remained acutely aware of his weakness in the Ardennes. It was a chance, he felt, that he had to take. He had instructed Middleton, commanding the U.S. VIII corps, to "simulate the movement of additional units into his area in order to draw enemy divisions to his front. He had carried out part of these activities early in the month (December) and was told to resume the program later."[1]

These instructions indicate that neither Bradley nor Middleton could have realised the enormous power the enemy was amassing in the Eifel. The intention to 'draw enemy strength' denies the possibility that the intention was to deceive the enemy in regard to American strength, and to deter an attack. The enemy, in any case, observed the simulations and was not deceived.

It is fair, I believe, to postulate that the only indications of a massive enemy assault, as opposed to counter-attack or attack on a divisional level, must come from intelligence sources. In view of the Ardennes experience one wonders whether intelligence might ever be able to state categorically that an enemy attack would occur on a given date, and that even if it were able to do so, would the commander concerned do anything about it?

It is an easy question to ask, and a difficult one to answer.

What did the situation seem like to Bradley, or to any other observer in the field on the eve of the enemy counter-offensive? We have the answer to this question.

II

On the eve of the enemy counter offensive the commanders in the field believed that they were confronted by a beaten enemy, and said so. On 12th December the 12th Army Group Head-

[1] Pogue, *The Supreme Command*, p. 371.

quarters issued a report couched in unusually flamboyant terms:

'It is now certain that attrition is steadily sapping the strength of German forces on the western front and that the crust of defenses is thinner, more brittle and more vulnerable than it appears on G-2 maps or to troops in the line.'[1]

Major Ralph McA-Ingersoll was the author of this document. He had been instructed 'to put some color' into it.

Field-Marshal Montgomery's Headquarters would not have dissented from these views, and on 16th December 21st Army Group issued a statement:

'The enemy is at present fighting a defensive campaign on all fronts; his situation is such that he cannot stage major offensive operations. Furthermore, at all costs he has to prevent the war from entering on a mobile phase; he has not the transport or the petrol that would be necessary for mobile operations, nor could his tanks compete with ours in the mobile battle.

'The enemy is in a bad way; he has had a tremendous battering and has lost heavily in men and equipment. . . .'

After the war Bradley generously commented: 'Had I been preparing an estimate of my own on the same day, I would not have changed a word of Monty's, for his appraisal was identical to my own.'[2]

Thus on the very day of the counter offensive the Allied Commanders brushed the enemy aside. Were they justified? Did it seem credible, or should it have seemed credible, that the enemy, despite the immense battering he had taken, despite all his difficulties, could, or would, mount such an offensive? It would mean predictably the committal of whatever strategic reserve he had been able to build up and to assemble throughout the atrocious conditions of the winter. It would mean the assembly of transport and petrol beyond the means believed to be available to him.

The Allied difficulty in assessing 'courses open to the enemy', and the factors involved, was in part the difficulty of thinking in terms of the possible reactions of Hitler to the military situation, and of deciding the balance of military decision in the field between Hitler and his generals. Into whose mind had the Allies to penetrate?

[1] Pogue: *The Supreme Command*, pp. 369, 369n.
[2] Bradley: *A Soldier's Story*, p. 460.

Field-Marshal Montgomery considered the courses open to the enemy, as I have stated, in terms of a military mind of the calibre and experience of a von Runstedt. This is reasonable, but I feel that it was always necessary to be alive to the unknown factor of Hitler, that 'suicide' actions were always 'on the cards'. In fact Montgomery always tried to put himself into the enemy's shoes, even to the extent of confronting the photographs of his adversaries. His task was difficult for him because the enemy's shoes did not fit, nor were they shoes he could imagine himself wearing. The enemy, as the Americans observed and stated, was fighting a 'poor man's war', and had been doing so for many months, even in Normandy. In logistical terms the enemy had fought magnificently on little more than half of the supplies the Allies found necessary. By December such a relative scale was far in the past, and the enemy was constantly achieving the impossible. In von Runstedt's shoes it is improbable that Montgomery would have opened fire, and to mount an attack would have been unthinkable. In orthodox military terms the actions embarked upon by the enemy under military commanders of great skill and experience were unthinkable.

Thus Montgomery was perfectly correct in his appreciation if he had been commanding the enemy. Nothing would have induced him to mount a counter offensive through the Ardennes or anywhere else. He could imagine himself defending on a 'shoe-string', but not attacking on a 'shoe-string', least of all a threadbare shoe-string at breaking point. . . .

Even in terms of the desperate situation of the enemy perhaps no one, and certainly not anyone with the orderly mind of Montgomery, could appreciate an enemy act of military suicide with von Runstedt in command, or even in nominal command. And the Ardennes offensive was an act of military suicide. There was not enough transport, petrol, ammunition, even on the bare minimum scale with which the enemy had made do. Any kind of partial success must be dependent upon overrunning Allied supply dumps, particularly of fuel, within not more than 72 hours. And indeed, success was to be feared even more than failure, for no one in his senses could have believed that the long exposed flanks success would entail could be held against the powerful Allied armies poised on these flanks. The success in coming within sight of the Meuse on the enemy left flank cost the enemy at least half the man-power of three armies plus an enormous weight of material.

Nevertheless, one feels, or at least I feel, that with the knowledge of the existence of three enemy armies, two of them Panzer armies, assembled immediately east of the Eifel, the Allies should have paid particular heed. It was the Supreme Commander's problem and General Bradley's problem, and only Montgomery's in a secondary degree. It was Montgomery's job to appreciate possible situations prejudicial to his coming offensive through the Reichswald forest to the banks of the Rhine, and as far as he, or his Staff could see, no such situation was developing.

It is not possible to acquit the Supreme Commander and General Bradley. They turned a 'blind eye' to the whole Ardennes front, and refused to believe what they did not want to believe. Admitting the great reluctance of Bradley to modify his offensives north and south of the Ardennes, and the Supreme Commander's pre-occupation at the time with the situation on his extreme right flank, it was militarily indefensible to leave the entire Ardennes front so thinly and inadequately defended. In particular the gap between VIII corps and V corps was gross military carelessness. The Losheim gap was virtually wide open to the enemy, and the enemy went through it. That even such pieces of monumental luck could not give the German 6th Panzer Army the impetus on his right flank upon which the success of the whole operation depended, reveals the desperate nature of his venture.

Bradley and Hodges should have taken precautions, and could have done so without prejudicing the attacks in progress. Making allowances for the Allied shortage of man-power a strategic reserve other than the two airborne divisions withdrawn from Holland to refit at Rheims, should have been created. Early on the 16th the 7th Armoured division of the U.S. 9th Army was ordered south at full speed, and as soon as he took control of the northern salient of the battle, Montgomery swiftly organised reserves by withdrawing VII corps from U.S. 9th Army, and moving it south.

But on the morning of 16th December when all seemed quiet on the western front except to the poor unfortunates caught up into the enemy tide, Field-Marshal Montgomery decided to play a few holes of golf at Eindhoven. The Eindhoven Golf Club was the headquarters of the Royal Air Force Group supporting the 2nd Army, and by a stroke of fortune Dai Rees, the golf professional at Hindhead in civil life, was serving as driver to the Air Officer Commanding. In the midst of the game news of the enemy attack was brought to the Field-Marshal, and he flew at once to his tactical headquarters at Zonhoven. He was very much 'on the ball'.

III

The enemy counter offensive launched through the Ardennes out of the rugged and thickly wooded Eifel in the grey and bitter dawn of 16th December provided Field-Marshal Montgomery with a challenge uniquely suited to his talents. He responded brilliantly. It is difficult to fault his handling of the Ardennes battle, his creation of reserves, his rapid covering of the Meuse bridgeheads, and his steady production of order out of a confusion that must have shocked, even if it failed to alarm, his meticulous military mind. His presence produced immediate confidence in the shaken 1st U.S. Army Headquarters, even though his manner and bearing, 'like Christ come to cleanse the Temple', as Wilmot[1] put it, may have caused slight irritation. Refusing the courtesy of the Army Commander's table, he ate his sandwiches and consulted his own small map of the area, and became immersed in his problem. His personal liaison officers, enjoying an unusual co-operation from the Americans, were already providing him with information.

It is not surprising that the four weak infantry divisions strung out thinly over the 75 miles of the Ardennes front were overwhelmed by the weight of enemy attack. They were, they thought, in spite of the heavy barrage preceding the attack, which many of them believed 'friendly', in a quiet sector, almost a rest and rehabilitation area where green troops might become accustomed to the discomforts of the 'front line' without too much danger. Of the three infantry divisions of the U.S. VIII corps under General Middleton, two, the 4th and

[1] Wilmot: *The Struggle for Europe.*

28th, had sustained severe hammerings and suffered heavy casualties in the grim autumn battles further north. They were dog weary, and plagued by trench foot, bronchial troubles and other minor disorders. The third infantry division, the 106th, had relieved the 2nd division in the line four days earlier after an exhausting truck journey in biting cold across France and Belgium. They were a 'green' division. Attached to the 106th, the 14th Cavalry Group patrolled an eight mile wide gap between the VIII and V corps. It was a dangerously weak 'seam'. The right flanking infantry division of the V corps, the 99th, completed the picture. It was an inexperienced, but well trained division. It proved itself.

A combat command of 9th Armoured division strengthened the right centre of the VIII corps line, and the relieved 2nd division had not moved out of the Ardennes area to the north. The reserves available were hopelessly inadequate, consisting of four Engineer combat battalions.

In the first forty-eight hours of the battle these were the troops in the path of an avalanche of men and armour coming upon them with little warning under a solid leaden sky like a lid, reflecting the 'artificial moonlight' cast by the enemy searchlights. Long before the dawn the leading enemy troops had begun to infiltrate the American positions, yet the Americans, swiftly disintegrating as organised units, unaware for the most part of what was happening, their communications totally disrupted, and virtually cut off from effective command, imposed initial delays upon the enemy that were to prove decisive. The impetus vital to German success was never attained, nor were the firm 'shoulders' established essential to the security of their flanks.

The Battle of the Ardennes was won, and a heavy defeat inflicted upon the enemy, by fine generalship supported by able commanders in the field, by heroic defensive actions, notably at St. Vith and Bastogne, and by the swift and skilful creation and deployment of reserves. All these deeds have been 'sung' and will live in military annals, but the disruption of the enemy plan and the imposition of delays from which it was impossible to recover was brought about by anonymous men, anonymous groups, often of stragglers of no fixed intention, whose deeds will never be known.

'The historian ... must tread warily through the maze of recrimination and highly personalized recollection which surrounds this story,' wrote the Official historian, Hugh M. Cole.[1] He was referring especially to the disaster overtaking the 106th division, but it is broadly true for the whole of the first three days. What happened may only be known from reliable fragments, but too many pieces are missing to build a complete picture. A tank in charge of mechanics, either on its way to repair, or repaired, held up an enemy column for precious minutes on a key road by the accident of being there, and enabled a handful of engineers, equally unknown, to blow a bridge. No one will ever know who they were, or why they were there. A signalman quietly repairing signal wires suddenly saw an enemy column approaching. He leapt into his jeep and raced back to warn some tank destroyers a few miles behind him. They imposed a serious delay upon the enemy column. They are anonymous, and the fact that they were there comes mainly from searching through enemy records.

"A platoon of engineers appears in one terse sentence of a German Commander's report," wrote the official historian.[2] 'They fought bravely, says the foe, and forced him to waste a couple of hours in deployment and maneuver. In this brief emergence from the fog of war the engineer platoon makes its bid for recognition in history. That is all. A small group of stragglers suddenly becomes tired of what seems to be eternally retreating. Miles back they ceased to be a part of an organized combat formation, and recorded history, at that point, lost them. The sound of firing is heard for fifteen minutes, an hour, coming from a patch of woods, a tiny village, the opposite side of a hill. The enemy has been delayed; the enemy resumes the march westward. Weeks later a graves registration team uncovers mute evidence of a last-ditch stand at woods, village or hill.'

That is from the detailed official history of this strange affair. For the first forty-eight hours very little of the shape, purpose and portent of the battle was known to the corps or army command. This was the situation Field-Marshal Montgomery

[1] Hugh M. Cole: *The Ardennes*, battle of the bulge, Office of Chief of Mil. Hist. Washington D.C.
[2] Hugh M. Cole: *The Ardennes*, battle of the bulge. Office of Chief of Mil. Hist Washington, pp. 310-311.

confronted on the morning of 20th December. It was a strange situation for Montgomery, and it was a strange situation for the enemy. It is tempting to surmise that the disintegration of the U.S. infantry, and the patterns of behaviour, confronted the Germans with situations alien to their military experience. Here were troops who neither stood, nor withdrew, nor actually fled. On the disastrous evening of 19th December nearly 10,000 officers and men of 106th division, surrounded in the Schnee Eifel, surrendered with all their arms and equipment to an enemy they outnumbered. 'The Schnee Eifel battle ... represents the most serious reverse suffered by American arms during the operations of 1944–45 in the European theater.'[1] It is useless to speculate on precisely why this disaster occurred. It made it seem even more strange to the enemy that instead of rounding up stragglers they found themselves engaged with furious groups of men, sometimes a mere handful, sometimes a score, fighting to the death. There is a sense of American folk history in this story, of men reacting to a tradition peculiar to their country.

It may seem curious that the Supreme Command and 12th Army Group command had permitted such a situation to arise, and were slow to recognise its nature when it did arise. In the Autumn General Eisenhower had remarked casually to General Bradley that they might have 'a little Kasserine'[2] in the Ardennes. Nothing was done about it. It had been, they said in retrospect, 'a calculated risk'. It would have been more true to say that it had been a risk which they had failed, or refused, to calculate; for while they believed that the risk was there, at the same time they contrived not to believe it. Naturally there were grounds for this attitude. It was part of the price paid for General Bradley's uncompromising support of General Patton's 3rd Army, and his determination to maintain his offensive south of the Ardennes in competition with Montgomery in the north. The burden fell constantly upon the shoulders of General Hodges and the U.S. 1st Army. From the end of October Hodges had been forced to fight his battles in the Hürtgen Forest and the Roer as best he might, under-manned, under-

---

[1] Cole: *The Ardennes*.
[2] A reference to the serious reverse suffered by U.S. armour in the Kasserine Pass, Tunisia, 1943.

supplied, and denied artillery support above a minimum scale. No Allied army faced a more powerful enemy backed by a greater weight of reserves, and no sector of the whole Allied front from the Swiss frontier to Arnhem held the terrors and difficulties of terrain of the Hürtgen forest and the Roer. And perhaps no sector had a greater tactical importance than this key region to the Cologne plain and the northern Rhineland. General Hodges was showing signs of strain when Bradley ordered him to attack the Roer dams and on 13th December Hodges ordered General Gerow, commanding V corps, to move into the attack.

No one on the operational side of the Allied campaign from north to south considered any possible enemy intentions. The Supreme Commander was pre-occupied with the Colmar pocket in the extreme south. Bradley and Patton were mounting their offensive in the Saar. Montgomery had asked the Supreme Command if he might take a week's leave, and his Chief of Staff had gone on leave on 15th December.

'One of the greatest skills in the practice of military art,' observed the Official historian, contemplating this situation, 'is the avoidance of the natural tendency to overrate or underestimate the enemy. Here, the enemy capability for reacting other than to direct Allied pressure had been sadly underestimated. Americans and British had looked in a mirror for the enemy and seen there only the reflection of their own intentions.'[1]

[1] Cole: *The Ardennes*.

CHAPTER FOURTEEN

Montgomery's predicament

I

WHEN Field Marshal Montgomery took command of the allied armies north of the Ardennes soon after noon on 20th December he was almost certainly ignorant of the agonizing appraisal and thought preceding the Supreme Commander's reluctant decision to call upon him. For the Field-Marshal it was a military challenge of a particularly stimulating kind; it was also a great deal more than that. It was a wound to American pride at a moment when the command situation had become a political and social issue on both sides of the Atlantic. If the allied command could have been disrupted beyond repair, which is unthinkable, the appointment of Montgomery at this time, and in this particular circumstance, would have done it. All the rivalries, the jealousies, the suspicions and criticisms, seething just beneath the surface since Patton had joined Bradley and the command had begun to split on an Army Group level, were ready to explode. And Montgomery was the yeast in this unhappy mixture. I believe that Montgomery was saved by his innocence and by his intense professionalism. If he was critical of the performance of the American soldier, he did not show it by word or slightest gesture. Instead he reacted with soldierly sympathy, not unaware of the agony of American wounds. He saw these wounds raw and uncovered, the embarrassing wound of the disaster in the Schnee Eifel with its echoes of the Kasserine Pass in American minds, even if in no one else's. Thus for three weeks Montgomery was a man walking in a minefield. His behaviour throughout the battle was impeccable. The almost unimaginable chaos, the virtual absence of lines of communication or of any safe ways forward from corps to division even, was accepted without comment. From division forward each man took his life in his hands, moving through uncharted seas. Yet without going forward it was impossible to understand the nature of the battle. Montgomery knew through his dedicated young men, and his mind fastened at once upon essentials, ignoring all that had flown apart and concentrating on the pieces that had come together. Steadily order began to prevail. He appreciated at once the nature of the dangers and that these dangers were limited and local. He was one of the few to maintain a sense of proportion. The worst that could possibly happen would be a severe set-back to civilian morale in Belgium, for it was clear that the greater success the enemy might enjoy, the greater must be the disaster soon to overwhelm him. Thus to his impatient allies Montgomery seemed excessively slow and cautious as the days passed and the counter-attack they longed for was delayed. The counter-attack might easily be too soon for maximum results; it could scarcely be too late.

Immediately upon his return to his Tactical headquarters on the afternoon of the 16th December, Montgomery had begun to appreciate the probable enemy intentions and to take steps to preserve his own forthcoming offensive while screening the road to Brussels and reinforcing the Meuse bridgeheads. He quickly realized that an enemy break through the centre of the U.S. VIII corps would split the 12th Army Group command in halves. The thought may not have been distasteful to Montgomery. The U.S. 1st Army was virtually on its own, in tenuous contact by telephone with Bradley's headquarters in Luxembourg. After the 17th personal contact between Bradley and his northern generals was at an end. At the same time Luxembourg itself was under threat from the German 7th Army, whose role was to protect the southern flank of General Manteuffel's 5th Panzer Army.

On the 19th Bradley had ordered Patton to move his 10th armoured division with all possible speed, not only to relieve the threat to his headquarters but to aid the defenders of the road centre of Bastogne. The situation was complicated by a barrage of V weapons descending upon the Meuse bridgeheads, and threatening Liege. V-2's had begun to descend upon Antwerp. These dangers injected an extreme sense of urgency into the Supreme Command.

On the evening of the 19th Major-General Strong at

SHAEF confided his fears to Major-General Whiteley, deputy Chief of Staff, Operations. Both men were British and acutely conscious of 'the smoldering animosity toward the British in general and Montgomery in particular which existed in the headquarters of the 12th Army Group and Third Army, not to mention the chronic anti-British sentiment which might be anticipated from some circles in Washington.'[1]

Nevertheless it seemed to the British Staff Officers that the rapidly developing situation had created the two commands, one north of the Ardennes, and one south of the Ardennes, for which Montgomery had argued for many weeks. It was in any case beyond doubt that the situation on the northern flank demanded at once a powerful and experienced hand, and Montgomery was the only answer. Yet with some trepidation Generals Strong and Whiteley confronted General Walter Bedell Smith, the Chief of Staff, with their conclusion. Bedell Smith, while on good terms with his British staff was antipathetic to Montgomery, and shared the distaste of his countrymen for the British. Moreover he was a man of uncertain temper, capable of explosions of anger and periods of melancholy. The Americans were well aware of his 'hair-trigger temper'. His first reactions were negative and angry, but he 'cooled off and admitted the logic of the proposal.'[2] Having reconciled himself to the inevitable Bedell Smith recommended the appointment to General Eisenhower, and telephoned the unpalatable news to General Bradley. Bradley, loathing the proposition, none the less reacted very well. He commented that Montgomery would use his reserves if he were appointed, and might not be so keen to do so otherwise. This is to misinterpret Montgomery as a general and as a man. He was dedicated to the common cause and had reversed the movement of 30th Corps from north to south as soon as he appreciated the situation. The form of 'personal warfare' and animosity indulged by Generals Bradley and Patton, and the growing influence of public opinion in the United States upon the strategy of the campaign, would have shocked Montgomery profoundly. I do not think it occurred to him that Eisenhower, Bradley and Patton were in any way ill disposed towards him.

[1] Cole: *The Ardennes*, p. 424. Office of Chief of Mil. Hist. Washington.
[2] Ibid.

He had pressed his views because he believed them to be militarily correct, and in the three days from 16th to 19th December the enemy seemed to be proving him right. That was that. If he felt a sense of triumph he didn't display it. He was, as one American remarked, 'chipper as always', but to others he was nauseatingly pleased with himself. At Maastricht the Field-Marshal had laughed and joked with the Supreme Commander and his colleagues in a comradeship that had seemed real, even though the decisions taken at Maastricht had been wrong-headed in Montgomery's view.

'Certainly if Monty's were an American command, I would agree with you entirely,' Bradley said to Bedell Smith. 'It would be the logical thing to do.' It was the logical thing to do, and there was no way out. Later Bradley wrote: 'Had the senior British field commander been anyone else but Monty, the switch in command could probably have been made without incident, strain or tension.' He went on to say that Montgomery 'could not resist this chance to tweak our Yankee noses' and 'Eisenhower held his tongue only by clenching his teeth.'[1]

The last thing Montgomery wanted to do was to tweak American noses, and his treatment of Hodges, the weary and rattled 1st Army Commander, was patient and sympathetic, so much so that Hodges quickly regained his poise. In the event Montgomery's position was far from enviable, and whatever he said or did would fail to calm the bitter resentments of Bradley, or stem the flow of derisive and contemptuous remarks aimed at Montgomery and the British by General Patton.

Montgomery had been informed of the change in command on the night of the 19th, and the next morning Bedell Smith discussed the position with the Supreme Commander. Eisenhower at once telephoned Bradley to assure his troubled Army Group commander that the appointment of Montgomery was simply temporary. If the temporary nature of the change in command had been made public, a great deal of trouble might have been avoided.

At that time Bradley and Patton had not appreciated the extent of enemy action, and it had not emerged from Bradley's talk with Eisenhower on the morning of the 19th. His reaction was to assume that Supreme Headquarters had an 'acute case

---

[1] Bradley: *A Soldier's Story*, p. 477.

of the shakes'. He was also concerned that this might be a blow to American prestige and to his own position. He had, in fact, reacted to the enemy threat with great speed, ordering the 9th army to transfer the 7th Armoured division to 1st Army on the 17th and the division was moving south to reinforce the remnants of the 106th infantry holding on at St. Vith with the help of the engineer battalions. On the southern flank he had persuaded the reluctant Patton to move 10th Armoured division to secure the flank and safeguard 12th Army Group headquarters from the threat developing from the German 7th Army. By the 19th December two airborne divisions completing their 'rehabilitation' near Rheims were ordered into the battle, the 101st to rush to the aid of the 110th Regiment of the shattered 28th division, disputing the road to Bastogne yard by yard, and the 82nd to hold the dangerous salient in the Vielsalm area west of St. Vith. Thus the two vital nodal points and road junctions essential to enemy success were swiftly reinforced.

When Montgomery took command in the north on the 20th the scaffolding of containment was in position, and the situation was not quite so 'unpleasantly vague' as it had been a day or two earlier. He had covered the Meuse bridge-heads, and four divisions of the British 30th corps with three armoured brigades rapidly concentrated in positions blocking the way through to Brussels and Antwerp. There was little to fear, for it was already apparent that the enemy, should he succeed in bouncing the Meuse between Liege and Givet, would be unable to do so in sufficient strength to cause much anxiety to 30th Corps.

In moving his reserves in this manner Montgomery had been studiously careful to avoid any possible crossing of the British and American lines of communication. Moreover he realised very clearly that this was, and must remain, an American battle. This was the heart of the challenge facing him. He was in direct and intimate command of an alien army already in the midst of a confused battle, and suffering the dismay of serious reverses. He had to deal with men whose training, whose concepts of life, whose values, were different from his own, and he was dealing with these men face to face at a time of personal crisis for many of them. General Hodges, commanding the U.S. 1st Army, was in a highly nervous condition which might demand action, even relief. It is difficult to imagine a more delicate situation. The fact that Montgomery's presence, his immediate grasp of the situation, his rapid moves to create reserves with which to counter-attack at the precise moment of his choosing, calmed Hodges. In a day or two Hodges was himself again, one of the most competent and experienced commanders in the American camp. The Supreme Commander, who would have had the unhappy duty of relief and replacement, was as glad as was Montgomery.

From the outset Montgomery had to persuade, rather than to command, soldiers to take actions often against their traditions and remarkable emotions. To create his reserve for counter-attack he withdrew divisions from battle in the north, and faced the indignation of the commanders involved. He was adamant in his choice of men and insisted upon Lieut.-General Lawton Collins to lead his VII corps in the counter-attacking role. Collins, nick-named 'Lightning Joe' by the Americans, was not an easy man to hold, and Montgomery's choice of him is revealing. One of the Field-Marshal's early and important decisions was the withdrawal of the U.S. 7th Armoured division covering St. Vith. General Hasbrouck, commanding the division, was a commander of rare quality and courage. On the 22nd, with his division under tremendous pressure, Hasbrouck had drafted a long message to his Corps Commander, General Ridgeway. His position was worsening rapidly, and he was throwing in 'his last chips' in an attempt to stave off violent attacks. He added a postscript to Ridgeway: 'In my opinion if we don't get out of here and up north of the 82nd (Airborne) before night, we will not have a 7th Armoured division left.'

To Ridgeway this meant that the 7th Armoured division had no alternative but to stand and fight to the last man. Fortunately Montgomery was fully informed, and was able to combat Ridgeway's refusal to order the division to withdraw. Hasbrouck had spoken frankly to one of the Field-Marshal's liaison 'Phantom' group. 'Montgomery had consulted with the Army commander, and here showed the ability to honor the fighting man...' wrote the U.S. Official historian.[1] The Field-Marshal's order would live in U.S. Military history: 'They can come back

[1] Cole: *The Ardennes*, battle of the bulge. Office of Chief of Mil. Hist. Washington.

with all honor. They come back to the more secure positions. They put up a wonderful show.'

Thus the 7th Armoured division was not only preserved, but remained a vital force blocking the further advance of the enemy. The U.S. Official Historian added: 'The First Army Commander, tired and worried from the strain under which he had lived since 16th December, agreed to withdrawal.'

In fact, the severe strains afflicting General Hodges had grown out of the long series of winter battles his army had fought in appalling conditions. No troops from north to south had sustained a comparable ordeal, and the 1st Army had been neglected long before the enemy drove a wedge through the middle of the 12th Army Group.

No sooner had Montgomery saved the 7th armoured division than he faced an even more delicate task in achieving the withdrawal of the 82nd Airborne division, against the will of its commander, General Gavin, of General Ridgeway, the Airborne corps commander, and of the unhappy Hodges. Gavin's heart-cry that his division had never withdrawn in 'its combat history' revealed a tragic weakness. In common with his commanders he was not able to understand at that time that to withdraw was his duty, and that by refusing to consider this course he was depriving his troops of tactical flexibility, and making a gratuitous present to the enemy. For only in the last extremity, in the isolated holding of a vital bastion which must be denied to the enemy at all costs—and Bastogne was such a bastion—may a commander honourably ask his men to die with him.

The situation was vastly complicated by General Ridgeway's inflexible support for his divisional commander. Ridgeway was an airborne version of General Patton, rather less flambuoyant and explosive, and wearing clusters of hand grenades instead of the pearl handled revolvers affected by Patton. Both men had considerable soldierly virtues, but part of their growing-up had been stunted in childhood, crippling them as adult members of society, even of a restricted military society.

While Montgomery summoned all his tact and patience to save the 82nd division the enemy moved with speed to force Ridgeway's entire reserve into the battle, and to gain a local tactical victory. Only then was Montgomery able to insist upon the withdrawal of the 82nd, and to re-group all available troops for the counter-attack he was resolved to mount in the greatest possible strength.

On 23rd December a spearhead of Manteuffel's Fifth Panzer Army had a brief glimpse of the Meuse near Dinant, but the enemy had shot his bolt, and knew it. The U.S. 1st Army, having held the major attacks of the German 6th Panzer Army between Spa and Malmedy in the north, had made the enemy plan impossible to carry out. The enemy progress in the centre was never more than a local danger born of enemy failure on the flanks, and the denial of the vital road centres of St. Vith and Bastogne. Without control of these nodal points he was forced to attempt to move through the centre on narrow, hopelessly inadequate roads which would prove death traps when the skies cleared and ice and snow replaced mud and rain. No major threat to the allies could be mounted or sustained on that line.

Meanwhile growing failure induced the enemy to concentrate all available force upon Bastogne and to free his left centre and flank to create whatever havoc might still be possible. The defenders of Bastogne, unlike the defenders of St. Vith, were completely cut off and isolated, until Patton's armour, disengaging from the Saar and racing north could force a corridor.

That day, the 23rd, was the beginning of the end for the enemy, even though this was not apparent to most observers. The leaden sky was clearing, and the first waves of the Allied Air Force began to take a terrible toll of enemy transport, armour, guns and men. By Christmas Day masses of men and and material were bombed and 'throttled', as Manteuffel put it, in the narrow chasms of the roads, unable to go forward or back. Denied hope of orderly withdrawal or reinforcement, not only by their Führer, but by the rapidly deteriorating conditions, the Germans continued to batter against the American right, left and centre, long after their cause was lost. They had failed in their objects, but the longer they were able to engage the allies, the greater would be the tactical reverse the western allies would suffer. Moreover, while the Allies were off balance the enemy contrived to maintain pressure in the north, and was also ready to mount an attack in an attempt to gain the Saverne Gap, disrupt the U.S. 7th Army, and even encircle the troops in the Colmar pocket. The U.S. 6th Army Group had been dragged out of position in support of Patton's 3rd Army, and Strasbourg was threatened early in the New Year. Militarily the Germans had known that they were going down fast to defeat long before they launched the counter-offensive through the Ardennes. Their aims were political rather than military, inspired by the forlorn hope, valid in the Führer's mind, if in the minds of very few others, that some startling success against the Anglo-American armies might give some bargaining power and disrupt the alliance between the Western allies and the Soviet Union. At any hour the Soviet armies would move into the offensive out of their bridgeheads across the Vistula, and the vice would begin to close upon the German heartland from east and west. Time was running out fast.

II

The problems confronting Field-Marshal Montgomery and General Bradley in their separate halves of the Ardennes battle were simple and local compared with the difficulties facing the Supreme Commander. The weaknesses in his 'Broad Front' strategy were ruthlessly exposed, and against a powerful enemy, adequately supported in the air and logistically on the ground, the Allies would have been open to defeat. As it was, the holes had to be plugged, and Strasbourg had to be held in spite of the military advantages of withdrawal. It might have been a minor lesson to the Supreme Command, and U.S. Joint Chiefs of Staff, that politics and military action are indivisible. They were in no mood to learn.

Meanwhile Montgomery handled his difficult command with patience and skill. He controlled 'half a battle', and was not kept sufficiently informed on progress on the southern front. His own half of the battle was very clear, and he had made great headway in restoring the balance of the 1st Army, freeing its troops from all anxieties other than those they faced on the immediate battlefield. The awful confusion in the rear areas was slowly coming under control, but plagued by rumours of enemy infiltration in U.S. uniforms and of plots to assassinate the Supreme Commanders, Montgomery and

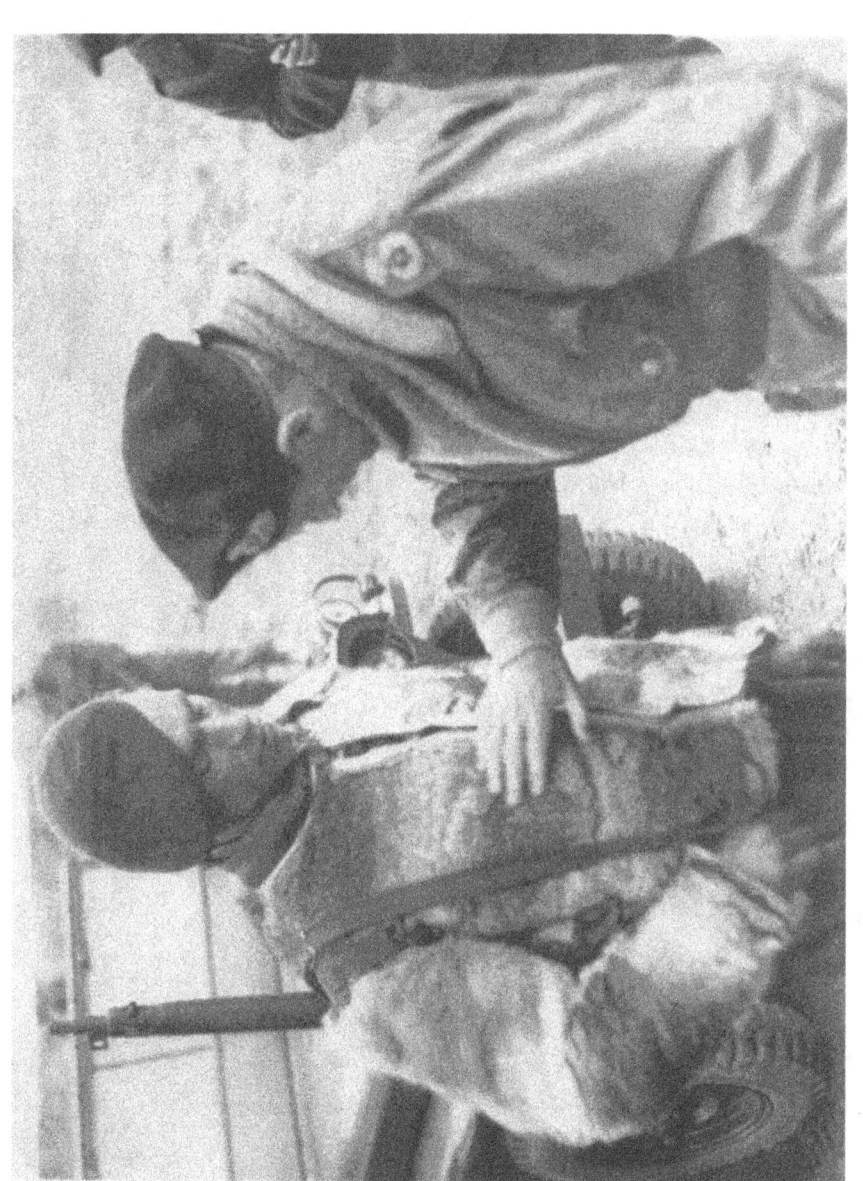

7. The C-in-C, on tour of forward areas, interested in a fur jacket captured from the enemy and worn by a Canadian infantryman

Bradley. While corps and divisions were gravely under strength, especially in infantry, Military Police and security forces seethed in the rear areas, providing the Supreme Commander with too much protection for his liking, hampering his movements, and drawing his attention to considerable numbers of men available for non-combatant duties. Montgomery had reported anxiously that 'the V Corps divisions were under strength by some 7,000, mostly in infantry, and asked if something could be done to get replacements "for this serious discrepancy".'

The shortage of infantry men was a sore point with Americans in high places, but it may not have been known to Eisenhower at that time just how dangerously low U.S. man-power had become. In analysis of the man-power situation William Bradford Huie arrived at alarming figures ... 'one youth out of every eight was excused from military service for reasons other than physical ... their number was 1,532,500—the temperamentally unstable, the maladjusted, the sexually perverted, and the overly nervous ... Of the 10,110,103 who were inducted only 2,670,000 were trained for actual ground combat; and of these a very large number, believed to be as high as a million men, soon managed to escape combat by such devices as bad-conduct discharges, or self-inflicted wounds, or being excused by psychiatrists for some form of mental insufficiency ... Among those who evaded combat were about forty thousand who were believed to have 'taken off' or 'bugged off' or 'deserted before the enemy.'[1]

Even a partial awareness of this situation, and it was at times manifest in particular divisions, added to the embarrassment of a disaster such as had recently occurred in the Schnee Eifel, may in some measure account for the bitterly ultra aggressive attitudes of Bradley, Patton and others towards the British.

Meanwhile Montgomery, short of news and doubting Patton's ability to reach Bastogne in time to relieve the beleaguered garrison, and to hold the German 7th Army away from its objectives, sought contact with Bradley. In fact, Patton, responding with immense enthusiasm to orders from the Supreme Commander, had swung a substantial force of the 3rd Army through a 90 degree arc and set them racing

---

[1] William Bradford Huie: *The Execution of Private Slovik*.

north at great speed. On the 26th December, a day after Montgomery had had a miserable meeting with Bradley, Patton's leading column began to open a narrow corridor through to Bastogne.

General Bradley appeared to have a very limited understanding of the nature of his battle on the southern flank, and of Montgomery's in the north and centre. He was lyrical in his praise of Patton's brilliant disengagement, and thrust to the north. He seemed to confuse the necessity for Patton to attack with all speed with the very different priorities in the north. Bradley and Patton coming in from the south had no option, for the alternative to attack was to fail to confront the German left, abandon Luxembourg and probably Bastogne, and give Manteuffel's 5th Panzer Army a clear run through to the Meuse. And, of course, the U.S. 3rd Army had been ordered to intervene with all possible speed. The two halves of the battle were in no way comparable.

On 25th December, Christmas Day, Bradley journeyed unhappily to Montgomery's tactical headquarters, resolved to urge Montgomery to counter-attack without more delay. He had begged General Eisenhower to 'prod Montgomery in an effort to speed up the counter-attack.'[1]

The meeting was disappointing. Montgomery, exuding the calm and confidence he felt, explained his plan with his usual clarity and economy. Bradley seems to have listened without comment, simply recording, 'Not until he was certain the enemy had exhausted himself would Montgomery plunge in for the kill.'[2]

Bradley saw himself as vital and enthusiastic opposed to the brick wall of Montgomery's extreme caution. Through Montgomery's eyes the meeting seemed very different. Bradley had neither argued nor disagreed. 'He (Bradley) looked thin, and worn and ill at ease,' the Field-Marshal wrote to Brooke. 'He agreed entirely with all I said. Poor chap; he is such a decent fellow and the whole thing is a bitter pill for him. But he is man enough to admit it and he did... He stayed only half an hour and flew straight back.'[3]

---

[1] Bradley: *A Soldier's Story*, p. 480.
[2] Ibid.
[3] Bryant: *Triumph in the West*, p. 368.

In fact Bradley was unaware that he had agreed with Montgomery, or that he had anything to admit. On 26th Bradley wrote a personal letter to Hodges, saying that although he 'was no longer in my command, I would view with serious misgivings the surrender of any more ground.' This letter seems a breach of etiquette, indicative of Bradley's nervous condition.

It is curious that while Bradley nagged incessantly about Montgomery's slowness in mounting a counter-attack in the north, he was full of praise for the U.S. 1st Army, ascribing its recovery and great endeavours solely to the brilliance of General Hodges, who 'gathered his VII Corps on the flank in preparation for a counter-attack.' Moreover, 'This remarkable regroupment of 1st Army while under attack equalled even the astonishing performance of 3rd Army.'[1] None of this achievement, apparently, was due to the strong command of Montgomery. All that could be credited or debited to the Field-Marshal was his extreme caution, his desire to 'tidy up', and his refusal to counter-attack until he was ready, and the enemy ripe.

General Bradley's lack of a real command, his fear that he might lose face with his troops and with the American public, and even that he might not regain command of his army group, tried him sorely.

Meanwhile the pressure of the German 6th Panzer Army was still powerful and persistent, and severe attacks were expected in the north until the end of the year. Eisenhower was well informed on the situation, and it is doubtful that he shared Bradley's view in regard to Montgomery's timing. He appreciated that Bradley wanted his command back, and his image restored. The elevation of Bradley to five-star General had mollified the 12th Army Group commander, but had not dispersed his fears. The sooner Montgomery counter-attacked, and brought the battle to an end the sooner Bradley would be restored. This factor, quite properly, did not influence the British Field-Marshal, nor was he influenced or greatly disturbed by the battle of words raging in the British and U.S. newspapers. Montgomery was in the full limelight as the saviour of the situation in many eyes, including many Belgians and Dutch, whose fears abated as soon as they heard that 'Monty'

---

[1] Bradley: *A Soldier's Story*, p. 478.

was in command. These reactions added fuel to the fires that were already burning with too much heat. The British press, naturally, but unfortunately, chose this moment to criticise the Supreme Command, while the U.S. press reacted angrily to Bradley's seeming replacement by Montgomery, and the general frustrations on the Western front.

For his part Montgomery seemed totally unaware of the storm on both sides of the Atlantic, and of the intense dislike generating against him in the American camp. When at last he became aware of the feeling against him he was 'dumbfounded', but it was doubtful, as Bradley wrote, that he ever 'knew just how exasperated we had become.'

In the midst of this crisis and outburst of popular feeling the Supreme Commander met Montgomery at Hasselt on 28th December. Eisenhower had had a frustrating journey, hemmed in by security guards, and plagued by delays and detours caused by enemy action. Montgomery was his usual 'chipper' self. He had a right to be. He had brought order out of chaos, organized powerful reserves for counter-attack, stabilized the U.S. 1st Army (and its commander), and used his own troops with care, speed, and skill. He expected at least one enemy attack in the north, and this would provide him with the timing for his counter stroke. He would be ready, he estimated, on 3rd January. Meanwhile the frustrated German 5th Panzer Army, unable to break loose, and the German command, had begun to throw its remaining strength into the battle for Bastogne, for no strategic purpose, but as a kind of 'Epilogue', as Manteuffel put it, to the whole wrong-headed offensive. The line of the Allied counter-attack was clear. The 1st Army would assault to cut off the salient and join hands with the 3rd Army at Houffalize on the Ourthe. The enemy would be confined within a constricting bulge, harassed mercilessly from the air, and forced to attempt to withdraw in hopeless conditions. The snow had begun to fall. Carpets of bombs 'throttled' the whole enemy supply system on the icy roads and made all troop movement impossible in daylight.

Unhappily, but reasonably, as it seemed to him, Montgomery chose the Hasselt meeting to urge the establishment of one command in the north upon the unhappy Supreme Commander. In spite of Eisenhower's strong feelings on this subject he left Montgomery believing that he had carried his point, and writing to Brooke happily that all would now be well. Brooke expressed his doubts in his diary: 'According to Monty, Ike agrees that the front should now be divided in two and that only one major offensive is possible. But I expect that whoever meets Ike next may swing him to another point of view.'[1]

This, I believe, is to misjudge Eisenhower. His fault was not that he could be easily swayed, but that he must have failed to express himself clearly and beyond a shadow of a doubt to the Field-Marshal. As Supreme Commander, and in this extremely important and delicate matter, he had an absolute duty to do so. Montgomery was difficult, but he could understand plain words spoken plainly as well as anyone. It is not possible that the Supreme Commander could have spoken clearly and unequivocally at Hasselt on 28th December. Had he done so, a great deal of trouble and misunderstanding might have been avoided. It is a curious situation. Months earlier Eisenhower had deplored Montgomery's failure to attend conferences, remarking that when they all got together and talked things out, problems would be solved. But it seemed that they did not talk things out, and problems were worse confounded. Bradley also failed to express himself, and in this the Americans failed in their duty to themselves and to Montgomery.

All that might have been hoped for in January, 1945 was a strengthening of ground force command. If Eisenhower had been prepared to assume a close ground force command himself, it would have satisfied Montgomery. But Eisenhower could not do so without failing in his even greater duties. Thus he must, in the British view, appoint a ground force commander, or a new deputy commander capable of performing that role. One thing should have been clear to Montgomery in early January, 1945, and that is that the Supreme Commander could not and would not put one army group commander under the other, whichever way about. The American public would have roared with rage, and many in Washington, including the Joint Chiefs of Staff, would have refused to accept such an appointment. Bradley would have resigned, and possibly Patton with him. They had come a long way since Normandy, and by different routes.

[1] Bryant: *Triumph in the West*.

Perhaps it was as well that Montgomery, in accordance with his custom, committed his views in writing to the Supreme Commander immediately after the Hasselt meeting. It was a strangely worded memorandum:

'It will be necessary for you to be very firm on the subject (of command), and any loosely worded statement will be quite useless. I consider that if you use the word "co-ordination", it will NOT work. The person designated by you must have powers of operational direction and control of the operations that will follow on your Directive... One commander must have powers to direct and control the operations; you cannot possibly do it yourself and so you would have to nominate someone else. I suggest that your Directive should finish with this sentence:

> 12th and 21st Army Groups will develop operations in accordance with the above instructions. From now onwards full operational direction, control, and co-ordination of these operations is vested in the C in C 21st Army Group, subject to such instructions as may be issued by the Supreme Commander from time to time.[1]

'The arrival of this uncompromising document at S.H.A.E.F. coincided with a major crisis in Anglo-American relations,' Brooke commented.

But the 'uncompromising document', worded as might a tutor to a rather dim pupil, and not very far removed from a 'reprimand', did not cause the crisis. The document was blunt even for Montgomery, and it may have reflected his exasperation at being so consistently misunderstood. Predictions in the British Press that Montgomery would take command in the north sparked off attacks against the Field-Marshal in the American Press, and on 30th December General Marshall, U.S. Chief of Staff, cabled the Supreme Commander:

> My feeling is this: under no circumstances make any concessions of any kind whatsoever. You not only have our complete confidence but there would be terrific resentment in this country following such an action. I am not assuming that you had in mind such a concession, I just wish you to be

---
[1] Montgomery: *Memoirs*, p. 318.

certain of our attitude on this side. You are doing a fine job and go on and give them hell.[1]

Whether or not Eisenhower could 'possibly do it' himself, he was going to do it. On that day, the 30th, Eisenhower held a meeting with his Staff officers. The fear that Montgomery was far behind Bradley 'when it came to the need for offensive action,' may have been justified by the Field-Marshal's performances in the past, but was doubtful judgement in the context of the Ardennes battle under discussion. In that battle 'They feared his (Montgomery's) alleged over-careful policy would cause the Allies to miss a chance to inflict a severe defeat on the enemy in the immediate future.'[2] In this appreciation the Supreme Commander's Staff revealed that they lacked Montgomery's intimate knowledge of the battlefield, and of the enemy intentions. While the enemy continued to commit forces, and to change direction to the south-west to concentrate upon Bastogne, the chances of a kill would increase rather than diminish. In fact the American desire for instant counter-attack was based upon personal grounds and emotions rather than on the military situation.

Nevertheless the feeling at Supreme Headquarters had reached the boil, alarming Montgomery's Chief of Staff, Major-General de Guingand. After a talk with Bedell Smith de Guingand reported back urgently to Montgomery, warning him that if it came to a showdown, 'someone would have to go and it would not be the Supreme Commander.'[3]

The Supreme Commander's reply to the Field-Marshal's 'uncompromising document' was very clear. After thanking Montgomery for his 'frank and friendly counsels, he wrote that he would deplore the development of such an unbridgeable gulf of convictions between us that we would have to present our difficulties to the Combined Chiefs of Staff. The confusion and debate that would follow would certainly damage the goodwill and devotion to a common cause that have made this Allied force unique in history.'[4]

Immediately on hearing the warning of his Chief of Staff,

[1] Pogue: *The Supreme Command*, p. 386. Eisenhower personal file.
[2] Pogue: *The Supreme Command*, p. 386n (80).
[3] De Guingand: *Operation Victory*, p. 434. M. *Memoirs*, p. 319.
[4] Pogue: *The Supreme Command*, p. 386n.

Montgomery had decided in his own phrase to 'pipe down'. He wrote at once to the Supreme Commander, that he was 'very distressed that my letter may have upset you and I would ask you to tear it up. Your very devoted subordinate Monty.'

But the command situation continued to rankle, and Brooke noted that Montgomery was still turning it round and round in his mind at the end of January.

III

On the 3rd January Montgomery launched the U.S. VII Corps into the counter-attack, and the vice began to close upon the enemy. Four days later, feeling that his task in the Ardennes, was virtually done, Montgomery gave his famous, or infamous, Press Conference in an endeavour to set the record straight, and to 'put in a strong plea for Allied solidarity.' He had sought and gained Churchill's approval for this move, and ignored the rather tentative suggestions of his more intimate staff that it might be better for him to say nothing at all. It was remarkable then, and it may appear even more remarkable now, that the Field-Marshal's simple account of the course of the battle, his praise of American troops and commanders, should have set off a storm of anger and vilification. It is a measure of the intensity of the feelings he had innocently aroused, and it is a reflection of the isolation suffered by those who control in some measure the destinies of their fellow men. To the lay mind it is difficult to grasp. One would have thought that men like General de Guingand, supported by Generals Strong and Whitely, even General Bedell Smith, the Chief of Staff to the Supreme Commander, might have put the situation clearly to Montgomery. Surely there must have been a way for men of this seniority to 'get through' to the Field-Marshal, to convince him of the feeling against him, and of the danger of words. Perhaps Field-Marshal Brooke, more than anyone, should have intervened. No one was in closer contact with Montgomery on a high level, no one was more aware of the dangerous situation.

Perhaps such a revelation of the truth would have been too

wounding to Montgomery. It would have been a risk worth the taking, a risk if taken much sooner, even years sooner, might have released the Field-Marshal from a seeming lack of sensitivity. On the other hand it might have damaged him severely, for a man is compounded of strengths and weaknesses, and of strange conceits. It is dangerous to tamper with these things. Montgomery was Montgomery, for better or worse. Yet it is worth remembering that the probable effects of Montgomery's words, *whatever he might say*, were foreseen, and those who gathered to hear them, and to report them, were curiously agog.

There is no doubt that Montgomery was upset by the attacks against the Supreme Commander in the British Press. He wanted to set the record straight. He wanted to make it clear beyond a doubt that the Ardennes had been an American battle, and that U.S. forces had won it. He described the U.S. soldier as 'a brave fighting man, steady under fire, and with that tenacity in battle which stamps the first class soldier; all these qualities have been shown in a marked degree during the present battle . . . I salute the brave fighting man of America; I never want to fight alongside better soldiers . . . I have tried to feel that I am almost an American soldier myself so that I might take no unsuitable action to offend them in any way.'[1]

The reaction of the American Press was reassuring. The *New York Times* commented in an editorial on 9 January that, 'no handsomer tribute was ever paid to the American soldier than that of Field-Marshal Montgomery in the midst of combat.'

That was at least a valid view of the Field-Marshal's words, yet General Bradley was outraged, and his staff with him. Did he detect some shade of irony, a feigned goodwill disguising malice? Or had the Field-Marshal's 'chipper', almost schoolboy, delight in himself, become, as such things may, intolerable. It was a serious matter. 'Weeks after the Montgomery interview, General Eisenhower was still getting strong reactions from his U.S. commanders and the U.S. press.'[2]

On the 8th February the Supreme Commander wrote to General Marshal: 'No single incident that I have ever encountered throughout my experience as an Allied commander

[1] Montgomery: *Memoirs*, p. 313.
[2] Pogue: *The Supreme Command*, p. 388.

has been so difficult to combat as this particular outburst in the papers.'

No wonder Montgomery wrote in his Memoirs, 'All of which shows that I should have kept my mouth shut.' At the time Montgomery remained happily unaware of the *gaffe* he had perpetrated. He believed himself to be on the best of terms with Bradley, and on the 12th January, two days after he had issued the final order jointly with Bradley for the last phase of the counter-attack, he wrote to the 12th Army Group commander most warmly and generously.

> 'My dear Brad,
> It does seem as if the battle of the "salient" will shortly be drawing to a close, and when it is all clean and tidy I imagine that your armies will be returning to your operational command.
> I would like to say two things:
> First: What a great honour it has been for me to command such fine troops.
> Second: How well they have all done.
> It has been a great pleasure to work with Hodges and Simpson: both have done very well.
> And the Corps Commanders in the First Army (Gerow, Collins, Ridgeway) have been quite magnificent; it must be most exceptional to find such a good lot of Corps Commanders gathered together in one army.
> All of us in the northern side of the salient would like to say how much we have admired the operations that have been conducted on the southern side; if you had not held firmly to Bastogne the whole situation might have become very awkward.
> My kind regards to you and to George Patton.
>
> > Yours very sincerely,
> >
> > B. L. Montgomery.'

The Field-Marshal sent a copy of the letter to the Supreme Commander with a covering note stating: 'It has been a very great honour to me to command two American armies.' It acted like gall in Bradley's wounds, for the enemy offensive had revealed a weakness in Bradley's command of his Army Group. His choice of his headquarters at Luxembourg, a mere ten minutes from General Patton and the 3rd Army headquarters, and a two hour journey or more from General Hodges and the 1st Army, indicated his preference and his bias. After the Ardennes the Supreme Commander insisted upon Bradley setting up his headquarters at Namur, allowing him equal access to both his 'wings', and more convenient for liaison with Montgomery's 21st Army Group. Perhaps Bradley felt some sense of guilt for the terrible battle of attrition.

IV

In the early hours of the 17th January the U.S. 1st Army joined hands with the U.S. 3rd Army across the river Ourthe at Houffalize. The ruined bridge could still be crossed by agile men. It was a scene of pitiful desolation, and a symbol of American victory. Until the end of the month the retreating enemy fought desperately to save what they could from the wreck of their hopes, but mainly to attempt to regroup, to fight again, and on to the bitter end. For there were no more hopes. The 6th Panzer Army had been withdrawn to be moved as swiftly as possible to reinforce the eastern front against the devastating torrent of the Russians.

There was now a consciousness that the war had changed its entire nature; that in a sense it was over, and that all that remained were the final catastrophic chords, the 'last Trump'!

'You will enter the continent of Europe, and, in conjunction with the other United Nations, undertake operations aimed at the heart of Germany and the destruction of her armed forces.'

The hour was at hand. Two million men were lining up in the West, ready for the final bound. Perhaps twice that number in the East were already launched into the last assault. It was awe inspiring, tragic and terrible, and there was no way out. War was dead. Something new was about to take place. The Eastern front had suddenly made the Western front seem small, and the Ardennes almost an insignificant incident. Yet there was nothing insignificant about it, nor about the smallest particle of battle, the death of the individual.

At dawn on 12th January Marshal Koniev advanced from his bridgeheads on the Vistula, and two days later the armies of Marshal Zhukov, crossing on his right flank, swung north over the Pilica, while on his left General Petrov's Army threatened Jaslo. On the extreme right of this violent assault, which swiftly enveloped Warsaw and Cracow, Marshals Rokossovsky and Chernyakhosky advanced upon Tilsit, obliterated East Prussia, and gained bridgeheads across the Vistula in the north to join with the right wing of Zhukov's armies. In the south, stiffening the pressure which they had never relaxed throughout the winter, Malinovsky and Tolbukhin enveloped Budapest, and the roads to Vienna and Berlin opened ahead. In three weeks, moving at an average rate of 14 miles a day as the crow flies, the Russians were on the river Oder 280 miles from their start point. From north to south 300 Russian divisions backed by 25 tank armies and tens of thousands of Cossacks, rolled back the Germans with an irresistible force.

It was the knowledge that this dreadful blow was impending that had induced Hitler to launch his desperate gamble in the Ardennes. It was the knowledge also that injected urgency into the British pursuit of a change in the command structure in the West, hoping that at the eleventh hour a political object might be imposed upon the crazy pattern of destruction. All Churchill's hoped for strategies in the Mediterranean and the Balkans had failed. Not only Vienna and Prague would be at any moment in Soviet hands, but Berlin itself might be engulfed. In Churchill's strategic thinking this was a matter of overwhelming importance. It made him, supported by his Chiefs of Staff, press the Americans for a Deputy Ground Force Commander to replace Tedder in the hierarchy. They wanted Alexander. This, they thought, would strengthen the northern attack, and give the northern armies the tight command for which Montgomery had argued for so long. British hopes died at Malta at the end of the month in arguments that were 'vehement as well as prolonged,' provoking 'the most acrimonious dispute between the Combined Chiefs of Staff during the war.'[1] Harry Hopkins, President Roosevelt's personal emissary and aide, commented: 'One can read the official minutes of

---

[1] *Grand Strategy*, vol. vi, p. 89 and see '*Argonaut*'.

these meetings without suspecting that a single harsh word had been exchanged. But they were very angry men.'[1]

As for Eisenhower, he remained immune to Churchill's pleas to the end, refusing to regard Berlin as more than 'a geographical abstraction'.

Against this vast backcloth of war Field-Marshal Montgomery became the David leading the David of British arms, not so much against 'Goliath', but in the midst of 'Goliaths'. His importance in British eyes had increased rather than diminished, and there had emerged a limit to this war that had at times seemed without limits. The last chapter was at last in sight, the meeting of the two jaws of the vice somewhere in Germany. Everyone knew that it must be as far east as possible, and there was a nightmare that it might be on the Rhine, that we should lose this last race. The river Elbe was a very long way away.

There was a great need for leadership and inspiration in this sodden month of January on top of the sodden months of December and November. Montgomery's triumph in the Ardennes—for it was a triumph in British eyes—had been well timed, furbishing the Field-Marshal's image. The Ardennes had been Montgomery's best battle in many ways. General Hasso von Manteuffel, commander of the 5th Panzer Army, believed that one of the main factors in the defeat of the offensive, not simply in its failure as an offensive, was that the allied counter-measures were co-ordinated as a single plan. 'On the other hand,' he wrote, 'one can now say that the enemy's counter-attack began too soon.'[2]

But for Montgomery the co-ordination would have been doubtful, and the counter-attack would have been launched much more prematurely, and with doubtful results. As it was the enemy had suffered losses in men and material which it was impossible for him to make good. The balance sheet was in favour of the Americans, especially in materiel, but in manpower it had been a harsh reckoning on both sides. The German casualties may have been as high as 120,000 men; the Americans had lost 80,000 men, and the British a few more than 1,000. It had left a bitter taste. I wrote soon afterwards

[1] *The White House Papers*, vol. ii.
[2] *The Fatal Decisions*, Part Six. *The Ardennes*. Manteuffel.

that Montgomery had probably saved the American 1st Army 20,000 casualties, including the U.S. 7th Armoured division. Perhaps it was this that Americans could not forgive. The blood was American, the brains, the firm hand, the moral courage were Montgomery's.

On 17th January the British 30th Corps had been pinched out of the battle and Montgomery's ordeal was over. He had concentrated upon the maintenance of his objective in the north, preserving his battle of the Rhineland. The battle of the Ardennes had cost him time, but less, I think, than he believed. He was glad to return to his own troops.

CHAPTER FIFTEEN

The race for the Rhine

I

MONTGOMERY returned to his command in the north with pleasure and relief. He was about to launch the battle for the Rhineland with three armies under his command, and with an airborne corps at his service should he call upon it. The priorities were his, and he had cause for satisfaction. There was no doubt by that time that the enemy had resolved to fight for every yard of German soil, and it seemed improbable that it would be possible to organize armies east of the Rhine to do much more than hinder the advancing allies. The Wehrmacht, engaged desperately on the eastern front in a struggle to the death rather than for survival, could still organize nearly eighty divisions to face the western allies, but they were divisions on paper and not on the ground. The poverty of their equipment and supply, their battered armour and threadbare artillery, was in marked contrast to the massive wealth of the Allies. Their man-power had become heavily impregnated with boy-power, and their once magnificent training cut to the bone. It would have been dangerous to under-estimate their fighting quality, and no one did, least of all Montgomery. The battle for the Rhineland might be the last battle.

An enormous wealth of supplies was flowing in from the port of Antwerp, and freight trains reinforced the great fleets of trucks struggling over the battered and sodden roads. The great stockpiles were building up to immense proportions to sustain 21st Army Group into the heart of the Reich. The only supply problems would be those of abundance rather than shortage. By the end of January the 1st Canadian Army had built up a reserve of 250,000 tons and deliveries were rising to a peak of 10,000 tons a day. The activities in the rear areas were awe inspiring, and the Dutch countryside from Antwerp to Nijmegen resembled Britain in the last days before D-Day. Every available space was crammed not only with the individual equipment of the soldier, the ammunition, the guns, but with armoured vehicles in great variety, and a wealth of amphibians. Engineer and signals stores were startling in magnitude. Dumps of petrol and lubricants seemed more than adequate for an army to drive on to the ends of the earth, and nothing that might be wanted in any foreseeable emergency was forgotten. Anticipation of extensive flooding had caused the assembly of more than half a million gallons of fog oil for burning in 100,000 smoke generators. This would enable the army commander to mask the whole of his left flank with smoke. The wealth of a nation was distributed over the countryside, and all of it expendable. The organization and distribution was superb.

There was no doubt that the enemy would call in water and flood to his aid from the great Roer dams to the Rhine bunds. The heavy and persistent rains, the melting snow and slush, the rivers bursting their banks, the bomb craters sometimes twelve feet deep and seventy feet across, had demanded the building of 95 bridges to keep the troops and transport moving. All the region had become a morass. The River Maas, swollen up to 1,000 yards beyond its banks confronted the engineers with an immense challenge, and eastward the River Niers had become a major waterway. Seven bridges would be built across the Maas and nearly 2,000 tons of bridging was moving forward through the narrow bottleneck between Nijmegen and Grave. There was no other way.

During Montgomery's absence in the Ardennes planning and preparations had gone ahead with urgency, but the demands of the Ardennes, especially on the U.S. 9th Army, had delayed the final clearance of the enemy from a difficult salient known as the Heinsberg triangle. Its elimination called for a full scale attack by four divisions. By the 25th January the Heinsberg triangle had been dealt with, and Montgomery's whole front was as tidy as he could make it. The U.S. 9th Army, reduced to five divisions by the demands of the Ardennes, had been promised twelve divisions by the Supreme Commander. Montgomery had asked for sixteen, but was content.

Yet there was much with which the Field-Marshal was not content. The command situation still nagged, and he was not in full control of his own battlefield. On the right of the 9th Army the U.S. 1st Army had been ordered to launch an attack upon the Roer dams, an unmistakable and vital part of Montgomery's battle. The failure to take the great Schwammanuel dam controlling the waters of the Roer and Erft rivers might prove costly, for if the enemy opened the sluices, as they were almost bound to do, the U.S. 9th Army would be immobilized behind the Roer river until the floods abated. Repeated attempts to destroy the dams by air attack had failed.

It had become glaringly obvious at this moment when the command arguments were at an end, at least in the field, that the whole area north of the Ardennes was one battlefield. The argument for a Ground Force commander in the north was as valid as it had been in Normandy, but those men and those circumstances had disappeared. No one disputed the nature of the battlefield in the north, not even General Bradley. Part of his 1st Army must be involved in it, and he regretted that profoundly. The defeat of the enemy in the Ardennes had presented him with a wonderful prospect. He wanted to press on through the Eifel with the 1st Army, and direct the 3rd Army on the Kyll river. Frankfurt, always the dream of Bradley and Patton, seemed more real than ever before.

Bradley abandoned his golden prospect with reluctance, blaming it on to the machinations of Montgomery. But there had been no machinations. The Supreme Commander had given the main role to Montgomery in the north because he was committed to do so, and because it was strategically right. With the loss of Silesia to the Soviet armies, and the imminent loss of all that remained of the Saar to Patton's army, the Ruhr had become not only the greatest, but the only power house remaining to Germany. How it continued to produce the sinews of war was a miracle, but it did. It had become a complex fortress of ruin defended by an army knowing all its ramifications. That must be the main target of allied attack.

Montgomery, according to Bradley, had 'insisted that Hodges be shifted back to our pre-Bulge sector on the Roer where he would attack to secure those river dams in preparation for Simpson's crossing . . . Eisenhower had little choice but to accede to Monty's demand.' Of course, Eisenhower had no choice, and Bradley knew it. 'While I did not relish the dam mission, I could not dispute Ike's choice,' he wrote. 'By shunting 1st Army north, we would link our U.S. strength to that of the British in a concerted push to the Rhine just below the Ruhr.'

It seems that Bradley's real place was in the north, commanding the U.S. 9th and 1st Armies on Montgomery's right as he had done in Normandy. It was a thought that did not enter his head or the Supreme Commander's. It would have been a sensible command move, but for the fact that Bradley would not serve again in that capacity. There was no room on that battlefield for two equals, and there was no commander, even had Eisenhower been prepared to contemplate such an appointment, who might have been given the Ground Force Command in the north to drive this difficult team. U.S. 3rd Army would then have been grouped with Devers and the U.S. 7th Army. It would have been in every way, except for the personalities involved, a good pattern. It would have held the main thrust in the north to the end. It would almost—but for Patton—have satisfied the American people.

In any case, the 1st Army had to shield the right flank of the U.S. 9th and co-ordinate its attack across the Roer, and advance to the Erft, screening the 9th Army's right flank. The alternative must have been to halt Montgomery, and to switch the main attack from the north to the centre. That would have been a treachery of which the Supreme Commander was incapable. Moreover it would have confronted him with the truth he refused to recognise that only one main thrust was the correct strategy to pursue, and destroyed his 'Broad Front' strategy, which was no more than a strategy of *laissez-faire* and compromise.

Incapable of treachery the Supreme Commander certainly was, but his weakness convicted him of compromise and subterfuge. Bradley knew that he would not be halted, that he would cajole support, that his front runner, General Patton, would not be out of the race for the Rhine, or late in the final run. Montgomery was aware of this, and in spite of the Supreme Commander's support, he remained uneasy and watchful. On the 18th January Bradley had visited Montgomery in the north, and once again there was a complete failure to communicate, of which Montgomery remained unaware. He imagined that he was in full agreement with Bradley, and that he and the American general were the best of friends.

At home, Field-Marshal Brooke, the C.I.G.S., knew otherwise. The question of a Ground Force Command and of the power and purpose of the main thrust in the north was of more concern to Brooke and to Churchill than it was now to Montgomery. For the Prime Minister it was not simply a question of strategy in the field, but of Grand Strategy, of what the Object was. And of course there was no Object. Unconditional Surrender and the destruction of the German armies had replaced the ancient European meanings and purposes of war. The split between the Allies, manifest in this long and irreconcilable argument, was historical and geographical. The division of war and politics into compartments seemed to the British barbaric, primitive and naive. But the Americans had not lived in a Continent maintaining for centuries balances of power, corrected by wars when other means failed. The First World War had underlined a turning point in European history, and almost certainly in World history, but the need for a balance of power had become more urgent, and the point of balance lay in Central Europe.

While it was essential for Britain and France to maintain the enemy as a nation, it was the American purpose to destroy, to underline Unconditional Surrender, to propagate and discuss possible divisions of Germany into many parts, even to convert it into a 'potato patch', and thereby to unite the enemy, stimulated by the brilliant distortions of Dr. Goebbels, to fight to the last.

In terms of Total War that was realistic. In that context the fall of Berlin, the pre-occupation of Churchill, might be, as Eisenhower said, no more than a 'geographical abstraction.' It would not bring about the capitulation of the enemy. And it may be that upon this all arguments and speculations as to whether or not the war could have been won in 1944, founder. Winning the war and the destruction of the German armies had become the same thing. Even the Wehrmacht generals who recognised the wonderful opportunity missed in the north in September, could not have understood that the Allies had accepted 'Total War', and that the German Reich had ordained its own destruction. There could not be surrender, or negotiations for an armistice, while the Führer lived and retained control.

The Soviet Union had watched the disappearance of British hopes, first in the Balkans, then in Italy, and now fast disappearing in Central Europe, with delight. At last the strategy pursued by the Tsars might be realized, and it behoved the Russian armies to press on westward beyond the Oder-Neisse line, and to meet the Western Allies as far west as possible. It was becoming apparent that the only race in which the Americans were interested was a race with the British on the left, first to the Rhine, and on to the end.

Bradley and Patton maintained a limited offensive in the south, alert to strengthen it into full scale attack as opportunity offered. It 'was kept quiet so as not to draw objections from Field-Marshal "Montgomery".' But it was not kept quiet enough, and at the end of January Field-Marshal Brooke persuaded Eisenhower's Chief of Staff, General Bedell Smith, to safeguard Montgomery's battle in the north.

As for the Ground Force Command, Eisenhower had told Montgomery that he was perfectly capable of exercising adequate control over the battlefield himself. He had co-opted Generals Whiteley and Lowell Rooks to 'stay on the road constantly', acting as his eyes and ears. General Bull was also a traveller. There would be no further question of a Ground Force Commander, and Montgomery had at last accepted that. The matter was closed. The Supreme Commander was prepared to accept Field-Marshal Alexander as a deputy in place of Air-Marshal Tedder, 'whose only difficulty arose from the unwillingness of senior ground commanders to take his opinion on purely ground matters.' Alexander might have strengthened the Supreme Command, but the idea was finally abandoned.

The arrival of the American newspapers in Bradley's headquarters at the end of January left him in no doubt that the American public had become a governing factor in Allied strategy. They wanted American armies in the vanguard, and could not be denied. Churchill had been about to write a letter to soothe Bradley's feelings. The newspapers changed his mind.

II

During Montgomery's absence in the Ardennes 1st Canadian and British 2nd Army headquarters had pushed ahead with detailed planning while improving their positions in the Nijmegen bridgehead, and mounting 'Operation Blackcock' to clear the Heinsberg triangle. On 21st January the Field-Marshal was able to issue orders for the advance to the Rhine, 'Operation Veritable', with a target date of 8th February. The 1st Canadian Army, reinforced by the British 30 Corps with the bulk of 2nd Army under command, would assault across the Maas to destroy the enemy between the Maas and the Rhine from Nijmegen to Wesel. Two days later the U.S. 9th Army would assault across the Roer river in support on a line Jülich to Düsseldorf. By early March Montgomery hoped to have closed the Rhine from Nijmegen-Emmerich to Düsseldorf.

It is unlikely that Montgomery believed that the U.S. 9th Army would be able to move across the Roer on the target date, or even for two to three weeks thereafter, unless the enemy failed to unloose the waters of the Roer and Urft dams. The Field-Marshal was prepared, and probably even glad, to go ahead alone with the greatest confidence. His army commanders handled their armies and carried out all the elaborate and complex preliminary manoeuvres with skill and smoothness. The planning was meticulous. By the end of January 500,000 rounds of ammunition of 350 varieties had been moved forward ready to serve the battery sites. 11,000 tons of high explosive would fall upon the enemy forward positions in the Reichswald forest from more than 1,000 guns in the hours immediately preceding the assault. Heavy bombers of Bomber command would obliterate the key points in the Siegfried defences, and erupt the ancient towns of Cleve and Goch into chaos on the eve. Emmerich, Udem, Weeze and Calcar, links in the enemy defensive network, would also be reduced to rubble.

The mark of Montgomery, the massive artillery and air support, the unchanging pattern of the set battle, was very clear. He ordained it. His generals would carry it out faithfully. No detail had been overlooked. 800,000 maps had been distributed and supplemented by half a million air photographs. All these were studied by commanders down to platoons and sections. Each man knew the nature of the ground, the extent of the enemy defensive positions, and lay-out of the Reichswald State forest through which they would have to penetrate. The forest was a coniferous mass intersected by lateral and transverse 'drives', and covering an area 10 miles wide and five miles across. Behind it to the east lay the Hochwald forest, and the escarpment from which at least they would look down over the narrow plain to the Rhine. It promised to be a very tough and difficult battle.

The German 1st Parachute Army under Army Group H would fight to the end to defend the approaches to the Rhine and their last line of defence. They were not paratroops, but they were the finest troops available to the enemy, young, fanatical, well trained. The 84th Division defended the Reichswald forest with three divisions in close reserve. A total of 114 guns had been assembled with difficulty, and air support would be negligible.

Nevertheless if the U.S. 9th Army was unable to move in the first weeks of the battle, the enemy forces in the Cologne plain would be sucked into Montgomery's battle. Once more, and for the last time, the British would fight the battle of the 'hinge', as they had done in Normandy, opening the way for the Americans on their right. South of the 9th Army the 1st Army would be ready to move across the Roer to protect the entire flank. The British role would not be spectacular, but it would be hard.

On 1st February the Supreme Commander ordered General Bradley to use a force of two or three divisions to 'seize the dams on the Roer and 'Urft rivers', and on 4th February the U.S. V Corps moved into the attack. On that day four armies north of the Ardennes were moving onto their 'start lines'. It would be the greatest battle since Normandy. In pitch darkness and through relentless rain the British divisions in the north moved to their assault positions. Nothing moved by day. The road

Eindhoven-Mook-Nijmegen collapsed and became a morass of liquid mud over which engineers, pioneers and provost companies lay mattresses of logs. There was no comfort and no hope of comfort for anyone, yet there was a new, a revived, spirit in the troops. They knew at last where they were going. The order to move, the knowledge that the last battle must be near, aroused men from their long winter of discontent.

On the afternoon of 7th February the rain abated, and soon after 9 o'clock that night 200,000 men on the banks of the Maas from Nijmegen to Cuick heard the muffled roar of fleets of bombers and felt the shock and shudder of the immense bombing assault a few miles ahead. At five in the morning 1,000 guns opened fire. Underneath the great weight of the barrage of heavy and medium artillery, the Bofors were firing flat, while the tanks of the armoured brigades and the machine gunners of three battalions drenched the enemy forward positions with fire.

It was an easy crossing, but there was no ease thereafter. The Canadians and British were on their own. On 9th February the U.S. V Corps, bearing down in the last phase of its assault to seize the Roer and Urft dams, was too late. Holding their positions to the last the enemy blew the sluices to send a cataract of water surging through Düren in a great wave to join the flooded Maas at Roermond, and for thirteen days the U.S. 9th Army, poised on the western bank of the Roer could only watch and wait. For two weeks the British and Canadians were locked in a life and death struggle with the enemy in forest, splintered to matchwood, and in mud, bog and flood. They were almost surrounded by water. In the extreme north the enemy had breached the main Rhine dykes, and the weight of flood water had collapsed the Quer dam. To reinforce this flood the enemy then blew the northern gates of the Spoy canal, and the whole area north of the Cleve—Calcar road became an inland lake. As a result of this immense flooding the rivers Maas and Niers, which had begun to subside, rose again steadily to hamper the engineers, and the movement of support troops. The bridge at Gennep proudly displayed a sign, 4,008 feet. Even the railway line on the line of advance through Kranenberg was under water, and the main axis of advance was under three feet of water.

In attempts to counter the floods Royal Engineers blew the dykes north east of Nijmegen on the advice of the Dutch, and sent two million gallons of water an hour in a counter barrage to roll back water with water. The enemy countered at once by breaching the dykes of the Alter Rhine. Yet these great floods, seeming almost 'Biblical', were of no real service to the enemy. No army was better equipped for water warfare than the British, and over all the left flank 'flotillas' of amphibians, 'Buffaloes', 'Weasels' and amphibious jeeps, navigated the dangerous waters deeper into Germany. Nevertheless by the end of the second day Operation Veritable had become a tactical tangle, impossible to unravel, and the story of the battle may only be built up from a mass of fragments. Orders from the top had become meaningless, and the struggle devolved upon brigade, battalion and company commanders, each one improvising according to his situation. The elaborate movements and timings, the steady leap-frogging planned for infantry and armour, had become impossible.[1]

'Progress was slow and costly,' General Eisenhower wrote in his assessment of the battle, 'and opposition became stiffer as the Germans began moving their forces from the Roer into the path of the Canadian advance. Montgomery was not too displeased by this transfer of German weight because of the promise it held that, once the American attack began, it would advance with great speed.'[2]

It is a remarkable tribute to the Field-Marshal, for it is difficult to imagine General Bradley being 'not too displeased' to draw enemy strength in order to open the way for the British. His frustrations seemed to consume him as he agitated incessantly, whatever the Supreme Commander's commitments to Montgomery in the north, for his own armies to be unleashed in the race for the Rhine. There could be little doubt that his armies would win the race, for the British were not racing. It is strange that Bradley's attitude did not seem to arouse the thought in Montgomery's mind that his 'temporary' command of the U.S. 9th Army might be precarious, nor persuade him to pay some special consideration to General Simpson, suffering his own frustrations as he waited for the

[1] Thompson: *The Battle for the Rhineland*.
[2] Eisenhower: *Crusade in Europe*, p. 410.

Roer floods to abate sufficiently for him to mount an assault crossing. In regard to Simpson, Montgomery had revealed his seeming inability to consider anyone's feelings but his own.

On 23rd February the 9th Army crossed the still flooded Roer and bulldozed its way through the minor industrial complex and fortifications of Jülich and Linnich, and in five days burst out into the open, taking München Gladbach, the first enemy town of consequence to fall into allied hands. As they moved swiftly on the Rhine, linking their left flank with the British right, and over-running enemy positions, a harvest of prisoners fell into their hands. On 2nd March 9th Army spearheads reached the Rhine bank at Neuss opposite Düsseldorf.

The last of the enemy rearguards to escape across the Rhine reached the Wesel bridge late on the evening of 10th March, fighting furiously to the end, and 21st Army Group lay upon the Rhine bank from Nijmegen to Düsseldorf. A series of rumbling explosions told those who still fought on that the Wesel bridge had been blown. They had fought bravely to gain time for those more fortunate.

In the last stages of the battle the enemy had mustered more than 1,000 guns and 717 mortars to subject the Canadians and British to the heaviest volume of fire experienced in the campaign. The battle yielded a total of 51,618 prisoners, 29,379 of them to the U.S. 9th Army, and 22,239 to the Canadians and British. They came from eighteen divisions and many hastily organised battle groups. At least three quarters of these troops had fought the Canadians and British.

In addition it was estimated that the enemy had lost 38,000 killed and wounded. The remnant of the First Parachute Army had withdrawn across the Rhine leaving behind some 90,000 casualties.

The Allied losses had not been light. The U.S. 9th Army in its rapid advance had lost 7,300 killed and wounded, and the 1st Canadian army 16,000 killed and wounded, two thirds of them British. By this battle of the Rhineland the Canadian 1st Army had cleared the road to Cologne for the U.S. 1st Army.

It seemed peaceful on the eastern bank. The river itself was the last defensive barrier and it held few terrors for troops accustomed to being waterborne. The total enemy strength in the west, in spite of numbering sixty divisions 'in name', was estimated by the Supreme Command to be equivalent to twenty-six full strength divisions. That night of the 10th March, and on the nights that followed, there could have been very little to prevent 21st Army Group seizing and developing a bridgehead.

III

Field-Marshal Montgomery called the tunes on 21st Army Group front, but the man who played the tunes and conducted the orchestra, directed detailed planning, and fought the battles was Lieut.-General Sir Miles Dempsey.

'It is strange that one who not only looked like a great army commander but actually was and behaved like one, should be so little known' wrote one of Dempsey's brigadiers. 'Like Germanicus, the whole world would have judged him capable of commanding had he never commanded.'[1]

At the end of July, 1944, in the midst of the 'sticky' time in Normandy, the C.I.G.S. wrote to Montgomery: 'Ike considers that Dempsey should be doing more than he does; it is equally clear that Ike has the very vaguest conception of war. I drew his attention to what your basic strategy had been.'

Montgomery replied at once: 'Gave orders to Dempsey this morning that attack is to be pressed with utmost vigour and all caution thrown to winds and any casualties accepted and that he must step on gas to Vire.'[2]

While Montgomery had been absent in the Ardennes, Dempsey had held a front of 125 miles on the Maas, alert to meet an enemy threat aimed through Breda on Antwerp in support of the main German offensive. He had moved 30 Corps south with four divisions, stripping his own front, while also adapting to the loss of the bulk of the U.S. 9th Army, and the shelving of its heavy commitments in the Roermond-Venlo area. His whole front had been incessantly active while the 1st Canadian Army consolidated and improved its positions

---
[1] Major-General Essame: *The 43rd Wessex Division at War*, 1944-45, p. 188.
[2] Bryant: *Triumph in the West*, p. 245.

in the Nijmegen bridgehead ready for the assault to the Rhine.

2nd Army headquarters had been involved in preliminary planning for the Rhine crossing since October, and at the end of January Field-Marshal Montgomery issued orders for the final planning, setting 15th March as the target date. Dempsey withdrew 12th Corps headquarters into reserve at Maesyck to prepare for the assault role, and placed it close to a reach of the Maas with some similarities to the Rhine between Emmerich and Wesel. There detailed planning began, and the troops embarked upon extensive exercises and rehearsals. At the same time Dempsey was given the responsibility of assisting U.S. 9th Army in planning its role.

There was at once an explosion of anger and dismay. As soon as General Simpson, commanding U.S. 9th Army, read his copy of Montgomery's directive to Dempsey he was furious and 'flabbergasted'. There was no command role for his army in the Rhine crossing. Instead, a U.S. Corps would support the 2nd Army crossing on the right flank. It was an intolerable omission, for not only in American eyes, but in fact, the Rhine crossing was the 'symbol' for the final defeat of the enemy, and to deny a forward army on the Rhine bank a part in it for any reason but absolute operational necessity, was unforgivable.

It must be understood that Montgomery was innocent of any intention to insult or to provoke, and indeed it was against all his interests to do so. The U.S. 9th Army had worked with the British with less friction than would have been the case with any other U.S. Army, mainly due to Dempsey's close liaison with Simpson, and the mutual respect arising from their association. The omission was one of Montgomery's blind spots.

General Simpson had suffered a good deal of banter from his fellow generals when he had been placed under Montgomery's command. He had been urged to take a course in 'Limey' ways and brush up his English usage. Simpson was a quiet American, an able commander, resourceful and highly intelligent. While he longed to be back under Bradley's 12th Army Group he was completely loyal to his commitments to 21st Army Group. Naturally he maintained contact with General Bradley and with his friends at Supreme Headquarters. He knew that

Bradley would have the 9th Army back under his command at the first opportunity, and since Montgomery wanted to retain the U.S. 9th Army under his command to the end his omission of a special role in the Rhine crossing was the more remarkable. Perhaps the Field-Marshal feared that if Simpson crossed the Rhine in strength south of Wesel the balance of power might swing to the south, and Bradley's feared major thrust in the centre would become more probable. The signs of Bradley's intention were evident even at the end of January, and Montgomery may have reasoned that to hold U.S. 9th Army to a minor role in the early stages would be more likely to ensure his hold upon Simpson. It is more likely that Montgomery did not reason at all on these lines. His approach was purely military. According to Supreme Headquarters the main thrust in the north was official policy, and the commitments in the north were of a magnitude not generally appreciated. Perhaps they justified 21st Army Group's immense build-up of resources and elaborate preparations, including naval units and landing craft under Admiral Burrough. All Holland 'north of the rivers' remained to be liberated from a still considerable enemy army, and the sufferings of the Dutch people were intense and desperate. The Baltic was also a major target, but these vital objectives must not prejudice the main thrust of 2nd Army to the Elbe, and, it was still hoped, on to Berlin.

Yet in view of rapid developments on the battlefields, the enormous preponderance of American man-power, and the determination of Bradley and Patton to beat Montgomery, no one but a dreamer could have believed that the major role would remain with the British.

Whatever may or may not have lain behind Montgomery's instruction of 31st January, General Simpson at once approached General Dempsey. The two generals studied the situation carefully, and Dempsey advised the Field-Marshal to revise his plans and to give U.S. 9th Army a more impressive role. On 4th February Montgomery ordered Simpson to plan a crossing of the Rhine at Rheinberg and develop a bridgehead south of the River Lippe, while Dempsey planned the 2nd army assault north of the Lippe. The intention then was to envelop the Ruhr, and imprison its garrison of mixed troops under Field-Marshal Model. It was a garrison, swollen to a total of more than 300,000 by 100,000 anti-aircraft troops. It was not a mobile army.

IV

Following this contretemps of early February, Simpson's rapid advance to the Rhine posed immediate problems. The arrival of his spearheads on the river opposite Düsseldorf on the 2nd March spurred him to enthusiasm, and by the 5th he had closed the Rhine bank from Neuss to Mors. Complaining to Eisenhower that he had seven divisions idle, Simpson at once requested permission to seize a bridgehead.

Montgomery's bleak refusal was staggering, not only to the Americans. There was no doubt that Simpson could have succeeded, and opened up a running sore which the enemy would have found it impossible to relieve or to contain. Had such a crossing been followed up urgently by 2nd Army before the enemy had time to organize his defences, disaster would have overtaken the very few organized formations in the north, and produced Dempsey's 2nd Army on the north German plain in a matter of days rather than weeks.

Moreover Hitler's orders forbade the destruction of the Rhine bridges while his troops still fought west of the Rhine. They must be denied to the enemy and kept open as an escape route. Such an order was unrealistic, creating alarm and despondency in the minds of those responsible for carrying out the order on pain of death. General Schlemm, commanding the 1st Parachute Army, caught in a life and death dilemma, might have presented 21st Army Group with a chance to seize the Wesel bridge between the 5th and 10th March.

While General Simpson chafed with intense frustration, the U.S. 9th Armoured division of 1st Army's 3rd Corps reached and seized the Remagen bridge on 7th March, rubbing salt into Simpson's wounds. Brigadier Hoge crossed the bridge on his own initiative, but he would not have done so without the knowledge that he would be fully supported by his army and army group commanders. Alas, no forward troops of 21st Army group had any doubts about the lack of comparable support.

Generals Bradley and Eisenhower at once reacted to the news with the wild enthusiasm of 'fans' at a football match, and Hodges put four divisions into the bridgehead with all speed, drawing enemy strength away from the closely threatened north. The enemy was clearly *in extremis*.

Throughout these developments Field-Marshal Montgomery remained unmoved and adamant in his refusal to permit General Simpson to force a crossing. The formidable barrier of the river Rhine was diminishing as an obstacle in all minds, save only in the Field-Marshal's. 'He preferred the planned assault of the Rhine on a broad front between Rheinberg and Emmerich,' commented the Supreme Command, and it seemed that the Field-Marshal felt that there was something improper in seizing a bridgehead, and gaining time. The Rhine crossing had grown in his mind over the months as an operation only slightly less complex and formidable than D-Day itself. Perhaps his immense preparations had imprisoned him, denying all flexibility.

The Americans did not share his views, and even before U.S. 1st Army seized the bridge at Remagen, the final pattern was becoming clear. In the first week of March General Patton had his armour on the move through the Eifel on his left flank, and was gathering momentum to close the Rhine from Coblenz to Mainz. No one doubted his intention to assault across the river without delay as soon as he reached the bank. It was rumoured that he 'towed his Rhine bridge behind him wherever he went', and Bradley's efforts to restrain his army commander were half-hearted, and only 'for the record'. After Remagen, all plans went by the board.

'To hell with the planners!' Bradley had shouted in excitement when Hodges had telephoned the news. The Supreme Commander's verdict was not in doubt. 'Get across with whatever you need,' Eisenhower ordered—but make certain you hold that bridgehead.' A week later, U.S. 1st Army had occupied Cologne without difficulty and closed the Rhine to Coblenz. The situation General Bradley had longed for and planned for was rapidly taking shape, and no one doubted where Eisenhower's heart was in the matter.

'Here on the Rhine plain,' wrote Major Ingersoll, a member of Bradley's Tactical headquarters staff, 'they (the Americans) got the green light to end all green lights—"Take off into Germany and keep going".[1]

On 2nd March U.S. 3rd Army crossed the Kyll river, seized Trier, forced crossings of the Moselle, and raced for the Rhine. Just before midnight on 22nd March, Patton made an assault crossing of the river at Oppenheim, and had six battalions in the bridgehead before the enemy aroused. The cost was 37 casualties.

General Patton's reaction was wildly juvenile: 'Brad,' he shouted over the telephone and his treble voice trembled, 'for God's sake tell the world we're across. We knocked down 33 Krauts today when they came after our pontoon bridges. I want the world to know 3rd Army made it before Monty starts across.'[2]

General Patton's liaison officer left no doubt of Patton's feeling of triumph:

> Without benefit of airborne drop, without benefit of the United States *or* British Navy, and not having laid down the greatest smoke-screen in the history of modern war, and without either a three months' build-up of supplies *or* a whole extra American army, and with no preliminary bombardment, and finally without even a code word, Lieutenant General Patton and the 3rd Army crossed the Rhine yesterday.

Field-Marshal Montgomery had not been racing, but the question is, should he have been? Curiously a Supreme Headquarters Directive dated 8th March changed the crossing date for 21st Army Group from Montgomery's 15th to the 24th March. The Field-Marshal obeyed orders, while his opposite number, General Bradley, turned a deliberate blind eye. There was no longer even the pretence of priority in the north. The Supreme Commander's mind had joined his heart in the centre.

[1] Ingersoll: *Top Secret*.
[2] Bradley: *A Soldier's Story*, p. 522.

CHAPTER SIXTEEN

Plunder

I

IT was Field-Marshal Montgomery's intention to cross the Rhine with two armies between Rees and Rheinberg, to envelop the Ruhr, relying on the left wing of the U.S. 1st Army, advancing out of its bridgehead at Remagen, to complete the encirclement in the region of Paderborn, and to advance to the Elbe. Thereafter the Field-Marshal hoped to press forward with his right to Berlin. But the Field-Marshal's commitments in the North, North-West and North-East, were very great, involving the 1st Canadian Army in the liberation of Northern Holland, clearing the Wilhelmshaven Peninsula, and covering the left flank of the British 2nd Army. The 2nd Army role was to drive through to the Elbe, clearing Bremen and Hamburg, and anchoring its left on the Baltic. Montgomery believed that the U.S. 9th Army would remain under his command, and his plans were based on that assumption. New divisions arriving from the Italian front would assist the Canadians by the middle of April.

The code name for this offensive across the Rhine was 'Plunder'.

'The all important factor,' Montgomery emphasised, 'was to follow up the enemy as quickly as possible, and we were able to achieve this speed of action mainly because of the foresight and preliminary planning that had been devoted to this battle for some months.'[1] He regarded the time available as very short. 'I intended that the bridgehead should extend to the south sufficiently far to cover Wesel from enemy ground action, and to the north to include bridge sites at Emmerich; the depth of the bridgehead was to be made sufficient to provide room

[1] Montgomery: *Normandy to the Baltic.*

to form up major forces for the drive to the east and north-east. I gave 24 March as target date for the operation.'[1]

No one would dispute that to launch an offensive on this scale, to move a million men with all their impedimenta of war over two major rivers and many lesser waterways, while constructing roads and railways in a severe winter, was an immense undertaking demanding administration and organisation of the highest order. The date of 24th March for the assault to the east across the last and greatest river barrier was chosen by the Supreme Commander to conform to the timings all along the line from Holland to the Swiss border, and involving seven armies.

What must be arguable is that Montgomery could have, and should have, gained a bridgehead across the Rhine from which to launch his offensive at the earliest opportunity, thus gaining space and time, as Hodges had done, and Patton was to do in much lesser degree. This would not have interfered with the timings of the Supreme Command or advanced the date of the offensive, but it would have advanced the speed of Montgomery's offensive. Why did the Field-Marshal deny himself an advantage there for the taking, and alienate the U.S. 9th Army commander in the process? On 7th March the U.S. 1st Army had shown the way.

Assault crossings of the river could have been achieved almost without opposition anywhere on the 21st Army Group front with the exception of a direct assault upon the key town of Wesel. The meanders of the Alter Rhine, the course of the River Lippe, the wet dykes and 'drains', the former watercourse of the river, produced difficult water obstacles at certain points. The river Ijssel, 15,000 yards to the east, was a considerable tank obstacle, and there were two lakes just east of Mehr joined to the Rhine by streams and drains. Time would not eliminate these obstacles, and would render them more formidable as the enemy used the respite to strengthen his weak defences. To gain these objectives before the offensive would have been of incalculable value. It would have mitigated against the congestion in the bridgehead which had become almost a feature of Montgomery's methods.

By his initiative at Remagen the American Brigadier-General

[1] Montgomery: *Normandy to the Baltic.*

Hoge had established an offensive platform of inestimable value not only to the 1st Army, but also to the 3rd Army on its right. By the time the offensive was launched General Hodges had extended 1st Army bridgehead to the Frankfurt autobahn, opening the way for Patton's armour, and he had relieved the pressure opposite the U.S. 9th Army as the enemy strove to seal off the running sore. It was Patton's swift movement out of his bridgehead, coupled with the rapid advance of the 1st Army that enabled Bradley to seize the priority of the main assault for himself, to take back the 9th Army, and with 45 divisions under his command to dominate the end-pattern of Allied victory. Thus, it may be argued, that Montgomery's failure to establish a bridgehead east of the Rhine before 24th March cost the British the last remaining chance of the main thrust in the north.

It must be evident that Montgomery could have gained a great advantage by permitting General Simpson to seize a bridgehead soon after his spearheads reached the river. Simpson's success (or failure) would have encouraged Montgomery to permit General Dempsey to follow suit, or to bide his time. Opposition was negligible, and defensive works almost non-existent. The enemy had lost 2,000,000 men on the Western front since Normandy, and suffered even greater casualties in the East. The severe casualties the enemy had sustained in the Rhineland battles had sapped the last of his effective strength in the West, reducing his few existing formations to shadows, and his equipment in armour and artillery to less than that enjoyed by a single allied division. The remnants of the First Parachute army escaping over the Wesel bridge had no time to reform, and the support available could not present a serious military threat. Even after two weeks of frantic endeavour resistance remained pitifully inadequate, and largely confined to sporadic bursts from desperate groups in buildings and improvised strong points.

'If the enemy chooses to fight west of the Rhine, that's easy,' Montgomery had said in the Autumn. He had done so, and it was easy.

To 52nd Mountain division, with the task of patrolling the west bank of the Rhine, the river, flowing at under $3\frac{1}{2}$ knots and 500 yards wide, seemed a far less formidable obstacle than

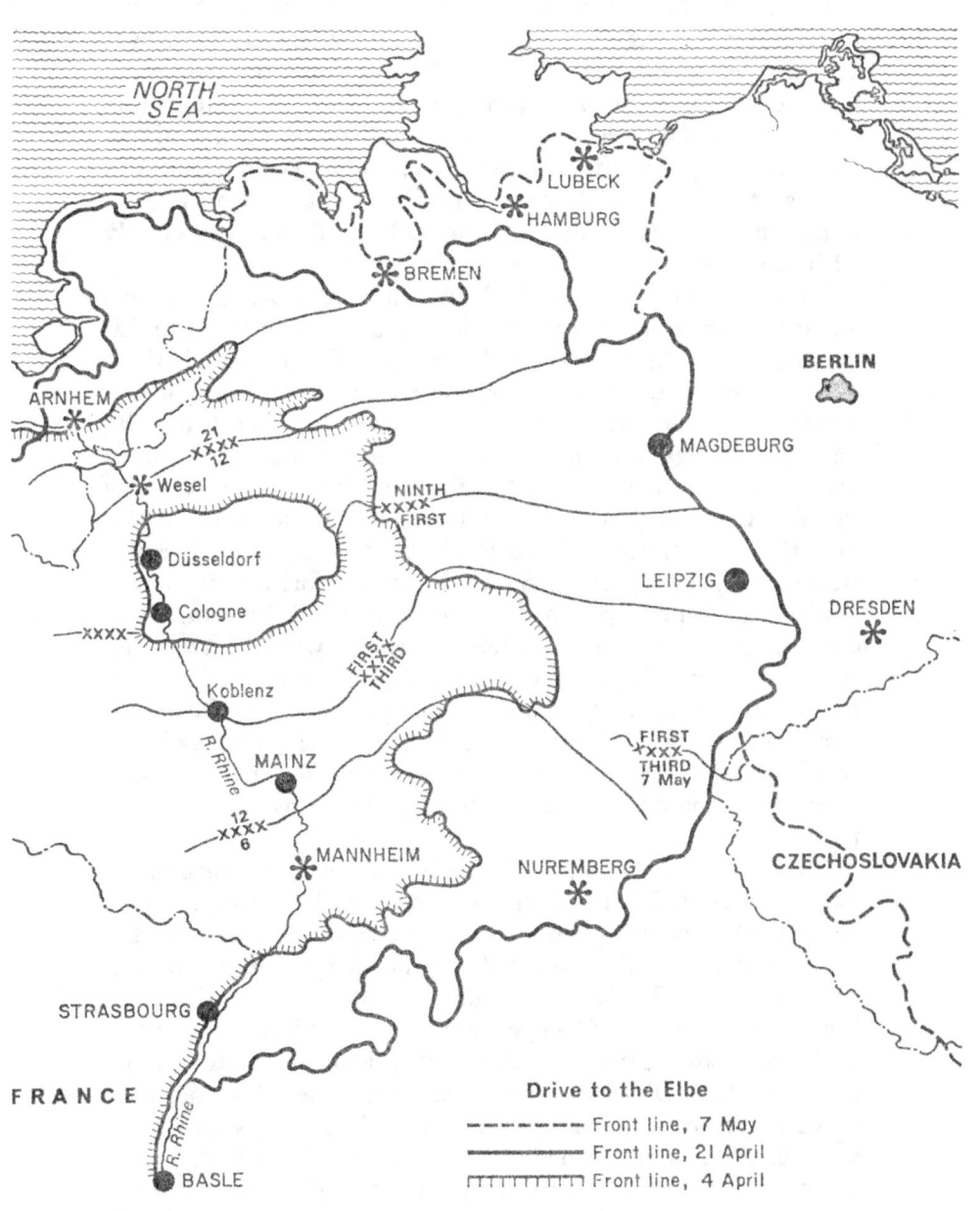

the one they had faced in October in their crossings of the Scheldt estuary against the enemy heavy batteries. It was certainly less formidable than the Maas in flood, backed by the Siegfried defences. From a vantage point near Xanten officers looked across the river to what seemed to be a peaceful countryside. The high ground of the Diersfordter Wald stood out against the sky line beyond the Church tower of Bislich. Farm buildings at Riswickhof and Lohr could be seen clearly with binoculars.

From 12th March onwards the weather was fine, and for two weeks the British looked at the view while the enormous build-up continued behind them. A smoke screen veiled these activities from the enemy, but it would have brought the enemy nearer to despair to have shown him everything. By seizing crossings it is probable that a week could have been saved, together with a wealth of ammunition, the services of the Royal Naval units, and at least half of the great assault from the air by the British 6th and U.S. 17th Airborne divisions. In the course of a week U.S. 9th Army and British 2nd Army might have joined up a bridgehead, and established start lines east of the lesser water obstacles. Space would have been created to enable the advance to flow—even to surge—eastward. For at least a week, from 7th to 14th March the east bank of the Rhine was highly vulnerable, its totally inadequate defences hastily manned by exhausted men escaping from the last battle, and desperately short of arms and ammunition.

The failure to exploit this situation, or even to consider it, must be sought, I believe, in Montgomery's leadership, and in his dedication since his earliest days to the 'set-piece battle', the meticulous preparation *irrespective of the enemy to be encountered*, and his fear of flexibility and the 'expanding torrent'. As an instructor at the Staff College his students had learned that any deviation from the strictly orthodox frontal assault would not be tolerated. In a Divisional attack exercise those who would lay down a preliminary barrage and move their troops into a full scale direct assault gained full marks. Those who suggested reconnaisance to discover the strength and dispositions of the enemy were frowned upon. Ahead lay enemy territory. It must be attacked with all available strength in a set-piece battle. That was in the early 1930's.[1] It had been so in 1943 in the assault across the Messina-strait. And now it was 1945 and the Lieut.-Colonel of the Staff College had become the Field Marshal commanding armies. He had marshalled a great mass of artillery to smash the Reichswald forest to matchwood, and heavy bombers to reduce the towns to rubble before crossing the Maas. Now he marshalled far greater resources in men, artillery and airborne troops, supported by galaxies of armour and amphibians, including landing craft of the Royal Navy, and all services disposed by 21st Army Group. 'A tremendous weight of day and night heavy bombers, medium bombers and Allied Tactical Air Forces' would make it almost impossible for the enemy to move.

It was immensely impressive, but it seemed irrelevant to the task which would confront the British and Canadian armies in the assault. Even on paper, in 2nd Army estimates, the enemy did not sound formidable. Field-Marshal Kesselring had inherited the hopeless end-play from Field-Marshal von Runstedt. It was a formality. The remains of Army Group H under General Blaskowitz faced 21st Army Group. It had three corps forward on the river line with 47th Panzer Grenadier Corps fifteen miles north east of Emmerich in reserve.

The enemy formations were below strength to the point that their 'titles' were meaningless. Two so-called divisions were disposed forward to meet the British onslaught, 7th Parachute division and 84th division, both reduced to weary battle groups. Under 100 Field and Medium guns were believed to be available to the enemy, with perhaps a mixed bag of 800 light and heavy A.A. guns. It was doubtful whether 150 'runners' could be gathered together out of the enemy's once formidable armoured strength in fighting vehicles.

It is certain that no organised defence or adequate opposition could have been found even seriously to challenge the British assault, or to provide any defence in depth to the offensive. The British Army waited; the U.S. 9th Army waited, while Allied bombers systematically isolated the battlefield. I do not believe that it can be questioned that Field-Marshal Montgomery's leadership lacked inspiration at this stage. He had failed to imbue his commanders with the sense of excitement,

[1] *The Montgomery Legend*, p. 91.

K*

of daring and initiative that had enabled Brigadier-General Hoge to seize the Remagen bridge for the U.S. 1st Army. Montgomery's leadership not only failed to inspire, it inhibited and denied initiative. It had been responsible for the failure of the 11th Armoured division to seize bridgeheads across the Albert canal, and to advance to seal off the Bevelands—and an army. The opportunity had been there for the taking, and it was unforgivable not to take it. Lieut.-General Horrocks said: 'I did not anticipate at that time any serious resistance on the Albert Canal. It seemed to us that the Germans were totally disorganised.'[1]

And so they were; but not for long.

General Dempsey, the army commander, had not felt a sense of urgency. Such failures stemmed directly from Field-Marshal Montgomery through his army commander. You did what you were told, and you played safe. And yet Montgomery had said that his idea was, 'To keep the enemy on the run straight through to the Rhine, and "bounce" our way across that river before the enemy succeeded in re-forming a front to oppose us.'

But these words could only have been turned into deeds if the commanders had been inspired with that kind of spirit of daring. Brigadiers, Lieut.-Colonels, even company commanders, seize bridges and bounce rivers, not Field-Marshals.

Thus there was no major-general or brigadier on the Rhine bank with the sense of excitement and initiative inherent in the Americans at their best, and coming down from the top. It would not have occurred to anyone to have suggested a crossing to the Field-Marshal. His plans were inflexible, and his leadership was that of the infallible 'father figure'. Even General Simpson's request had met with a bleak uncompromising refusal. A British general might well have been consigned to the 'bottom of the class', or sent home.

II

The preparations and precautions for the last assault and advance into Germany were of a magnitude to excite a sense

[1] B. H. Liddell Hart: *Private Papers*.

of wonder, not entirely reassuring. They could not have been greater, or more cautious, if the British and Canadians were preparing to face the full might of the German army and air force. Since the opening of the port of Antwerp the growth of supplies, workshops, repair units, warehouses, vehicle parks, and dumps of many kinds had been staggering. The voracious appetite of 21st Army Group demanded a constant stream of vessels across the North Sea, reflecting the massive production of the munitions factories. It was becoming more than clear that not only logistics, but technological progress, had added a new dimension to warfare which would have, and was having an impact upon tactics and strategy. The problem was to use these advances to the greatest advantage, and Montgomery constantly chose the most expensive methods to achieve results. His passion for bombardment, his profligate use of artillery and heavy bombing, and the consequent demands on shipping space, had evoked criticism and alarm in many quarters in Italy, and more recently at Caen. Destruction appeared not only wanton, but counter-productive.

On the west bank of the Rhine the enormous panoply of weapons, the proliferation of armoured fighting vehicles and amphibians, the unending lines of trains and transport unloading at rail and roadheads, and building up vast dumps, caused many to wonder and worry. Field-Marshal Montgomery seemed to suffer from a compulsion to use everything because it existed, and the point had come, or was about to come, when it might be suggested that weapons and 'gadgetry' were using Montgomery. The possession of such an overwhelming power and variety was tactically crippling, mitigating against surprise and speed. Infantry had become so accustomed to their assaults being preceded by massive bombardment that many would have been dismayed had they been ordered simply to advance or to assault under covering fire provided by their brigade or divisional resources. Like the Commander-in-Chief men no longer questioned the presence of the enemy, or his strength, or the nature of the opposition. The enemy must be neutralised. The role of the infantry was subtly changing.

It may be invidious to single out a particular branch of the service for distinction, but it was very clear that the Royal Engineers had become paramount in assault. Not only were they responsible for the detection and clearance of mines and booby traps, but for road construction and bridging under difficulties and dangers which were often greater and longer sustained than those faced by leading infantry. In addition to their qualities as fighting soldiers, responsible often for forward reconnaisance, they needed also skills of a very high order.

In the preparations for the forthcoming assault across the Rhine Engineer resources were strained to the limits. They had opened the way across Holland by road, rail and bridge, across the Maas in flood, to enable fleets of trucks and trains to serve the great dumps as far forward as the shattered town of Goch, once the southern lynch pin of the southern defences of the Reichswald. 70,000 vehicles, including 4,000 tank transporters, were under movement control of 2nd Army alone in the early days of March, as well as hosts of armoured fighting vehicles and amphibians, all demanding space, the construction of roads, and the services of a host of men. It seemed to at least one observer that the 21st Army Group suffered an *embarras de richesse*, and that this was the factor perhaps more than any other which, added to the natural caution of the Field-Marshal, prevented a crossing of the Rhine and the establishment of a bridgehead from which the 2nd Army might have seized crossings over the Dortmund-Ems canal and other obstacles, inadequately defended, and erupted to 'crack about', as they had been promised, over the North German plain.

But it was clear, irrespective of the situation and the overwhelming defeat suffered by the enemy, that the Field-Marshal was resolved to mount an assault, second only to D-Day, with which it was compared. It would be, beyond all doubt, a tremendous spectacle, but could it be necessary?

While the build-up was taking on its final shape an extensive air interdiction programme isolated the battlefield, and heavy bomber fleets, 1,400 strong, ranged far into the heart of Germany attacking airfields to neutralise the stricken Luftwaffe. These heavy attacks reflected fear of the jet aircraft trickling into service at the last moment with the enemy, and almost in the nature of a 'secret weapon'.

Apart from the impressive array of Army Group resources, especially in artillery, the 2nd Army had brought forward 750,000 rounds of ammunition to serve its 700 guns, of which the hard core consisted of 25 pounders, and 5.5 in. mediums, supported by 3.7's to 8 in. and 240 mm super heavies. Twelve rocket projectors, each of thirty barrels, which had created astonishing destruction in the Rhineland battle, added to the fire power. These twelve projectors, served by 68 men, could devastate an area of more than 68,000 square yards in 4 seconds at a range of 7,600 yards and using fifteen tons of ammunition. This was a remarkable saving in man-power. Four and a half medium regiments of Royal Artillery, served by 612 men, and firing at a rate of 2 rounds per 4 seconds, would be needed for an equivalent performance. The entire range of weaponry, much of it novel, available to the 21st Army Group, demands a special study.

As D-Day approached 3,000 Royal Engineers and 1,000 lorry loads of equipment moved down behind the bunds of the river bank ready for the early bridging tasks. The sappers had carried out their own reconnaisance, and employed two forces each of 9,000 men to meet the demands of 2nd Army.

In the last days the 21st Army Group front seemed isolated from the Supreme Command, indifferent to the activities southward, and to Patton's enormous exertions. The troops coming forward from their rehearsals on the Maas looked in fine shape. The British and Canadians had sustained nearly 170,000 casualties since D-Day, and there were many men on the Rhine bank who had been present on that day, and many more had served in Normandy. Yet it was not a weary army. Leave arrangements had been very good, and were getting better. The end was near, and morale was high. Few men seemed to give much thought to what might lie ahead, or showed signs of natural tension. You could not go by old Monty and his preparations!

No one doubted that everything would go according to plan, and the planning for the assault was meticulous, the timings split second, units moving into position 'like clockwork'. Last light on the night would be at 19.45 hours, and the Commando brigade on the right would enter the water in Buffaloes at 10.00 hours, objective Wesel. Half an hour later heavy bombers would turn Wesel into a furnace and reduce much of it to rubble.

H hour for the main assault was 02.00 hours, and by first

light the D.D. tanks would be climbing ashore in support.

On D minus three the artillery overture began, working up to its crescendo on the night. Coupled with a programme of harassing bombing the enemy communications would be in chaos, and the enemy, it was hoped, would be 'punch drunk'. Right back to the Maas the processions of men, armour and equipment, moved steadily forward filling almost every square yard of available space. 5,000 tons of engineer stores were loaded on lorries at Kevalaer ready for action, and twenty Field Companies of Royal Engineers were at their posts.

At 10.00 hours on the morning of the first day the Airborne Corps would fly in from British and French fields, converging between Brussels and Namur to land its gliders in the midst of the enemy, and to seize crossings of the Ijssel on the left and storm the Diersfordter ridge. On the right the Airborne troops would encircle Wesel.

Soon after 20.00 hours on the night of 23rd March 27 bombers lit fires over Wesel to guide the 200 heavy bombers to their target. Two hours later the first of the Commando troops entered the water. There was a three quarter moon, and under the searchlights the shells of many calibres poured across the sky, and burst in torrents of high explosive amidst the enemy.

III

In the twelve hours from ten o'clock on the night of 23rd March to ten o'clock on the morning of the 24th, Montgomery's huge pyrotechnic display, reaching its airborne climax, dazzled the eyes of the privileged spectators, while those assaulting across the Rhine went quietly about their business.

At ten o'clock on the night of the 23rd the directional tracer streaming overhead illuminated the river faintly, and a fire on the distant shore made a trail across the water, which combined with the moonlight deprived the night of cover. The first wave of the Commandos, their faces smeared black, embarked quietly into the Buffaloes, and within ten minutes touched down on the east bank without meeting more than desultory spandau fire. Within half an hour the first of the Buffaloes climbed back up the west bank, the water pouring from its bows. One by one the craft lifted their great shapes over the low dyke barrier and reformed to ferry the second and third waves. Overhead the perfect sky was filled with vast red sheaves of tracer pouring from Bofors, and the harsh muttering of massed machine guns weaved incessantly under the whiplash of the heavy guns.

Landing in silence the first wave of the commandos had ripped a few dazed enemy out of their positions and the prisoners stood huddled in small groups on the east bank, their hands clasped above their heads as they waited to be taken into safer captivity. They were quite docile.

At half past ten o'clock a great weight of bombs seemed to tear the town of Wesel, and the very earth, into a torment of fire and explosions, and at once a great crimson stain of smoke and flame turned the Rhine to the colour of blood. Here and there bombs bursting in the water heaved the assault craft about like corks, and the whole sky line as far as one could see was lit with gun flashes. For hour after hour through the night the uproar of flame and sound, of flares and signals, of red and green tracer floating lazily over the river, created a wild chorus to the end of war.

All this time there was scarcely a sound from the enemy, but at last a pitiful handful of 88's and mortars began to range on the western shore, and a few shots smacked into the dyke banks. The enemy was almost paralyzed.[1]

Through all the days and nights following the landing craft, the Buffaloes, the storm boats, moved steadily from the marshalling areas and out of their 'hides' to the Rhine bank and took to the water. At 02.00 hours the main assault began and twenty minutes later the first waves of infantry were landing dry shod to winkle the enemy out of holes, cellars, houses, barns, wherever they might be found. Within half an hour the vehicles and support guns were following, and the engineers on the east bank were laying specially prepared 'carpets' to help the D.D. tanks to climb up out of the water when their time came at first light.

By that time small pockets of enemy had begun to come to life, but not with any possibility of exacting more than a token price in blood for the final intrusion into the Reich. A dozen women armed with rifles were among the early

[1] Despatch, ex Thompson: 23rd March, Rhine.

prisoners taken by Scottish troops. Chance shells and mortar bursts killed and maimed men on the west bank, especially engineer working parties. Desperate and short lived attacks checked forward troops, while the engineers worked steadily on their many tasks of bridging, the establishment of ferries, rafts and folding boat equipment to move guns armour and vehicles in support while the Bailey bridges grew steadily. Within six days continuous streams of heavy traffic fed a great mass of armour and ammunition out of the dumps and vehicle parks and across the Rhine. Casualties to engineer working parties and pioneers were often heavier than those suffered by assault troops, but there was no serious interference from the enemy.

After a night gaudy with the thunderous din of massed artillery, the Allied air fleets flew out of the west on time to the minute and disappeared into the pinkish haze of morning mist and smoke. Out of the west and into the east they roared with the fighters high above them like tiny silver fish. Here and there the Dakotas towing the gliders showed the ruddy glow of fire in wings and bodies. From some the parachutes came out; one, two, three, four ... and the crews came safely down while the aircraft suddenly dived steeply to crash to earth in spouts of fire and flying fragments of flame as wings and tails flew off like meteors. But it was not always so. Sometimes the thick pillars of smoke and flame were the funeral pyres of men.[1]

Soon after noon on 24th March the airborne troops had silenced most of the enemy guns in the rear areas. Small arms fire and the occasional 88 firing over open sights took a toll of the gliders, but casualties were slight to the air landings, except in the cases of individual gliders, when the casualties were total.

Churchill had joined Field-Marshal Montgomery to watch this last great performance, and the old warrior was thrilled by all he saw, by the artillery programme of bombardment by 2,000 guns,[2] and by the magnificent organization. Once again, as he had done in that fateful August in the Western Desert, he listened to the Field-Marshal expounding his plans in his map wagon, and was entranced:

[1] Thompson: *Men Under Fire*.
[2] Churchill: *Triumph and Tragedy*, vol. vi, p. 360-361.

'Here were displayed all the maps kept from hour to hour by a select group of officers. The whole plan of our deployment and attack were easily comprehended . . . All our resources were to be used . . . masses of boats and pontoons lay ready. On the far side stood the Germans, entrenched and organized in all the strength of modern fire-power.'[1]

Possibly Montgomery had convinced himself that this must be so, but it was not so. There was no strength of modern fire-power; no entrenched enemy to speak of. It was the Prime Minister's last taste of the battlefield spanning nearly fifty years of war. It was the victory he had worked himself and others almost into the ground to achieve over four long years. At times he had been gloomy, but never for an instant daunted. No man was more entitled to his visions. Yet the quietness of the crossing, the lack of incident brought about by enemy action, was in remarkable contrast to the kind of agonies demanded of the fathers and grandfathers of those who moved so easily across the Rhine. It was a measure also of the defeat suffered by the enemy. The ordinary wire fences of the farmers were often the worst of the obstacles encountered.

For four days movement in the bridgehead was almost impossible as the enormous numbers of vehicles, guns and armour, churned the soft wet earth into seas of mud. Groups of prisoners, often unguarded, walked timidly over the battered tracks seeking their own ways to captivity. And then after four days of frustrating congestion in the mud the thin crust of resistance burst, and there was no more stopping, no more battle, but only sporadic 'guerilla' type attacks and stubborn pockets of defence, hastily organized. Battle groups from local battle schools fought with the fury of young despair at a few points where ambush was possible, contested crossings of the Dortmund-Ems canal, strove to defend airfields, and made it dangerous to neglect reconnaisance of woodland ridges. But for the most part towns and villages awaited the oncoming columns, the people, civilians, children, soldiers alike in a state of apathy, almost of indifference, and an infuriating complacence.

Thus at the end of March seven armies burst out of their bridgeheads over the length of the Rhine from Arnhem to

[1] Churchill: *Triumph and Tragedy*, vol. vi, pp. 360-361.

Basle and raced into Germany to the limits ordained by the Supreme Commander, backed uncompromisingly by the U.S. Chief of Staff, General Marshall. On the left by the end of April the British 21st Army Group lay upon the Baltic, embracing the coast on a line from Wismar, Lubeck, Hamburg, Bremen, Emden to Zwolle, the Ijssel Meer and Arnhem. In the centre the U.S. 9th, 1st and 3rd Armies lay with their left upon Wittenberge, south through Magdeburg to Chemnitz and the outskirts of Karlsbad. On the right the U.S. 3rd Army easily penetrated into Czecho-Slovakia, enveloped Pilsen and Linz, and stopped, obedient to the command of General Eisenhower in personal communication with Stalin, and impervious to British plans and anxieties.

For nearly two weeks the capital city of Prague lay open awaiting the advancing armies of the Soviets. The U.S. 7th Army with the 1st French Army covered the southern flank on the Austrian and Italian frontiers to meet the advance guards of the Allied armies that had fought up the length of Italy to emerge at last through the Resio and Brenner passes.

Meanwhile the Russian armies under Chernyskhovsky and Rokossovsky in the North, with Zhukov and Koniev in the centre, and Malinovsky and Tolbukhin in the South, had moved out of their bridgeheads across the Oder and Neisse rivers to join hands with the Western Allies on the rivers Elbe and Mulde. Berlin, Vienna and Prague had become symbols of Russian victory, and the Communist Dictator had fulfilled the dreams of the Tsars, and gained the buffer states against Western aggression that had been a Russian nightmare since 1812; a nightmare renewed by Bismarck, by the Kaiser, and by Hitler.

From the beginning Stalin had had a clear vision of his Object.

IV

Churchill had argued urgently with the Supreme Command and with Washington for some clear political purpose to be injected into the final pattern of war. It had been a long struggle, and perhaps Churchill's hopes had been finally denied by 'Anvil-Dragoon', the landings in the South of

France so joyfully welcomed by Stalin. Possibly, but improbably, if Roosevelt had been in full command in the last months of the war, Churchill's final pleas might have been answered, but Roosevelt was at Warm Springs, there to die on 12th April. The Prime Minister's urgent messages were answered by General Marshall, and it is unlikely that they were shown to the ailing President. The last chapters of 'Triumph and Tragedy'[1] reveal the depths of unease Churchill shared with the British Chiefs of Staff. Let us, he begged, join hands with the Russians as far East as possible. Let us drive for Berlin.

'Berlin was the prime and true objective of the Anglo-American armies; the liberation of Czecho-Slovakia and the entry into Prague of American troops was of high consequence.' These were but two of the eight decisive points the Prime Minister spelled out. But he was ignored.

According to Admiral Leahy Churchill's pleas and arguments were not even considered by the Joint Chiefs of Staff, and Forrest Pogue comments:

'On the broader political question of getting to Berlin before the Russians, the U.S. Chiefs of Staff reacted as they had done formerly in regard to proposals of Balkan operations. Their view was that the business of the armed forces was to get the war ended as soon as possible and not to worry about the matter of prestige which would come from entering a particular capital.[2]

As though Berlin were merely a 'particular capital', or the future of Western Europe no more than a matter of prestige. There was in fact no common political ground between Churchill's European thinking and American detachment of the military from politics. Also, as Pogue points out, the Supreme Command did not believe that the allies had a chance of racing the Russians to Berlin in early April.

These were Churchill's major anxieties, but he was also deeply concerned with the impending loss of the U.S. 9th Army as an essential wing of 21st Army Group. As early as 30th March Eisenhower wrote to the Prime Minister that 'as soon as the U.S. 9th and 1st Armies join hands and enemy encircled in the Ruhr area is incapable of further offensive action I propose driving eastward to join hands with Russians

---
[1] Churchill: *Triumph and Tragedy*, Chapter xxvii.
[2] *The Supreme Command*, pp. 444-445.

or to attain general line of Elbe.' The main axis would be on the line Kassel-Leipzig, and Bradley would command the 1st, 3rd and 9th Armies. 'He (Bradley) will have Montgomery protecting his left flank.'[1]

On the 4th April, without real warning or formality, U.S. 9th Army joyfully went back under Bradley's command to join in the central thrust, mainly on firm ground and with a clear run ahead.

At the same time, Churchill learned with dismay, and not without anger, that Eisenhower had announced his policy in a direct communication to Marshal Stalin on 28th March. This was a breach of the Supreme Commander's prerogatives. Eisenhower at once argued that since Stalin was the Commander-in-Chief of the Soviet forces, his action was perfectly correct. 'Yet,' Churchill observed, 'it was not with the President of the U.S. that he (Eisenhower) corresponded, who was also the head of military forces, but with General Marshall.'

It was useless to protest further. The Americans were in a position to call whatever tune they pleased. There were some who believed that General Bradley had virtually taken over the military command. Eisenhower had discussed the whole problem, including Berlin, with Bradley, and Bradley wrote:

'Had Eisenhower even contemplated sending Montgomery ahead to Berlin, he would have had to reinforce that British flank with not less than one American Army. I could see no political advantage accruing from the capture of Berlin that would offset the need for quick destruction of the German Army on our front. As soldiers we looked naively on the British inclination to complicate the war with political foresight and non-military objectives.'[2]

The passage, as Pogue wrote, is 'significant'. And, of course, it was not a matter of 'either or'.

Montgomery, for his part, was remarkably philosophical. He had agreed with the Prime Minister's views from the beginning, and had deplored the South of France landings, revealing the shape of things to come. More in sorrow than in anger he wrote:

'The Americans could not understand that it was of little

[1] Churchill: *Triumph and Tragedy*, p. 401.
[2] Bradley: *A Soldier's Story*, pp. 535-536.

avail to win the war strategically if we lost it politically; because of this curious viewpoint we suffered accordingly from VE-day onwards, and are still so suffering. War is a political instrument; once it is clear that you are going to win, political considerations must influence its further course. It became obvious to me in the autumn of 1944 that the way things were being handled was going to have repercussions far beyond the end of the war: it looked to me then as if we were going to "muck it up". I reckon we did.'[1]

Montgomery looked to his very heavy commitment, and there was an end to 'bellyaching'. He had to seize the Baltic ports and coast line as far east as possible, to seal off the enemy escape routes from Denmark and Schleswig, and pay great attention to the still agonizing problems of North Holland. Dempsey handled the 2nd Army with great tactical skill, and persuaded the U.S. General Gavin, whose 82nd Airborne division had been lent to strengthen his left, to move rapidly across the Elbe in the north to the Baltic. This was no small achievement. Indeed the achievement of Montgomery's 21st Army Group in proportion to their size and the difficulties of the terrain they had traversed, was a matter for pride and satisfaction. They had come far. They had not 'bounced' many rivers, nor had they 'cracked about' very much in the North German plain, as their fanciful commander had put it before the event. But they had done more than well.

Nevertheless, as the army moved deeper into Germany, occupying the ruin of Bremen, and receiving the surrender of Hamburg, there was an absence of *élan*. By the end of April it was realised that the end was very near, but it did not lift the heart. Soldiers experienced only those things they saw on their lines of march, but there were some things all saw. Some had had a few stiff encounters, others had moved forward almost without incident. There was a remarkable contrast between town and country, between the appalling destruction that had overtaken Bremen and Hamburg, and had raised small anonymous places to the ground, and the apparently well fed complacency of the country folk. It was very beautiful in that April, but there was no Spring in the heart.

Through all that lovely countryside the great trails of the

[1] Montgomery: *Memoirs*, p. 332.

refugees wove like tragic and terrible threads of misery, caught between armies, between life and death, homeless, stateless, anonymous. The tragedy overlaid the triumph, and perhaps many felt, or began to feel, that this tragic country was the graveyard of Western civilisation.

Tremendous problems confronted the Military government sections attempting to organize local government. A junior officer and half a dozen men often found themselves confronted by a column of one thousand bewildered, hungry and vermin ridden refugees, not knowing which way to turn. The German civil population reacted to these agonizing columns without a trace of guilt, and complained indignantly to the authorities that such people should be permitted to move among them, and demanded protection. I remember one young corporal losing patience with a travesty of a woman:

'Don't you know about the way you have treated these people in your filthy horror camps!'

'Yes,' she said, 'but they still steal my chickens.'

But neither the corporal, nor the woman, knew much about the horror camps. Very few were inside Belsen, Buchenwald, Auschwitz in the first hours, to find themselves like mutes, confronted with the unthinkable beyond cruelty and ordinary horror. The deliberate reduction of human beings to beasts, stripped of all dignity, and starved to the point where the living and the dead were not to be distinguished. It had been a slow, cold, calculated process. It was the destruction of the soul, and it seemed then the ultimate crime against God and man.

And in some strange way very few felt guiltless. The laughter, the vitality, that had been on the faces of troops on the long journey from Normandy, the sense of pride in the liberation of the French, the Belgians, the Dutch, all was gone. There was no 'liberation' here, no joy, no triumph even. An understanding of some of the realities of the war began to grow as men came face to face with truths they had not even considered. The cheers for victory would not be on the battlefield, and relief that it was almost over was tempered with unease.

Right to the end there was death and danger to be faced, a truck load of infantry blowing up on a mine on the last day, almost in the last hour; an almost spent bullet lodging in a heart. In the north an enemy Panzer division continued to fight against the 51st Highland division, careless of the 'armistice' already signed. It was late afternoon on 6th May before Major-General Roth, commanding the 15th Panzer division together with General Raaspe, commanding a formation he designated as 'The Ems Corps', surrendered nearly 100,000 men to 30th Corps and the Highland division. They wished, they said, with great hauteur 'to surrender with honour', but there was no honour. The war had reached its bitter end.

V

Luneberg Heath, 5th May, 1945

Tomorrow, Saturday, at 08.00 hours British double summer time, the cease fire sounds on the 21 Army Group front and the extensive flanks of our armies. This is the end. It would be premature to call it peace, but at least it is the 'Armistice'.

For an hour we waited on the edge of the Luneberg Plain, the training ground of the armies of Nazi Germany, and the scene of many encounters. The sky was cold and grey, and a fine rain was driving in the blustering wind. A small group of us waited silently, our minds filled with the 'history' that we all felt was about to take place before our eyes. It was the kind of moment when small things impress themselves on the mind. We stood at the fringe of a clump of firs, and before us the spires of the two churches of Luneberg stood out sharply above the sombre darkness of the forest, lit only by the pale green of birches. It was a sombre scene, with that curious darkness that seems always intrinsic in Germany.

As we waited, searching the horizon for the thin clouds of dust that would mean the return of the German delegates, two British soldiers came slowly over the sandy loam with three prisoners they had picked up. The sky was darkening, and the lush green of the young corn was bright, almost yellow, against the blue-green darkness of firs that clothe the low rolling hills.

Rain began to drive in the wind. It was five o'clock, and suddenly a staff officer announced that the Field-Marshal was coming to talk to us, to tell us the story of these last hours. So we sat on the brown heather in the gloom of a large tent and waited. Precisely at five-fifteen Montgomery came in, hands stuffed deep into the pockets of his light naval dufflle-coat. The sound of rain driving on the canvas top of the tent was loud in our ears. Then the Field-Marshal began to talk. He was calm, almost jaunty.

'I'm going to tell the story of what's going on,' he said. And then, suddenly: 'Had a good tea?'

In short, General Blumentritt, who commands all the forces between the Baltic Sea and the river Weser, approached the 2nd Army on 2nd May, wishing to surrender 'Army Group Blumentritt'. This, as the Field-Marshal explained, was not an Army Group as we know it, but more like a 'Brigade Group'. The proposal was accepted. But on the morning of the 3rd when Blumentritt was due to arrive he sent a message in these terms:

'As far as I know, something is going on above my level, and therefore I am not coming.'

Instead there arrived at Montgomery's headquarters four Nazi officers: General-Admiral Friedenburg, C-in-C German Navy, succeeding Admiral Doenitz; General Kinsel, Chief of Staff to Field-Marshal Busch; Rear Admiral Wagner, Staff Officer to von Friedenburg, and a 'Major Freide'—'a kind of G-2,' Montgomery called him, to General Kinsel.

These officers lined up outside Montgomery's caravan in the woods, and the Field-Marshal came out on to the steps and surveyed them, saying curtly, with that snap he gets into his voice at times:

'What do you want?'

'We have come,' they said, 'from Field-Marshal Busch to ask you to accept the surrender of three German armies now withdrawing in front of the Russians in Mecklenburg.'

These armies were the 3rd Panzer Army, the 12th Army, and the 21st Army.

'And we are very anxious,' they said, 'about the conditions of German civilians who are being driven along as these armies are fleeing from the advancing Russians.'

They might well be anxious, and their anxiety grew as Montgomery answered curtly: 'No. Certainly not! The armies concerned are fighting the Russians. If they surrender to anybody it must be the Russians. Nothing to do with me.' With that the Field-Marshal turned back to his caravan.

But these high ranking Germans were near to despair. They had come, as they thought, with full baskets, and they dared not go away empty handed. Montgomery gave them a brief ultimatum:

'Are you prepared,' he asked, 'to surrender to me the German forces on my western and northern flanks? All forces between Lubeck and Holland, and all forces in support of them—such as Denmark?'

The reply was an instantaneous 'No!' But it was far from as decisive as it sounded. It was the 'No' of men who did not know that their country and their power was vanishing with the passing minutes.

'We are very anxious indeed about the conditions of civilians in those areas,' they said, with amazing effrontery, 'and we would like to come to some agreement with you whereby they will not be slaughtered.'

They then went on to suggest that we should advance slowly by agreement as they retreated.

Montgomery's 'No' was emphatic, and unmistakable even to the representatives of this race that lives on illusions. 'I am not going to discuss any conditions with you. Nothing,' he said. And then said very coldly, 'I wonder whether any of you know the battle situation on the Western front?'

It was then that he showed them his battle map, and in his own words, 'It was a great shock to them. They were amazed and very upset.'

The General-Admiral broke down and cried. He burst into tears and he wept all through his lunch, the Field-Marshal told us.

'No doubt that when they saw the situation on the map they were in a condition—a good condition, a good ripe condition— to receive a further blow,' Montgomery said. 'You must clearly understand three points: You must surrender to me unconditionally all the German forces in Holland, in Friesland, including the Friesian Islands, in Schleswig Holstein, and in Denmark. Two: Once you have done all that I shall be prepared to discuss with you the implications of that surrender— that is, how we shall dispose of those forces, our occupation, and so on. Accept point one, and discuss two. Three: If you don't agree to Number One, I shall go on with the war, and will be delighted to do so, and all your soldiers and civilians will be killed.'

That was the ultimatum to which we were awaiting the answer.

'No alternative. Accept One, Two, Three. Finish!' Montgomery rapped out.

The immediate reply was: 'We came here entirely for the purpose of asking you to accept the surrender of our armies on your eastern flank, and we have been given powers to agree to that only. We have not power to agree to your demands. Two of us will go back, and two will remain until we return.'

And so, yesterday afternoon General-Admiral von Friedenburg, accompanied by Major Freide, went back into the German lines in the Hamburg area, while General Kinsel and the Rear Admiral stayed behind.

Suddenly Montgomery said: 'The General-Admiral will be back about five. Ha! He is back! He was to come back with the doings. Now we shall see what the form is!'

At this moment Montgomery was superb, the complete master of the situation. 'My intention is,' he said, 'that they shall sign a piece of paper I have prepared. I am dealing with the command of forces facing me. I am demanding from him complete tactical surrender of forces fighting me. And I have absolutely excluded anything that might be an Allied matter.'

Then gaily, like a boy, he chuckled: 'No doubt that if the piece of paper is signed forces to be surrendered total over a million chaps. Not so bad, a million chaps! Good egg!'

The Field-Marshal left us. For a short time we waited, and then just before six we walked up the narrow sandy track through the firs. Above the cluster of caravans that is Montgomery's Tactical headquarters the Union Jack fluttered in the stiff cold breeze. A square table with a plain grey army blanket showed under the raised flaps of a tent, and around it were placed six hard brown chairs, their varnish shining under the electric lamps. In this tent the 'piece of paper' drawn up by the Field-Marshal would be signed.

There was complete stillness. The dark woods clothing the rounded slopes girdling the plain, seemed to enclose a kind of vacuum in which we waited. The rain was driving in the wind and it was bitter cold.

Presently Montgomery walked down the steps of his caravan. Fighter planes roaring overhead emphasized the stark bluntness of the ultimatum, and the might of the Allies. The Field-Marshal strolled casually under the awning nets of his caravan, the 'piece of paper' in one hand, the other stuffed deep into his battledress pocket.

And then they came. Through the woodland, over the crisp brown heather, over the path we had traversed five minutes earlier, the delegates owning the utter defeat of Nazi Germany. Two British Staff officers walked with General-Admiral von Friedenburg, and behind them followed in pairs, General Kinsel and Rear Admiral Wagner followed by Major Freide, and a new arrival, Colonel Polleck.

They came slowly, the Admirals in blackish-grey raincoats, the soldiers in their long grey coats tight-belted at the high waists, the skirts swinging round their black jack-boots. Only the bright scarlet of General Kinsel's lapels relieved the drabness of their appearance, this solitary little procession bringing with it the submission of a once mighty nation ... So they walked, General Kinsel, thick-set, tall, monocled, and the shorter, more thick-set naval officers, to the steps of the Field-Marshal's caravan. General-Admiral von Friedenburg climbed the steps alone, and entered. The others waited, as we all waited. And above these four figures the Union Jack fluttered, the flap of its bunting almost the only sound in this quiet woodland setting.

It was six-twenty when the General emerged from the caravan, and the small cavalcade, led by two British Staff officers, walked across the fifty yards of sandy loam to the tent with the simple table. And there they stood, each at his chair, waiting.

Two minutes later Field-Marshal Montgomery followed. The five Germans saluted stiffly and seated themselves after the Field-Marshal. Montgomery wore his tortoiseshell rimmed spectacles. On his left General Kinsel, monocled, heavy jowled, red colour in his face. The rest, grey, all hard eyed, beaten men. They sat in silence, only jaw muscles betraying their emotions as Field-Marshal Montgomery read clearly the text of the 'piece of paper' . . . 'The German Command agree to Surrender all German forces . . . to Commander-in-Chief Twenty-one Army Group . . . All hostilities to cease eight hundred hours British Double Summer Time Fifth of May 1945 . . . The decision of Allied powers . . . final . . .' The voice was cold and clear and hard as stone.

The face of General Kinsel betrayed his effort at control. His eyes moved from the Field-Marshal's face to the grey cloth of the table. The faces of the others were literally grey, save for Major Freide whose cheeks had a youthful bloom.

Then Montgomery said: 'The German delegation will now sign. They will sign in order of seniority.' The words were like hammer blows, each one dropping into the minds of us all indelibly. 'General-Admiral von Friedenburg first.'

The Admiral rose, and with the simple army issue pen, signed. Then General Kinsel, the only one who showed emotion in the working of his face. As he raised himself from bending over the table he licked his dry lips.

So they followed as the Commander of the British Armies called their names: 'And Major Freide will sign last.'

Only Montgomery's voice rose above the click of the cameras, and then he said: 'Now I will sign on behalf of the Supreme Allied Commander, General Eisenhower.' His lips were firm, and as he finished signing he sighed faintly, sat back, and removed his tortoiseshell rims, relaxed. 'That concludes the surrender,' he said.

The tent flaps were let down, and we walked away over the brown heather.[1]

[1] R. W. Thompson: *Despatch*, Luneberg Heath, 5th May, 1945.

Belchamp Walter
27th October, 1968.

Epilogue

IT is no part of my purpose to pursue the Field-Marshal beyond the battlefield. His tenure of the office of Chief of the Imperial General Staff, his service as Deputy Supreme Commander in N.A.T.O., cannot add to or subtract from his performance as a commander in the field. Nor, it must be hoped, will his phenomenal success as a writer and publicist in his 'retirement', and his remarkable obsession with the 2nd battle of Alamein, be permitted to blur or to obscure his real worth as a soldier. It is as a soldier that the Field-Marshal must be judged, and it is upon his performance in the field that his place in history will be assessed.

I do not think that the Field-Marshal's command of the 8th Army from Alamein to the Sangro will long remain a matter for controversy. The facts are simple, even though the words are often devious and the political machinations following upon Auchinleck's strategic defeat of the enemy at 1st Alamein are discreditable and distasteful. The Field-Marshal cannot be blamed for that. He came upon the scene with very little warning, unaware until it happened that such a task awaited him.

There is nothing complicated about the battle he fought at 2nd Alamein. Occupying an impregnable position, and refusing to be hurried, he was able to concentrate an overwhelming weight of men and matériel upon an exhausted and overstretched enemy. The ground was so much in his favour that his superiority was greatly enhanced. His opponent, General von Stumme, having no Ruweisat Ridge to help him, had felt bound to string out his troops over his whole front. He had failed to concentrate his armour, as Rommel would almost certainly have done, and had distributed it in six 'packets' behind the front.

But it is idle to speculate upon what Rommel would have done, had he been there, for the sick and weary general, when he returned to face the defeat of his army and to reap the bitter fruits of failure, refrained from criticizing the man who had done his best in his absence, and had died on the second day of the battle.

Yet in spite of all the Field-Marshal's advantages at 2nd Alamein, a terrible battle of attrition developed, at times seeming to teeter on the edge of failure. The Field-Marshal had not a shell or a tank too many. He looked failure in the eye, and it is to his everlasting credit that his nerve held, that he regrouped, changed direction, and battered on. He was slow, and unimaginative, but he did not falter.

It is curious in the whole context of these events and those preceding them, to look again at the reactions of the Prime Minister and the C.I.G.S. to this battle.[1] Both men were in a state of extreme anxiety, and it is difficult to believe that a few weeks earlier the commanders in the desert had been vilified for not defeating the enemy on equal terms, and often with inferior weaponry.

On 28th October, with the battle raging, Churchill cabled the Prime Ministers of Canada, New Zealand and Australia: 'The great battle in Egypt has opened well, although one cannot yet forecast its result. The enemy are short of ammunition and fuel... Our forces are substantially superior in the air, in armour, including best armour, in artillery fire, and in numbers, and they have far easier lines of communication. Rommel is seriously ill, and has only been brought back as an extreme measure.'

The next morning, the 29th, the Prime Minister's fears of failure led to an explosion of temper which fell upon the faithful Brooke, himself a prey to dreadful doubts. At the same time Whitehall was thick with rumours. 'After a week's hard slogging and ten thousand casualties,' Brooke noted, 'the offensive seemed little nearer its goal than at the beginning.'

There is no doubt that the battle was a tremendous personal ordeal for Montgomery, and he was very much on his own. It was his 'baptism of fire' as an army commander. Alone in his caravan in the last days of October he must have contemplated, however briefly, the possibility that he might lose, or fail to win, an unlosable battle. I believe that the ordeal marked him for life. Pre-eminently a general of *matériel*, as Fuller remarked,

---

[1] Churchill: *The Hinge of Fate* (R.U. Edn.), p. 480. Bryant: *The Turn of the Tide*, pp. 511-512.

his caution was underlined. Henceforth, as the Americans were quick to observe, he would not move unless his superiority ensured success.

It must be clear that this battle of 2nd Alamein impressed itself indelibly upon the Field-Marshal's mind, almost to the exclusion of all else. Month after month and year after year he re-lives it, and always with a greater degree of fantasy. Nothing would be more unfortunate than for his performance as a soldier to be judged by 2nd Alamein, and for it to be forgotten that he was very much the victim of the immense floodlight of publicity and propaganda cast upon him. Thus in the immediate aftermath of the battle, in his intense reaction and relief, he suddenly found himself a hero, acclaimed not only by his own countrymen, but by a vast public in the United States. And upon the instant, this dry and solitary professional soldier, was transformed.

The timing of the battle, the alignment with the North African landings, proclaimed to the world in unmistakable terms, that the tide had turned, and that at last, plain for all to see, the enemy had begun to withdraw, and must withdraw on all fronts. The relief of the British people was manifest in their hero worship of Montgomery who, naturally, had become the symbol of victory. The slow follow up of the defeated enemy to Tunisia drew out the sense of triumph and the savour of victory. No one was disposed to quibble.

In Sicily Montgomery failed dismally to add to his laurels. He had largely called the tune in the planning stages, and chosen his dominant role. He would lead his victorious army to the straits of Messina and thence into Italy. The American General Patton in a supporting role, and finding his vital road usurped by Montgomery, was forced to cover the long west coast route. In the event, as Martin Blumenson put it, 'What should have been Montgomery's "cup of tea", turned out to be Patton's bowl of milk.' Against all odds the American beat Montgomery to the winning post.

Montgomery's long pause at Messina was significant in underlining not only his extreme caution, but his disregard of the enemy condition, his failure to appreciate enemy strength or weakness, or even whether the enemy was there. The delay while he gathered together his wealth of artillery support might have—and probably did—jeopardize the success of the American landings at Salerno. A valuable two days had been lost, and in the event more flowers than bullets greeted British troops on the Italian shore.

It is Montgomery's concentration on his North African campaign, and this whole phase of his generalship, and particularly his obsession with the 2nd battle of Alamein, that has made it difficult for many to see the Field-Marshal whole, and to begin to assess his place as a commander in the field. Even in his own mind all the rest of his generalship seems forgotten.

II

It is in his conduct of the campaign in north west Europe in 1944/45, in his command of the ground forces in the battle for Normandy, in his command of the 21st Army Group, that his merits will be assessed. Alamein was a traumatic experience; the conduct of the campaign in north west Europe revealed his quality as a commander in the field, his strengths, his weaknesses, his limitations.

The criticisms of the Field-Marshal's conduct of the battle for Normandy began at once. The criticisms focussed upon his alleged failure to take the city of Caen. His principal critic was Tedder, the Deputy Supreme Commander, supported by the air force commanders. Perhaps his most dangerous critic was the British General Morgan, the architect of 'Overlord', and deputy chief of staff to the Supreme Commander under General Walter Bedell Smith. The critics alleged that the city of Caen was a vital objective, if not the vital objective, on the first day. The attitudes of the airmen could be understood by their need for airfields and space, and their persistent over-estimates of the power of air bombardment to defeat the enemy. But Morgan was a soldier, a soldier moreover who should have known. No nuance of the Overlord plan or of the D-Day plan could have escaped his notice. Thus the professional support for the criticisms of Montgomery were very powerful.

A great deal of this argument seems to me irrelevant to the battle for Normandy. Beyond a shadow of doubt all the commanders were immensely pleased and relieved by the D-Day result. The Prime Minister, the C.I.G.S. and the Monarch, all of whom suffered grave fears and forebodings, were jubilant. It seems, therefore, improbable that the landings fell far short of the targets. The intention, the absolute 'Object', was to get ashore and stay there.

Later, of course, critics would draw attention to the phase line estimates of advance and stress their wide divergence from the progress actually made. The phase lines were estimates made long in advance mainly for the guidance of the logistical planners, and it was this tight planning carried to its conclusion that so hampered the developments on entirely different lines when the break-out from the Seine occurred. The phase lines on the Normandy plans indicated hopes and possibilities.

I do not believe that it was, or could have been, the direct intention of Montgomery to take the city of Caen on D-Day, or immediately thereafter. It probably figured as a hope, an outside chance. If it was a direct intention, a vital objective of D-Day or D plus 1, as Morgan's criticism must imply, then the planners were hopelessly at fault. The strength deployed on the left flank of the D-Day assault could not have encouraged the greatest optimist to regard the fall of Caen as more than an outside possibility. Caen was at the hinge of the German 15th Army in the Pas de Calais, and the German 7th Army defending Normandy. It was a great and vital road centre, essential to communications. It was the 'gateway to Paris', and a valuable minor port. How could such a heavily defended key centre of the enemy be expected to fall without the most powerful and concentrated assault directed upon it?

And, of course, it did not fall, nor was it threatened.

The battle for Normandy developed on lines I have sought to describe carefully. The congestion in the bridgehead grew very serious indeed, giving rise to many agonizing frustrations and hampering the development of airfields on the scale longed-for by the Air-Marshals. But the Field-Marshal was a soldier, not unmindful of the value of air power in support of his armies, but concerned to win the battle with his ground forces. And he did. It was a battle, in my estimate of the Field-Marshal's abilities as a commander in the field, peculiarly suited to him. His over use of air bombardment against Caen in his final assaults upon the city may have had their genesis, not only in the Field-Marshal's tendency to over bombardment, but in these early criticisms and frustrations of the Air-Marshals.

Even if it had been the intention to take Caen on the first or second day, the fact is that the city was not taken and the battle as fought was the battle that confronted the Field-Marshal when he stepped ashore to take the ground force command directly into his hands. It is on that battle, not on a might-have-been, that he must be judged. He inflicted a decisive and terrible defeat upon the enemy, a defeat from which the enemy should not have been permitted to recover. The fact that the fruits of the Field-Marshal's victory were squandered, not least by himself, must not detract from his performance in Normandy.

Yet the 'might-have-been' of Caen, the 'if' history, is dangerous and fascinating. It is dangerous because some of those who construct well reasoned and convincing accounts of what might have happened tend to convince themselves, and others, that their accounts would have happened, and are not merely speculation. It is fascinating because the possibilities of the campaign in north west Europe had Caen fallen to the British on the first day, or even in the first week, provide a fascinating exercise for military students. Certainly the whole course of the campaign would have been very different. A host of new factors would have come into play, and many of them, it may appear, in favour of the enemy. Perhaps the enemy, who would have been able to deploy his armour with much greater facility in the early stages, might have imposed a slower tempo upon the whole campaign, avoiding a major defeat comparable with that suffered in Normandy. No one knows; no one will ever know. For my part I regard it as fortunate that Caen did not fall. I feel sure that the ensuing battle had Caen fallen would not have suited the Field-Marshal's abilities so well as the reality.

The Field-Marshal's failure to seize Antwerp entire and to advance across the Albert canal to cut off the Bevelands—and the German 15th Army—is his most agonizing failure. It was a dreadful omission, and the temptation to speculate is very strong. There is not much one may deduce with any degree of certainty.[1] Again the campaign would have been very

---

[1] I believed and still believe that the advance should have continued at least to Woensdracht. It might, of course, have closed the Maas.

different. Certainly the left flank of the British 2nd army would have been covered on its isolated dash to Nijmegen and its attempt on Arnhem, and the difficult logistical situation confronting all armies throughout the winter would have been greatly relieved.

The failure to open the Scheldt and the port of Antwerp with all speed was inexcusable. It could have been relegated to a second priority (and I do not mean that the crossing of the Albert canal and the sealing off of the Bevelands should have been relegated in any circumstances) if the British 2nd Army had pressed on relentlessly in pursuit of the enemy. Antwerp and Arnhem were not alternatives. The Scheldt failure is in a different category from the Field-Marshal's failure to take Arnhem and make good a crossing of the Rhine. That failure is a failure due to caution and delay, and impossible to reconcile with Montgomery's declared intention on his drive to the Seine, 'to keep the enemy on the run straight through to the Rhine, and "bounce" our way across that river before the enemy succeeded in reforming a front "to oppose us".'

In battle Montgomery had his feet firmly on the ground, too often, perhaps, rooted to the ground. But in his hour of victory, in his sense of elation, a new and daring Montgomery was manifest—in words. Perhaps inside him was a daring and dashing commander struggling to get out.

'Persistent pace and pressure,' Liddel Hart emphasized, 'is the key to success in any deep penetration or pursuit, and even a day's pause may forfeit it.'[1] Montgomery paused at Brussels from 4th to 7th September. Excuses abounded, mainly involving logistics, but they are not good enough. Nothing, absolutely nothing, should have imposed a pause upon the British 2nd Army. The fact is that the 2nd Army and its commanders thought that they had earned a respite from their exertions. They believed the enemy incapable of rallying, and in those wasted days, the real hope of winning the war in 1944 was lost. There was the moment of truth, the supreme moment of opportunity.

After the failure of the belated Arnhem adventure, and the slowing down of the armies all along the line, the broad front pattern took shape, inevitably, and only the enemy break-

[1] *The Listener*, 3rd September, 1964.

through in the Ardennes relieved the long bitter tedium of the winter. Throughout that long winter the Field-Marshal fought his most difficult 'battles' with the Supreme Command. It was in many ways a brave fight, but a hopeless one, for as Michael Howard was to write:[1] 'There comes a point in the conduct of strategy when calculations valid at a lower level no longer apply; when conditions other than military have to be taken into account and the problems of personal, party or national susceptibilities can no longer be brushed aside. To cope with such problems the qualities of a statesman, or at the very least of a diplomat, are as necessary as those of a soldier; and these qualities the Field-Marshal signally failed to acquire. In a phrase he used lavishly of others, he had risen above his ceiling.'

The Field-Marshal's logic was impeccable, his reasoning on his level very sound, his expositions clear and lucid. But he was arguing from a lower level, and his reasoning did not apply. He was, moreover, an army commander rather than an army group commander, concentrating as did Bradley also, upon one of his armies. But he commanded an army group which must, absolutely must, coordinate and integrate with other, and *alien*, army groups. This posed problems the Field-Marshal did not seem to understand. Inevitably he was the odd man out, not one of the 'family', as were Bradley, Patton, Devers, and, of course, Bedell Smith. In that gathering Montgomery, lacking the easy fellowship of his Chief of Staff, de Guingand, was an outsider, and nothing that Eisenhower could do, or anyone could do, would alter that. It must have been strange for Montgomery to mix closely with American generals, to be Ike, Brad, George and Monty. What did it mean? It sounded like friendship, an easy relationship. But these nick-names may have indicated how far apart they were, rather than how close.

In the midst of the worst of the command troubles the Field-Marshal took up the challenge in the Ardennes. It was a situation cut to his measure, and at the end he was unable to conceal his triumph. His prestige with the liberated peoples of Belgium and Holland was greatly enhanced. Perhaps, whatever he had said in the hour of victory would have angered the hyper-sensitive Americans, and Bradley in particular; perhaps his only course would have been to creep silently away, and back

[1] *New Statesman*, 8th November, 1958.

to his battle of the Rhineland. He was not made that way, and I find it difficult to blame him. I feel certain that when he returned to his own command he was unaware of the powerful feelings he had left behind him in the American camp.

The Field-Marshal's last great opportunity came when his armies lined up on the west bank of the Rhine. In his long and meticulous preparation for crossing the river he was himself, unhurried, cautious, confident, the same man who had lectured his senior students at the Staff College 25 years earlier on the proper way to mount a divisional assault, the same man who had refused to be hurried before 2nd Alamein, the same man who had demanded invincible strength before the assault upon Sicily.

But he was an immensely professional soldier. The Americans, disliking him intensely, gave him credit for his handling of the 'set-piece' battle. He had learned to do that very well, and had become a more flexible tactician than he had been at 2nd Alamein. Moreover he had a fine army commander in General Dempsey. And perhaps the Field-Marshal knew in his heart his limitations; perhaps he always had. That is why his way was the 'set-piece' battle whether or not the situation demanded it.

When his armies including the U.S. 9th Army under his command, lined up along the Rhine he needed American confidence, but they had never believed him capable of 'keeping the enemy on the run . . . and "bouncing" rivers'. Had they had confidence in the Field-Marshal for that kind of role he would have won, I believe, all the backing he needed. But the Americans did not believe that he would drive the U.S. 9th Army with the speed and élan of Bradley, and he lost it. He might have kept it under his command at least until the encirclement of the Ruhr, but he had held General Simpson in leash too long, and his caution played into Bradley's hands.

Yet it is unlikely that whatever the Field-Marshal had done the final pattern could have been greatly changed. He might have played a more forceful part in the final stages, but it would have been essentially the same pattern. A sense of inevitability broods over the whole campaign, of the too great control of logistics over strategy and tactics. It is this, I think, that makes one seek constantly—and to long for (as one did at the time), the 'great Captain', for military genius that alone could have broken loose.

There was no 'great Captain'. The Field-Marshal directed his armies with thoroughness and skill to the end. At Luneberg he had earned his considerable victory. It had been a long hard haul from the Normandy beaches.

III

A handful of serious and critical assessments of the Field-Marshal have been attempted on both sides of the Atlantic. Writing in the U.S. publication 'Armor' Martin Blumenson,[1] the distinguished Historian, summed up:

'Well-schooled, well-trained, experienced, Montgomery was competent, adequate. He was not great... He is, I think, vastly overrated, the most overrated general of World War II.'

It is a harsh verdict, but essentially just. American involvement in the European Theatre began after 2nd Alamein, and Blumenson is one of those who accepted the enormous propaganda build-up of Montgomery at something near its face value. Thus he expected too much. He caught up with Montgomery as a general in the last stages of the North African campaign, and in the assault on Sicily. The Field-Marshal was bound to fall far short of the 'image' created at Alamein.

Montgomery was certainly overrated, but in my view all the allied generals in the European Theatre of operations were overrated in the second half of the war, just as many of the generals of the first half were, often shamefully, underrated. Those who struggled and held on bravely through more than two and a half years of terrible shortages, against an enemy on the rampage, tend to be forgotten. They made victory possible. No one knows what those who came afterwards in the days of plenty and when the tide had turned would have done in their shoes. Liddell Hart wrote:

> Those who commanded in the field during the later phase of the war operated with an advantage of strength over the

[1] One of the U.S. team of official historians. Author of *Break-Out and Pursuit* Office of Chief of Mil. Hist. Washington.

enemy too large to form an adequate test, or a basis of comparison with the best of their predecessors... Moreover, none of them in the main theatre proved their capacity to *master* adverse conditions and out-manoeuvre opponents of superior strength—which is the greatest test of generalship. On the other side, a number of leaders did so—particularly Manstein, Guderian and Rommel. The most successful of the Allied commanders enjoyed such an immense quantitative advantage that the qualitative value of their own performance cannot be gauged.

The fortunes of war were kind to Field-Marshal Montgomery and his associates, Bradley, Devers, Patton, Clark. The Field-Marshal stands very high among them, and his was the testing role. I hope that he will be remembered for what he was, a very professional and dedicated soldier.

Bibliography

Biennial Report of the Chief of Staff of the United States Army, July 1st 1943, to June 30th, 1945, to the Secretary of War.

Report by the Supreme Commander to the Combined Chiefs of Staff on the Operations in Europe of the Allied Expeditionary Force.

Operations in North-West Europe from June 6th, 1944, to May 5th, 1945, Despatch submitted to the Secretary for War, June 1st, 1946, by Field-Marshal, The Viscount Montgomery of Alamein, K.G., G.C.B., D.S.O. (Supplement to *London Gazette*, 3rd September, 1946 (No. 37711).

Air Operations by the Allied Expeditionary Force in N.W. Europe from November 15th, 1943, to September 30th, 1944, Air Chief Marshal Sir Trafford Leigh Mallory, K.C.B., D.S.O., Fourth Supplement to *London Gazette*, 31st December, 1946.

The Assault Phase of the Normandy Landings, Admiral Sir Bertram Ramsay, K.C.B., M.V.O., Supplement to *London Gazette*, 28th October, 1947.

History of the Second World War, United Kingdom Military Series.
Victory in the West, Ellis, (London, H.M.S.O.)
Grand Strategy, vol. iii, Part II, Butler, (London H.M.S.O.)
Grand Strategy, vol. v, Ehrman, (London, H.M.S.O.)
Grand Strategy, vol. vi, Ehrman, (London H.M.S.O.)
The Strategic Air Offensive against Germany, 1939–1945, (four vols.) (H.M.S.O.)
By Air to Battle: The Official account of the British 1st and 6th Airborne divisions, (H.M.S.O.)
North West Europe, 1944/1945, John North, (H.M.S.O.)

United States Army in World War II.
Office of Chief of Military History, Dept. of the Army, Washington, D.C.
The Supreme Command, Pogue.
Cross-Channel Attack, Harrison.
Break-out and Pursuit, Blumenson.
The Lorraine Campaign, Cole.
The Ardennes: Battle of the Bulge, Cole.
Three Battles, MacDonald & Ors. (Special Studies).
Command Decisions.

The Logistical Support of the Armies, two volumes, Ruppenthal.
American Forces in Action Series, Historical Division, Dept of Army, Wash. D.C.
Utah Beach to Cherbourg.
Omaha Beachhead.

Ottawa: The King's Printer.
The Canadian Army, 1939/45, Stacey.
Canada's Battle in Normandy, Stacey.
American Contributions to the Strategy of World War II, Samuel Eliot Morison, (Oxford Univ. Press)

Regimental and Divisional Histories.
The Royal Hampshire Regt. Vol. iii. Daniell, (Gale and Polden.)
Borderers in Battle: The War Story of the Kings Own Scottish Borderers, 1939/45, Gunning. (Printed for the Regiment by Martin's of Berwick upon Tweed.)
Assault Division, (3rd British Infantry), Scarfe, (Collins.)
The 43rd Wessex Division, Essame, (Clewes.)
The 15th Scottish Division, 1944/45, Martin, (Blackwood).
The Story of the 79th Armoured Division, Oct. 1942/June 1945, (Hamburg.)
Mountain and Flood, (52nd Lowland Div.) Blake, (Jackson.)
The Path of the 50th (Div.) Clay, (Gale and Polden.)
Guards Armoured Division, 1941/45, Rosse and Hill, (Bles.)
The Red Beret: The story of the Parachute Regt. at War, 1940/45, Saunders, (Michael Joseph.)
The Green Beret: The Story of the Commandos, Saunders, (Michael Joseph.)
The Tanks: The history of the Royal Tank Regiment, vol. ii. 1939/45, B. H. Liddell Hart, (Cassell.)

The Second World War, vol. v. Closing the Ring, vol. vi. Triumph and Tragedy, Churchill, (Cassell.)
The White House Papers of Harry Hopkins, two vols. Sherwood, (Eyre & Spottiswoode.)
Triumph in the West, (The Alanbrooke Diaries.) Bryant, (Collins.)
Eisenhower's Six Great Decisions, Bedell Smith.
Operation Neptune, Edwards, (Collins.)
Overture to Overlord, Morgan, (Hodder & Stoughton.)
Operation Victory, de Guingand, (Hodder & Stoughton.)
The Struggle for Europe, Wilmot, (Collins.)
Top Secret, Ingersoll, (Harcourt Brace.)
My Three Years with Eisenhower, Butcher, (Heinemann.)

Crusade in Europe, Eisenhower, (Heinemann.)
A Soldier's Story, Bradley, (Eyre & Spottiswoode.)
The Rommel Papers, Ed. Liddell Hart, (Collins.)
War as I knew it, Patton, (W. H. Allen.)
The Second World War, Fuller, (Eyre & Spottiswoode.)
Decisive Battles of World War II, (German view), Jacobsen & Rohwer, (Deutsch.)
With Prejudice, Tedder, (Cassell.)
Memoirs of Lord Ismay, Ismay, (Heinemann.)
The Fatal Decisions, (Michael Joseph.)
Panzer Leader, Guderian, (Dutton.)
Arnhem, Urquhart, (Cassell.)
The Business of War, Kennedy, (Hutchinson.)
Phantom was There, Hills, (Arnold.)
Memoirs of Field Marshal Montgomery, Montgomery, (Collins.)
Normandy to the Baltic, Montgomery, (Hutchinson.)
The Path to Leadership, Montgomery, (Collins.)
Montgomery, Moorehead, (Hamish Hamilton.)
The Nicolson Diaries, vol. ii. (Collins.)
The Execution of Private Slovik, Huie, (Jarrolds.)
The Virus House, Irving, (Kimber.)

Appendix

Specialised Armour, used in Normandy, Scheldt, Rhine crossing, and generally throughout the campaign.

AVRE: Armoured vehicle, Royal Engineers. A Churchill tank with or without turret, carrying a 12-inch spigot mortar PETARD, or, a small girder bridge, S.B.G. Or Trackway bridge, or, 'carpets' of various kinds for laying over boggy ground, and carried on large BOBBINS,
or FASCINES for filling ditches or craters,
or Tank Dozers.

CDL Tank. A Grant tank without turret armament, replaced by CDL searchlight. Invulnerable to small arms and M.G. Fire. Light able to switch on and off or flicker at will.
The tank used 75mm gun from right hand sponson on targets illuminated by searchlight.

CROCODILE: A Churchill VII tank with flame thrower in place of hull M.G. Carried 400 gallons special fuel in armoured trailer. Range 110 yards. Normally armed with 2–7.92 besas plus 1–75mm.

CRAB (or Flail): Sherman V tank fitted with rotating drums mounted in front. 43 chains rotating at 180 r.p.m. flailed ground at 2–3 m.p.h. Armament, 1–75mm, 2–.300 Brownings, 1–17 pounder. Carried less than normal Sherman V ammo.

D.D.: Duplex Drive amphibious Sherman V (or III), fitted with a collapsible canvas scree supported by air pillars and steel struts. Height 13 ft. Propelled by two propellers driven by main engine. Speed in water $4\frac{1}{2}$ knots, draft 9 feet. On land reverts to normal Sherman.

SPs.: Canadian RAM (Sherman chassis) 25 pdr. field gun firing 25 lb shell 13,300 yards. Crew 6, weight 24 tons, speed 25 m.p.h.
VALENTINE 17 pdr. anti-tank gun, 17 lb shell, 6,500 yards H.E. crew 4, weight 16 tons, speed 20 m.p.h.
USA M10, 17 pdr., range 7,700 yards, H.E.
crew 5, weight 28 tons, speed 30 m.p.h.

APC (or KANGAROO), a Sherman or Canadian RAM tank without turret, carrying one section of infantry.

APPENDIX

BUFFALO (or LVT.): Tracked landing vehicle, personnel and stores. Adapted to carry 17 pdr. and M.G. in well. No doors. Could take Weasel, Scout car (Dingo), Jeep, Airborne bull dozer. Very light armour in front. Sometimes equipped with 20mm Polsten gun. Load 4 tons water speed 6 knots, land speed 30 m.p.h. Absolutely invaluable in Scheldt crossings, Bevelands, Walcheren, and in Rhine floods. Able to climb 29 degrees gradient. Wonderful except in deep mud. Only 2 feet belly clearance. Very noisy, Cut roads to ribbons.

WEASEL: Light amphibious tracked vehicle. Excellent cross country in waterlogged conditions, but mechanically delicate. Not reliable for crossing Rhine under own power.

R.E. Bridging equipment available to 21 A.G., and timings for Rhine Crossing.

Stormboat: Built of plywood. 22 H.P. Outboard Motor, tended to 'play up'. Engine needed 3 men to carry it, and 14 men to carry boat. 3 feet of water essential before starting up, preferably quiet 'lagoon' or sheltered spot. Lifts one section of infantry.

Class 9 raft: Constructed of light pontoons and a trackway superstructure. Driven by motors. Royal Engineer personnel needed special training in watermanship. Rafts carried up to a D 3 tractor or 15 cwt APC or half track.

Took 4 hours to construct. Carried 12 vehicles per hour per rafting site in daylight and 9 vehicles per hour by night.

Class 50/60 raft: Heavy raft of metal pontoons and girder superstructure carrying trackway. Run on cables across river hauled by balloon winches on banks. Equipment carried on special trailers towed by MATADOR wheeled tractors or sledges hauled by AVRE's. Movement difficult.

Assault Squadrons Royal Engineers specialised on this job. Raft carried one tank or M10 SP Anti-Tank gun, or two Kangaroos or 15 cwt armoured half tracks. Could also lift small vehicle at same time, jeep or scout car.

9 vehicles per hour by day, 7 vehicles per hour by night, per rafting site.

Class 9 FBE: (Folding boat equipment). Light bridge of canvas and wood, folding boats and trackway. Delicate stuff. Needed approximately 8 hours maintenance in each 24 hours.

BAILEY Pontoon equipment: Carried on pontoons with special landing bays to carry bridge from land to floating bays, varying standard equipment enabled engineers to construct any bridge from Class 9 to Class 70.

APPENDIX

Timings: Rhine Crossing.

H plus 1 hour. 25 storm boats in use.

H plus 9 hours. Four Class 9/12 close support raft ferries, each ferry two working rafts and one spare.

H plus 12 hours. Two class 50/60 ferries, each of two working rafts, and one spare.

H plus 18 hours. DUKW ferry.

H plus 36 hours. Class 9 FBE bridge.

H plus 48 hours. Class 15 Bailey pontoon.

H plus 60 hours. Class 40 low level Bailey pontoon bridge.

H plus 120 hours. Class 40 all-weather Bailey Pontoon bridge.

Author's note: But the Buffaloes were the great work horses. With these and DD Tanks substantial bodies of men and armour could be landed at maximum speed.

INDEX

Aachen, 206
  break-through to, 210
Aachen-Maastricht Gap, seizure of, 160
Aide-Mémoire (Churchill), 17, 20n.
'Air Transportation Plan'
  effects of before D-Day, 24, 61, 82
Albert Canal, 177, 188, 294, 319
  bridges of blown up by Germans, 174
  failure to seize the bridges across the, 170-71
Alencon, 106
Alexander, General Sir Harold, 18, 20, 31, 37, 40, 48, 87, 111, 115, 181, 217, 230, 268, 276
Allied Airborne Army, 1st, 149, 159, 160, 172, 193
  frustration of, 183
Allied Air Force, 24, 82, 98, 103, 141, 277, 293
  entering the battle in the Ardennes, 255
  role in 'Overlord', 69-71
Allied camp
  disunity in, 107, 110
  rivalry in, 126, 131-2, 142-3, 250-51
  see also Anglo-American relations
Allied counter-attack in the Ardennes, 260
Allied reinforcement and supply
  difficulties in keeping up, 78-82
  see also Supplies for Allied forces
Allied Strategic bombing programme, 277
  before D-Day, 24, 82
After Rhine, 289
American commanders
  discounting German thread in the Ardennes, 235-41
  susceptible to public opinion, 112, 250, 276
American public as governing factor in Allied Strategy, 276-7
Americans
  aggressive tactics of, 138-9
  determining events in Europe, 111-12
  view on 'Operation Overlord', 26-9
  war casualties of, 123
Anderson, General Sir Kenneth
  replaced by Dempsey, 36
Anglo-American relations
  conflict in, 15-16, 20-21, 26, 42-3, 136, 167, 212, 262
  see also Allied camp
Antwerp, 184, 224, 318, 319
  allied attack on, 206
  German V-bomb attacks from, 177
  importance of to allied troops, 59, 134, 155, 162, 167, 208
  liberated (Sept. 1944), 148, 209
  Montgomery's failure to capture, 170-71, 174, 176-9, 203, 213
Anvil Decisions, The (M. Matloff), 49
Anvil Deadlock, The (Thompson), 49
Anvil (plan for an attack on the South of France), 17, 27, 31, 112, 302
  conflict over, 46-48
  changed to code *Dragoon*, 48
Ardennes
  background to the battle of, 233
  battle of, 214, 244, 250, 263, 268
  counter-offensive in, 233-247
  launching of German attack in, 243-5
Ardennes, The (Cole), 235n, 245n, 246n, 247n, 250n, 253n
Ardennes, The (Manteuffel), 269
Argentan, 106
  Patton's troops at, 107-8, 142, 143
Armistice (5th May 1945), 307
Armoured fighting vehicles
  development of under Hobart, 22
Arnhem, 319
  aftermath of, 220
  failure of, 197-202, 203
  Montgomery's advance towards, 186-202
  Montgomery's plan to seize, 177-9

INDEX

Arnhem (R. E. Urquhart), 193n, 197n, 200n
Arnold, General, 30
'Artificial harbours', production of, 23, 28
A Soldier's Story (General Bradley), 100n., 108n., 109n., 120, 132n., 142n., 143n., 160n., 168n., 237n., 240n., 258n., 259n., 287n., 304n.
Atlantic, battle of, 28
'Atlantic Wall', 61, 149
Atomic bomb, 24
Auchinleck General, 60, 111, 159
Aure, river, 61
Auschwitz, 306
Arranches, 108, 166, 234

Bailey bridges, 165, 300
Bastogne, battle of, 254, 260, 263
Battle for France, 104, 133, 224
Battle for Normandy, 69, 113n., 124, 135, 166, 192, 234, 316, 317
   decisive battle of the campaign, 83
   development of, 83–4
   fought in three main phases, 88–101
   taking shape, 93–107
Battle for the Rhineland, 210, 224, 270, 271, 290, 321
Battle for the Rhineland (R. W. Thompson), 210n., 214n.
Bayerlein, German General, 98
'Beach Groups' engineers, 23
Bedell Smith, Lieut-General Walter, 33, 34, 39, 44, 46–7, 93, 127, 128, 225, 226, 228, 237, 238, 250–51, 263, 264, 276, 320
   visit to Montgomery, 117–18, 177
Beeringen, struggle for the bridgehead at, 182
Belgian-Dutch border, fighting at the, 188
Belsen, 306
Berlin, 154, 155, 275, 302
   Montgomery's plan to seize, 172–6
'Blackcock, Operation', 277
Blumenson, Martin, 148n., 150n., 322
Blumtritt, General, 154, 155, 308
Bofors, 279, 299

Bradford Huie, William
   analysis of the man-power situation by, 257
Bradley, General Omar N., 33, 34, 37, 90, 97, 105, 106, 108, 111, 114, 116, 119, 120, 123–6, 130, 131, 140–42, 143n., 151, 153, 157, 159, 160, 163, 167, 168n., 172, 175, 206, 212, 215–18, 224–30, 246–9, 260, 263, 265, 273, 275–7, 287n., 290, 304 *passim*
   aggressive attitude towards the British of, 257–8
   assuming command of 12th U.S. Army, 42, 99–100, 110
   breakdown of command of, 184–5
   capturing St. Lo, 97
   criticising Montgomery, 107
   crossing the Rhine, 283–4
   foresight of, 56–7
   German threat to assassinate, 257
   ignoring warning of German attack in the Ardennes, 236–9
   influenced by public opinion, 136
   in Normandy, 94, 96, 98
   in Paris, 109
   meeting Eisenhower in Maastricht, 229
   personal tribute to Montgomery of, 132
   position of in the Ardennes, 250–59
   racing to the Rhine, 280–81
   rejecting Hobart's armour, 78
   role of at D-Day operations, 60–61, 70
   setting up headquarters at Namur, 267
Break-Out and Pursuit (Blumenson), 148n., 150n.
Bremen, 305
Brereton, Lieut.-General Lewis, 149 160, 176, 183
Bridgeheads in Normandy, 94–5, 187
   congestion in the, 78–80
Bridging, importance of, 165
Britain
   decline of military power of, 16
   import crisis of in (1943), 27
   preparing for 'Operation Overlord', 25, 27

INDEX

B.B.C. (British Broadcasting Corporation), 231
British 1st Airborne division, 189, 200, 202
  holding out under impossible circumstances, 196-8, 201
British 2nd Army ('British Liberation Army'), 18, 120, 132, 141, 148, 206-7, 210, 211, 292
  advancing to the Rhine, 284-5
  at Reichswald forest, 205
  crossing the Seine, 168, 169
  held up by Bradley's troops, 167
  in Normandy, 75-87, 97, 102-3
  under the command of Dempsey, 36-7
British forces, 156
  dwindling manpower of, 126
  parting from U.S. forces, 114
  war casualties of, 123
British-Indian divisions
  in the Mediterranean, 112
British industrial production of war materials, 23-4
'British Liberation Army, The'
  see British 2nd Army
British press, 110-21, 138-9, 259-60, 262
Brittany, Patton's troops advancing through, 102
Broadhurst, Air Vice Marshal, 92
Broad Front strategy ('No-Plan'), 115, 116, 154, 183, 184, 206, 274
  established, 203
  weaknesses in, 256
Brooke, General Sir Alan, 16, 18, 19, 20, 29, 31, 39, 56, 58, 65, 72, 85, 96, 101, 111, 115, 127, 128, 133, 140-41, 152, 219, 226, 228, 229, 230, 261, 262, 264, 275, 276, 314
Browning, General, 149, 160, 172, 176, 183, 193
Brussels
  liberated (Sept. 1944), 148, 170
Bryant, 31n., 72n., 73n., 112n., 128n., 141n., 226n., 227n., 258n., 261n., 282n., 314n.
Buchenwald, 306
Buckley (War correspondent), 19n., 139

BUCO (Organisation), 44
Budapest, taken by Russian army, 268
'Buffalos' used to cross the Rhine, 280, 297-9
Bull, General, 276
Burrough, Admiral, 284
Busch, Field-Marshal, 308
Butcher, Capt., 19n., 34, 128

Cairo-Teheran conferences (1943), 28-9
Caen, 83, 86, 141, 165, 295, 318
  Dempsey's position at, 94
  German 21st Panzer division in, 78-9, 80
  major objective in cross-channel assault, 44, 58, 78
  misunderstanding over, 128, 138
  Montgomery's battle of, 96, 97, 139
Canadian 1st Army, 102-3, 106, 120, 148, 166, 168-9, 184, 207, 208-10, 211, 213, 271, 277, 282
  fighting of in Sept. 1944, 174
  liberating Northern Holland, 288
Carentan, liberation of, 136-7
Caumont, Dempsey's army concentrated against, 98
Censorship, necessity of, 137
Chambois, 106, 108, 123
Chartress, 106, 108, 109
  supreme command meetings in, 174-5
Cherbourg, 128
  as major objective in cross-channel assault, 44, 59, 94
  as U.S. supply point, 124n.
  taken by the Americans, 84
Chernyakhosky, Marshal, 268, 302
Chevallerie, 147
Chiang Kai Sheks, the, 26, 29
Churchill, Sir Winston, 28-30, 31n., 38, 56, 58, 70, 92, 111, 112, 140n., 147, 152, 216, 226, 230, 264, 269, 275, 300, 301n., 302, 314 *passim*
  anxiety over Eisenhower's talks with Stalin, 303-7
  convalescing in Marrakesh, 31-2
  illness of in Africa, 16-17
  opinion on 'Overlord', 20, 64-5
  overall activities of, 54-5

Churchill, Sir Winston—*cont.*
  plea of to take Berlin, 303
  preparing 'Overlord', 50–52
  relationship with Montgomery, 128, 133
  visit to Montgomery, 80, 141
Clark, General Mark, 18, 31, 323
Clausewitz, 150
Clifford (War correspondent), 139
Closing the Ring (Churchill), 17n., 51n.
COBRA—the break-out, operation, 97–8
Cole, Hugh M., 235, 245, 246n., 247n., 250n., 253n.
Collins, Lieut.-General Lawton, 100, 253, 266
Colmar pocket, 247, 256
Cologne, occupied, 286
COMET, operation, 176
Command Decisions (M. Matloff), 49, 108n., 142n.
Coningham, Air Marshal, 92, 128, 130
COSSAC organisation, 33, 43, 46, 47, 53, 58
  outline of plan for 'Overlord', 34, 36
Cross-channel assault
  in jeopardy, 27
  on North-West Europe (1943), 15–32
  preparation for, 40–41
  see also 'Operation Overlord'
Cross-Channel Attack (G. A. Harrison), 29n., 47n., 61n., 76n.
Cross Roads of Strategy (M. Matloff), 49
Crusade in Europe (Eisenhower), 120n.
Czecho-Slovakia, taken by U.S. 3rd Army, 302

Dakotas, 300
Dawnay, Colonel
  sent to London by Montgomery, 85
D-Day, 297, 317
  bad weather conditions for, 67
  hazards of, 73–87
  inter-service difficulties before and after, 70
  last preparations for, 58–71
  postponement of, 67–8
DA (swimming tanks), 76
  used for crossing the Rhine, 298–9

Deception plans
  in Normandy, 122
  on the East and South coast of England, 53, 74
De Gaulle, General, 109
De Groote, bridgehead at, 188–9, 193
De Guingand, Major-General, 35, 38, 63, 70, 116, 117, 139, 220, 223, 231–2, 263, 264
Dempsey, General Sir Miles, 60, 95, 120, 123, 131, 132, 139, 148, 153, 167, 176, 202, 282, 285, 290, 294, 305, 321
  as commander of the 2nd Army, 36–7
  concentrating against Caumont, 98
  influenced by public opinion, 136
  in Normandy, 81
  position at Caen of, 94
  preparing for an assault on the Rhine, 283–4
  qualities of, 38
Devers, General, 119, 124, 153, 217, 274, 320, 323
Dickson, Colonel
  warning of German attack from, 236
Dieppe Raid, 22
Diersfordter Wald, 292
Dill, Sir John, 30
Diplomatic privileges for all Embassies, restrictions of (April 1944), 53
Dives, river, 94, 97
Doenitz, Admiral, 308
Dollmann, 147
Dragoon (assault (former *Anvil*), 302
  launched, 112
  taking place in August (1944), 48, 153–4
Dreux, 106
DUKW, amphibious, 50
Dunkirk, Montgomery's retreat at, 19
'Dunkirk' rescue of 2,000 men, 202
Dupuy, Colonel, 136
Dutch-Belgium border, fighting on the, 188

EAGLE TAC, 108
Eastern front
  expanding of, 59, 147, 204
  re-inforced by the Germans, 267

INDEX

East Prussia, obliterated by Russian armies, 268
Eberbach, Heinrich, 103, 147
  replacing von Schweppenberg, 84
Ehrman, 17n., 29n., 31n., 47n., 49, 82, 112n., 113, 150n., 152n., 184n.
Eifel
  Bradley's advance on, 273
  German troops amassing in, 239, 242
  Patton moving through the, 286
  see also Schnee Eifel battle
Eighty-five Days, The (Thompson), 178n., 179n., 209n.
Eindhoven Golf Club, Montgomery at, 243
Eisenhower, General Ike, 15, 18, 20, 29, 32, 61, 108, 111–15, 117, 118, 130, 131, 132, 138–42, 152, 154, 158, 163, 172, 183, 206, 212, 215, 218–19, 227–9, 250, 258, 265, 269, 273 *passim*
  appointed as Supreme Commander, 25, 33, 110
  approving Montgomery's Arnhem plan, 178–9
  assessing the battle of the Rhine, 280
  at the final 'Presentation of Plans', 63–4
  badly placed headquarters of, 158–226
  characteristics of, 34–5
  decision to launch 'Overlord' of (June 1944), 68
  difficulties of in establishing Supreme Command, 179–85
  difficult task in Britain of, 42–3
  emphasizing the importance of Antwerp, 177–9, 207–8
  German threat to assassinate, 256–7
  in communication with Stalin, 302–7
  influenced by public opinion, 136
  in Normandy, 95
  in Paris, 109
  meeting at Hasselt held by, 260–62
  mistrusting Montgomery, 127–8
  misunderstanding of Montgomery's plans at Caen, 90–101, 127–43
  overall military power of, 43
  preparing for 'Operation Overlord', 33–5
  rejecting Montgomery's plan to take Berlin, 175
  reorientation of plans of, 214
  taking over Supreme Command in the field, 116, 124, 157
  touring army camps in Britain, 56–7
  views of German counter-attack, 237–9
Elbe, river, 269, 302, 305
  thrust of 2nd Army to the, 284
Elboeuf pocket, scene in the, 108
Ellis, 49, 103n., 105n., 117n., 118n.
EPSOM, operation, 96
  misunderstanding regarding, 96–7
Equipment used to cross the Rhine, 296–8
Erft, river, 273, 274
Essame, Major-General, 198, 282n.
Execution of Private Slovik, The (W. Bradford Huie), 257n.
Exercises for troops
  carried out on simulated beaches in Britain, 44

Falaise, 83, 104, 106, 107, 108, 165
  allied attacks on, 97, 98, 142, 143
Fatal Decisions, 269n.
Faulknor, destroyer H.M.S.
  Montgomery aboard the, 72
Fighter-bombers, 141
First World War, 26
Frankfurt, 218
  bridgehead to, 290
  importance of, 229, 273
  thrust on, 212
Freide, Major, 308–12
French Resistance, aiding Allied landing, 61–2
French 1st Army, 211, 302
Friedenburg, General-Admiral, 308–12
Fuller, 19n., 314–15

Gassicourt, 122
Gavin, General, 199, 254, 305
Gehr von Schweppenberg, General Leo Freiherr (German commander), 62, 73, 98

336 INDEX

Gehr von Schweppenberg—*cont.*
  accounts of on the position in Caen, 86
  disappearance of, 84, 89
George VI, King, 39–40
  visit to Holland, 220–21
German command
  failure of on D-Day and after, 73–87
Germany, battle for, 234
German industrial production
  increase of, 24
  of secret weapons, 24
German troops
  collapse of on the Western front, 150–52, 158
  defending channel ports, 166
  fighting over the Albert Canal, 174
  heavy resistance of at Gheel, 188–9
  inadequate transport of, 235
  offence in the Ardennes launched by (Dec. 1944), 153, 233–47
  penetrating the Ardennes, 234–5
  powerful defensive position at Woensdrecht of, 204
  prolonged resistance of, 152–3
  under bombing day and night, 147
  unprotected against air attack in Normandy, 76
German 7th Army, 249, 257
German 15th Army, 166, 169, 173, 318
  resistance of, 188–9, 204
Germany
  allied plan to advance into, 117
  hopeless situation of, 188
Gerow, General, 247, 266
Sheel, struggle for the bridgehead at, 182, 188–9
Ghent, 169
  liberation of, 148
Goebbels, Dr, 275
GOODWOOD, Montgomery's operation, 90, 96, 98
  misunderstood by Eisenhower, 90, 97
Grand Strategy (Ehrman), 17n., 29n., 31n., 47n., 49, 112n., 113n., 150n., 152n., 184n., 268n.
Grave, seizure of the bridge at, 192, 196
Grigg, Sir James (P.J.), War Minister, 39, 219

Ground Force Command
  necessity of in the north, 275
Guderian, 149

Haislip, General, 142, 148, 170
Hakewill Smith, Major-General, 38
Hamburg, 305
Harbours, artificial
  badly damaged by storms, 88–9
  completion of (spring 1944), 54–5
  construction of, 23, 41
  production of, 28
  taking shape on French beaches, 82
Harrison, G. A., 29, 47n., 61n., 76
Hasbrouck, General, 253
Hasselt, Allied meeting at, 260–62
Hausser, 103, 147
Hasso, General, 269
Hechtel, enormous array of troops assembled at, 195
Heinsberg triangle, 272, 277
Hinge of Fate, The (Churchill), 314n.
Hitler, Adolf, 25, 103, 106, 122, 134, 141, 142, 147, 148, 153, 156, 240, 285
  failure to assassinate, 152
  last attempt to drive back the Allies, 99
  launching the counter-offensive, 235, 268
  refusal to withdraw of, 82–7
  unaware of the grave situation, 155
Hobart, Major-General Sir Percy, 22, 63
  first days on Normandy beaches, 76
  important friend to Montgomery, 221
Hockweld forest, 278
Hodges, General, 119, 153, 154, 161, 175, 236, 246–7, 251, 255, 259, 266, 267, 273, 289, 290
  discounting German attack in the Ardennes, 242
  influence of Montgomery on, 251–3
Hoge, Brigadier-General, 290, 294
  crossed Remagen bridge on his own initiative, 285
Holland, Northern
  liberated by the Canadian army, 288
Hopkins, Harry, 30, 268

INDEX

Horrocks, Lieut.-General, 37, 169, 173, 190, 197, 210, 294
Howard, Michael, 320
Hurtgen forest, battle of, 209, 246

Ijssel, river, 190, 194, 289
India, 111
   defended by Indian troops, 26
Infantry men, acute shortage of, 257
Ingersoll, Major, 286, 287n.
Initial Joint Plan, *Neptune*, 50
Initial Maintenance Plan, 50
Intelligence Committee, Joint, 150, 152
Intelligence officers
   British, 224
   U.S., 224
   warning of the German attack from, 235-9
Intelligence, Supreme Headquarters concerned about German troops in the Ardennes, 236
Irving, David, 24n.
Italy, campaign in, 19, 26, 31, 48

Jeeps, amphibious
   used for crossing the Rhine, 280
'Jerrycans', disappearance of, 137, 162
Junction canal, 188

Kassel-Leipzig line, 304
Kennedy, General, 101
Kesselring, Field-Marshal, 106, 293
King, U.S. Admiral, 30, 48
Kinsel, General, 308-12
Kock, General, 151
Konier, Marshal, 268, 302
Kyll, river, 273, 287

Landing-craft
   assault troops in, 76
   development of, 23
   on the Normandy beaches, 73-6
   shortage of, 26, 46, 48-9
   used for crossing the Rhine, 284
Leahy, Admiral, 30, 303

Le Clerc, General, 109
Le Havre, fortress port of, 167-8
Leigh Mallory, Air Chief Marshal Sir Trafford, 44, 57, 61, 92, 160
   disliked by Montgomery, 128, 130
Leighton, Richard, 16
Leipzig-Kassel line, 304
Le Mans, 106
'Liberation' army
   see British 2nd Army
Lidell Hart, Sir Basil, 90n., 154, 164, 294n., 319, 322
'Lightning Joe'
   see Collins, Lieut.-General Lawton, 253
Lippe, river, 284, 289
Logistical Support of the Armies (Ruppenthal), 22n., 50n., 52n., 134n., 150n., 162
Logistics
   governing the war, 22, 59
   importance of, 81, 109, 121, 122, 143, 150, 154-5, 161-2, 180-81, 209, 241, 257, 319
   main factor in operation 'Overlord', 49, 134
Losheim gap, 242
Lowell Rooks, General, 276
LUCKY FORWARD, operation, 142

Maas, river, 190, 196, 205, 210, 214, 277, 282
   crossing of, 279
   flooded, 272, 292, 296
Maastricht meeting, 229, 251
MacArthur, General Douglas, 60, 159, 231
Mail and Communication system
   subject to strict control (Spring 1944), 53
Malinovsky, 268, 302
'Manhattan Project, The', 24
Mantes, 122
Manteuffel, General, 235, 249, 255, 258, 260
'Market Garden', operation, 190-202
   airborne troops used in, 193-202
   reason for the failure of, 197-202

Marshall, General George (U.S. Chief of Staff), 25, 27, 28, 29, 30, 110, 113, 128, 206, 230, 262, 265, 302, 303, 304
Matloff, Maurice, 48–9
McAingersoll, Major Ralph, 240
McLean, Brigadier, 47
Mediterranean operations
   end of Churchill's, 16–17
   American, 27, 31
Memoirs (Montgomery), 65n., 70n., 80n., 114n., 117n., 118n., 132n., 140, 158n., 228n., 262n., 263n., 265n., 305n.
Men Under Fire (Thompson), 300n.
Metz, Patton in, 155, 205, 211
Meuse bridgehead, 243, 252
   reinforcing the, 249
Middleton, General, 239, 243
Military government sections
   attempting to organise local government, 306
Mine-sweeping flotillas clearing the Channel (3rd June 1944), 67
Ministry of Supply, role of, 51
Model, Field-Marshal, 106, 148, 156, 173, 174, 190, 199, 204, 234–5, 285
   replacing von Kluge, 84
Montgomery, General Sir Bernard, 23, 25, 31, 103n., 110–15, 117n., 118n., 147, 151, 155, 158–60, 163, 167n., 169, 183n., 188, 201, 212, 216, 227, 228n., 233, 262n., 288n., 289n. *passim*
   acting as Supreme Commander in January 1944, 39
   administering the *coup de grâce* in France, 104
   administration in Belgium and Holland, 220
   appointed Field Marshal, 119, 124, 126
   battle at Caen, 96
   battle in Normandy, 83–4, 93–107
   breakdown of command of, 184–5
   British confidence in, 21
   characteristics of, 34–5, 41–2, 55–7, 221–3, 231–2
   Churchill's and Morgan's visit to, 79–80, 82
   churlish attitude to Eisenhower, 225
   clashing with the War Minister and the King, 39–40
   complimenting the Americans, 265–6
   concentrating on Antwerp, 208
   conception of Ground Force command of, 120
   considering Eisenhower incompetent, 219
   control over the battle of Normandy, 93
   criticism from Bradley and Patton of, 107
   criticized for using expensive warfare equipment, 295
   crossing the Rhine, 298–302
   dealing with the German counter-attack, 248–70
   deceiving the enemy at Caen, 139
   defeating Germans in August 1944 in Normandy, 122
   demands for support to advance on Arnhem, 177–9
   directive of to open Antwerp from Eisenhower, 208
   effect of public opinion on, 136
   end of the strategy of, 102–9
   enlarging 'Overlord' plans of, 43–9
   established the 'Broad Front', 203
   failing to inspire initiative, 293–4
   failure of operation 'Market Garden', 196–202
   failure to establish a bridgehead east of the Rhine, 285–94
   failure of to open up Antwerp and Northern Holland, 172–81, 203, 213
   German threat to assassinate, 256–7
   handling of the Ardennes battle, 243
   headquarters of in Portsmouth (May 1944), 64–5
   Hobart's friendship with, 221
   in close touch with the battlefield, 223–4
   in conflict with Tedder, 69–71
   in the Western Desert, 19
   keeping Churchill informed, 140

INDEX

Montgomery, General—*cont.*
  major operations of in June and July 1944, 96–8
  making conditions for surrender of Northern Germany, 308–12
  meeting Churchill in Marrakesh, 32
  meeting Eisenhower in Maastricht, 229
  misunderstood by the Supreme Command, 85, 89–90, 127, 138
  mounting a major attack in Normandy, 89
  obsession of to strike due North, 168–85, 193
  ordeal of, 72–87
  plan for total defeat of Germany, 112–14
  planning a trap for the enemy, 99
  plans to take Berlin, 175–6
  preparation for D-Day of, 58–71
  preparing for 'Overlord' (Spring 1944), 51–55
  Press Conference of (Jan. 1945), 246–66
  provoking a command crisis, 175
  reaching Antwerp, 170
  receiving Nazi Officers, 308
  refusing Simpson permission to cross the Rhine, 285–6
  relations with Bradley, 98
  re-opened criticism on Supreme Command, 213
  retreat of at Dunkirk, 19
  rivalry with Patton, 119
  seemingly unaware of command positions, 112–18
  seizing Baltic ports, 305
  'set-piece battle' of, 292–3
  social difficulties of, 90–92
  statement on German counter-offensive, 240–41
  subject to harsh criticism, 127, 130, 132, 137
  tactics and strategies of, 88–101, 141
  tactics for taking the Rhine outlined by, 279–81
  tactlessness of, 42–3
  taking command in the North, 250–56
  touring Britain, 55–7
  triumph of in the Ardennes, 269
  understanding of military problems of, 40–41
  using misleading phrases in public statements, 139, 222
Montgomery Legend, The, 173n., 293n.
Moorehead, Alan (War correspondent), 139, 223
Morgan, Lieut.-General Sir Frederick (C.I.G.S.), 27, 36, 43, 58, 92, 101, 132, 225
  attitude to Montgomery, 69, 128, 130
  plan of 'Overlord', 28, 33
  views on 'Overlord' and 'Anvil', 47–8
  visit to Montgomery in France, 80
Mortain, German attack on the 1st U.S. Army at, 104–5
Mortars, used by German troops, 84–5
Moselle, river, 108, 148, 149, 150, 166, 205
  crossing of, 287
Mulde, river, 302
MOVCO (Organisation), 44

Nebelwerfer regiments, German inflicting heavy losses on British troops, 85
Neder Rijn, 190, 195
'Neptune, Operation', 50, 63
New York Herald Tribune, The (newspaper)
  reports of, 140,
New York Times, 265
Nicolson, Harold
  disliked by Montgomery, 219
Niers, river, 214, 272, 279
Nijmegen bridgehead, 195–7, 199, 202, 277
Norfolk House, importance of, 33
Normandy, Battle for
  see Battle for Normandy
Normandy beaches
  assaults on at D-Day and after, 73–87
  congestion on, 76–8
  importance of a foothold on, 61–3
  'Operation Overlord' launched on, 63

Normandy to the Baltic (Montgomery), 103n., 114n., 167n., 172n., 183n., 288n., 289n.
North, John, 172n., 179n.
North-West Europe (C. J. North), 172, 179n.
Nye, Lieut.-General, 115

Oder-Neisse line
  Russian troops pressing beyond the, 276, 302
Oder, river, 268
Odon, river, 97
Omaha beaches
  Americans fighting for a toe-hold on, 78, 139
'Operation Crossbow', 24
'Overlord', operation of, 18, 22, 26, 84, 116, 122
  American appointment of a Supreme Commander for, 30-31
  American opposition to, 20, 24, 28
  Anglo-American command over, 15-16
  Churchill's opinion on, 20
  enlargement of endorsed by Eisenhower, 43-9
  General Eisenhower as Supreme Commander of, 30
  logistics of, 134
  Montgomery appointed as commander of, 15-17
  Morgan's plan of, 28
  preparations made for in London, 34-5
  postponed until June 1944, 49
  sailing of (6th June 1944), 68
  success of, 73-87
  U.S. Army in Britain for, 38-9
  see also Cross-channel assault
Operation Victory (De Guingand), 263n.
Orne, river, 44, 58, 78, 137
  bridgehead across the, 94, 165
Ourthe, river, 267
Overture to Overlord (Morgan), 15n., 130n.

Paget, General Sir Bernard, 18, 27, 36, 56, 58, 86

Paris, allied troops in (Aug. 1944), 109
Patton, General George, 23, 37, 60, 90, 103, 105, 106, 111, 114, 116, 121, 124, 126, 141, 142, 148-54, 157, 160, 163, 164, 175, 205, 211, 212, 216, 222, 228, 238, 239, 246-9, 252, 254-6, 260, 266, 267, 273-5, 284, 286, 289, 297, 315, 320, 323 *passim*
  advancing through Brittany, 103
  aggressive attitude towards the British, 257-8
  assuming command of 3rd U.S. Army, 99-100
  at Argentan, 108
  break-through at Avranches of, 166
  criticising Montgomery, 107, 119
  moving through the Eifel, 286
'Peace imports', cutting of, 51
Peenemünde, rocket development centre
  air attack on, 24
Petrov, General, 268
Ploesti oil-fields
  seized by Russian troops, 156
'Plunder', operation (code name for offensive across the Rhine), 288-312
Pogue, Forrest, 15n., 49, 61n., 99n., 102n., 103n., 111n., 113n., 119, 136n., 151n., 157, 158n., 163, 175n., 178n., 206n., 208n., 213n., 215n., 216n., 229, 235, 236n., 237n., 238, 239n., 240n., 263n., 265n., 303, 304
Polish airborne brigade, 200
Political importance of the war, 302-7
Polleck, Colonel, 311-12
Portsmouth
  headquarters of the Supreme Commander (1944), 64
Prague, 154, 302
'Presentation of Plans', final, 63-4, 65
Press, influence on Generals and Public, 110-21, 138-9, 259-60, 262
Price of Victory, The (Thompson), 49, 50n., 62n., 68n., 76n.
Prisoners, German, 299-300
Progress reports, official
  issuing of, 137

Public opinion
  powerful factor in strategy, 135, 143, 250, 276-7

Quebec Conference (1943), 16, 27
Quer dam, blown up by Germans, 279

Raaspe, General, 307
Ramsey, Admiral (Naval force commander), 46, 67, 160
'Rankin' operation, 20, 134
Reichswald forest, 199, 200, 205, 210, 242, 277, 278, 293, 296
Reinforcement and supply, Allied difficulties in keeping up, 78-82, 89, 158
Remagen bridge, seized, 285, 294
R.E.M.E. workshop, 133
Republican Guards in Paris, 109
Rhineland, Battle for the
  see Battle for the Rhineland
Rhine, river, 116, 119, 126, 155-7, 214, 274
  battle at, 281
  crossing of, 284, 287, 319
  drive towards the, 172
  engineer resources used for crossing of, 296-7
  equipment used for crossing the, 296-8
  floods of, 272
  race for the, 271-87
  reached by 2nd March (1945), 281
  Simpson's advance to the, 285
Ridgeway, General, 254, 266
Road to Rome (Buckley), 19n.
'Rock Soup' method, 175-6, 181
Roer dams, 272, 277
  German control of, 205, 214, 233
  U.S. attack launched on, 273
Roer, river
  attack across, 274
  floods of, 279-81
  order to seize the, 278
Rokossovsky, Marshal, 268, 302
Rommel, Field-Marshal, 70, 73, 80, 83, 103, 147, 173, 313, 314
  anticipated difficulties of, 79, 96
  defensive tactics on Normandy beaches of, 62
  restricted movement of, 95
  suicide of, 84, 89
Rommel Papers, The, 62n.
Roosevelt, President, 27, 28, 152, 216, 230, 268, 302
  choosing a Supreme Commander for 'Overlord', 29-30
Roth, Major-General, 307
Rotterdam
  importance of, 134, 182
  V-bomb attacks from, 177
Rouen, 167
'Round-Up': code-name for an assault (1943), 25
Royal Engineers, importance of, 295-6, 298
Royal Navy, role of in 'Operation Overlord', 70, 292
Ruhr
  Montgomery's plan to seize the, 172, 183, 284
Rumania, collapse of, 156
Ruppenthal, 22n., 50n., 52n., 134n., 149n., 150n., 162n.
Russia
  growing military power of, 16
  victories of in Germany, 147
Russian armies, 59, 204, 302
  advance of, 267
  in Warsaw, 156
  pressing beyond the Oder-Neisse line, 276
  reaching the Oder, 268
  taking Silesia, 273

St. Bastogne, battle of, 244
St. Lo
  air attack on, 98
  American struggle for, 97
  captured by Bradley, 97
  vital American objective, 79, 94
St. Odenrode, road near
  cut by German troops, 196
St. Paul's School
  headquarters of Montgomery, 35, 58-60, 63
St. Vith, battle of, 244, 252, 253, 255

Scheldt estuary, 168, 169, 176, 185, 292, 319
  battle of, 204, 210
  first cargo ship sailing up the, 227
  improvised German defence of, 148
  taken by allied troops, 208–9
Schlemm, General, 285
Schmidt, battle at, 209, 214
Schnee Eifel battle, 246
  disaster in the, 248, 257
Schwammanuel dams, 273
  German control of, 209–11
Second World War, The (Fuller), 19n.
Seine, river, 108, 118, 120, 123, 124, 135, 143, 158, 165–7, 233
  breakout and advance to the, 125 map
  bridgeheads on, 169
SHAEF, 58, 109, 119, 140, 250, 262
  G2 intelligence summaries of, 151
Sherwood, 26n., 29n., 30n.
Siegfried Line, 173, 182, 204
  obliterated, 277
Simpson, General, 206, 266, 273, 280–1, 283, 290, 294, 321
  Montgomery's refusal to permit the crossing of the Rhine, 285
  rapid advance to the Rhine, 285
Skorzeny, Waffen SS Colonel Otto, 236
'Skyscraper' plan, 18, 36
'Sledgehammer' assault, 25
Smith, General, 136
Smuts, General, 63, 65
Somme, river
  British advance towards the, 169
South-East Asia
  British commitments in, 111
Soviet Armies
  see Russian troops
Spectator, The (Gehr von Schweppenberg), 87n.
SPOBS (Organization), 44
Spoy canal, 279
Stagg, Group Captain, 68
Stalin, Marshal, 29, 302, 304
  in communication with Eisenhower, 302
Stimson, Henry (U.S. Secretary of State for War), 26, 30, 140

Strong, Major General, 225, 249, 250, 264
  warning of German attack from, 236–9
Struggle for Europe, The (Ch. Wilmot), 37n., 127n., 243n.
Student, General, 148, 152, 155, 174
Submarine cables (oil pipeline)
  invention of, 53
Supplies for Allied forces
  difficulties over, 124, 158, 162
  landed over Normandy beaches, 78–87, 89
  wealth of, 271–2
Supreme Command, The (Pogue), 15n., 43n., 49, 61, 99n., 102n., 103n., 111n., 113n., 119n., 136n., 151n., 157n., 158n., 163n., 175n., 178n., 206n., 213n., 215n., 216n., 229n., 236n., 237n., 238n., 239n., 240n., 263n., 265n., 303n.
'Supreme' Supreme Commander
  appointment of, 29

Tank Landing Ships
  caught by the enemy E boats, 50
Tanks, The (L. Hart), 90n.
Tedder, Air Chief Marshal, 67, 92, 226, 228, 268, 276
  criticism of Montgomery of, 69–71, 130
  in Normandy, 95
  misunderstanding Montgomery's tactics, 100, 128
TEWTS, Importance of, 187
The 43rd Wessex division at War (Essame), 198n., 282n.
Three Years with Eisenhower (Butcher), 19n., 128n.
Thompson, R. W., 49, 50n., 62n., 68n., 76n., 178n., 179n., 209n., 210n., 214n., 228n., 299n., 300n.
Times, The (newspaper)
  reports of, 139–40
Todt organization, 61
Tolbukhin, 268, 302
Top Secret (Ingersoll), 287n.
Tournai, 160–61
Transportation plan, 92

INDEX

Trenchard, Lord, 92
Trier, seized by the U.S. 3rd Army, 287
Triumph and Tragedy (Churchill), 300n., 301n., 303, 304n.
Triumph in the West (Bryant), 31n., 72n., 112n., 128n., 141n., 226n., 228n., 258n., 261n., 282n.
Troyes, 106, 122
Trun, 106, 108, 123
TURCO (Organization), 44
Turn of the Tide, The (Bryant), 314n.
Typhoons, British, 105-7, 123
    rocket firing of, 193

Unconditional Surrender, importance of, 25, 28, 59, 147, 275
United States
    Army imports, 53
    growing military power of, 16
U.S. 1st Army, 42, 118, 119, 120, 148, 156, 158, 176, 184, 206, 209, 210, 212, 216, 230, 246, 249, 252, 255, 267, 274, 289, 302
    attacked by Germans at Mortain, 104
    attacking the Roer dams, 255, 259, 273
    in Normandy, 102
    Intelligence officers of, 236-7
    taking Cologne, 286
U.S. 3rd Army, 157, 246-7, 257, 258, 267, 273, 274, 287, 302 *passim*
    crossing of the Rhine of, 287
    Intelligence officers of, 151
    Patton in command of, 99, 124, 148, 184, 211, 217, 228
U.S. 7th Army, 211, 274, 302
    withdrawal of, 253-4
U.S. 8th Air Force
    bombing St. Lo-Lessay area, 98
U.S. 9th Air Force
    bombing the St. Lo-Lessay area, 98
U.S. 9th Army, 205, 206, 209-11, 216-17, 230, 272, 274, 277, 278, 279-86, 283, 284, 289, 290, 292, 293, 303, 304, 312
U.S. 12th Army Group, 42, 157
    Bradley in Command of, 99
U.S. 82nd and 101st Airborne division, 190, 194, 199, 202

U.S. forces
    in Britain (Jan. 1944), 40
    occupying south-west England, 40-41
    parting from British forces, 114
U.S. VII Corps
    suffering casualties from U.S. bombers, 98
U.S. press, 110-21, 138-9, 259-60, 262
Urft, dams, 277-8
Urquhart, Major-General R.E., 193-4, 197, 200
Utah beach (Normandy)
    landing plans for, 61

V-bomb attacks
    on England, 177
    on the Meuse bridgehead, 249
'V' bomb sites (Pas de Calais), 166
    taken by the Canadians, 168
'Veritable', operation, 210-11, 214, 277, 280
Vernon
    British advance led out of, 169
Victory in the West (Ellis), 49, 85n., 86n., 87n., 103n., 105n., 116n., 117n., 118n., 127n., 130n., 131n.
Vielsalm area, battle of, 252
Villers Bocage, 141
    heavy fighting in the region of, 94-5
    vital objective for 2nd Army, 79
Vire, river, 44, 58, 61, 98, 282
Virus House, The (D. Irving), 24n.
Vistula, bridgehead on the, 268
Von Arnim (in Tunisia), 173
Von Funck, General, 104
Von Kluge, Field-Marshal Gunther 84, 97, 99, 103, 104, 105, 147
    taking cyanide, 106
Von Runstedt (German Commander-in-Chief West), 62, 73, 79, 80, 96, 103, 147, 156, 204, 234, 241, 293
    disappearance of, 84, 89
    moving all available armour to Normandy, 83
    restricted movement for troops of, 95
Von Speer
    providing replacements of arms etc., 204, 213

Von Stumme, General, 313
Von Zangen, General, 148, 169, 204

Waal, river, 190, 195
Wagner, Admiral, 308–12
'Walrus' aircraft, 68
War as I Knew it (Patton), 102n., 107n., 164n., 175n.
War Correspondents, 183
   creating a rivalry between U.S.A. and Britain, 137
   frustrations of, 137
   influence of, 110—21
   influence on Generals and public, 135–43
   not realizing Montgomery's plan, 138–9
Warlimont, German General, 99, 147

Warsaw, Russian troops in, 156
Water proofing, of allied vehicles etc., 51, 66
'Weasels' used in crossing the Rhine, 280
Wesel
   bombing of the town of, 299
   bridge of, 281, 285
Westphal, General, 154
White House Papers, The (Sherwood), 26n., 29n., 30n., 269n.
Whiteley, Major General, 225, 250, 264, 276
Wilmot, Chester, 37, 127, 139, 163, 231, 243
With Prejudice (Tedder), 67n., 226n.
Woodward (War correspondent), 139

Zhukov, Marshal, 268, 302

For Product Safety Concerns and Information please contact our EU
representative GPSR@taylorandfrancis.com
Taylor & Francis Verlag GmbH, Kaufingerstraße 24, 80331 München, Germany

www.ingramcontent.com/pod-product-compliance
Lightning Source LLC
Chambersburg PA
CBHW071233290426
44108CB00013B/1403